The Regional Economics of Knowledge and Talent

NEW HORIZONS IN REGIONAL SCIENCE

Series Editor: Philip McCann, *Professor of Economic Geography, University of Groningen, The Netherlands and Professor of Economics, University of Waikato, New Zealand*

Regional science analyses important issues surrounding the growth and development of urban and regional systems and is emerging as a major social science discipline. This series provides an invaluable forum for the publication of high quality scholarly work on urban and regional studies, industrial location economics, transport systems, economic geography and networks.

New Horizons in Regional Science aims to publish the best work by economists, geographers, urban and regional planners and other researchers from throughout the world. It is intended to serve a wide readership including academics, students and policymakers.

Titles in the series include:

International Knowledge and Innovation Networks
Knowledge Creation and Innovation in Medium Technology Clusters
Riccardo Cappellin and Rüdiger Wink

Leadership and Institutions in Regional Endogenous Development
Robert Stimson and Roger R. Stough with Maria Salazar

Entrepreneurship and Regional Development
Local Processes and Global Patterns
Edited by Charlie Karlsson, Börje Johansson and Roger R. Stough

Endogenous Regional Development
Perspectives, Measurement and Empirical Investigation
Edited by Robert Stimson, Roger R. Stough and Peter Nijkamp

Media Clusters
Spatial Agglomeration and Content Capabilities
Edited by Charlie Karlsson and Robert G. Picard

Spatial Scenarios in a Global Perspective
Europe and the Latin Arc Countries
Edited by Roberto Camagni and Roberta Capello

Creative Knowledge Cities
Myths, Visions and Realities
Edited by Marina van Geenhuizen and Peter Nijkamp

Societies in Motion
Innovation, Migration and Regional Transformation
Edited by Amnon Frenkel, Peter Nijkamp and Philip McCann

Innovation, Global Change and Territorial Resilience
Edited by Philip Cooke, Mario Davide Parrilli and José Luis Curbelo

The Regional Economics of Knowledge and Talent
Local Advantage in a Global Context
Edited by Charlie Karlsson, Börje Johansson and Roger R. Stough

The Regional Economics of Knowledge and Talent

Local Advantage in a Global Context

Edited by

Charlie Karlsson

Professor of the Economics of Technological Change, Jönköping International Business School, Jönköping University, Jönköping, Professor of Industrial Economics and Organization, Blekinge Institute of Technology, Karlskrona, Sweden, Guest Professor of Economics, University West, Trollhättan, Sweden and President, European Regional Science Association (ERSA)

Börje Johansson

Professor of Economics, Jönköping International Business School, Jönköping University, Jönköping and Director, CESIS (Centre of Excellence for Science and Innovation Studies), Royal Institute of Technology, Stockholm, Sweden

Roger R. Stough

Vice President for Research and Economic Development, NOVA Endowed Chair and Professor of Public Policy, George Mason University, USA

NEW HORIZONS IN REGIONAL SCIENCE

Edward Elgar

Cheltenham, UK • Northampton, MA, USA

Published by
Edward Elgar Publishing Limited
The Lypiatts
15 Lansdown Road
Cheltenham
Glos GL50 2JA
UK

Edward Elgar Publishing, Inc.
William Pratt House
9 Dewey Court
Northampton
Massachusetts 01060
USA

A catalogue record for this book
is available from the British Library

Library of Congress Control Number: 2012935265

MIX
Paper from
responsible sources
FSC® C018575
FSC
www.fsc.org

ISBN 978 1 84844 328 0

Typeset by Servis Filmsetting Ltd, Stockport, Cheshire
Printed and bound by MPG Books Group, UK

Contents

PART III THE GLOBAL CONTEXT

Contributors

Martin Andersson, Jönköping International Business School, Jönköping and Royal Institute of Technology, Stockholm, Sweden

Corinne Autant-Bernard, University Jean Monnet Saint-Etienne, Saint-Etienne, France

Pascal Billand, University Jean Monnet Saint-Etienne, Saint-Etienne, France

Gary A.S. Cook, University of Liverpool, Liverpool, UK

Urban Gråsjö, University West, Trollhättan, Sweden

Juan Julio Gutierrez, George Mason University, Fairfax, USA

Tsuyoshi Hatori, Tokyo Institute of Technology, Tokyo, Japan

Börje Johansson, Jönköping International Business School, Jönköping and Royal Institute of Technology, Stockholm, Sweden

Sara Johansson, Swedish Board of Agriculture, Jönköping, Sweden

Charlie Karlsson, Jönköping International Business School, Jönköping and Royal Institute of Technology, Stockholm, Sweden

Kiyoshi Kobayashi, Kyoto University, Kyoto, Japan

Hans Lööf, Royal Institute of Technology, Stockholm, Sweden

Nadine Massard, University Jean Monnet Saint-Etienne, Saint-Etienne, France

Kakuya Matsushima, Kyoto University, Kyoto, Japan

Peter Nijkamp, VU University, Amsterdam, The Netherlands

Désirée Nilsson, Swedish Institute for Transport and Communication Analysis, Östersund, Sweden

Kristina Nyström, Royal Institute of Technology, Stockholm, Sweden

Michael Olsson, The University of Skövde, Skövde, Sweden

Naresh R. Pandit, University of East Anglia, Norwich, UK

Mediha Sahin, VU University, Amsterdam, The Netherlands

Robert J. Stimson, The University of Melbourne, Australia

Roger R. Stough, George Mason University, Fairfax, USA

Alina Todiras, VU University, Amsterdam, The Netherlands

Preface

The contributions forming the different chapters in this book were first presented and discussed at the Tenth Anniversary Uddevalla Symposium on: 'Institutions for Knowledge Generation and Knowledge Flows – Building Innovative Capabilities for Regions', held at University West, Campus Uddevalla, Sweden, 14–16 June 2007.

The aim with this international conference was to explore and analyse further the challenges of transmission of knowledge and the assumptions for creating regional innovations. The contributions cover a significant range of topics within the field of entrepreneurship and regional economic development in a global market context.

The symposium was organized by University West, Uddevalla, Sweden in cooperation with the School of Public Policy, George Mason University, Fairfax, USA and Jönköping International Business School, Jönköping, Sweden.

The symposium was sponsored by CESIS (Centre of Excellence for Science and Innovation Studies), Stockholm and Jönköping, Sweden; Centre of Higher Education in Bohuslän, Uddevalla, Sweden; Formas (the Swedish Research Council for Environment, Agricultural Sciences and Spatial Planning), Stockholm, Sweden; Gustaf B. Thordén Foundation, Sweden; Preemraff Lysekil, Sweden; School of Public Policy, George Mason University, Fairfax, VA, USA; University West, Uddevalla, Sweden; The Bank of Sweden Tercentenary Foundation, Stockholm, Sweden; The Municipality of Lysekil, Sweden; The Municipality of Uddevalla, Sweden; VINNOVA (Swedish Governmental Agency for Innovation Systems), Stockholm, Sweden; and Västra Götalandsregionen, Göteborg, Sweden.

The organizers of the symposium thank Swedbank, Uddevalla, Sweden for sponsoring the Best Paper Awards Programme.

The authors and the editors thank Iréne Bernhard, University West, Sweden and Ulla Forslund, Jönköping International Business School, Sweden, for editorial assistance.

Charlie Karlsson Börje Johansson Roger R. Stough

Jönköping and Fairfax, VA, March 2010

1. Introduction – human capital and agglomeration

Charlie Karlsson, Börje Johansson and Roger R. Stough

In recent decades, we have witnessed an increasing interest in phenomena associated with the emerging knowledge economy. However, the concept as such was launched in the late 1950s and early 1960s (Drucker, 1959; Machlup, 1962). The fundamental characteristics of the global knowledge economy of today are on the one hand a continuous increase in knowledge investments such as education and knowledge production, and on the other hand, a widening application of knowledge in the development, production, distribution and use of goods and services. In this context, knowledge can be defined to comprise the abilities, capabilities, methods, creativity and persistence in identifying and solving problems by collecting, selecting, interpreting and applying existing knowledge and information (cf. van Oort and Raspe, 2007).

The above observations imply a distinction between knowledge as 'an object' and knowledge as talent, skills, know-how and understanding embodied in individuals. The concern of this book is primarily the latter aspect, including creativity as a dynamic and knowledge-enhancing capacity. It is individuals and teams of individuals who identify and solve problems and pursue activities that involve creation of new knowledge. It is also individuals who are responsible for advancing formal and informal education, where teaching, tutoring and other forms of exchange of ideas transfer knowledge to other individuals. Thus it is only natural that skills and abilities of individuals to solve problems and transfer knowledge are a focal point in the knowledge economy. These skills and abilities are built up in investment processes, which involve formal and informal education as well as learning by doing, learning by using and accumulation of experiences. Normally, we view the value of these skills and abilities of an individual as his or her human capital.

The increased interest in the knowledge economy has led to the development of new models of economic growth, frequently referred to as the theory of endogenous growth, in which the production of knowledge is endogenously determined, and in which the spillover of knowledge plays a critical role in the growth process (Romer, 1986; Lucas, 1988). The foundation for the role of knowledge was in principle introduced several decades earlier in Arrow (1962) and Solow (1956, 1957), who both advocated the significance of learning mechanisms for increasing productivity. In the original versions of the endogenous growth theories, knowledge was assumed to move instantaneously and without friction between economic agents. However, it is obvious that the spread of knowledge is far from perfect and that knowledge transfer is a both time- and resource-consuming process (Karlsson and Johansson, 2006). This implies that different economic actors located at different points in geographical space have different knowledge access, even if they are in the same trade. Assuming that knowledge is essential in the growth process, this implies that different locations have different growth prospects given the differences in their knowledge accessibility. On top of this we can observe that the critical input in the knowledge economy – the human capital – is strongly concentrated in geographical space, much more so than most other types of economic resources and activities. In other words, we can conclude that human capital exhibits strong tendencies to agglomerate in certain locations.

In this discourse, it is interesting that economists have for a long time stressed that there exists a link between the agglomeration of human capital, sometimes called talent (Florida, 2002), and regional development and growth (Myrdal, 1957; Hirschman, 1958; Kaldor, 1970). The contributions from these scholars observe that urban regions function as seedbeds of creativity and innovation, and that human capital, in particular, is an important factor in stimulating economic growth (Park et al., 1925; Jacobs, 1961; Thompson, 1965; Lucas, 1988).

Park et al. (1925) were probably the first to stress the role of urban regions in concentrating and stimulating human creativity. Jacobs (1961) illustrated how urban regions function as open systems, which attract talented individuals from different backgrounds and spur their creative capacities. Lucas (1988) presented a formal theory showing how urban regions function as attractors for human capital, thereby forming an arena for the generation of new ideas and economic growth. It is in this connection important to observe that large urban regions are also the dominant communication and transport network nodes and as such the primary locations of emission and reception of knowledge and information. Because these regions contain concentrations of complex communication arrangements and transport terminals, information diffuses more easily from and to urban regions than it does within the hinterland of each urban region and otherwise peripheral areas (Florax and Folmer, 1992; Guillain and Huriot, 2001).

In recent years, the literature on urban and regional economics has revealed a substantial increase of interest in how agglomeration in general and knowledge spillovers in particular affect the regional growth process at the firm level, the sector level and the overall level. This interest has developed into enquiries into how agglomeration economies can explain differences between regions in terms of the knowledge intensity of firms, and the knowledge spillovers between firms have been highlighted (Rosenthal and Strange, 2003; Capello and Nijkamp, 2004; Cheshire and Duranton, 2004). We can observe that human capital measured in terms of people with higher education[1] levels tend to agglomerate to a substantially higher degree than the population at large.[2] This naturally raises the following questions: Why do highly educated people, i.e. the carriers of human capital, tend to concentrate in large agglomerations? What are the agglomerative forces? How does this agglomeration of human capital affect different types of economic activities and in particular their location behaviour?

All these questions are formulated in the spirit of urban agglomerations as magnets, which attract persons who embody knowledge. They are assumed to select such locations, but why? How does the agglomeration of human capital and certain types of related economic activities affect regional growth and development? Other pertinent questions concern to what extent knowledge-intensive labour (i) becomes more productive in urban agglomerations; (ii) has greater opportunities to harvest the fruits of its knowledge investments in urban milieus; and (iii) does not crowd out others in the knowledge-rich regions.

These questions are examples of issues raised and discussed in this book. The purpose of this introductory chapter is to discuss these questions at an overall level as well as to provide an overview of the contributions by the different chapters in this book. The outline of this chapter is as follows: in Section 1.1 we discuss and try to explain why human capital tends to agglomerate in large urban regions. How this affects the location of different types of economic activities is analysed in Section 1.2. In Section 1.3 we discuss the effects that human capital agglomeration can have on regional growth and development. The contributions collected in this book are presented in Section 1.4.

1.1 THE AGGLOMERATION OF HUMAN CAPITAL AND TALENT

The tendency of human capital and talent to concentrate in cities and urban regions, i.e. to urbanize, has been known for centuries. In synthesizing the literature, the formation and growth of industrial as well as modern cities at a general level are explained by benefits or more precisely spatially bounded externalities arising from a variety of market and non-market forces. At the same time, many researchers in the USA have advocated models of a representative city, characterized by an 'optimal size'. This phenomenon is often referred to as an inverted U-shaped (concave) curve, describing the relationship between the utility or real income per worker and the city's population or employment (Mills, 1967; Henderson, 1974). When smaller cities grow, workers benefit in terms of rising real per capita incomes due to the localized agglomeration benefits from increasing scale.[3]

The identified market and non-market forces include division of labour, lower search costs for matching specialized labour and firms, market size and non-traded intermediate inputs. Bigger and more dense local markets can, for example, support more varieties, and hence offer economies of diversity both in household consumption and in the use of local intermediate inputs (Krugman, 1991), where diversified inputs are assumed to improve innovation and efficiency among local producers (including exporters). Another important force is information spillovers, i.e. technological externalities from human capital, within industries and in input and output markets from economic agents in close proximity, which generate localized benefits for clustered firms when the spatial information decay is rapid (Henderson and Thisse, 2004; Rosenthal and Strange, 2004).

Duranton and Puga (2004) make a distinction between matching, sharing and learning mechanisms. The matching mechanisms work in such a way that the larger the number of employers and workers in a regional labour market, the higher are the chances for a good match between the needs of the employers and the skills of the workers, which increases regional labour productivity. Sharing mechanisms imply that spatial proximity between producers and customers allows both to reduce their spatial transaction costs, which induces lower prices, increased demand, higher output and higher wages. Learning mechanisms, finally, imply that the larger the number of people brought together in an urban region, the higher the potential for learning, which implies that knowledge production as well as knowledge diffusion becomes more efficient. In this case, one may wish to add that there is more to learn in knowledge-rich regions – and even more in large knowledge-rich places. Nevertheless, the general conclusion from this discussion is that clustering of firms and people may arise due to a number of different underlying forces generating spatially concentrated increasing returns to scale (Marshall, 1890; Duranton and Puga, 2004). With the general rise in real incomes, cities have also become centres of arts, entertainment and other amenities. Brueckner et al. (1999) show how the concentration of human capital increases with the supply of regional amenities. A more general understanding of the urbanization process also demands that issues such as the development of infrastructures and institutions are brought into the picture (North, 1981).

To understand the underlying urbanization processes it is necessary to start from a microeconomic framework, which contains centrifugal as well as centripetal forces. There are numerous models of urbanization in the literature on regional and urban economics. The original two-sector models were set up to explain urbanization in general and not specifically the agglomeration of human capital. In the original models people move from a rural sector to a general urban sector as an effect of exogenous factors, such as (unexplained) technology shifts (Lewis, 1954). These two-sector models focus on questions such as the existence of urban bias, the effects of public policies on urban–rural development, and the efficient allocation of population between the rural and the urban sector at a given point in time. What is typical of these models is that they are static and that urbanization is driven by exogenous technological factors that favour either the urban sector or the terms of trade of the urban sector. Extending the microeconomic issues in this type of model would include questions such as: (i) does urban productivity rise because in-migrants are more productive, or (ii) do migrants and already established workers become more productive because a growing urban region gets augmented agglomeration economies, or (iii) because of the interaction effects of both individual effects?

In recent decades, another type of two-sector model – the core–periphery model – has been used to explain urbanization (Krugman, 1991; Puga, 1999). These models usually specify two interacting regions. The core question in these two-sector models is the following: what conditions will retain two agglomerations, and what conditions will channel urbanization towards one of the regions? When the latter happens, an important and disproportional share of economic activities becomes concentrated in one of the regions. These models assume that there exists one sector characterized by monopolistic competition. The normal starting point is two identical regions that initially are affected by some external factor such as an exogenous (historical) location decision, which makes one of the regions the largest, or a technological improvement, which reduces transport costs in one region relative to the other. This external factor induces the development of an expanding core and a declining hinterland due to the existence of increasing returns. These models have a limited focus, since they target the analysis on what happens to the core–periphery relationship, when, for example, transport costs fall. This implies that even if these models are spatial models, their power to highlight agglomeration and urbanization in general and the agglomeration of human capital in particular remains unexploited. To provide a better understanding of agglomeration and urbanization in a more comprehensive way, the models must be capable of depicting the city formation process more generally. In this sense, there is a need for formulations with several urban regions, whose number and size are determined endogenously in a dynamic process. Fujita et al. (1999) struggle with this issue, and Fujita and Thisse (2002) suggest alternative ways to elaborate such ideas.

Within the framework of an exogenous growth model, it is possible to illustrate how increases in national population are accommodated through increases in the number of cities in the national system of cities (Henderson and Ioannides, 1981). Efficient city size will also grow due to exogenous technological changes, which increase agglomeration economies or reduce the commuting costs in urban areas. These basic ideas were developed by Black and Henderson (1999) in an endogenous growth model, where there are two types of cities, each using different technologies and having different human capital intensities. In their model, members of growing dynastic families are allocated between the two types of cities. Human capital is the only capital in the model and there is no formal market for human capital. However, there exists an intra-family capital market with family members in low capital-intensity cities lending to those in high capital-intensity cities. People in cities with a high human capital intensity earn a (positive or negative) premium relative to those in the other type of city, but their nominal wages must be high enough to pay back the human capital they have borrowed in order to earn the returns of their higher required levels of human capital.

Assuming conditions allowing for steady-state growth, people accumulate human capital continuously. The regional stock of human capital within cities generates a knowledge externality, which is translated into improved production efficiency and thus the efficient city sizes grow continuously. The urban knowledge externalities are the source of national economic growth. Hence urban and national growth processes are interdependent, parallel processes. In the Black and Henderson model, both types of cities grow at the same rate in terms of their size, and if the national population growth is high enough, both types of cities grow in number at the same rate.

What more can be said about the agglomeration of human capital and talent? In terms of modelling, there exist endogenous urban growth models with human capital agglomeration. In the model presented by Henderson and Wang (2005), there is a migration from rural to urban sectors driven by increased human capital and per capita income. The urban sector consists of many cities, which grow in size with human capital accumulation and in number as the national population increases and people move from the rural to the urban sector. The demand for food products produced in the rural sector is assumed to be income inelastic. This implies that as real incomes increase, the relative demand for food products will decline at the same time as the productivity in the food sector increases. Thus labour will be pushed out of the rural sector, and induced to move to the urban sector as the relative demand for urban products increases over time. However, to get a deeper understanding of the agglomeration of human capital there are a number of further questions that need to be considered:

- What induces people to invest in human capital?
- What is the composition of the labour demand in the rural and the urban sector, and how does it change over time?
- What factors induce educated, knowledge-intensive labour to move from the rural to the urban sector?
- Why do certain activities prefer to locate in cities and urban regions?
- How does the composition of urban activities change over time?
- What role do infrastructure and institutions play in the urbanization process?
- Is there an inter-urban equilibrium that is consistent with a change process involving both expanding and declining urban regions?

1.2 HUMAN CAPITAL AGGLOMERATION AND THE LOCATION OF ECONOMIC ACTIVITIES

To more fully understand why human capital has such a high tendency to agglomerate in cities and urban regions, one needs to fully explore urban regions as places for both production and consumption. It seems obvious, starting with the production aspect, that certain industries and activities in the economy at each point in time prefer an urban location, and thus can be classified as urban industries and activities. Certain industries such as universities have largely been urban for centuries with a few noted exceptions, at least in the USA, of universities located in more rural and isolated places. Other industries, such as many of the manufacturing industries that developed in the city centres during the industrial revolution, have with few exceptions left the city centres to locate either in the outskirts of the city region or in more peripheral places, including totally non-urban locations. Recent decades have witnessed how, for example, knowledge-intensive business services agglomerated historically in urban centres and, in particular, in the core of large urban regions.

One major reason for the agglomeration of production in urban regions and metropolitan areas today is the existence of various positive externalities such as:

- the potential to realize internal economies of scale in a larger and denser market;
- the existence of a larger labour market with a more diverse and specialized labour force;
- the existence of a larger supply of specialized input services;
- the existence of well-developed intra- and interregional infrastructures, which allow for frequent local face-to-face interaction with customers and suppliers in the region as well as planned face-to-face interaction with customers and suppliers in other regions.

Industries and firms with knowledge-intensive and knowledge-creation activities that demand accessibility to a labour force with deep and varied knowledge and specialization, as well as labour equipped with special talents, will be attracted by the labour market in large and dense urban regions. The underlying reason is that the competitiveness of firms in these industries is critically dependent upon their creativity (Andersson, 1985; Fujita and Thisse, 1996). The level of creativity is a function of personal communication within groups of people with common interests and goals (Lucas, 1988). However, distance is a barrier to the spread of information and knowledge (Hägerstrand, 1965). Thus efficient communication within such groups is dependent upon the options for face-to-face interaction (Saxenian, 1994), since the knowledge to be exchanged is often complex, uncertain and developing. The incentives to develop interactive communication come from the need to avoid the risk of misunderstanding when the knowledge involved is complex (Gaspar and Glaeser, 1998). Here frequent encounters are critical for an efficient diffusion and good understanding of information and knowledge (Leonard and Strauss, 1997). A prerequisite for efficient communication is that the individuals involved understand things in the same way and thus share the same culture (Arrow, 1974; Cohen and Levinthal, 1990). Proximity between economic agents favours the establishment of a common language and thus facilitates the understanding of the information and the knowledge exchanged (Guillain and Huriot, 2001). Proximity is a vehicle for calibrating the processes of encoding and decoding complex messages.

The size of the communication groups is critical, since people have different skills. To solve complex problems and to create new knowledge, the groups must be large enough to contain the necessary complementary skills and experiences. Knowledge creation and problem solving are critical for competitiveness in the modern knowledge economy, which implies that the most important activity of economic agents to achieve this is information and knowledge exchange. Due to their rich and specialized supply of arenas for such exchange processes, large and dense urban regions offer the best conditions for arranging such communication activities – ranging from congress meetings to bars – and it is natural that such information-intensive activities agglomerate in large urban regions (Fujita and Ogawa, 1982).[4] Florida (1995) characterizes such regions as 'learning regions', although the label 'creative regions' seems more to the point. In Florida's interpretation firms benefit from concentrating their activities in such regions, because such locations allow them to minimize transport (contact) costs for a given level of learning, and to maximize their learning with a given budget for interaction costs. Firms striving to augment their creative capabilities have strong incentives to locate in these learning regions.

Consider now that new problems to be solved are emerging. Under such conditions, there is a need to change the composition of the creative groups. Large urban (metropolitan) regions are proper places for such rearrangements. This implies that large and dense urban regions give rise to substantial static and dynamic scale and scope effects, because in such regions it is possible to have many creative groups as well as to change the composition of each group over time. It must also be acknowledged that ideas and knowledge have public-good characteristics, which implies that the communication processes will generate localized spillover effects. This implies that the creative processes in large urban regions themselves can induce strong agglomeration tendencies (Fujita and Thisse, 1996).

Large urban regions and, in particular, metropolitan regions are centres of innovation, headquarters and the locus of advanced business services. Large urban regions are normally highly diversified,[5] making it possible for new firms but also for development units in established firms to experiment with different technologies until they learn what technology best satisfies their goals (Duranton and Puga, 2000). When firms have adopted a standard technology, production will be decentralized to smaller, more specialized urban regions. According to this model, large diversified urban regions function as centres for R&D and innovation and as incubators for new high-tech products. The market penetration and routine development of these products follow the product cycle model in the sense that once a product has become standardized and its production process has become routine, the location of its production will move to smaller cities or be off-shored to countries with lower land and labour costs.

Duranton and Puga (2005) present a model of functional specialization in large urban regions. For the organization of production and final sale, the large multinational firms need specialized business services, which Duranton and Puga summarize as 'headquarter functions'. Due to the improvements in transportation and communication technologies, these headquarter functions can be localized in large urban regions, often far away from many of the production facilities located in smaller cities all around the world. Such a location makes it possible for the headquarters to buy inputs locally from specialized business service firms in areas such as R&D, marketing, financing, law, exporting, logistics etc. The co-location of headquarter functions in large urban regions generates agglomeration benefits due to the shopping behaviour of these headquarters. Together they create the foundations for a wide variety of specialized intermediate business service firms from which the headquarters can buy locally when they want to outsource various services.

As the urban demand for educated and experienced individuals expands, wages for such kinds of employees will increase, and more and more of these individuals are attracted to these regions. A large market is attractive for individuals who are rich in human capital, because it provides better expected job matches and thus a higher wage (Kim, 1990), but probably also a more interesting job. It also offers lower risks for unemployment in case of idiosyncratic employment shocks. Large urban regions generally offer more 'liquid' labour markets to people with specialist skills. In order to attract human-capital-rich employees, knowledge-intensive firms may be forced to offer jobs in large urban regions with liquid labour markets. To attract these employees to other regions they would normally need to pay substantially higher wages.

Urban regions are also the location of institutions of higher education, which implies that they also attract households that give priority to education possibilities for their children. In addition, the location of one or several universities in an urban region means that the conditions for communication externalities are greater in these locations.

1.3 HUMAN CAPITAL AGGLOMERATION AND REGIONAL GROWTH AND DEVELOPMENT

The early development economists in the postwar period emphasized that the spatial agglomeration of human capital generated benefits over and above the private returns reaped directly by the individuals themselves. Today these social benefits are usually considered the result of either market-mediated or extra-market-mediated[6] human-capital externalities (Moretti, 2004a). Contributions by Arrow (1962), Romer (1986) and Lucas (1988) stress that human-capital externalities arising from uncompensated learning processes between individuals are an important source of economic growth, underpinning the importance of arguments, which refer to technological non-market externalities. However, pecuniary market externalities related to human capital, for example, may arise if firms choose their investments in physical capital in anticipation of the expected average human capital of their future employees (Acemoglu, 1996). It is in this context important to distinguish between (i) static externalities, which imply that increases in human capital have a one-time effect on output (Lucas, 1988), and (ii) dynamic externalities, which imply that increases in human capital make the economy grow faster, due either to a larger number of innovations (Romer, 1990) or to more efficient imitation of technologies developed by others (Nelson and Phelps, 1966). If we are able to demonstrate that there exist human-capital externalities, this has indeed strong policy implications (Aghion and Howitt, 1998).

Obviously there are strong theoretical arguments but also tentative empirical evidences that the agglomeration of human capital contributes to regional development and growth. Empirical studies, for example, have found that an urban region's supply of educated people plays an important role in generating urban growth in metropolitan areas in terms of population, employment and incomes (Glaeser et al., 1995). Glaeser (1994) showed that the association between human capital and growth seems to get stronger over time. Black and Henderson (1999) found in a panel context for the USA that cities with higher shares of college graduates grow faster in each decade during the period 1940–90.[7]

Rauch (1993) found empirically that the geographic concentration of human capital significantly increases productivity and wages. He approached his research problem by augmenting the standard wage regression of the Mincer type (Mincer, 1974; Card, 1999) with data on the properties of the cities where individuals are located. In his empirical modelling, he related the wage w of individual i in city c to basic characteristics of the individual, such as education and experience, X_{ic}, to the average level of schooling in city c, S_c, and to other characteristics of city c, Z_c, using the equation

$$\log w_{ic} = \alpha X_{ic} + \beta S_c + \gamma Z_c + \varepsilon_{ic},$$

where ε_{ic} accounts for all unobserved factors influencing individual wages across cities. By estimating the above equation using data for US cities in 1980, he found β to be significantly positive, indicating the existence of human-capital externalities at the city level in the USA. Rauch's approach has certain drawbacks: (i) it does not account for unobserved city characteristics, which are time-invariant, while still affecting both schooling and wages; and (ii) it assumes city-level schooling to be exogenous.

Rosenthal and Strange (2004) report in their literature survey that there seems to be a consensus that a doubling of the size of cities is associated with a productivity increase in the range of 3 to 8 per cent. Other studies have shown that if the employment density is doubled, wages and productivity increase by about 6 per cent in the USA (Ciccone and Hall, 1996), by about 5 per cent in European countries (Ciccone, 2002), and by 4 per cent in the UK (Anastassova, 2006). Karlsson and Pettersson (2005) show in panel study of urban centres in Sweden that a 10 per cent increase of local accessibility to population, i.e. labour, increases gross regional product per square kilometre by more than 5 per cent. Furthermore, the share of the labour force with three or more years of university education also has a significant positive effect on regional product. For Germany, Möller and Haas (2003a, 2003b) found that a doubling of the employment density tended to raise individual wages by about 2.5 per cent and that these benefits increased with the skill level. However, this is not a measure of human-capital externalities, since it also includes the effects of other influences. Suedekum (2006) analyses human-capital externalities in a study of the effect of regional human capital shares on regional employment growth. He finds that regional human-capital accessibility has a positive impact on subsequent employment of low-skilled workers, indicating a complementary relationship between skilled and unskilled workers. Moretti (2004b) reports that he found the largest wage increases for college students between 1980 and 1990 in the US cities where the share of college graduates had increased most. In another study using plant-level data, he found that the output of plants in high-tech city industries did rise with the levels of schooling in other high-tech industries in the same city (Moretti, 2004c), which is consistent with the existence of human-capital externalities. However, there is an alternative explanation. It could be that skill-based technological progress is translated into productivity and wage increases of college graduates in high-tech industries. In such a scenario, cities specializing in industries having rapid productivity growth would experience faster growth and attract more college graduates from other regions. The period 1980–90 was characterized by increased wage premiums for college graduates, which Katz and Murphy (1992) explain by skilled-based technological progress, which supports the alternative hypothesis.

It has been questioned to what extent the urban wage and productivity premium can be ascribed to human-capital externalities. Glaeser and Mare (2001) argue, for example, that a large part of the urban wage premium is due to spatial sorting of workers with respect to observable and unobservable characteristics. Still, they find that human-capital externalities increase wages in urban regions by about 12 per cent. For French cities, human-capital externalities are estimated to increase wages in urban regions by about 3 per cent (Combes et al., 2008).

One reason for the current uncertainty concerning the size of the human-capital externalities is the critical identification problems involved (Angrist and Kreuger, 2001). Omitted variables in the econometric specification may imply that human-capital externalities are not properly identified. If, for example, shifts in the supply of and demand for different skills in urban regions, i.e. structural change, are not acknowledged in the analysis, this could lead to substantially biased estimates. Ciccone and Peri (2006) show, using a Mincerian wage equation, that a positive effect of average schooling may not be due to human-capital externalities. Instead, they suggest an alternative approach, which starts from the fact that the wage differential between workers with low and high education mirrors differences in marginal social products between the two types of workers when human-capital externalities are absent. According to their results, there is no significant evidence of human-capital externalities at the level of US states and cities.

It is also interesting to note that the use of instrumental variables in some cases, as in the study by Acemoglu and Angrist (1999), has reduced social returns from education to below 1 per cent, which is substantially lower than in earlier studies. They assume that US states rather than cities are the relevant aggregates when estimating the equation used by Rauch (1993). They show that at the state level changes in compulsory schooling and child-labour laws can be used as instruments for changes in average schooling at the state level. According to their study, there is no evidence between 1960 and 1980 of significant schooling externalities.

However, Heuermann (2008), using instrumental variables in a study in Germany, finds human-capital externalities to be an important wage-determining factor. According to his estimations, the regional share of highly qualified workers increases wages by 1.8 per cent for highly qualified workers and by 0.6 per cent for other workers. He claims that human-capital externalities are underestimated by about 50 per cent in simple regressions for workers at all qualification levels. He interprets his results to indicate that knowledge externalities emerging through communication and learning processes are of greater importance for highly qualified workers, while other workers are influenced primarily by pecuniary externalities coming from investment decisions by firms affected by the overall regional human-capital endowments.

This introductory overview has highlighted some of the current knowledge as regards three critical questions related to the emerging knowledge economy: (i) why do human capital and talent tend to agglomerate in large urban regions? (ii) how does this agglomeration affect the location of different types of economic activities? and (iii) how does this agglomeration affect regional growth? In this way we have presented important aspects of the state of the art in the field, which serves as a foundation for the different contributions contained in this book. The contributions in this book extend the current research frontier in three directions, with their focus on the role of human capital and talent for creativity, entrepreneurship and regional development, the role of institutions for the behaviour of firms and entrepreneurs and the influence of the global context for the location, export and innovation behaviour of firms in a knowledge economy.

1.4 STRUCTURE AND CONTRIBUTIONS

The content of this book is presented in the subsequent 13 chapters as well as in this introductory chapter. The 13 chapters are organized in three subparts: Chapters 2–7 focus on human capital and talent, Chapters 8–10 on institutions, and Chapters 11–14 on the global context.

1.4.1 Human Capital and Talent

Chapter 2, by Charlie Karlsson and Börje Johansson, is a conceptual effort that seeks to underpin the other contributions in this book with a solid review and synthesis of the relationship between creativity, knowledge and regional development. The understanding of economic development in regions in developed countries has gone through a fundamental change during recent decades. Nowadays, regions are increasingly looked upon as quasi-independent, dynamic marketplaces that are connected via flows of interregional and international trade, and via knowledge flows. Regional development is driven by changes in the economic specialization, which can be explained by two different, but complementary, theoretical frameworks for analysing location and trade, one old and one new. The old theoretical framework assumes that changes in the economic specialization of regions depend upon changes in the supply of durable and semi-durable regional characteristics. The new theoretical framework, known as the new economic geography, assumes that changes in the economic specialization of regions are driven by the dynamic interaction of regional market potentials and rational firms experiencing increasing returns. In their pure form, these theoretical frameworks can explain changes in regional economic specialization and consequently regional development without any reference to knowledge creation and other changes in knowledge assets. This is certainly a bit odd for a period of history often referred to as the era of the knowledge economy. So, does knowledge have no role to play as a force driving regional specialization and regional development? Or, is it the case that the traditional 'knowledge-free' explanations of changes in regional specialization and regional development are missing important points? In this chapter, the authors claim that knowledge infrastructure, human capital, talent, creativity, knowledge generation, knowledge protection, knowledge accumulation, knowledge appropriation, knowledge flows etc., as well as the creative use of knowledge, are basic factors that influence the specialization of regions and hence of regional development in both a regional and a global context.

In Chapter 3, Corinne Autant-Bernard, Pascal Billand and Nadine Massard stress that science has always been 'cooperative' in the sense that, with the development of modern scientific methods and the scientific journal system, scientists have communicated their findings to each other, both formally and informally. However, to anyone concerned with the creation and diffusion of knowledge and its application, it is clear that we are in a time of intense change. The main feature of this change is probably the increasingly networked nature of knowledge creation. The innovation process involves more and more actors, and more interconnected actors. These transformations are likely to affect both the location of R&D and the nature of new knowledge creation. Therefore they bring forth new issues for the geography of innovation. The aim of this chapter is to point out the main questions that arise when mapping knowledge diffusion over space and to suggest some research directions to deal with these questions.

In Chapter 4, Mediha Sahin, Alina Todiras and Peter Nijkamp argue that migrant entrepreneurs are new opportunity seekers in the urban economy and essential for a vital modern city. The phenomenon of 'migrant entrepreneurship' refers to business activities undertaken by migrants with a specific sociocultural and ethnic background or migrant origin. Migrant entrepreneurship distinguishes itself from 'normal' entrepreneurship though its orientation to migrant products, to migrant market customers or to indigenous migrant business strategies. Migrant groups that produce a strong entrepreneurial group can be of great economic significance for the migrant business community as well as for the total community, through job and opportunity creation. Recent literature has documented that migrant businesses are one of the fastest-growing sectors in the Dutch economy.

However, knowledge and information that documents entrepreneurial differences among migrants is lagging far behind this rapid growth. Previous research has mainly focused on knowledge of native entrepreneurs that informs mostly policy, education and research. Against this background, this chapter aims to investigate entrepreneurial similarities and differences from a multicultural perspective on migrant entrepreneurs. The authors focus mainly on four active and prominent migrant groups in the Netherlands: Turks, Moroccans, Surinamese and Antilleans.

First, they give a brief historical overview of migration from and to the Netherlands with an emphasis on postwar immigration and its impact on Dutch society. Next, they discuss the living and working conditions of migrant groups and they compare these groups with each other as well as with native Dutch groups in terms of their entrepreneurial behaviour. Their comparison and evaluation are, of course, limited by the available data. After evaluation of the development of migrant entrepreneurship in the Netherlands, they examine the basic concepts of migrant entrepreneurship on the basis of the main characteristics and psychological, sociological, economic and demographic determinants. Finally, they consider some socioeconomic and sociocultural effects of migrant entrepreneurship on the national economy, sustainability and diversity.

Juan Julio Gutierrez in Chapter 5 explores the determinants of three innovation outputs in low- and medium-technology (LMT) manufacturing factories located in El Salvador, Guatemala, Honduras and Nicaragua. These countries are participants in the Central American Free Trade Agreement with the USA. Three types of innovations are discussed in this chapter: (i) new products; (ii) new production processes; and (iii) small or incremental changes in product performance, which may over a long time period have major technological and economic effects. The theoretical basis for identifying the determinants of innovation outputs builds upon two strands of literature. First, innovation is dependent on the factory's networks of internal and external relationships. The internal network is equated to intrafirm cooperation, which encompasses the relationship of local foreign-owned factories with their headquarters. The external network is divided into inter-factory and interfirm relationships and institutional relationships. Second, innovation inputs that produce technological change are: (i) adaptation and development within the factory; (ii) acquisition of machinery and equipment; and (iii) human capital. The analytical framework is applied to a cross-country factory-level database of LMT manufacturing industries (the World Bank's 'Investment Climate Survey'). The results support the idea that external networks, mainly interaction with universities, and purchasing of foreign licences constitute a mechanism for generating innovation outputs in LMT sectors. However, foreign ownership does not seem to have a positive impact on innovative output, which indicates enclave characteristics of foreign-owned factories. On the input side, the results show importance and robustness with regard to: (i) machinery and equipment acquisition, where new technology is embodied in those capital goods; (ii) adaptation and development within the factory, where learning by doing is an integral component in the process of making incremental output innovations in LMT manufacturing industries; and (iii) the hiring of new personnel, which helps absorb, use and adapt new technology, assuming that technological know-how is embodied in technical personnel.

There is an increasing interest in the role of endogenous factors in regional development. The literature places emphasis on factors such as regional industrial structure and diversification/specialization, human capital, population size and growth, leadership and institutional arrangements, in addition to the traditional concern with regional resource endowments. Robert J. Stimson in Chapter 6 reviews the evidence from Australia on the role some endogenous factors play in differentiating regional performance in mainly non-metro settings.

Michael Olsson in Chapter 7 stresses that the mobility of workers is important, not least as a source of knowledge transfer. In the labour market, unemployed persons face accessibility to vacancies, and employers with vacancies face accessibility to unemployed persons. In a country like Sweden, the unemployment insurance regulations state some rather strict mobility requirements for those unemployed who are insured against unemployment. If these regulations were used in practice by the labour market agencies, the two accessibilities would change substantially compared to the current practice. Moreover, this would have consequences for the flow of knowledge.

1.4.2 Institutions

In Chapter 8, Kristina Nyström uses an institutional approach to investigate the relationship between the regional institutional environment and regional new firm formation. The importance of perceived attitudes regarding private enterprises, local taxes, political majority, the size of the government sector, and perceived rules and bureaucracy on new firm formation in 286 Swedish municipalities are investigated. The empirical findings show that perceived positive attitudes towards private enterprises and political governance by a right-bloc majority tend to have positive effects on new firm formation. A large local government sector, on the other hand, tends to have negative (crowding-out) effects on regional new firm formation. This chapter also explores if the effect that different regional institutional arrangements have on new firm formation is similar across industries. The pattern in the private service sector industries is most similar to the general pattern in the economy, while perceived rules and bureaucracy is the only institutional–environment variable that has an impact on new firm formation in manufacturing industries.

Referendums in which imperfectly informed individuals are called to vote for or against an innovative project can bring about inefficient outcomes, as compared to the outcomes that would arise with completely informed individuals. In Chapter 9, Tsuyoshi Hatori and Kiyoshi Kobayashi present an incomplete information game to investigate the influence of interest groups' voices on judgements of individuals. It is shown in the chapter that, because of the lack of knowledge of individuals about an innovation project, a limited number of interest groups that disagree with the innovation can use their voices in strategic fashion and try to prevent a referendum outcome containing the majority will. Alternative institutional designs are introduced to overcome this inefficiency, and some problems regarding the referendum process are outlined.

In Chapter 10, by Kakuya Matsushima and Kiyoshi Kobayashi, the risk-sharing structure between the firm providing transportation services and the customers of the pre-paid and post-paid systems is investigated theoretically. The pre-paid systems refer to the complete contracts that have to be established before service transactions, while the post-paid systems refer to the incomplete contracts, where the application of the pre-paid specified fare structure is described in the contract, and the actual payments are conditional upon the actual consumption by the consumers. The three-period contract model is formulated to investigate the impacts of pre-paid and post-paid systems upon the firm's profit and the consumers' welfare. The chapter concludes that social welfare can always be improved by introducing a post-paid system in addition to the conventional price system.

1.4.3 The Global Context

Gary S. Cook and Naresh R. Pandit in Chapter 11 examine the small but growing literature that offers explanations for the location of multinational enterprises (MNEs) in clusters. It tests propositions of this literature against the findings of a study that compares MNEs and non-MNEs regarding the advantages and disadvantages of a location in the City of London financial services cluster, which has an extraordinarily large MNE component. As such, it makes a contribution towards current efforts to bridge the gap between the established theories of MNEs and those of industrial clustering. The evidence presented in the chapter is based on 39 semi-structured interviews with very senior managers across seven major subsectors of the financial services industry in London and 310 postal questionnaires. The primary conclusion in this chapter is that MNEs and non-MNEs have different and multiple motives for locating in the cluster. MNEs perceive significantly higher benefits of close proximity in terms of competing with rivals and benchmarking against them compared to non-MNEs. Moreover, they perceive significantly higher benefits in terms of ease of communication and ability to have face-to-face contacts than non-MNEs, undermining popular 'end-of-geography' arguments. The authors also reach two auxiliary conclusions. Strong clusters generate disadvantages in the form of congestion and the like, and this is perceived as a disadvantage by MNEs. Moreover, since disadvantages may change over time, MNEs need continually to assess which activities they need to locate in a cluster. The second auxiliary conclusion is that for MNEs, clusters may provide advantages over and above those available to non-MNEs.

During the 1980s, many economists started to use the term globalization as a catchword for an increased interaction between countries in world trade. However, the literature does not provide a clear definition of globalization. In Chapter 12, Börje Johansson and Desirée Nilsson set up a number of criteria and formulate hypotheses about globalization, which they explore for Swedish export flows during the period 1965–2000. Globalization, in this chapter, is referred to as increases in country diversity, extended export radii, less effect of distance on trade flows, and increases in the ratio of exports to importing countries' incomes. However, the results from the empirical analysis do not support the hypotheses of increasing trade globalization. It is rather the case that export flows are becoming more internationally regionalized.

Martin Andersson, Sara Johansson and Hans Lööf in Chapter 13 present a comprehensive description and analysis of the international trading activities of firms based on new detailed Swedish data. As a small open economy with a limited domestic market, Sweden constitutes an interesting contrast to existing evidence. The authors show that many of the stylized facts from large countries (specifically the USA) about firms' participation in international trade also pertain to a small open economy. They provide robust evidence of selection operating from market to market, which is consistent with the hypothesis that firms with a low productivity level are confined to markets with low productivity thresholds. Furthermore, they show that selection also applies to the number of products traded. Both export and import productivity premiums increase with the number of markets and number of products traded, respectively. There is a substantial heterogeneity among exporters and importers in terms of the number of markets they trade with, and in terms of the number of products they trade.

The purpose of the final chapter in this book, Chapter 14, written by Urban Gråsjö, is to analyse the effects of national and international knowledge flows on innovative activity. Therefore a knowledge production function is estimated with patent applications in Swedish municipalities as the measure of innovation. The knowledge resources applied are R&D investments and high-value imports. In order to account for the importance of proximity, the knowledge resources are expressed as accessibilities. The total accessibility of a municipality is decomposed into local, intraregional and interregional accessibility. The main results indicate that the knowledge resources in a given municipality tend to have a positive effect on the innovative activity of another municipality, given that the municipalities belong to the same functional region. Thus the results of the analysis indicate that knowledge flows transcend municipal borders, but that they tend to be bounded within the functional region. This result holds for both R&D investments and high-value import products.

NOTES

1. According to the human capital theory, education enhances an individual's skill level and thereby his or her human capital (Schultz, 1961; Becker, 1964). A workforce with a higher skill level increases the production capacity of an economy.
2. In the Nordic countries, for example, this evolution is combined with an increased share of knowledge-intensive labour in medium-sized urban regions as well (e.g. NUTEK, 2006).
3. The inverted U-shaped (concave) form implies that at some point the marginal benefits of increasing city size are overtaken by rising marginal costs for commuting and other diseconomies. The idea of a concave curve is at best a 'tentative simplification' and discussions of the pertinent diseconomies are beyond the purpose of this introductory chapter.
4. Actually, Beckmann (1976) suggested the need for interaction among individuals as an explanation for the existence of cities.
5. Baumont et al. (1998) maintain that cities and urban regions can be defined basically by the concepts of agglomeration and diversity.
6. Extra-market externalities from human capital accumulation include reductions in crime rates, better-informed voting decisions, improved health-related behaviour etc. (Davies, 2002).
7. The association between human capital and urban growth also holds for much longer periods, as shown by Simon and Nardinelli (1996) using data for England.

REFERENCES

Acemoglu, D. (1996), 'A micro-foundation for social increasing returns in human capital accumulation', *Quarterly Journal of Economics*, **111**, 779–804.

Acemoglu, D. and J. Angrist (1999), 'How large are the social returns to education? Evidence from compulsory schooling laws', NBER Working Paper, no. 7444, Cambridge, MA: National Bureau of Economic Research.

Aghion, P. and P. Howitt (1998), *Endogenous Growth Theory*, Cambridge, MA: MIT Press.

Anastassova, L. (2006), 'Productivity differences and agglomeration across districts of Great Britain', CERGE-EI Working Paper no. 289, Center of Economic Research and Graduate Education, Charles University of Prague.

Andersson, Å.E. (1985), *Kreativitet – Storstadens Framtid*, Stockholm: Prisma.

Angrist, J.D. and A.B. Kreuger (2001), 'Instrumental variables and the search for identification: from supply and demand to natural experiments', *Journal of Economic Perspectives*, **15**, 69–85.

Arrow, K.J. (1962), 'The economic implications of learning by doing', *The Review of Economic Studies*, **29**, 155–73.
Arrow, K.J. (1974), *The Limits of Organization* (The Fels Lectures on Public Policy Analysis), New York: W.W. Norton.
Baumont, C., H. Beguin and J.-M. Huriot (1998), 'An economic definition of the city', in D.A. Griffith, C.G. Amrein and J.-M. Huriot (eds), *Econometric Advances in Spatial Modelling and Methodology: Essays in Honour of Jean Paelinck*, Dordrecht: Kluwer Academic Publishers, pp. 15–31.
Becker, G.S. (1964), *Human Capital: A Theoretical and Empirical Analysis with Special Reference to Schooling*, New York: National Bureau of Economic Research.
Beckmann, M.J. (1976), 'Spatial equilibrium in the dispersed city', in Y.Y. Papageorgiou (ed.), *Mathematical Land Use Theory*, Lexington, MA: Lexington Books, pp. 117–25.
Black, D. and J. Henderson (1999), 'A theory of urban growth', *Journal of Political Economy*, **107**, 252–84.
Brueckner, J.K., J.-F. Thisse and Y. Zenou (1999), 'Why is central Paris rich and downtown Detroit poor? An amenity based theory', *European Economic Review*, **43**, 91–107.
Capello, R. and P. Nijkamp (2004), *Urban Dynamics and Growth. Advances in Urban Economics*, Amsterdam: Elsevier.
Card, D. (1999), 'The causal effect of education on earnings', in O. Ashenfelter and D. Card (eds), *Handbook of Labour Economics*, Amsterdam: North-Holland, pp. 1801–63.
Cheshire, P. and G. Duranton (2004), *Recent Developments in Urban and Regional Economics*, Cheltenham, UK and Northampton, MA, USA: Edward Elgar.
Ciccone, A. (2002), 'Agglomeration effects in Europe', *European Economic Review*, **46**, 213–28.
Ciccone, A. and R.E. Hall (1996), 'Productivity and the density of economic activity', *The American Economic Review*, **86**, 54–70.
Ciccone, A. and G. Peri (2006), 'Identifying human capital externalities: theory with applications', *Review of Economic Studies*, **73**, 381–412.
Cohen, W.M. and D.A. Levinthal (1990), 'Absorptive capacity: a new perspective on learning and innovation', *Administrative Sciences Quarterly*, **35**, 128–52.
Combes, P.-P., G. Duranton and L. Gobillon (2008), 'Spatial wage disparities: sorting matters!', *Journal of Urban Economics*, **63** (2), 723–42.
Davies, J.B. (2002), 'Empirical evidence on human capital externalities', Working Paper 203–11, Department of Finance, Canada.
Drucker, P. (1959), *Landmarks of Tomorrow: A Report on the New Post-modern World*, New York: Harper.
Duranton, G. and D. Puga (2000), 'Nursery cities: urban diversity, process innovation, and the life cycle of products', *American Economic Review*, **91**, 1454–77.
Duranton, G. and D. Puga (2004), 'Micro-foundations of urban agglomeration economies', in J. Henderson and J.-F. Thisse (eds), *Handbook of Regional and Urban Economics*, Vol. 4, Amsterdam: Elsevier, pp. 2063–117.
Duranton, G. and D. Puga (2005), 'From sectoral to functional urban specialization', *Journal of Urban Economics*, **57**, 343–70.
Florax, R. and H. Folmer (1992), 'Knowledge impacts of universities on industries: an aggregate simultaneous investment model', *Journal of Regional Science*, **32**, 437–66.

Florida, R. (1995), 'Towards the learning region', *Futures*, **27**, 527–36.
Florida, R. (2002), *The Rise of the Creative Class*, New York: Basic Books.
Fujita, M. and H. Ogawa (1982), 'Multiple equilibria and structural transformation on non-monocentric urban configurations', *Regional Science and Urban Economics*, **12**, 161–96.
Fujita, M. and J.-F. Thisse (1996), 'Economics of agglomeration', *Journal of the Japanese and International Economies*, **10**, 339–78.
Fujita, M. and J.-F. Thisse (2002), *Economics of Agglomeration. Cities, Industrial Location, and Regional Growth*, Cambridge: Cambridge University Press.
Fujita, M., P. Krugman and A.J. Venables (1999), *The Spatial Economy: Cities, Regions and International Trade*, Cambridge, MA: MIT Press.
Gaspar, J. and E.L. Glaeser (1998), 'Information technology and the future of cities', *Journal of Urban Economics*, **43**, 136–56.
Glaeser, E.L. (1994), 'Cities, information and economic growth', *Cityscape*, **1**, 9–48.
Glaeser, E.L. and D.C. Mare (2001), 'Cities and skills', *Journal of Labor Economics*, **19**, 316–42.
Glaeser, E., J. Scheinkman and J. Shleifer (1995), 'Economic growth in a cross-section of cities', *Journal of Monetary Economics*, **36**, 117–43.
Guillain, R. and J.-M. Huriot (2001), 'The local dimension of information spillovers: a critical review of the empirical evidence in the case of innovation', *Canadian Journal of Regional Science*, **24**, 313–38.
Hägerstrand, T. (1965), 'Aspects of the spatial structure of social communication and the diffusion of information', *Papers of the Regional Science Association*, **16**, 27–42.
Henderson, J. (1974), 'The sizes and types of cities', *American Economic Review*, **61**, 640–56.
Henderson, J. and Y. Ioannides (1981), 'Aspects of growth in a system of cities', *Journal of Urban Economics*, **10**, 117–39.
Henderson, J. and J.-F. Thisse (2004) (eds), *Handbook of Regional and Urban Economics*, Vol. 4, Amsterdam: Elsevier.
Henderson, J. and H.G. Wang (2005), 'Urbanization and city growth', *Journal of Economic Geography*, **5**, 23–42.
Heuermann, D.F. (2008), 'Human capital externalities in Western Germany', Institute of Labour Law and Industrial Relations in the European Community, University of Trier, Trier (mimeo).
Hirschman, A.O. (1958), *The Strategy of Economic Development*, New Haven, CT: Yale University Press.
Jacobs, J. (1961), *The Death and Life of Great American Cities*, New York: Random House.
Kaldor, N. (1970), 'The case for regional policies', *Scottish Journal of Political Economy*, **17**, 337–48.
Karlsson, C. and B. Johansson (2006), 'Dynamics and entrepreneurship in a knowledge-based economy', in C. Karlsson, B. Johansson and R.R. Stough (eds), *Entrepreneurship and Dynamics in the Knowledge Economy*, New York: Routledge, pp. 12–46.
Karlsson, C. and L. Pettersson (2005), 'Regional productivity and accessibility to dense markets and knowledge', CESIS Working Paper No. 32, The Royal Institute of Technology, Stockholm and Jönköping International Business School, Jönköping.

Katz, L.F. and K.M. Murphy (1992), 'Changes in relative wages 1963–1987: supply and demand factors', *Quarterly Journal of Economics*, **107**, 35–78.
Kim, S. (1990), 'Labour heterogeneity, wage bargaining and agglomeration economies', *Journal of Urban Economics*, **28**, 160–77.
Krugman, P. (1991), 'Increasing returns and economic geography', *Journal of Political Economy*, **99**, 483–99.
Leonard, D., and S. Strauss (1997), 'Putting your whole company's brain to work', *Harvard Business Review*, **75** (4), 110–21.
Lewis, W. (1954), 'Economic development with unlimited supply of labour', *Manchester School of Economic and Social Studies*, **22**, 139–91.
Lucas, R.E. (1988), 'On the mechanics of economic development', *Journal of Monetary Economics*, **22**, 3–42.
Machlup, F. (1962), *The Production and Distribution of Knowledge in the United States*, Princeton, NJ: Princeton University Press.
Marshall, A. (1920 [1890]), *Principles of Economics*, 8th edn, London: Macmillan.
Mills, E. (1967), 'An aggregative model of resource allocation in a metropolitan area', *American Economic Review*, **57**, 197–210.
Mincer, J. (1974), *Schooling, Experience and Earnings*, New York: Columbia University Press.
Moretti, E. (2004a), 'Human capital externalities in cities', in J.V. Henderson and J.F. Thisse (eds), *Handbook of Regional and Urban Economics*, Amsterdam: Elsevier, pp. 2243–91.
Moretti, E. (2004b), 'Estimating the social return to higher education: evidence from longitudinal and repeated cross-section data', *Journal of Econometrics*, **121**, 175–212.
Moretti, E. (2004c), 'Workers' education, spillovers and productivity: evidence from plant level production functions', *American Economic Review*, **94**, 656–90.
Myrdal, G. (1957), *Economic Theory and Underdeveloped Regions*, New York: Duckworth.
Möller, J. and A. Haas (2003a), 'The agglomeration differential reconsidered – an investigation with German micro data 1984–1997', in J. Bröcker, D. Dohse and R. Soltwedel (eds), *Innovation Clusters and Regional Competition*, Berlin: Springer, pp. 182–215.
Möller, J. and A. Haas (2003b), 'Die Entwicklung der räumliche Lohnstruktur – empirische Befunde für Westdeutschland im Zeitraum 1984–1997', *Jahrbuch für Regionalwissenschaft*, **23** (1), 55–89.
Nelson, R.R. and E. Phelps (1966), 'Investment in humans, technological diffusion and economic growth', *American Economic Review*, **56**, 69–75.
North, D. (1981), *Structure and Change in Economic History*, New York: W.W. Norton.
NUTEK (2006), 'Metropolitan development fostering national growth' (in Swedish), Report B 2006:4, Verket för Näringslivsutveckling, Stockholm.
Park, R., E. Burgess and R. McKenzie (1925), *The City*, Chicago, IL: University of Chicago Press.
Puga, D. (1999), 'The rise and fall of regional inequalities', *European Economic Review*, **43**, 303–34.
Rauch, J.E. (1993), 'Productivity gains from geographic concentration of human capital: evidence from the cities', *Journal of Urban Economics*, **34**, 380–400.
Romer, P.M. (1986), 'Increasing returns and long-run growth', *The Journal of Political Economy*, **94**, 1002–37.

Romer, P.M. (1990), 'Endogenous technological change', *Journal of Political Economy*, **98** (5), S71–S102.
Rosenthal, S.S. and W.C. Strange (2003), 'Geography, industrial organization and agglomeration', *Review of Economics and Statistics*, **85**, 377–93.
Rosenthal, S.S. and W.C. Strange (2004), 'Evidence on the nature and sources of agglomeration economies', in J.V. Henderson and J.F. Thisse (eds), *Handbook of Regional and Urban Economics*, Vol. 4, Amsterdam: Elsevier, pp. 2119–71.
Saxenian, A. (1994), *Regional Advantage: Culture and Competition in Silicon Valley and Route 128*, Cambridge, MA: Harvard University Press.
Schultz, T.W. (1961), 'Investment in human capital', *American Economic Review*, **51**, 1–17.
Simon, C. and C. Nardinelli (1996), 'The talk of the town: human capital, information and the growth of English cities 1861–1961', *Explorations in Economic History*, **33**, 384–413.
Solow, R. (1956), 'A contribution to the theory of economic growth', *Quarterly Journal of Economics*, **70**, 65–94.
Solow, R. (1957), 'Technical change in an aggregative model of economic growth', *International Economic Review*, **6**, 18–31.
Suedekum, J. (2006), 'Human capital externalities and growth of high- and low-skilled jobs', IZA Discussion Paper No. 1969, IZA, Berlin.
Thompson, W. (1965), *A Preface to Urban Economics*, Baltimore, MD: Johns Hopkins Press.
van Oort, F.G. and O. Raspe (2007), 'Urban heterogeneity in knowledge-related economic growth', in J. Suriñach, R. Moreno and E. Vayá (eds), *Knowledge Externalities, Innovation Clusters and Regional Development*, Cheltenham, UK and Northampton, MA, USA: Edward Elgar, pp. 280–303.

PART I

Human capital and talent

2. Knowledge, creativity and regional development

Charlie Karlsson and Börje Johansson

The understanding of economic development in regions in developed countries has gone through a fundamental change during recent decades. Nowadays, regions are increasingly looked upon as independent, dynamic marketplaces that are connected via flows of interregional and international trade. Regional development is driven by changes in economic specialization, which can be explained by two different, but complementary, theoretical frameworks for analysing location and trade, one old and one new.

The old theoretical framework assumes that changes in the economic specialization of regions depend upon changes in the supply of durable and semi-durable regional characteristics. The new theoretical framework, known as the new economic geography, assumes that changes in the economic specialization of regions are driven by the dynamic interaction of regional market potentials and rational firms experiencing increasing returns. In their pure form, these theoretical frameworks can explain changes in regional economic specialization and thus regional development without any reference to knowledge creation and other changes in knowledge assets. This is certainly a bit odd for a period of history often referred to as the era of the knowledge economy. So, does knowledge have no role to play as a force driving regional specialization and regional development? Or, is it the case that the traditional 'knowledge-free' explanations of changes in regional specialization and regional development are missing important points?

In this chapter, we claim that knowledge infrastructure, human capital, talent, creativity, knowledge generation, knowledge protection, knowledge accumulation, knowledge appropriation, knowledge flows etc., as well as the creative use of knowledge, are basic drivers of the specialization of regions and hence of regional development. The purpose of this chapter is to discuss the role of knowledge and talent in regional development seen in both a regional and a global context.

This chapter is organized as follows: in Section 2.1 we introduce the concept of creative regions and discuss the role of these regions. This discussion is followed up in Section 2.2, where creative regions are treated within a framework of trade and location. Section 2.3 deals with the international system of creative regions and the links between these regions. The special role of large urban regions as creative regions is highlighted in Section 2.4. In Section 2.5, we highlight the role of spatial product cycles for regional development. Section 2.6 concludes.

2.1 CREATIVE REGIONS

Social scientists have for several decades pointed out that during the postwar period the developed economies have gone through fundamental changes. Different authors have used different concepts to characterize what they have seen as the most basic aspect of these changes. Thus concepts such as the information society, the service society, the post-industrial society, the knowledge society etc. have been introduced. As early as the 1980s the Swedish economist Åke E. Andersson started to describe the dynamics of the long-term changes in Western societies and to analyse the underlying driving forces (Andersson, 1985a, 1985b, 1988, 1989; Andersson and Mantsinen, 1980; Andersson et al., 1984; Andersson and Strömquist, 1989; Matthiessen and Andersson, 1993). According to him, the major driving force in the modern economy is creative activities, which generate new knowledge spurred by culture and communication. Development, handling and presentation of new knowledge and information employ a steadily increasing share of the labour force and are assumed to have strong spillover effects on industrial activities in manufacturing as well as in service production.

In the picture painted by Andersson, economic life is undergoing steady change towards more dynamic product competition. The resource base in developed economies is no longer natural resources, energy etc., but education and assets based on creative activities. The development in these economies is based upon new complementary infrastructure. Traditional means of transportation are complemented and sometimes also substituted by the communication networks created by modern information technology. Among the traditional means of transportation, road and air transport gradually get a more and more dominating role. Access to material and immaterial networks is becoming more and more critical.

To be able to understand, predict and/or influence regional development in the creative society, it is, according to Andersson (1985a), necessary to understand how the economic system can be divided into game or play and scene or arena. The economic and the political game with rapid and sudden changes is played out in an arena where changes are slow. The arena consists of material infrastructure (transport systems, buildings etc.), immaterial infrastructure (knowledge stocks, knowledge networks etc.) and institutions (formal and informal behavioural rules, property rights etc.).

A fundamental difference between the knowledge society and earlier societies is that its infrastructure consists in a profound way of many interconnected layers. The material infrastructure not only consists of road, rail, air and sea traffic networks. Rail, for example, serves local, regional, national as well as international transport demand. Rail traffic is complemented with increasingly advanced information systems for traffic control as well as for planning and booking trips, even in combination with other means of transport. The immaterial arena consists of knowledge and information assets. What is typical for the modern society is that knowledge and information flows are distributed over many different media and that electronic media increase its market share rapidly.

As regards institutions, the trends seem to go in different directions. On the one hand, there is an increasing stress on patents, copyrights etc. to protect property rights. On the other hand, there are signs that property rights are becoming less and less interesting in a rapidly changing society, which is illustrated by the increased reliance on 'open innovation' (Chesbrough, 2003). What seems to matter more and more is the position of individuals, firms and regions in different networks, i.e. what access they have to relevant knowledge and essential information.

As early as 1990, Andersson et al. demonstrated how industrial development and income growth in a region are positively influenced by a combination of universities and other research institutions, which grow synergetically with telecommunications and good accessibility to rapid transport systems in the form of air and road transport. The creative society emerges and creates growth and prosperity in regions that have this kind of potential.

In earlier phases, the military played the most important role internationally for stimulating creativity and innovation (Hall, 1990). In more recent phases, other sources, such as experiences, entertainment, health, environment and food, have become more and more important in generating a demand for creativity and innovation.

Fujita and Thisse (1996) suggest that human activities can be divided into two categories: production and creation, where the former represents routine methods of production. Creation, on the other hand, stands for the generation of new ideas, new knowledge, new technologies, new products etc. Andersson (1989) has analysed what characterizes dynamic creative activities. Successful dynamic creative activities are large logistical networks of small, creative units. The creative units have a non-hierarchical structure and are often self-organized. This implies that economics of scale are combined with, and complemented by, economies of scope. These characteristics have strong implications for the development of the system of functional regions.[1]

The difference between knowledge- and information-rich, and knowledge- and information-poor regions tends to grow. Regions with company R&D and research universities are centres for the development of fundamental research results, whether it occurs within the laboratories of universities or private companies. Such regions also offer deeper and more versatile knowledge, competence and supply of specialists as well as rich opportunities for personal contacts. There is a greater probability for spin-off growth if the regional milieu is information-rich (TV, radio, press, Internet, interregional and international information networks etc.) than if it is information-poor. It is also vital to have activities within the region that demand scientific results and can pay the price. With intraregional demand, spin-off effects occur, which stimulate further growth. There are ruptures from existing institutions and activities, since progressive inventors start their own businesses and become entrepreneurs.

For a creative region to grow and develop, it is important that the transport system has high quality and high capacity (Matthiessen and Andersson, 1993). Such a transport system allows contacts with and imports of new knowledge and innovations from other creative regions in the rest of the world. It is much better for a region to be an import centre than an export centre, even if exports also contribute to growth and prosperity. The reason is that the majority of all those ideas that generate new activities in a region get inspiration from other regions. Irrespective of how strong a region is in terms of R&D, it only produces a tiny share of all new knowledge in the world. Most of the ideas that are taken up in a given activity come from other creative regions. They are imported, they are used, they are developed, and they generate new production. The production of new goods or services places a firm among those firms that compete with product characteristics and have a capacity to pay high wages and salaries.

General import activities and knowledge-importing organizations are concentrated to a limited number of urban regions in each country. Production, which is based on imports, is generally a low-risk activity. That something has been imported implies that it has been possible to produce somewhere else and to sell. In a second round, the new products in the import regions spread to other (export) regions and thereby their exports are renewed (Jacobs, 1969, 1984).

There is a debate in the literature on whether diversified or specialized economic milieus offer the best conditions for creativity and innovation.

Vernon and Hoover (1959) and Vernon (1960) stressed the role of diversity in the New York region in its economic development. Thus, diversity seems to an important aspect of creative regions (Jacobs, 1961, 1969). Other important aspects of creative regions are, according to Andersson (1985a):

- flexibility in terms of social conditions, economic activities but also in terms of land-use planning;
- willingness to overcome political, language, cultural and physical barriers; and
- a sociocultural milieu marked by great openness and an atmosphere of tolerance.

The last aspect, especially, enhances the attractiveness of regions for creative talent and makes them an inspiration for cultural producers, etc. A marked social and cultural variety and openness, therefore, represent the specific cultural capital of a creative region, which makes it highly attractive for actors in the creative economy. At the local level, this cultural capital might also be characterized as a specific subcultural capital of particular districts within the region, i.e. creative activities might be highly localized within a creative region. These thoughts support the thesis advocated by Florida (2002) that the economic growth of creative regions is driven by the locational choices of creative people – the holders of creative capital – who prefer places that are diverse, tolerant and open to new ideas.

Andersson (1985a) summarizes the characteristics of creative milieus.[2] Many different factors work together in a creative milieu. The creative process can be seen as a form of dynamic synergy. To initiate a creative process many factors must be able to influence each other in a mutual ongoing interaction. This concurrence and this interaction imply great demands on the regional milieu. It appears that the regional milieu must be of large scale but still culturally versatile, rich in deep original knowledge and competence, and characterized by good communication possibilities, internally and externally.

For intraregional communication, physical nearness seems to be of great importance, since personal communication within groups of individuals with common interests seems to be a vital input to creativity (Jacobs, 1969; Lucas, 1988). To achieve significant synergy effects there is a need for variety. The different activities in a creative region are often of small scale as individual activities. Industries grow not by quantitative growth of the existing activities but through the emergence of new activities. The following seven factors seem to be fundamental conditions for creative processes, according to Andersson (1985a):

1. Benevolent or tolerant attitudes towards experiments.
2. Versatile composition of knowledge and competences.
3. Versatile and relatively unregulated financial basis for science, entrepreneurship and cultural life.
4. Good possibilities for spontaneous and informal personal contacts between different parts of the region and with other regions.
5. Many-sidedness rather than functional division of the social and physical milieu.
6. A feeling that the needs are larger than actual resources or possibilities.
7. A flexible social and economic organization, which sometimes goes beyond the borders to structural instability.[3]

It seems, according to Andersson (1985a), as if structural instability is a necessary condition for creativity from both a micro and a macro perspective. During the major part of each research, design or development process, the activities are mainly routinized, i.e. they proceed within a structurally stable equilibrium process. However, in a parallel process an internal instability in the main process may develop. Inconsistencies on a logical plane may become more and more obvious, concurrently with the attempts to increasingly generalize the basic ideas. Exceptions to basic principles may be discovered. The process might stagnate and come to an end if there is a lack of people with original, deep and varied knowledge and competence. However, if there are enough people with the right background and with possibilities of active mutual communication, the process can turn into a powerful bifurcation or a phase of structural instability with great uncertainty about the future development path and thus a great potential for creative acts.

Such a structural instability can at the regional level be perceived as a period of fundamental uncertainty about future development. Trend extrapolations do not work. However, this uncertainty also brings an advantage as well as a risk. Due to the lack of stability within the system, smaller groups of people can also influence the system and thus choose a new set course, which may open up the possibility for several different set courses. Of course, it is troublesome for regional planning and policy that creativity demands structural instability, variety and uncertainty. In addition, it may be difficult to combine creativity with short-term productivity. Furthermore, creativity at the regional level and social security can be assumed to be in opposition to each other.

Up to now, we have not provided any definition of creativity. Andersson (1985a) defines creativity as the ability to combine knowledge, i.e. familiarity and insights, and competence, i.e. the ability to use knowledge for one or several purposes, to create something new.[4] This implies that change is at the centre of creativity. It is possible to make a distinction between different types of creativity (cf. Florida, 2002): (i) scientific creativity; (ii) technological or innovative creativity; (iii) economic or entrepreneurial creativity;[5] and (iv) artistic or cultural creativity. These different types of creativity are probably to a certain extent mutually dependent in the sense that they may stimulate and reinforce each other when located in the same urban region. However, it is well known that artists, such as painters, may develop a high level of creativity also when forming artistic colonies in peripheral rural regions.

An understanding of the creative region presupposes some degree of understanding of the creative processes at the micro level, i.e. within individuals or small teams of individuals working together. Unfortunately, the knowledge about creative processes at the micro level is rather limited. The human brain has, however, certain abilities, which are interesting (Andersson, 1985a):

- the heuristic ability
- the ability to remember
- the ability to detect deep structures
- the ability to see and to use ambiguity and manifoldness
- the ability to appreciate paradoxes and surprises
- the ability to use disequilibria
- the ability to use fundamental uncertainty.

Another important question relates to why people are creative. This question is also discussed in Andersson (1985a), and he makes a distinction between individual intrinsic and social motivation. It seems as if internal reinforcement mechanisms have a greater importance for explaining the total creativity level of individuals than simple reward or coercion arguments. This suggests that it is difficult to stimulate the creative output of individuals, and thus that the creative output of regions depends upon the total number of creative persons. It is also important to observe that exaggerated demands for discipline and organization might strangle creative potential. Concerning the social motivation for creativity, it seems as if the right to take one's own initiatives, little work supervision, and employment and income security, if creativity fails, is important for generating creative working conditions.

There must obviously be rewards to creativity, since the creative process is a costly, uncertain process that includes the risk of failure, stress and other negative effects. Creative ideas challenge established norms and might bring disorder, which implies a risk for creative people, since they tend to be met by resistance and scepticism, which is typical not least within science (Kuhn, 1962) but also within, e.g., the arts, music and poetry (Boden, 2004), where the orthodoxy works as a constraint on novelty and new means of individual expression. On the other hand, to change the established norms might be the intrinsic motivation for creative people.

2.2 TRADE, LOCATION AND CREATIVE REGIONS

Going through the last 1000 years of economic history, it is obvious that fundamental changes in the geography of creative regions have taken place. Logistical revolutions have initiated periods with a high level of creativity, which have generated fundamental structural changes in the world economy (Andersson, 1985a, 1993). These periods have coincided with and been mutually dependent upon fundamental changes in institutions, technology and culture (Andersson, 1995). Different large city regions have been able to take advantage of the special conditions during each period, which has led to the emergence of new centres of creativity in the world economy during each logistical revolution.

The current epoch, which goes back some 30 years, has been characterized as the fourth logistical revolution (Andersson, 1985a). It involves the realization of a systems society, where computer and telecommunications systems make it possible to integrate the business community into a logistical system at a very rapid pace, but also with substantial risks for increased vulnerability.

The current logistical revolution coincides with the increasing dominance of the knowledge society. A rapidly increasing knowledge stock and an increasing number of highly educated people increase the creative potential in society and in the business community. Creative manufacturing and service industries imply that the number of new products and varieties of old products increases continuously. However, this gradually changes the basic conditions for the interregional and the international division of labour. At each point in time, certain large urban regions are centres for creativity in culture and industry. Due to their superior accessibility to demanding customers with high purchasing power, they also become centres for innovation of new products. Thus we can say that certain large urban regions will be the motors of global product cycles, whose speed of change is regulated by the size of the R&D investments. However, the relative importance of different urban regions as creative centres changes over time, so we must also ask what processes might bring about such changes.

Johansson (2000) suggests that, at a fundamental level, one may make a distinction between producer-driven and consumer-driven processes. A suitable starting point for producer-driven processes is Ricardo's model of comparative advantage. In general, conditions in regions differ, such that it is possible to state that individual regions have a comparative advantage in the production of one or more products. Specialization of production, exports and imports may then be assumed to follow the advantage patterns. The advantage can be defined using an opportunity-cost argument:

> A region has a comparative advantage in producing a product z, if the number of units of other products, y, that has to be given up to produce one extra unit of z, is smaller in the particular region than in other competing regions.

This basic idea was put forward by Ricardo about 200 years ago. The critical question is, however, how such advantages are generated. This question was analysed by Ohlin (1933). Ohlin's message was – in modern terminology – that patterns of comparative advantage are based upon the durable characteristics of each region, i.e. resources and other conditions, which are 'trapped' or change at a very slow rate. In the literature, the following four different causes of comparative advantages are put forward: (i) technology gaps between regions; (ii) spatial product cycles; (iii) differentials in the relative supply of production factors, including natural resources; and (iv) demand differentials, based upon variations between regions in willingness to pay for products. Also, variations between regions to take advantage of internal and external economies of scale influence comparative advantages.

The first aspect refers to region-specific conditions, which influence the capability of firms to generate, adopt and apply new technical solutions. Spatial product cycles represent a dynamic version of the technology gap theory. In such models, firms in different regions get different stimuli from their pertinent economic milieu to develop and initiate sales of products with new attributes, i.e. to be creative and to innovate.

Regional differences in the supply of production factors, such as capital and labour, require a certain degree of friction, making the supply of these factors in different regions semi-fixed (Johansson, 1998b). This implies that they are given exogenously in the short run and that they change at a slow rate only (Johansson and Wigren, 1996). Production capital, such as buildings, but also to a great extent machines, are region-specific for extended periods. In a similar manner, households with varying knowledge and competence may have a low mobility, i.e. slow adjustment to regional differences in labour market conditions. In particular, this is true for mobility between countries. What can be said about regional differentials as regards demand? The composition of household consumption varies between regions due to variations in income levels and culture. However, there is also another source of demand emanating from firms and entire industries located in a region. When a region is specialized in certain sectors, e.g. due to the existence of external economies of scale, this will generate a particular composition of demand for inputs, i.e. for goods and services.

In a modern version of the Ricardo model one could consider the educational level, i.e. the human capital, of the inhabitants in regions as a specific production factor. Human capital can also be seen as a durable or semi-fixed resource in economies where household migration adjusts to regional differentials in employment opportunities and wages at a slow pace.

This naturally takes us to the consumer-driven processes. We identify two types of consumer-driven processes. The first comes from the Tiebout model, in which households are assumed to migrate without friction (Tiebout, 1956). According to this model, individuals or households migrate from one local jurisdiction to another in response to differentials as regards the supply of local public goods and local taxes. Different mixes of local public goods and taxes in different local jurisdictions will attract different types of households.[6]

According to Tiebout's formulation, households vote with their feet, while simultaneously revealing their preferences and promoting an efficient differentiation of the supply of public goods across local jurisdictions. Of course, if all households are different, efficiency requires that there are many municipalities. This will not be possible if there are increasing returns to scale in the supply of public goods. The latter may, for example, require significant investments in the public infrastructure.

The second type of consumer-driven processes has been advocated, among others, by Quigley (1990). He argues that the driving forces shaping regional development to a great extent come from the spatial pattern of household location and the housing opportunities offered by different regions. One important condition behind this is the changes in the character of economic activities undertaken in advanced Western societies:

- manufacturing has become less important, and business services have become more important;
- technical progress has reduced the optimal scale for a great many types of economic activity;
- advances in transportation, communication and computation technology have eroded the traditional locational advantages and created new opportunities for outsourcing and off-shoring of

activities within the overall supply chain in both goods and services production.

As a result, larger firms can fragment their business activities both within and between regions. The confluence of these important trends on the production side has made new sites within regions and new regions suitable or even preferred as locations at the same time as firms have become much more footloose, i.e. have gained much more freedom to choose location interregionally as well as intraregionally for their different types of activities.

Another important background condition is the changes in the factors that influence the locational choices of households:

- the dramatic increase in female labour supply, making two-worker households with two spouses the norm;
- the reduction in transport costs and advances in computer and telecommunication technology;
- the rapidly rising real incomes of households.

This implies that households have become less sensitive to commuting costs and commuting distances due to, among other things, increased opportunities for distance-work. At the same time, they have become more sensitive to variations in housing quality and housing amenities in choosing residential location. In particular, highly educated and high-income households seem to be very sensitive when it comes to choosing regions as well as residential areas within regions.[7] Hence we can see, once more, that households vote with their feet and make distinct choices about where they prefer to live. Large urban regions have a special competitive advantage in this respect since they in general offer a higher density and a larger variation of amenities of importance in attracting highly educated and creative individuals and households (Glaeser et al., 2001).

In combination, the two conditions described above suggest that in competition for skilled and highly educated labour, firms will choose to locate in close proximity to their potential labour force instead of trying to attract the same labour to old established locations. This idea was later adopted by Florida (2002), who put forward the argument that the companies, the technologies and the venture capital of knowledge-intensive economic activities are moving to or forming in places that have the skilled and talented people. He (ibid., p. 7) emphasizes in particular the sociocultural properties that make certain regions particularly attractive to the creative class as a place for living and working: 'Creative people . . . don't just cluster where the jobs are. They cluster in places that are centres of creativity and also where they want to live.' Thus lifestyle attributes of the creative class and a supportive sociocultural milieu are at the centre of an urban region's attractiveness in the creative economy. The argumentation has several implications:

- urban regions or parts of such regions with unusually desirable natural, cultural and consumption amenities will experience continued competitive advantages in attracting firms employing highly qualified labour;
- urban regions or parts of such regions in which highly qualified workers already reside are prime candidates for the location of new employment in activities intensive in the use of highly qualified workers;
- public resources devoted to improving amenities in urban regions may reap rewards over and above their initial impacts upon the well-being of the current residents.

2.3 THE INTERNATIONAL SYSTEM OF CREATIVE REGIONS

The study of creative regions is always exciting. However, it also involves certain risks. One major risk stimulated by the focus on localized knowledge spillovers is a concentration on the individual creative regions, disregarding the fact that these large urban regions are closely connected in many ways and engaged in intense interregional interaction. To use the conceptualization of Johansson (2005), there has probably been too much focus on proximity externalities and too little focus on network externalities.

A long time ago, the Swedish location economist Palander (1935) observed that one of the most remarkable features of modern urban structures is the frequency and extension of the interactions between the activities carried out in different cities. Today the situation is very different in the sense that the infrastructures connecting in particular large urban regions are much more developed and advanced, offering superior accessibility to other large urban regions. As a result, human interaction, in particular between large urban regions, has increased in intensity but also in complexity (Karlsson and Westin, 1994). One fundamental force behind the 'new accessibility' and growth in complexity is found in the development of communication and information systems. The information and communication technologies revolution has lowered the marginal costs of information exchange between different locations to levels very close to zero (Karlsson and Klaesson, 2002), and the evolution of national and international air travel has significantly reduced the travel costs and travel times. Furthermore, the international scientific community is organized as a large number of big international knowledge networks, relying, for example, on scientific conferences and journals. Large multinational firms, not least within their R&D organization, often link a large number of large urban regions together. Still, it is often claimed that interregional and in particular international knowledge spillovers are limited in geographical scope (Jaffe et al., 1993; Audretsch and Feldman, 1996). However, there are a few authors who claim that the interregional and international knowledge spillovers have been underestimated, since there is abundant evidence that information and knowledge networks that enhance business efficiency can be and often are widely diffused geographically (Hansen, 2000).

It is obvious that creative regions throughout the world are closely connected and that they stimulate each other's creative processes and knowledge production processes.[8] The stimuli have two major forms: the flow of 'pure' knowledge and the import of products embodying new knowledge.

Knowledge flows take place in specialized interregional networks, i.e. 'knowledge networks' (Batten et al., 1989). These consist of a set of nodes and a set of links connecting them. The nodes are represented by human settlements, such as towns, cities and metropolitan regions, providing different instances of functional regions. The nodes can be characterized by their endowment of knowledge production capacities and related activities, including knowledge infrastructure such as universities, meeting infrastructure, stocks of knowledge and human capital, local knowledge networks etc. The links include transportation as well as communication channels.

No matter how large or creative an urban region is, it will fetch its strongest and most frequent impulses for new ideas, new products, improved production methods and new consumption patterns from import flows from other large urban regions in general and from creative regions in particular (Johansson, 1993a). The underlying reason is of course that the size of the R&D resources and the number of innovations in each individual region are only a tiny share of all R&D and all innovations in the world economy. The Swedish economist and economic historian Eli F. Heckscher coined the expression 'imports are more varying than exports'. The import flows provide information about 'news' developed in different creative regions around the world. Varied imports and dense import networks provide strong stimuli for innovation and imitation. The import flows stimulate firms in the import regions to develop new products and to develop substitutes and complements to the imported products. Thus there will be a strong tendency for new product cycles to be initiated in large import regions. However, as we will show in later sections, the import regions also play a central role in, in principle, all innovation processes in an economy and thus form a vital component in any innovation system.

It is a general observation that imports dominate exports in the large rich regions. There are two explanations. Imports are attracted to the richest regions with the highest purchasing power. However, a region also develops economic precedence by being an import node for a surrounding territory. It is from a development and innovation perspective that imports play their strategic function. New products are transmitted via imports. Imports, in particular to large urban regions, focus on development, new technology and investments. Imports play an especially important role when a firm or an organization is about to change and improve its technology, increase its capacity and/or change its line of business. The variety of imports is mirrored in the fact that the number of import firms is much larger than the number of export firms in large urban regions. Import flows generally contain a much larger share of innovations than export flows. Thus import flows give stimuli to start producing goods that are new to the importing region in the sense that they have not been produced there before.

There is much to gain for each region in following product development and technological progress in the world economy. Observations of new products in the import flows bring quite special information to the importing region. The new products in such a flow have passed two tests: first, it is made clear that there exist the technical possibilities to produce the product in question, and second, the import flow shows that there exist customers in the region, i.e. there is a market in the region and/or its hinterland. Thus the imitation of import products is a low-risk innovation strategy.

A focus on qualitative imports, i.e. imports with a high share of new products, is a form of regional specialization. Normally a small number of regions within each country are responsible for the lion's share of the total import value and for the import of new products. This is, in particular, true for import firms importing and reselling new technology, new equipment and knowledge. The import firms in these regions support customers in all parts of the country with import products via their customer networks.

Our main point in this section is that it is impossible to understand the role and function of creative regions without also acknowledging that they are specialized import regions with an open attitude to ideas, knowledge and technologies developed elsewhere. This also implies that among the critical knowledge and competence factors in creative regions are the knowledge and competence to scan the world economy for new products and to evaluate the potential of these new products to be the starting point for new product cycles.

2.4 THE ROLE OF LARGE URBAN REGIONS AS CREATIVE REGIONS

From the discussion above it is obvious that creative potential is not evenly distributed across space. In the last section, we illustrated that there are self-reinforcing processes working, where regions well equipped with highly educated labour function as an attractor for firms with activities critically dependent upon good access to highly educated labour. As more firms move into these regions, the demand for amenities as well as for highly educated labour stimulates investments in amenities as well as the immigration of such labour. Thus virtuous cycles might emerge stimulating agglomeration of knowledge and creative potential.

In particular, the large urban regions in developed economies can be understood as large, knowledge-intensive production systems. In most developed countries, a dominating share of all production takes place in the large urban regions. Most international and interregional trade takes place between the large urban regions. However, they are even more important as nodes in the international networks for knowledge generation and knowledge and information transfer. Milieus for creativity and innovation are largely found in large urban regions and, in particular, in those large urban regions that are characterized by variety and small-scale activities. One important reason behind this is that the new technologies that are developed have such a high complexity that the knowledge involved in their creation is dispersed and distributed over many individuals and organizational units (Karlsson et al., 2004). Thus only large urban regions offer a broad enough knowledge base for developing these new technologies.

The versatile large urban regions offer great advantages when it comes to introducing new economic activities. Large urban regions with their concentrations of human capital function as 'incubators' of creativity and innovation (Thompson, 1965). The role of (large) cities in concentrating and spurring human creativity was initially recognized by Park et al. (1925). Cities function as 'open systems', which attract talented people from various backgrounds and stimulate their creative capacities (Jacobs, 1961). Jacobs's ideas were later formalized by Lucas (1988) into a basic theory, which argues that cities function as collectors of human capital, thus generating new ideas and economic growth through human-capital externalities. However, the economic history of urban regions shows that such a relative advantage is easily lost and this loss often has a connection with the development of long-term product cycles (Andersson, 1985a).

The product cycle theory is an attempt to develop a pure dynamic explanation for the division of labour between regions and nations (Vernon, 1966). As such, it is a necessary complement to the classical theory of comparative advantage. The theories of long-term product cycles involve three types of industrial dynamics: (i) technological development, which introduces new products or changes the function or design of products; (ii) the introduction of new or improvements of old production processes; and (iii) changes of the market organization via the creation of new market channels or changes in pricing and marketing policies. Karlsson and Larsson (1990) emphasize that evolving product cycles involve a fourth type of dynamics, namely a change in competition strategies from product competition to price competition. Product competition signifies a market behaviour where the individual supplier uses the combination of attributes contained in his products, including delivery conditions and sales and after-sales services, as his most important measure to attract customers to himself and away from his competitors (Johansson, 1988). The two competition strategies correspond to two innovation strategies (Anderstig and Karlsson, 1989):

- dynamic innovations, which are measures taken by firms as a part of product competition strategy that increase the perceived quality of its old product(s), or that introduces totally new products on the market;
- cost innovations, which are measures taken by a firm as part of a price competition strategy that reduce its production costs for existing products.

All versions of the product cycle theory are founded upon a number of basic premises (Karlsson, 1988): (i) that tastes differ with income; (ii) that communication costs within the firm; and between the firm and the market, are significant and increase with distance; (iii) that as the product cycle of any new product unfolds, the product and its production technique pass through successive stages of standardization; (iv) that associated with these stages will be dynamic shifts in comparative advantage of predictable direction; and (v) that the market for technical knowledge is very imperfect.

The spatial product cycle theory is based upon the assumption that every new product will most probably be launched in one of the most advanced urban regions in the world after a phase of R&D, testing and production on a small test scale. Such regions offer dynamic comparative advantages, i.e. they are characterized by high R&D investments at the same time as they have good access to a human-capital-rich labour force. As a result, the first production of the new products will normally take place in the region where they were developed.

In the initial phase, other regions will import the new product. However, knowledge about the characteristics of the new product and its production technology will diffuse to other regions when they start to import the product. As the demand for the product expands, it is possible to introduce large-scale production technologies. The initiating region may then lose its comparative advantage over time, as the production process is simplified and/or automated. The term process here comprises all the operations or activities of a firm, as suggested by Nelson and Winter (1982). They argue convincingly that a firm has a set of interdependent sub-process routines, which combine to form a compound process. The compound process includes the following sub-processes: (i) distribution; (ii) production; (iii) 'routinized' design and construction; and (iv) management, administration and commercial activities. Improvements in all the above sub-processes are recognized as process innovations. Improvements here refer to reductions of costs and/or improvements in quality and accuracy (Fischer and Johansson, 1994). Only by ongoing development of the product's function and design can the initiating region continue to keep its advantage.

According to the basic assumptions of the product cycle theory, the production of new products can start to diffuse when they have become standardized. The degree of standardization of a product group has a major influence on the market structure and innovation behaviour of firms. It is possible to distinguish two basic levels of standardization (Fischer and Johansson, 1994):

1. A product group or, in other words, a market consists of product variants. The product group is standardized if all of the variants are equivalent to the extent that price is the only criterion for the decision-making of customers.
2. A firm may supply a standardized product, which at the same time competes in a market with either (a) standardized products, or (b) differentiated products.

In neither of the above cases does the individual firm adjust its deliveries and product attributes to customers who specify individual requirements or preferences with regard to attributes. In case 2(b) the firm has selected a particular market segment, i.e. a specific customer group. The first case refers to mass markets and mature products, including staple goods. In such markets, price competition prevails. A firm that supplies non-standardized products adjusts its product attributes to each specific customer group. Each delivery may be unique. For firms of this type, the capability to adapt product characteristics to specific requirements becomes an essential aspect of their everyday production activity. This makes them dependent upon high accessibility to customers with a high enough willingness to pay for specific product characteristics in the own region and in other regions, as well as to the relevant knowledge sources and qualified labour. In these markets, price is just one of several criteria that influence the decision-making of a customer.

Product standardization and process routinization are key notions in the model of product cycle dynamics developed by Johansson and Andersson (1998). Along a product cycle path, the knowledge intensity is high when a product is non-standardized and the production process is non-routinized. Standardization and routinization imply reduced knowledge intensity. This indicates that in the spatial product cycle theory, the change processes are influenced by the characteristics of the entire labour force and the knowledge accessibility in each region (Johansson and Karlsson, 1986). Such overall regional attributes describe the economic environment of individual firms and indicate their possibilities of acquiring knowledge and information pertinent to their production segment. The regional attributes also show which possibilities a firm has to adjust the competence profile of its staff. Regional labour market characteristics are closely related to the location of R&D activities, cultural opportunities and regional infrastructure.

Two aspects of the interaction between structural economic adjustments and pertinent changes in the labour market in individual regions and a system of regions are analysed in Johansson and Karlsson (1987). First, changing sectoral composition, new products and the introduction of new techniques affect the demand for different types of employment categories, i.e. types of jobs. This is a process with comparatively direct and fast impacts. The second aspect comprises a process that operates on a slower time scale. In this case, the gradual change in the competence profile of a region's labour force affects the location advantages of the region over time. This profile may change in such a direction that the region develops into an advantageous environment for product development and the creation of new production techniques. However, the labour force composition may also develop in such a way that the region gradually moves into a state of an economic periphery with unfavourable future employment prospects.

The spatial product cycle theory is based upon an assumption concerning the existence of economies of scale, which makes it difficult to associate it with the static theory of comparative advantage. In fact, the existence of economies of scale strengthens the advantages of trade and regional specialization. A region can, without having any comparative advantages in the classical sense, still gain from uniformly developing one line of production among many possible lines so that it can take advantage of economies of scale.

Economies of scale are not a special case for new products. It is the normal case. New products are normally introduced and tested in small markets. It is obvious that they have strong advantages of an expanded production scale. Thus R&D generating new products is a factor that through economies of scale can drive the specialization of regions much further than what is motivated by traditional economies of scale.

Summarizing the discussion so far makes it obvious that the spatial product cycle theory contains three basic elements that go beyond the traditional theory of comparative advantage: (i) R&D to generate new products and production processes; (ii) investments in a new market organization; and (iii) returns varying with the production scale.

The most critical part of a dynamic analysis using the spatial product cycle theory concerns the determination of which regions are most likely to function as recurrent creative milieus. As soon as a new product has been introduced in a national or an international market, the spatial product cycle theory predicts a spatial development over time of the type illustrated in Figure 2.1.

In the introductory phase of the product cycle, the initiating region has a monopoly through its unique competence. As the production scale increases and the production technology is successively improved, it becomes easier for other regions to adopt the product and its production technology. Often this is facilitated by the fact that production equipment is produced by specialized producers of machines and other equipment. In connection with the diffusion of production units, the production is routinized and simplified and the knowledge requirements reduced to a similar extent. The knowledge-intensive R&D regions often have a high general wage level and thus can not compete with regions that have a generally lower competence level and, hence, a lower wage level. Those conditions that in the early phases of the product cycle give the R&D regions their location advantages in later phases become their disadvantages.

Even if it is possible to delay and sometimes also to counteract this cyclical process by ongoing product development, i.e. improved design and function, it is a basic hypothesis that later stages of the product cycle involve a shift towards process development and market investments at the expense of product development. In connection with spatial diffusion

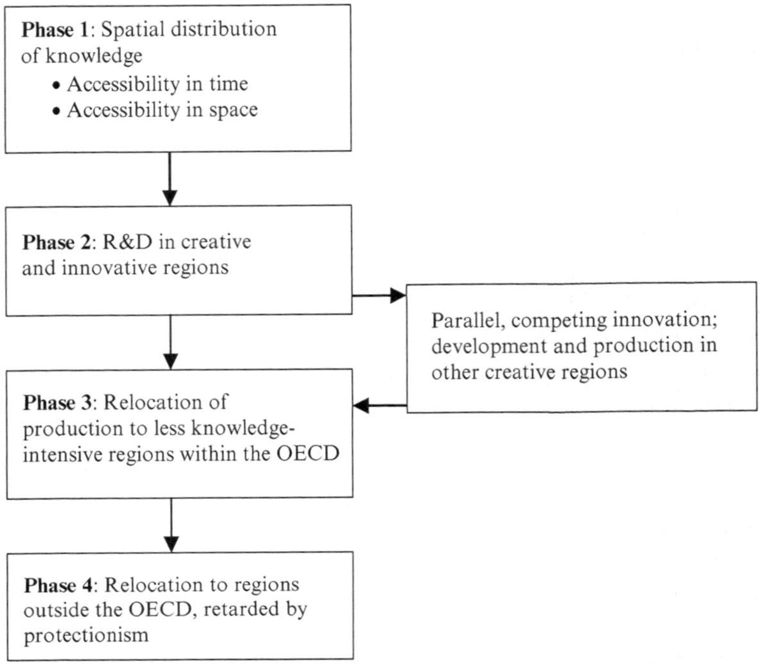

Source: Andersson (1985a).

Figure 2.1 The spatial location of production over time

of production and increased competition, R&D activities are gradually driven more and more towards labour- and general-factor-saving technological changes and improved logistical and distribution systems. In a parallel process, the demands for protective political measures increase.

Andersson and Johansson (1984a, 1984b) use microeconomic models to show how product cycle assumptions generate location and relocation processes (see also Johansson and Karlsson, 1987). They also demonstrate how clusters of product cycles can be observed empirically in the form of aggregate specialization patterns, which describe a time–space hierarchy. These results are in Johansson and Andersson (1998), reformulated into a more coherent framework, where new directions for this type of model formulations are emphasized.

Within the rich countries, a number of large urban regions have developed into international centres for R&D and product development. All these regions are characterized by a very good international accessibility by air, and a high intraregional accessibility to purchasing power, and to a diversified and highly developed R&D capacity. The development and the market introduction of new products presupposes a good intraregional accessibility for two reasons. The first reason is that the first market introduction of a completely new product is normally done as a trial and locally. In this initial phase, it is essential that the unit costs be reduced rapidly by a rapidly increasing production and sales volume. A substantial sales volume in the initial phase can only be achieved in a region with a large regional population and a large number of firms with a high purchasing power and an interest in new products. The second reason is that the development of new functions and new designs can only take place under synergistic and catalytical conditions, which implies that researchers, product developers and designers must be able to move easily between different research and cultural milieus (Andersson, 1985a). The contact needs of such an almost accidental nature can only be fulfilled in large and dense urban regions.

A large share of the goods production can be decentralized, its products transported with effective logistical systems and its production coordinated by modern computer and telecommunications systems. This applies to goods and to financial and technical data of a routine nature for which the transport and the transmission costs are low. For knowledge generation and transfer, creative and innovative processes and negotiations the conditions are different. In such processes face-to-face contacts are always important (Karlsson and Manduchi, 2001; Saxenian, 1994). They are particularly important in situations characterized by substantial changes, marked by negotiations, R&D aiming at new designs, and new functions of existing products or totally new products. In a similar manner, the transfer of knowledge and competence demands effective educational systems with frequent opportunities for face-to-face contacts. This implies that the transfer of knowledge and competence, creative processes and negotiations demand social milieus larger than a certain minimum scale in terms of individuals (with the relevant knowledge and competence). Furthermore, creativity in the form of R&D of new products and new processes needs variety and a high probability of random contacts in the regional milieu. Only a limited number of the large urban regions in the advanced countries fulfil at the same time all the necessary criteria in terms of size, purchasing power, knowledge and competence level, variety and general accessibility to the extent that they can function for extended periods as international centres for R&D, creativity and innovation.

The birth of new products is normally located in a limited number of large urban regions among the advanced countries. When the product has been introduced in its birth region, it is frequently strongly dependent upon continued development and improvements of its functions and design. Regularly, the production at this stage demands special professional skills, which opens opportunities for continuous changes in product characteristics. Thus it is necessary to keep production close to the R&D units. This implies that it is profitable to keep the production of the new products within or close to the creative regions, as long as the R&D efforts are substantial. Not until a later stage, when the product has come closer to a more final form and function, can the production process be routinized. Then, competence can be built into the machinery equipment. At this stage, cost considerations make it possible to decentralize production to regions with lower knowledge, competence and wage levels. However, it is also important to observe that the development of product concepts, experimentation with young products, and routinized processing of mature and ageing products all constitute distinct categories of activities. Each of these activities has its specific interaction characteristics and thus demands for particular combinations of infrastructure attributes of the built environment, which has implications for both location and relocation of activities (Johansson, 1993b).

Hence the basic hypothesis says that as a product matures, it gradually uses less and less of the competence-, knowledge- and creativity-dependent production factors, and more and more of standardized inputs. These standardized inputs are accessible at substantially lower costs in other regions within the country or in other countries with relatively lower knowledge and competence level, and with fewer possibilities for many-sided, informal and fast face-to-face contacts between persons with a high and varied knowledge and competence level.

An application of the spatial product cycle analysis to rich countries is illustrated in Table 2.1. In the table, different products are characterized according to their relative static and dynamic role among the rich countries. The table assumes that new products are born in the upper left corner, which delimits products with a high and non-declining specialization in the rich countries. This product group mainly consists of R&D-intensive, distance-sensitive high-income products, which need a well-developed infrastructure. Such infrastructure-dependent or systems-oriented product or production processes can only be successfully localized in highly developed urban regions in the rich countries with well-developed transport and communications systems, labour markets with a rich and varied supply of well-educated labour and good access to material and non-material infrastructure.

Products mature in a technical sense at the same time as the R&D share of the total costs and the investment costs decline, and the demands concerning the educational level of the labour force are lowered. On the other hand, this phase of the technological development

Table 2.1 The spatial product cycle applied to the OECD countries

R&D New products	The product specialization is stable in the OECD area	The product specialization is falling in the OECD area
High specialization level for the products in the OECD area	• R&D-intensive products • Knowledge- and competence-intensive products • Infrastructure-dependent processes • System products • Design-intensive products • Distance-sensitive products	• Capital-intensive processes, *but* • Not R&D-intensive • Not knowledge- and competence-intensive • Not infrastructure-dependent • Components
Low specialization level for the products in the OECD area	• Politically protected products • Products protected by market organization	• Not R&D-intensive • Not knowledge- and competence-intensive • Not infrastructure-dependent • Components • Labour-intensive • Raw material-intensive

Source: Andersson (1985a).

is often connected with high capital intensity. In the lower left corner of the table, products that have earlier contracted substantially in the rich countries are accumulated. For employment and other reasons the production of some of these products may be protected from international competition. However, it is obvious that the total share of the production protected in this manner among the rich countries cannot be larger than certain politically accepted protection levels. Thus it is obvious that most of these products will, after a quarantine period with political protection, move into the lower right corner of the table. Earlier, defence policy considerations could mean that products could return to the lower left corner.

The speed of the spatial structural change is to a great extent dependent on the level of R&D investments in the rich countries. The part of the table that contains product development can be seen as the driving force in the spatial product cycle. When the share of the value-added invested in product development increases, the speed of spatial structural change increases. Regions and nations among the rich countries are forced to improve their mutual division of labour and to accept a more rapid relocation of production to regions in countries outside the group of rich countries. This is a painful process and there are plenty of examples of rich countries trying to protect their own production.

2.5 KNOWLEDGE, SPATIAL PRODUCT CYCLES AND REGIONAL DEVELOPMENT

The above discussion of the spatial product cycle dynamics is for obvious reasons very stylized. In the abstract theoretical case it is assumed that products always go through a sequence of R&D, product development, introduction in an R&D region, continued improvements in function and design, improved and simplified production technology, routinization, increased production scale, decreased needs for knowledge and competence and relocation to regions and nations with lower educational and skills levels with or without protectionist retardation of the structural change process. The analysis above can be summarized in six statements:

1. R&D capacity, knowledge and competence decide the initial location of production. Large knowledge demands in production results in highly developed urban regions dominating the production of such products.
2. Relocation of production from highly developed urban regions happens when large-scale, routinized production becomes possible technologically, generally known and reasonable from an economic and a logistical point of view.
3. When a product matures technologically, the relative importance of market investments increases. After a period of large investments in improved process technology, firms tend to relocate their immaterial investments from R&D to investments in improved market organization and marketing.
4. The spatial structural change is retarded by protectionist measures in the rich countries and regions. When an industry approaches technological maturity and the market shares of the rich countries and regions decline rapidly, national and regional political bodies tend to introduce protective measures to slow the fall in employment, production and market shares.
5. R&D, product development design and other creative activities are mainly located in large urban regions with high internal and external accessibility for passenger transport. Professions dealing with creative activities primarily need good intraregional accessibility, i.e. the milieu of a large urban region.
6. Knowledge transfer via education or consultation has a somewhat lower need to be located in a large urban region.

The spatial product cycle theory offers an overall framework for understanding regional development in terms of changes in the specialization of regions of different sizes and with different conditions, and the role of knowledge in such change processes. However, the theory is less clear about the dynamic microeconomic processes working within regions and about the endogenous character of general regional development processes. Comparative advantages are not given forever. They can be gained and lost.

One important observation is that there is a dynamic interdependence between a region's durable characteristics and the possibilities of exploiting economies of scale (Johansson and Karlsson, 2001). We start by discussing how the existence of internal economies of scale influences the specialization and growth of regions (Karlsson and Stough, 2002). For regions with distance-sensitive transaction costs, the relevant demand depends on the region's internal market potential. Hence large urban regions with a high purchasing power are the only possible locations for new products with thin demand. Internal economies of scale are a consequence of technological features of an individual firm and are related to the existence of one or several fixed (indivisible) production factors in a firm's production (and cost) function. Furthermore, research institutes and units are characterized by internal economies of scale. They tend to be tied to large urban regions not by the demand side but by supply-side considerations. Only these regions can supply a varied and large enough supply of the highly qualified labour demanded for frontline research. The same is true to a great extent also of large research universities.

The concept of economies of scope is related to internal economies of scale. Such economies exist in their simplest form when the total costs of producing two different products within one firm are lower than the sum of the total costs of producing the two products in two different firms. Economies of scope, which arise in similar ways as internal economies of scale, are basically the result of several products using the same fixed resource within a firm. Hence economies of scope are a basic motive for product differentiation within firms. However, they are also a motive for differentiation of research and higher education within research institutes and research universities, making it rational for cost reasons to expand the scope and the size of such institutions, which adds to the motives to locate them in large urban regions.

In addition to internal economies of scale, a certain production activity may also be characterized by external economies of scale, i.e. agglomeration economies, along the lines suggested by Marshall (1920). External economies of scale appear when firms producing the same type of products (same industry or sector) locate themselves in the same region. Such external economies are therefore sometimes called location economies. Combinations of three major phenomena are assumed to cause external scale effects: (i) specialized labour markets; (ii) specialized neighbouring firms supplying inputs; and (iii) information spillover between the firms in the same sector.[9] Johansson (2005) deepens the analysis of external economies by making fundamental distinctions between (i) the source: proximity versus network externalities; (ii) the nature: pecuniary versus non-pecuniary externalities; and (iii) the consequence: efficiency versus development externalities.

External economies of scale normally refer to the advantages that a set of firms producing similar products can have just by being located close together in a region. However, the same is true for knowledge-generating activities within firms, research institutes and research universities. Karlsson and Andersson (2009) show, using a simultaneous equation approach, that company R&D is attracted to concentrations of university R&D and vice versa. A cluster of research performers can attract to the region a rich supply of varied labour categories, which are specialized to suit the research activities in question.[10] A concentrated demand from R&D activities in the region also attracts neighbouring firms, which are first of all input suppliers (of various kinds). These specialized input suppliers may have their own internal economies of scale, and then it is important to have accessibility to sufficient demand, which in this case is provided by the localized R&D performers. Neighbouring firms may in addition include specialized innovative firms of various sizes, which are attracted by the concentrated and varied supply of, in particular, new knowledge from the R&D performers in the region.

But why does it matter for these specialized neighbouring firms to locate in the same region as the R&D performers? The desire of the specialized input suppliers to be in the same region as their customers is determined by frequent interaction with their customers and distance-sensitive transaction costs. The specialized innovative firms have similar motivations for being close to the potential knowledge suppliers. However, their motivation is even stronger since new knowledge is a very particular commodity – tacit (Polanyi, 1966), sticky (von Hippel, 1994), complex, contextual, uncertain etc. – which implies that it can in principle be accessed only by means of face-to-face communication. A location in the region where the new knowledge is produced is more or less a prerequisite for being able to take advantage of it for product or process innovations or for future R&D. Even if much new knowledge is protected by means of patents, it is well known that small firms are able to do a substantial amount of innovation without doing any R&D of their own (Acs and Audretsch, 1988). Obviously it is possible for firms not doing any R&D to appropriate part of the new knowledge generated, given that they are close enough to the sources.

This observation about distance-sensitive interactions brings us to the third factor, i.e. information spillover between firms. Part of the new knowledge is spread in an intraregional neighbourhood without being priced, because in such a milieu it becomes prohibitively costly to privatize all information. Hence some of it will spill over to other R&D performers and to specialized innovative firms.

A major concern here is that different products (and knowledge is also a product) have different distance sensitivities. This sensitivity is derived from the more basic properties of products, such as the contact intensity needed for their transfer between economic agents, i.e. the complexity and contact requirements of the transfer process. The assumption that products vary with regard to the contact or interaction intensity associated with their input and output transactions has a long history in economic theory (von Thünen, 1926; Lösch, 1943; Hirsch, 1967). These authors also make an additional assumption, namely that interaction costs are much lower when a transaction is made inside a region than when it is carried out between regions. New knowledge is transferred under complex and contact-intensive conditions, which may involve frequent and many varieties of nearby contacts. Consequently the transfers of new knowledge can be assumed to have distance-sensitive geographical transaction costs and thus mainly take place within large urban regions

Summarizing the arguments in this section so far, it is obvious that knowledge-generating, knowledge-using and creative activities have location advantages in large urban regions. The existence of scale economies in knowledge generation implies that large urban regions have a location advantage with regard to all types of knowledge generation with thin demand. Thus large urban regions can specialize in knowledge diversity and rely on the double force of internal and external scale economies in knowledge production. Scale economies are vital when we want to explain the existence of geographical concentrations of knowledge generation.

As the knowledge-generating activities in a large urban region expand, productivity and output are enhanced and the cost level reduced due to internal and external scale economies, scope economies and improved input supplies with more and more specialized input suppliers. To the extent that this makes the price of knowledge fall, output will grow even further. The expansion of the output of new knowledge will stimulate the location and the growth of knowledge-using innovative firms in the region. A higher level of innovative activity in the region will stimulate income growth, which will be used partly to increase the knowledge-generating activities. Thus we can imagine an endogenous growth process in the large urban regions. As a modelling example, Kobayashi and Andersson (1994) propose a computable dynamic input–output model to examine the interactions between knowledge accumulation and economic growth with endogenous technical change. This model explicitly introduces new sectors called 'knowledge sectors' into the traditional dynamic input–output economic system. However, the regional growth may at the same time bring about congestion and increasing labour costs and land rents, phenomena that normally retard growth. Thus economic activities in large urban regions must under these circumstances be more productive to cover those extra costs for labour, land and premises. This applies in particular to new economic activities that have to pay their 'full' costs and that do not have the 'sunk cost advantages' of old economic activities.

However, the kernel of the innovative activities is that of stimulating the coming to market of more and more valuable products, i.e. products for which the customers have a high willingness to pay. The firms producing these products can normally pay the higher labour costs and land rents, since they produce valuable goods under conditions of monopolistic competition. The increasing costs and rents hit the production of somewhat older products, where competition is increasing, since their products and production processes have become standardized. The firms producing these products now get incentives to move production partially or totally to locations with lower costs and rents in other regions within the country or abroad.

Thus we can imagine a growth process where the continued knowledge-driven growth in the large urban regions stimulates the renewal of production in other regions. However, scale economies constitute an equally important phenomenon for medium-sized and small regions. Here specialization can take two basic forms. The first may be thought of as the classical Ricardian case, in which a medium-sized or small region hosts industries based on natural resources and for which internal economies of scale are important. If the natural resource is valuable enough, the necessary knowledge to exploit it can be brought from the large urban regions by means of direct investments, since the knowledge to exploit natural resources is established standardized knowledge. A similar case of large-scale specialization in medium-sized and small regions may develop when the production of products is relocated from large urban areas during their growth phase as part of the spatial product cycle. Such relocations also bring the necessary knowledge to produce the actual products.

The second form of specialization and thus growth mechanism refers to Marshall's idea about external economies of scale. In this case, medium-sized and small regions may develop a specialization in a self-organized way. In such a development, one can observe a narrow set of related industries or product areas, characterized by external economies of scale, i.e. localization economies. The development may be initiated by a relocation of production from large urban regions, imitation of products developed in large urban areas or in some rare cases by some original innovation. The cumulative sequence can be described as follows. Firms in the core industry with localization economies locate together in a region. Input suppliers and labour categories, which are specialized with regard to the pertinent industry, are attracted to the region. Sometimes one can also observe how industry-specific customers are attracted to the region. The environment of industry-specific input suppliers and employment categories as well as the core firms themselves form an economic milieu, i.e. a cluster, which attracts industry-specific firms to locate and to expand in the region (Karlsson et al., 2005). By means of development work within the core firms, learning by doing and complementary knowledge imported from large urban regions, such industry-specific concentrations of firms can develop into a creative cluster generating industry-specific new knowledge.

Using the terminology developed by Myrdal (1957), the above sequence can also be referred to as cumulative causation. It represents self-reinforcing, circular dynamics, which is constrained by the development of demand from the region and from its external markets. This form of positive feedback is in general constrained by the existing durable capacities in the form of built environment, accessibility based on transportation systems, production capacities and labour supply. For certain activities, these constraints may not be binding, whereas other activities require adjustments of the durable capacities. Generally, the market potential can be assumed to adjust at a faster rate than the durable capacities However, in the longer time perspective regional capacities and the economic milieu will adjust in a system of coupled feedback linkages. The interaction between scale economies and regional durable characteristics has the same nature in both medium-sized and small regions, although external linkages to other larger regions are more important for smaller regions. For medium-sized and small regions, the adjustment of durable capacities may be assumed to be rather specific with regard to the narrow set of industries that forms the specialization nucleus of each region. This implies that there is always a risk that, in particular, medium-sized and smaller regions may develop a specialized material and immaterial infrastructure, which in the long run can be a severe obstacle to a necessary structural change (Johansson and Karlsson, 1990). Using the German Ruhr area as an example, Grabher (1993, p. 256) illustrates how an earlier innovative milieu may lose its innovativeness: 'The initial strength of the industrial districts of the past – their industrial atmosphere, highly developed and specialised infrastructure, the close interfirm linkages, and strong political support by regional institutions – turned into stubborn obstacles to innovation.' Hudson (1994) draws the same conclusion based on analyses of a large number of industrial regions.

So far very little has been said about durable regional characteristics such as infrastructure and production factors, which have a fixed or semi-fixed location across regions. Durable characteristics can be divided into (i) local and external markets; and (ii) durable capacities (Johansson and Karlsson, 2001). The latter consist of the supply of different labour categories, existing production capacities with their specific techniques, R&D organizations, institutions of higher education, and material infrastructure in the form of facilities and networks (Johansson, 1995). The durable capacities generate comparative advantages in the Ricardian sense and influence the specialization profile of regions. Although these characteristics are more or less given in the short and medium term, a major part of the durable characteristics changes gradually over time and is to a large extent created by investment and migration-like processes. These processes are partly driven by the decisions of firms and households, but political decisions in many cases play a major role in reshaping the durable characteristics over time.

Turning to the size and the purchasing power of a region's local and external markets, we can observe that in the short and medium term the properties of markets are durable phenomena, which create comparative advantages in the pertinent regions. However, the dynamics of the interdependence between market size and economies of scale is essential. The interaction between market potential and the location of firms with scale advantages, which, in principle, can be seen as the initiation of new product cycles, is indeed intriguing. Firms with internal economies of scale are attracted to locate in a region with a large market potential, and a region in which firms want to locate develops a large market potential. This observation is further emphasized if we note that, for many activities, internal and external economies of scale coexist.

If we study the process of specialization on a slow time scale, the size and composition of a region's market potential become variables that evolve in a dynamic process. Similarly, we can observe an evolutionary process in which the specialized labour supply gradually adjusts in concordance with the specialization profile of the region. In a sense, the insights into this type of basic cumulative endogenous courses of events are not new. They can be traced back to the contributions by Marshall (1920), Myrdal (1957) and Kaldor (1970).

With this view of the world, the location of a particular industry is history dependent, due to the prevalence of multiple equilibria. This also implies that policy matters. However, it is by no means certain that policies can always change the ongoing processes. Once a pattern of specialization is initiated, for whatever reason, the pattern tends to get 'locked in' by the cumulative gains from trade and specialization. Thus there is a strong tendency towards 'path dependence' in the patterns of specialization and trade between regions. Since knowledge generation is cumulative, path-dependent and subject to increasing returns to scale, and since knowledge diffusion is subject to spatial frictions, spatial knowledge monopolies might very well emerge with asymmetric knowledge access (cf. Akerlof, 1970) between regions, making it possible for urban regions to keep their constructed competitive advantages for extended periods.

2.6 CONCLUDING REMARKS

The purpose of this chapter was to discuss the role of knowledge and talent in regional development in both a regional and a global perspective. Our starting point was the idea that knowledge infrastructure, knowledge flows, human capital, talent, creativity, and the generation, protection, accumulation, appropriation and creative use of knowledge are basic drivers of the specialization of regions and thus of regional development. We have discussed the characteristics of creativity and of creative regions, how human capital and knowledge-dependent firms are attracted to creative regions, characteristics of the international system of creative regions, the special role of large functional regions as creative regions and as initiators of new product cycles, and how knowledge-driven spatial product cycles function as motors in regional development.

Even though we are, at a more general level, able to describe theoretically how knowledge and creativity are at the heart of our understanding of regional development within both a regional and a global context, we still need to learn more about the underlying processes. For example, we need to learn more about the relative importance of learning and selection processes in regional development.

NOTES

1. A functional region is distinguished by its concentration of activities and of its infrastructure, which facilitates high factor mobility within its interaction borders. In particular, a functional region has an integrated labour market, in which commuting as well as job search is intensive (Johansson, 1998a).
2. The concept of creative milieu can be compared with the concept of 'milieu of innovation' introduced by Castells (1989, p. 82). 'by a milieu of innovation we understand a specific set of relationships of production . . . based on a social organization that by and large shares a work culture and instrumental goals aimed at generating new knowledge, new processes and new products.'
3. Rasulzada (2007) stresses that the social and organizational context often affects the level of creativity.
4. Amabile (1996) defines creativity as the development of new ideas that are potentially useful, i.e. that can be embodied in products, practices, services or procedures. It is important to observe here that creativity also develops ideas such as nuclear bombs and cluster bombs!

5. Sternberg and Lubart (1999) also look upon entrepreneurship as a form of creativity. As remarked by Baumol (1990), not all entrepreneurship is productive. Some of it is pure rent seeking and some of it is criminal.
6. This form of competition was suggested by Tiebout (1956) to improve multi-regional allocative efficiency. However, there are some technical problems with the Tiebout model, which will not be touched upon here (Bewley, 1981; Stahl and Varaiya, 1983).
7. Quality-of-life variables seems to play a major role in determining the migration patterns of households (Rosen, 1979; Roback, 1982).
8. The same is true for cultural activities, as pointed out by Lloyd (2006, p. 162). 'The social world of cultural production privileges particular locales. . . . Such locales are not self-contained, bounded entities, but rather operate in multiple networks of exchange – of products, ideas, and human capital – with other key sites, preceding the eventual dissemination of selected cultural commodities into the global marketplace.'
9. In line with Marshall's arguments, Duranton and Puga (2003) suggest three types of general microfoundations for agglomeration economies: (i) sharing; (ii) matching; and (iii) learning. It can be observed that these mechanisms not only explain the existence of agglomerations in general but also provide a microeconomic rationale for the continued expansion of large urban regions.
10. We must observe, given the discussion above, that there is a high probability that the R&D activities from the beginning are located in urban regions with a good supply of highly educated labour.

REFERENCES

Acs, Z.J. and D.B. Audretsch (1988), 'Innovation in large and small firms: an empirical analysis', *American Economic Review*, **78**, 678–90.

Akerlof, G. (1970), 'The market for "lemons": qualitative uncertainty and the market mechanism', *Quarterly Journal of Economics*, **84**, 488–500.

Amabile, T.M. (1996), *Creativity in Context*, Boulder, CO: Westview Press.

Andersson, Å.E. (1985a), *Kreativitet – Storstadens Framtid*, Stockholm: Prisma (in Swedish).

Andersson, Å.E. (1985b), 'Creativity and economic dynamic modelling', in D. Batten, J. Casti and B. Johansson (eds), *Economic Evolution and Structural Adjustment*, Berlin: Springer Verlag, pp. 27–45.

Andersson, Å.E. (1988), *Universitet – Regioners Framtid*, Regionplanekontoret, Stockholm (in cooperation with B. Hårsman and J. Linzie) (in Swedish).

Andersson, Å.E. (1989), *Sydsvensk Framtid*, Södertälje: Moraberg Förlag (in cooperation with I. Holmberg and D.E. Andersson) (in Swedish).

Andersson, Å.E. (1993), 'Economic structure of the 21st century', in Å.E. Andersson, D.F. Batten, K. Kobayashi and K. Yoshikawa (eds), *The Cosmo-Creative Society: Logistical Networks in a Dynamic Economy*, Berlin: Springer Verlag, pp. 17–29.

Andersson, Å.E. (1995), 'Economic network synergetics', in D.F. Batten, J. Casti and R. Thord (eds), *Networks in Action. Communication, Economics and Human Knowledge*, Berlin: Springer Verlag, pp. 309–18.

Andersson, Å.E. and B. Johansson (1984a), 'Industrial dynamics, product cycles, and employment structures', WP–84–9, IIASA, Laxenburg, Austria.

Andersson, Å.E. and B. Johansson (1984b), 'Knowledge intensity and product cycles in metropolitan regions', WP–84–13, IIASA, Laxenburg, Austria.

Andersson, Å.E. and J. Mantsinen (1980), 'Mobility of resources: accessibility of knowledge and economic growth', *Behavioural Science*, **25**, 353–66.
Andersson, Å.E. and U. Strömquist (1989), *K-samhällets Framtid*, Stockholm: Prisma (in Swedish).
Andersson, Å.E., C. Anderstig and B. Hårsman (1990), 'Knowledge and communication infrastructures and regional economic change', *Regional Science and Urban Economics*, **20**, 359–76.
Andersson, Å.E., G. Törnqvist, F. Snickars and S. Öberg (1984), *Regional Mångfald till Rikets Gagn*, Stockholm: Liber Förlag (in Swedish).
Anderstig, C. and C. Karlsson (1989), 'Spatial diffusion of information technology in Sweden', in Å.E. Andersson, D.F. Batten and C. Karlsson (eds), *Knowledge and Industrial Organization*, Berlin: Springer Verlag, pp. 157–76.
Audretsch, D.B. and M.P. Feldman (1996), 'R&D spillovers and the geography of innovation and production', *American Economic Review*, **86**, 630–40.
Batten, D.F., K. Kobayashi and Å.E. Andersson (1989), 'Knowledge, nodes and networks: an analytical perspective', in Å.E. Andersson, D.F. Batten and C. Karlsson (eds), *Knowledge and Industrial Organisation*, Berlin: Springer Verlag, pp. 31–46.
Baumol, W.J. (1990), 'Entrepreneurship: productive, unproductive and destructive', *Journal of Political Economy*, **98**, 893–921.
Bewley, T. (1981), 'A critique of Tiebout's theory of local public expenditures', *Econometrica*, **49**, 713–40.
Boden, M. (2004), *The Creative Mind: Myths and Mechanisms*, New York and London: Routledge.
Castells, M. (1989), *The Informational City*, Oxford: Blackwell.
Chesbrough, H. (2003), *Open Innovation*, Boston, MA: Harvard Business School Press.
Duranton, G. and D. Puga (2003), 'Micro-foundations of urban agglomeration economies', in J.V. Henderson and J.-F. Thisse (eds), *The Handbook of Regional and Urban Economics*, vol. 4, Amsterdam: North Holland, pp. 2063–117.
Fischer, M.M. and B. Johansson (1994), 'Networks for process innovation by firms: conjectures from observations in three countries', in B. Johansson, C. Karlsson and L. Westin (eds), *Patterns of a Network Economy*, Berlin: Springer Verlag, pp. 261–74.
Florida, R. (2002), *The Rise of the Creative Class. And How It's Transforming Work, Leisure, Community and Everyday Life*, New York: Basic Books.
Fujita, M. and J.-F. Thisse (1996), 'Economics of agglomeration', *Journal of the Japanese and International Economies*, **10**, 339–78.
Glaeser, E.L., J. Kolko and A. Saiz (2001), 'Consumer city', *Journal of Economic Geography*, **1**, 27–50.
Grabher, G. (1993), 'The weakness of strong ties: the lock-in of regional development in the Ruhr area', in G. Grabher (ed.), *The Embedded Firm: On the Socio-economics of Industrial Networks*, London: Routledge, pp. 255–75.
Hall, P. (1990), 'High-technology industry and the European scene', in *Urban Challenges*, SOU 1990:33, Stockholm: Allmänna Förlaget, pp. 117–33.
Hansen, N. (2000), 'The new economy: implications for peripheral regions', paper presented at the Annual Meeting of the Southern Regional Science Association, Miami Beach, Florida, 13–15 April.
Hirsch, S. (1967), *Location of Industry and International Competitiveness*, Oxford: Oxford University Press.

Hudson, R. (1994), 'Institutional change, cultural transformation, and economic regeneration: myths and realities from Europe's old industrial areas', in A. Amin and N.J. Thrift (eds), *Globalisation, Institutions, and Regional Development in Europe*, Oxford: Oxford University Press, pp. 196–216.

Jacobs, J. (1961), *The Death and Life of Great American Cities*, New York: Random House.

Jacobs, J. (1969), *The Economy of Cities*, New York: Random House.

Jacobs, J. (1984), *Cities and the Wealth of Nations*, New York: Random House.

Jaffe, A., M. Trajtenberg and R. Henderson (1993), 'Geographic localisation of knowledge spillovers as evidenced by patent citations', *Quarterly Journal of Economics*, **108**, 577–98.

Johansson, B. (1988), 'Innovation processes in the Swedish network of export and import nodes', Working Paper from CERUM, Umeå University, Umeå.

Johansson, B. (1993a), *Ekonomisk Dynamik i Europa. Nätverk för Handel, Kunskapsimport och Innovationer*, Malmö: Liber-Hermods (in Swedish).

Johansson, B. (1993b), 'Economic evolution and urban infrastructure dynamics', in Å.E. Andersson, D.F. Batten, K. Kobayashi and K. Yoshikawa (eds), *The Cosmo-Creative Society: Logistical Networks in a Dynamic Economy*, Berlin: Springer Verlag, pp. 151–75.

Johansson, B. (1995), 'The dynamics of economic networks', in D. Batten, J. Casti and R. Thord (eds), *Networks in Action. Communication, Economics and Human Knowledge*, Berlin: Springer Verlag, pp. 287–308.

Johansson, B. (1998a), 'Infrastructure, market potential and endogenous growth', Jönköping International Business School, Jönköping (mimeo).

Johansson, B. (1998b), 'Economic milieu, specialization and location dynamics', in A. Reggiani (ed.), *Accessibility, Trade and Location Behaviour*, Aldershot: Ashgate, pp. 121–52.

Johansson, B. (2000), 'Regional competition: endogenous and policy-supported processes', in P.W.J. Batey and P. Friedrich (eds), *Regional Competition*, Berlin: Springer Verlag, pp. 34–65.

Johansson, B. (2005), 'Parsing the menagerie of agglomeration and network externalities', in C. Karlsson, B. Johansson and R.R. Stough (eds), *Industrial Clusters and Inter-Firm Networks*, Cheltenham, UK and Northampton MA, USA: Edward Elgar, pp. 107–47.

Johansson, B. and Å.E. Andersson (1998), 'A Schloss Laxenburg model of product cycle dynamics', in M.J. Beckmann, B. Johansson, F. Snickars and R. Thord (eds), *Knowledge and Networks in a Dynamic Economy*, Berlin: Springer Verlag, pp. 181–219.

Johansson, B. and C. Karlsson (1986), 'Industrial application of information technology: speed of introduction and labour force competence', in P. Nijkamp (ed.), *Technological Change, Employment and Spatial Dynamics*, Berlin: Springer Verlag, pp. 401–28.

Johansson, B. and C. Karlsson (1987), 'Processes of industrial change: scale, location and type of job', in M.M. Fischer and P. Nijkamp (eds), *Regional Labour Markets*, Amsterdam: North-Holland, pp. 139–65.

Johansson, B. and C. Karlsson (1990), 'Stadsregioner i Europa', SOU 1990:34, Stockholm: Allmänna Förlaget.

Johansson, B. and C. Karlsson (2001), 'Geographic transaction costs and specialisation opportunities of small and medium-sized regions: scale economies and market extension', in B. Johansson, C. Karlsson and R.R. Stough (eds),

Theories of Endogenous Regional Growth – Lessons for Regional Policies, Berlin: Springer Verlag, pp. 150–80.
Johansson, B. and R. Wigren (1996), 'Production milieu and comparative advantages', in D.F. Batten and C. Karlsson (eds), *Infrastructure and the Complexity of Economic Development*, Berlin: Springer Verlag, pp. 187–211.
Kaldor, N. (1970), 'The case for regional policies', *Scottish Journal of Political Economy*, **17**, 337–47.
Karlsson, C. (1988), *Innovation Adoption and the Product Cycle*, Umeå Economic Studies, University of Umeå, Umeå (diss.).
Karlsson, C. and M. Andersson (2009), 'The location of industry R&D and the location of university R&D – how are they related?', in C. Karlsson, Å.E. Andersson, P.C. Cheshire and R.R. Stough (eds), *New Directions in Regional Economic Development*, Berlin, Heidelberg: Springer Verlag, pp. 267–91.
Karlsson, C. and J. Klaesson (2002), 'The spatial industrial dynamics of the ICT sector in Sweden', in Z.J. Acs, H.L.F. de Groot and P. Nijkamp (eds), *The Emergence of the Knowledge Economy. A Regional Perspective*, Berlin: Springer Verlag, pp. 243–75.
Karlsson, C. and J. Larsson (1990), 'Product and price competition in a regional context', *Papers of the Regional Science Association*, **69**, 83–99.
Karlsson, C. and A. Manduchi (2001), 'Knowledge spillovers in a spatial context – a critical review and assessment', in M.M. Fischer and J. Fröhlich (eds), *Knowledge, Complexity and Innovation Systems*, Berlin: Springer Verlag, pp. 101–23.
Karlsson, C. and R.R. Stough (2002), 'Introduction: regional policy evaluation in the new economic geography', in B. Johansson, C. Karlsson and R.R. Stough (eds), *Regional Policies and Comparative Advantage*, Cheltenham, UK and Northampton, MA, USA: Edward Elgar, pp. 1–21.
Karlsson, C. and L. Westin (1994), 'Patterns of a network economy – an introduction', in B. Johansson, C. Karlsson and L. Westin (eds), *Patterns of a Network Economy*, Berlin: Springer Verlag, pp. 1–12.
Karlsson, C., P. Flensburg and S.-Å. Hörte (2004), 'Introduction: knowledge spillovers and knowledge management', in C. Karlsson, P. Flensburg and S.-Å. Hörte (eds), *Knowledge Spillovers and Knowledge Management*, Cheltenham, UK and Northampton, MA, USA: Edward Elgar, pp. 3–31.
Karlsson, C., B. Johansson and R.R. Stough (2005), 'Industrial clusters and inter-firm networks: an introduction', in C. Karlsson, B. Johansson and R.R. Stough (eds), *Industrial Clusters and Inter-Firm Networks*, Cheltenham, UK and Northampton, MA, USA: Edward Elgar, pp. 1–25.
Kobayashi, K. (1995), 'Knowledge networks and market structure: an analytical perspective', in D.F. Batten, J. Casti and R. Thord (eds), *Networks in Action. Communication, Economics and Human Knowledge*, Berlin: Springer Verlag, pp. 127–58.
Kobayashi, K. and Å.E. Andersson (1994), 'A dynamic input–output model with endogenous technical change', in B. Johansson, C. Karlsson and L. Westin (eds), *Patterns of a Network Economy*, Berlin: Springer Verlag, pp. 243–59.
Kuhn, T.S. (1962), *The Structure of Scientific Revolutions*, Chicago, IL: University of Chicago Press.
Lloyd, R. (2006), *Neo-bohemia. Art and Commerce in the Postindustrial City*, New York: Routledge.
Lösch, A. (1943), *Die Raumliche Ordnung der Wirtschaft*, Stuttgart: Gustav Fischer.

Lucas, R. (1988), 'On the mechanics of economic development', *Journal of Monetary Economics*, **22**, 3–42.
Marshall, A. (1920), *Principles of Economics*, 8th edn, London: Macmillan.
Matthiessen, C.W. and Å.E. Andersson (1993), *Øresundsregionen – Kreativitet, Integration, Vækst*, København: Munksgaard (in Danish).
Myrdal, G. (1957), *Economic Theory and Underdeveloped Regions*, London: Duckworth.
Nelson, R.R. and S.G. Winter (1982), *An Evolutionary Theory of Economic Change*, Cambridge, MA: Harvard University Press.
Ohlin, B. (1933), *Interregional and International Trade*, Cambridge, MA: Harvard University Press.
Palander, T. (1935), *Beiträge zur Standorttheorie*, Uppsala: Almqvist & Wiksell.
Park, R., E. Burgess and R. McKenzie (1925), *The City*, Chicago, IL: University of Chicago Press.
Polanyi, M. (1966), *The Tacit Dimension*, London: Routledge & Kegan Paul.
Quigley, J. (1990), 'The quality of housing', in SOU 1990:33, *Urban Challenges*, Stockholm: Allmänna Förlaget, pp. 39–49.
Rasulzada, F. (2007), *Organisation Creativity and Psychological Well-being*, Department of Psychology, University of Lund, Lund (diss.).
Roback, J. (1982), 'Wages, rents and the quality of life', *The Journal of Political Economy*, **90**, 1257–78.
Rosen, S. (1979), 'Wage-based indexes of urban quality of life', in P. Mieszkowski and M. Strazheim (eds), *Current Issues in Urban Economics*, Baltimore, MD: Johns Hopkins University Press, pp. 391–429.
Saxenian, A. (1994), *Regional Advantage: Culture and Competition in Silicon Valley and Route 128*, Cambridge, MA: Harvard University Press.
Stahl, K. and P. Varaiya (1983), 'Local collective goods: a critical re-examination of the Tiebout model', in J.-F. Thisse and H.G. Zoller (eds), *Locational Analysis of Public Facilities*, Amsterdam: North-Holland, pp. 45–54.
Sternberg, R.J. and T.I. Lubart (1999), 'The concept of creativity: prospects and paradigms', in R.J. Sternberg (ed.), *Handbook of Creativity*, New York: Cambridge University Press, pp. 3–15.
Thompson, W. (1965), *A Preface to Urban Economics*, Baltimore, MD: Johns Hopkins Press.
Tiebout, C. (1956), 'A pure model of local expenditures', *Journal of Political Economy*, **85**, 865–72.
Vernon, R. (1960), *Metropolis 1985*, Cambridge, MA: Harvard University Press.
Vernon, R. (1966), 'International investment and international trade in the product cycle', *Quarterly Journal of Economics*, **80**, 190–207.
Vernon, R. and E.M. Hoover (1959), *Anatomy of a Metropolis*, Cambridge, MA: Harvard University Press.
von Hippel, E. (1994), 'Sticky information and the locus of problem solving: implications for innovation', *Management Science*, **40**, 429–39.
von Thünen, J.H. (1926), *Der Isolierte Staat in Beziehung auf Nationale Ökonomie und Landwirtschaft*, Stuttgart: Gustav Fischer.

3. Innovation and space – from externalities to networks

Corinne Autant-Bernard, Pascal Billand and Nadine Massard

3.1 INTRODUCTION

There are many studies describing the geographical structure of innovative activities within various countries, both in the American and European contexts.[1] All of these studies register a considerable spatial polarization of activities connected with innovation. They are accompanied by a relatively high theoretical production, which, since the end of the 1980s, has aimed to describe the different forms of local development through innovation. Local innovation systems, districts, technopoles, scientific parks, innovative environments, high-tech clusters – the terms are many and often correspond to differing views of the innovation processes and their inscription in space. Such differences are often the result of underlying theoretical traditions, as are the normative ambitions attributed to these concepts (Massard and Torre, 2005).

Beyond these differences, however, all have one term in common: they are based largely upon the notion of geographical externalities. The positive impact of geographical proximity upon innovation seems essentially to be due to a limiting of the diffusion of knowledge externalities in space. This simple hypothesis, for which the theoretical implications concerning 'local advantages' are quite heavy, has led to a few dangerous short-cuts in terms of public policies.

A review of the empirical studies that developed at the beginning of the 1990s, attempting, in particular, to measure the geographical dimension of these externalities, highlights the many subtleties of this hypothesis (Autant-Bernard et al., 2008). It provides elements for analysis that enable a finer understanding of the relations between innovation and space and the role played by the effects of proximity. Such a review specifically allows us to underline the shortcomings of those approaches that study the spatial diffusion of knowledge only from the angle of externalities.

Indeed, for anyone who, these days, is interested in the creation and diffusion of knowledge, as well as its various application, it is obvious that we are living in an era of great change (Wagner, 2004). The main feature of this evolution is without doubt the increasing influence of networks in the creation of knowledge. Innovation processes involve a growing number of different actors, who are increasingly interlinked. These transformations, however, cannot be reduced merely to effects of externalities as they are likely to affect both the localization of R&D activities and the nature of knowledge creation.

Thus, although having started with the simple measurement of the geographical dimension of knowledge externalities at spatially aggregated levels, the studies conducted in the geography of innovation have gradually turned towards the analysis of the mechanisms underlying the spatial diffusion of knowledge (absorption capacity, face-to-face exchanges, professional mobility). Pinpointing these mechanisms in turn justifies the research angles that endeavour to understand individual cooperative behaviour in terms of innovation. Such behaviour is at the base of the actor-networks dynamics that nowadays characterizes collective innovation phenomena and includes both local and global dimensions. A better understanding of the factors determining the spatial configuration of these networks appears to be necessary if we are to properly grasp innovation–space relationships.

In this chapter we aim to review the logic behind the research conducted in this field over the past few decades. The chapter is structured thus: Section 3.2 describes several stylized facts concerning the evolution of the geography of innovation over the past 30 years, and highlights the existence of highly concentrated specialized zones. Section 3.3 is a rapid survey of the theoretical founding of the economic geography of innovation before we review those works whose objectives are to provide empirical evidence in support of their main hypothesis: the existence of geographical knowledge externalities. In Section 3.4 we begin with the assumption that externalities are not diffused uniformly but rather transit via networks of interpersonal relationships. We then demonstrate how the progression towards a better understanding of the production and diffusion of knowledge mechanisms leads us to question the importance of deliberate individual initiatives to establish relationships. Leading on from this, Section 3.5 deals with the perspectives provided by the theories of relational networks for studying the innovation–space relationship. Section 3.6 is the conclusion.

3.2 SOME STYLIZED FACTS ABOUT THE GEOGRAPHY OF INNOVATION

The geography of innovative activities is distinguished by two essential features: a considerable spatial concentration on the one hand and a sectoral specialization of certain geographical zones on the other.

3.2.1 Heavy Spatial Concentration of Innovation Activities

One of the most striking characteristics of economic activity is its considerable spatial polarization. Innovation is no exception and is in fact even more concentrated than other production activities.[2]

From this point of view, America is without doubt the world leader. In 2005, not only was 40 per cent of the OECD's private expenditure for research concentrated there, but so also was 34 per cent of the inventors who had registered triadic patents (i.e. with the EPO – European Patents Office – the US Patent Trademark Office and the JPO – the Japan Patent Office). The EU appears in second place, with one quarter of the OECD's R&D expenditure, as well as 34 per cent of the triadic patents. Other countries are also present in certain specific domains (Japan, India, China). In these countries the spatial concentration is also striking. Hence, in the USA, innovation activity is mostly concentrated in the coasts of the states of California, New York and New Jersey.

In Europe, where the general context is one of stagnation with a ratio of R&D expenditure to GDP at around 1.9 per cent, the localization pattern of innovation is also characterized by a dense spatial polarization that is evident at both the state and regional levels. Thus the map of regional expenditure for R&D shows that the localization of technological activity forms an axis going from Holland to the south of Germany, the Paris area, the south-west of the UK, the Rhône–Alpes region and the north of Italy (see Figure 3.1). The map in Figure 3.2, showing the spatial distribution of the number of patents filed, reinforces this conclusion of spatial concentration in Europe as well as within each country.

These agglomerative tendencies of innovative activities are hardly recent. A study of the geography of such activities over the past 100 years in the USA (Vertova, 2002) shows that the phenomenon is long-standing even though it is now tending to intensify.

One might think that such spatial polarization of innovation is merely the result of the agglomeration of economic activity as a whole. Confronting the geographical distribution of innovation with that of production does indeed reveal strong similarities. The zones where innovative activity is concentrated are also the zones where there is a generally high level of

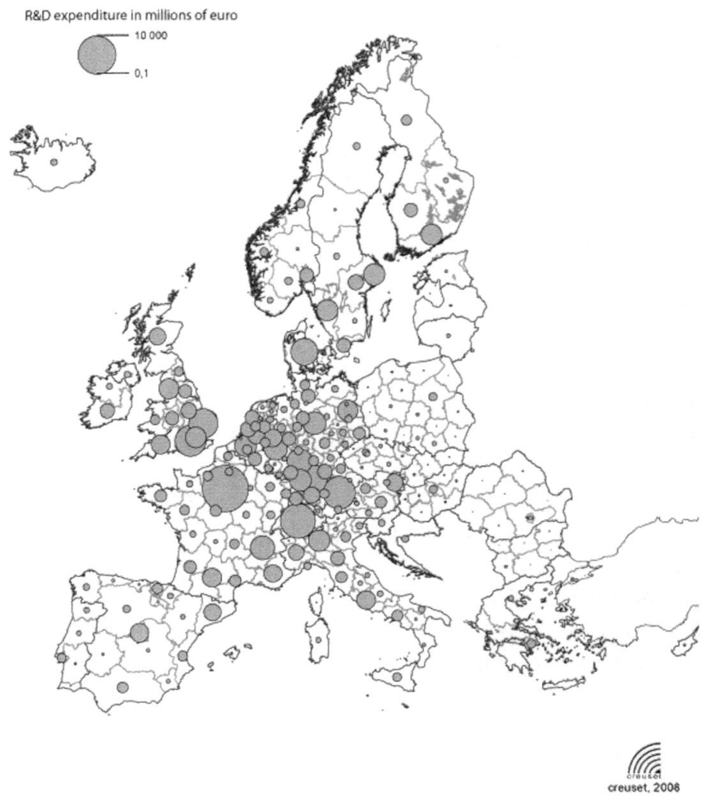

Note: Data in 2003 for Germany, Belgium, Bulgaria, Greece, Italy, Norway, Netherlands and Portugal.
Private non-profit sector not included in R&D expenditure in UK.

Source: Eurostat. © EuroGeographics for administrative borders (NUTS1 or NUTS2 according to countries).

Figure 3.1 R&D expenditure, 2004

activity. For the following two reasons, however, it seems simplistic to attribute the unequal geographical distribution of innovation solely to the concentration of production.

On the one hand, the areas where innovative activity is concentrated do not exactly cover those areas with a strong economic activity. For instance, the intensity of research and innovation, in relative terms when compared to the individual states' economic size (in terms of GDP), varies considerably from one region to another. In the USA, Massachusetts comes out as the most innovative state, ahead of New Jersey and California despite

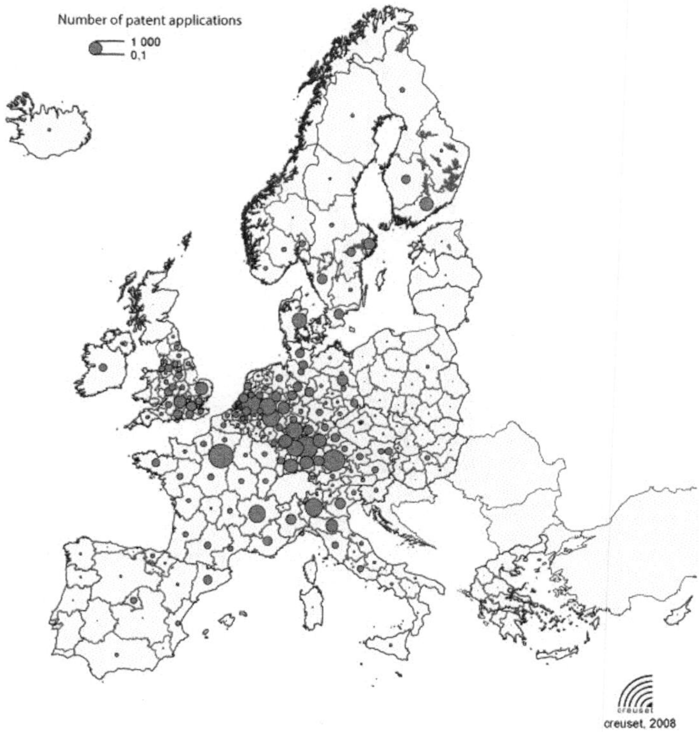

Source: Eurostat. © EuroGeographics for administrative borders (NUTS1 or NUTS2 according to countries).

Figure 3.2 Distribution of patent applications, 2002

their excellent position in terms of economic activity. In Europe, in 2005, the highest relative intensity of R&D (R&D/GDP) among the member states was recorded in Sweden (3.86 per cent of GDP), followed by Germany (2.51 per cent), Denmark (2.44 per cent), Austria (2.36 per cent) and France (2.13 per cent). The lowest intensity was recorded in Romania (0.39 per cent in 2004), Cyprus (0.40 per cent), Bulgaria (0.50 per cent) and Slovakia (0.51 per cent).[3]

On the other hand, production remains less agglomerated than innovation. Feldman (1994), when studying the American case, and Caniëls (2000) concerning Europe, in fact calculated concentration indices (Gini, Herfindahl, for instance) in order to compare the concentration of innovative activity with that of the rest of economic activity. The indices that were obtained for innovation were always distinctly higher than those obtained for production. In the same vein, the comparison carried out by

Source: Eurostat. © EuroGeographics for administrative borders (NUTS1 or NUTS2 according to countries).

Figure 3.3 Human resources in science and technology, 2006

the OECD (Science Technology Industry Scoreboard)[4] between the indices for the geographical concentration of patents and those of the population having been through higher education even shows that in most countries the highly qualified population (which is nonetheless more concentrated than productive activity) is less concentrated than are patents. The map in Figure 3.3, when compared with that of Figure 3.2, indicates the same for Europe. The polarization of productive activity is therefore insufficient to totally explain the geographical concentration of innovation.

Moreover, it would seem that there are both national and sectoral specificities that could explain the spatial organization of innovation. Indeed, the recorded levels of concentration vary from one country to another and from one sector to another.

The concentration indices elaborated by the OECD[5] show, for instance, that the geographical concentration of patents is particularly obvious in Australia, where 89 per cent of patents are registered by local inventors within less than 10 per cent of the country, in Japan (79 per cent), in Portugal (73 per cent), in Korea (72 per cent). By contrast, some countries show a less obvious concentration; this is the case for Poland (35 per cent), Belgium (39 per cent), the Netherlands (42 per cent) and Germany (43 per cent). What is more, we may clearly distinguish, among the members of the EU, those countries with multipolar structures where research activities are conducted in more than three or four regions of similar size: Germany, Austria, Belgium, Italy, Norway, Sweden, the UK, from countries with a monopolar structure where the greater proportion of R&D activity is concentrated in one or two regions at most: Spain, Finland, France and the Netherlands. International comparisons, however, remain extremely difficult. The geographical scales are not homogeneous. According to the level of observation, the indices' values may vary considerably.

The effects of spatial concentration upon the various industrial sectors are also very different. In France, for example, the activities connected to aerospace and computer science are highly agglomerated, whereas the research conducted on materials and in the food sector is much more widespread (Autant-Bernard, 2000). Added to these differing levels of concentration, from one industrial sector to another, are the effects of each region's technological specialization, which is at the origin of the different forms of agglomeration.

3.2.2 The Existence of Diversified Forms of Innovative Agglomerations

The spatial concentration of innovative activities is far from homogeneous and may take many different forms (Feldman and Massard, 2002). Innovative urban zones often have different natures. In particular, we may distinguish two main types of agglomeration: large diversified agglomerations on the one hand (in particular in association with finance and a variety of industries, such as New York), and often more reduced agglomerations that are extremely specialized. In global terms the latter are not first-ranking poles for innovation; they are, however, innovative leaders in one or more specific industries. Silicon Valley, as described by Saxenian (1994), is a case study for such an agglomeration, although many other regions also fall into this category, such as the famous Italian districts.

Despite the fact that, once more, international comparisons are difficult, it would seem that Europe is more highly specialized than the USA. Indeed, we may set alongside each other the results of Caniëls (2000) for the European context and those of Feldman (1994) for the USA. In Europe the most innovative region, for any industry, achieves, on average, half of the innovation for that industry, against only one-third for the Americans. This result, however, is conditioned by the number of industrial sectors taken into account and the size of the geographical zones concerned.

Beyond the simple distinction between specialized agglomeration and diversified agglomeration, observation of how innovative agglomerations have evolved shows that cities are tending towards functional specialization. It would seem that this phenomenon, put forward by Duranton and Puga (2005), is a result of the change in the way firms are organized, leading to the specialization of cities according to the type of activity rather than by sector. The specialization of large cities tends towards service functions, whereas smaller towns tend towards productive functions.

This tendency towards functional rather than sectoral specialization ought to coincide with an increase of the spatial concentration of innovative activity, certain countries and regions being specialized in R&D activities. This tendency ought also to reinforce agglomerations' sectoral diversification.

3.3 THE SPATIAL DIMENSION OF EXTERNALITIES AND THE ECONOMIC GEOGRAPHY OF INNOVATION

Essentially, the attempts made to interpret these facts theoretically are based upon the notion of the geographical externalities of knowledge.

3.3.1 The Theoretical Groundings

Alfred Marshall's work on districts provides the initial foundations for the microeconomic dynamics upon which agglomerations are based. The fact that, since the 1990s, they are once more in the limelight thanks to the development of the new economic geography has renewed the analysis of the innovation–space relationship.

A first fundamental element of this relationship concerns the geographical dimension of knowledge externalities. To be precise, while Krugman (1991) picks up on two agglomeration forces suggested by Marshall – pecuniary externalities connected to the backward–forward relationships within industries and the role of the labour market – he does not take geographical knowledge externalities into account, as according to him these cannot be measured and therefore remain impalpable. The theories of endogenous growth, however, insist upon the role of innovation and the processes of externalities linked to the diffusion of knowledge in growth dynamics.

Finally, the approach that synthesizes economic geography and endogenous growth brings these two perspectives together and provides a formalized analytical framework for the localized growth dynamics based upon innovation.[6] Beyond the traditional agglomerating factors of productive activity, technological externalities are central to the explanations concerning the highest polarization levels of innovative activities. The regions that benefit from such technological spillovers become more dynamic, in terms of innovation, and more attractive for new activities wishing to set themselves up. In this context, the hypothesis of a local dimension to these phenomena is essential. Where the externalities are localized, a region with a slight technological head-start will accumulate knowledge more rapidly. This, in turn, reduces the cost of innovation in that area and thus attracts more resources for that purpose. The result is an agglomeration of research and innovation activities for that region.

The second fundamental aspect of the innovation–space relationship concerns the degree to which local firms need to specialize in order for such externalities to exist. For Marshall (1890), then Arrow (1962) and Romer (1986) (MAR), knowledge externalities may only be transmitted where there exists a certain technological proximity.[7] In this case, high specialization, meaning the clustering of activities belonging to the same industry or related industries, determines the intensity of the knowledge externalities, the production dynamics of knowledge and the competitiveness of firms and regions. On the other hand, for other authors, externalities and local growth are positively affected by the grouping of a variety of activities in a same place. Jacobs (1969) holds this view. Thus the debate opposes the defenders of diversity and the defenders of specialization (review by Massard and Riou, 2002).

The second stylized fact that we have brought to evidence, that is the existence of differentiated forms of agglomeration according to their level of specialization, is then theoretically justified thanks to the idea of MAR or Jacobs externalities. It would seem that the larger, diversified agglomerations originate with the presence of Jacobs externalities, whereas the existence of specialized urban areas would be justified by MAR externalities.

Both types of agglomeration have been included in Duranton and Puga's (2001) simple model, which is based upon the existence of an innovation cycle. During the emerging, experimental phase of an activity, a firm has to face many uncertainties concerning the most efficient production process or the most appropriate qualifications of its employees. During this phase, then, firms will seek out diversified environments that offer proximity to other firms in the experimental stage. Although this diversity has a cost, due to the dispersion of competences over the given geographical area, the firms do not need to suffer these delocalization costs with each new experiment. The need for a diversified environment ends once the firm has found the appropriate production procedure. Then the firm will opt for a change of location for a geographical zone that specializes in its production procedure and where the production costs are less. The choice of location will then be governed by Marshallian externalities. Thus Duranton and Puga (2001) demonstrate how diversified and specialized urban fabrics may coexist, each answering firms' expectations at different stages of their life cycle.

These theoretical considerations on the localized nature of knowledge externalities have given rise, since the beginning of the 1990s, to several attempts at empirical validation.

First of all it should be noted that by placing itself at the junction between economics of innovation and spatial economics, the geography of innovation encounters not only the difficulties of modelling knowledge but also those of modelling spatial phenomena. The attempts that have been made to empirically evaluate the existence of technological externalities as well as their spatial dimension are therefore not so obvious. In fact the econometric literature concerning knowledge externalities seeks to report on these phenomena according to three research angles: analysis of the levels of concentration; patent citations; and the localized knowledge production functions.

3.3.2 Analysis of Concentration Levels

These analyses consist simply of studying the geographical distribution of research and innovation activities. With this in view, the work of Audretsch and Feldman (1996) and of Caniëls (2000) aims to explain the concentration levels of innovative activities, starting with the idea that if the spillovers are localized, then certain regions must benefit from the cumulative effects that favour the production of innovation.

The model initially presented by Audretsch and Feldman (1996) is based upon the estimation of a two-equation system: one equation for the concentration of production and one for the concentration of innovation. The results of the econometric estimations carried out by these authors, using 4200 innovations that were commercialized in the USA in 1982 are confirmed by Caniëls (2000), using European data from the 1990s: concerning the concentration of production, the first equation indicates that industries where research plays an important role have a greater tendency to be located near to each other.[8] Furthermore, industries where the qualified workforce represents an important part of the staff tend to be more concentrated than others.

Concerning the concentration of innovation, the second equation indicates that by neutralizing the effect of localization upon production, the factors related to new knowledge still lean towards a concentration of innovation. The concentration of innovative activity cannot therefore be entirely explained by production localization. The authors thereby deduce that it is not so much the localization of production that explains the concentration of innovation as the technological spillovers.

More recently studies have privileged methods that attempt to measure knowledge flows and their effects directly.

3.3.3 Patent Citations

The previous approach reveals considerable spatial disparities but offers no real modelling, as such, of spillovers. Other methods have therefore been considered. One was suggested by Jaffe et al. (1993), who oppose Krugman's view (1991) that knowledge externalities are impalpable with the idea that, on the contrary, they leave traces: patent citations, i.e. already existing patents that are cited when a new patent is applied for.[9] The purpose of these data, for the analysis of geographical spillovers, is to provide precise indications concerning innovators and their location. If the importance of the tacit nature of knowledge requires close proximity in order to enable the exchange and acquisition of knowledge, a firm will find it easier to use the local store of knowledge rather than that which is produced at a distance. We should therefore be able to find a connection between the location of new patents and that of the patents to which they refer (cited patents).

The principle of this method is the following: for the connection to be relevant, one must take into account the fact that technological activities may initially be geographically concentrated. It is likely, then, that patents become located in the same place as the patents that they cited, without this necessarily being proof for the existence of spillovers. We must therefore compare the probability that a patent is situated in a given place with the probability that it is situated in the same place as the patent to which it refers. For this purpose, Jaffe et al. compiled a control sample of patents.[10] The local dimension of spillovers is then highlighted if the frequency obtained for the co-localization of the cited patents is higher than that of the control sample.

The results obtained both for American data (Jaffe et al., 1993; Almeida and Kogut, 1997a, 1997b) and European data (Maurseth and Verspagen, 1999; Verspagen and Schoenmakers, 2000) corroborate the idea that localization influences innovation. Despite a few variations among the industrial sectors and within the time factors, the similarity of localization between the patents that are cited and the patents that cite them is generally stronger than that of the cited patents with the control patents.

The use of patent citations as 'markers' for knowledge spillovers is considered to give a good indication of the existence of a geographical dimension. Nevertheless, extrapolating about the means of transmission of spillovers from the results obtained for patent citations remains delicate. It relies upon the assumption that patent citations are good spillover indicators. It may be, however, that some citations do not always reflect spillovers, and vice versa: patent citations do not account for all spillovers.[11]

Moreover, defining localization is far from obvious, which would explain why other studies have turned towards alternative methods and abandoned the idea of spillover 'markers' in favour of analyses based upon work carried out in economics of innovation, and more specifically in R&D economics. The aim, then, is to test a knowledge production function while including spatial indicators.

3.3.4 Localized Knowledge Production Functions

The most frequently used knowledge production functions are based upon the one initially proposed by Griliches (1979). Griliches's function connects a firm's level of knowledge production or innovation to a set of explanatory variables. Alongside the variables that describe the firm's inherent features and the input of internal research, externalities are introduced as a stock of external research that is measured by the research expenditure of other firms and universities. If the research activity produces externalities, then the firm's innovation production must increase with the research efforts of other entities. In order to measure the geographical externalities within this framework, a spatial dimension is introduced into the estimations of such production functions. For this, different approaches have been considered. The first requires the measurement of the geographical coincidence, whereas the second compares different stocks of external research measured at different geographical levels.

The knowledge production function

The knowledge production function, as proposed by Griliches in 1979, is widely used in economics of innovation in order to provide a measurement for externality phenomena. This function, of a Cobb–Douglas type, explains internal innovation production (I_i) with the aid of variables that characterize the firm (E_i), the internal research input into firm (R_i) and a stock of external research (R_i^*):

$$I_i = \alpha(E_i)^{\beta_1}(R_i)^{\beta_2}(R_i^*)^{\beta_3} \quad (3.1)$$

The elasticity of innovation towards an evolution of external stock (β_3) measures the effects of externalities.

Although the existence of external effects is widely admitted, it is more difficult to measure the extent of their spatial diffusion. The literature suggests two approaches that allow the introduction of the spatial dimension into estimations.

Approach 1: This consists of measuring the effects of the geographical coincidence between private and public research laboratories upon innovative efficiency (Jaffe, 1989).

Jaffe (1989) devised an index for the geographical coincidence between industrial and university R&D at state level. Localization is determined by public expenditure on research and staff numbers of private R&D, measured at the metropolitan area level. This index is a non-centred correlation coefficient:

$$C_i = \sum_s U_{is} \cdot TP_{is} \Big/ \left(\sum_s U_{is}^2\right)^{1/2} \cdot \left(\sum_s TP_{is}^2\right)^{1/2} \quad (3.2)$$

where TP_{is} is the number of employees of private R&D in a metropolitan area s situated in a state i. The correlation is then calculated between the research expenditure and the number of workers in R&D, according to geographical zones.

Jaffe then integrates this index into a Griliches-type knowledge production function, aggregated at the level of the USA:

$$\log(P_{ik}) = \beta_{1k}\log(I_{ik}) + \beta_{2k}\log(U_{ik}) + \beta_{3k}\left[\log(U_{ik}) \cdot \log(C_{ik})\right] + \varepsilon_{ik} \quad (3.3)$$

where P being private patents, I is private R&D expenditure, U is university research expenditure, C is the geographical coincidence index between private R&D and university R&D within the state, ε is a random disturbance, i is the geographical observation unit (the state) and k is the technological area (i.e. the industrial sector).

In a more complete version of this equation, Jaffe also takes the size of the population into account in order to eliminate any effects due merely to the size of the state.

Based upon work carried out in spatial econometrics, Anselin et al. (1997) add three other indicators of geographical coincidence to Jaffe's index:

- A measurement that is close to Jaffe's but that uses counties instead of metropolitan areas. This indicator, noted as CUR_s, is given by $\Sigma_i\ \delta R_i \cdot \delta U_i / \Sigma \delta U_i$, where i is each of the counties within the state s. Thus it is possible to measure the proportion of regions where private R&D and public research are co-located.
- A gravity measurement: the C indicator of equation (3.2) becomes: $Grav_i = \Sigma\ U_j / (d_{ij})^2$, where i is the county where private R&D is located and j the county in which public research takes place. Variable d measures the distance between the two counties, i and j.
- Two covering indicators: $\text{Cov}_i = \Sigma\ \delta_{ij} \cdot U_j$. If the distance between counties i and j is less than 50 (or 75 miles), then $\delta_{ij} = 1$, otherwise $\delta_{ij} = 0$. An external research stock, which was constituted outside the zone being considered, is then integrated into the knowledge production function.

Approach 2: The second method studies the spatial interactions at different geographical levels.

In a second part of their work, Anselin et al. (1997) consider spillovers at different geographical levels, integrating the knowledge production function (K), private research expenditure (R) and public research expenditure (U) at the periphery of the metropolitan area (50 or 75 miles). The main equation is the following:

$$\log(K_i) = \alpha + \beta_3 \log(R_i) + \beta_4 \log(R75) + \beta_5 \log(U_i) + \beta_6 \log(U50) + \varepsilon \qquad (3.4)$$

The work of Autant-Bernard (2000) takes the same view by testing the following equation:

$$\log(I_i) = \alpha_1 + \beta_1 \log(R_i) + \beta_2 \log(R_{v(i)}) + \beta_3 \log(R_{v'(i)}) + \beta_4 \log(VA_i)\ u_1 \qquad (3.5)$$

where I is the innovation output (measured by the number of patents). R is the level of research input within zone i, in the zones bordering i ($v(i)$), and in the zones bordering i's boundary zones ($v'(i)$). α_1 is a constant term and u_1 is a random disturbance. VA is an indicator of added value that allows the effects of zone size to be taken into account.

A similar method has also been used by Bottazzi and Peri (2003). The production of patents by European regions is explained by research carried out at different geographical levels: within the region, in regions situated less than 300 km away, in regions situated between 300 and 6000 km away, 600–900, 900–1300, 1300–2000. A dummy variable is added to designate the country. The equation that is tested is:

$$\text{Ln}(Patent_i) = a + b_1 \ln(RD_i) + b_2 \ln(RD_{0\text{–}300}) + b_3 \ln(RD_{300\text{–}600}) + \ldots + d_i\, Country_i + u_i \quad (3.6)$$

The results of these studies basically confirm the idea that technological externalities are localized: only the research input of the zone and its immediate periphery have a significant influence upon innovation within the zone (what is more, the greater the distance, the more the parameters decrease). The spillovers appear to be more localized for private research than for public research.

Furthermore, the method used was reinforced by using spatial econometric tools. These help to evaluate the spatial extent of knowledge externalities by proposing a set of techniques for dealing with methodological questions taking spatial effects into account, and, more specifically, spatial autocorrelation and heterogeneity. Indeed, whilst using spatial data offers the opportunity for a richer analysis, allowing us in particular to relate the phenomena of spatial interdependence, the way in which these dependencies should be integrated into a regression is complex and has implications for the identification of parameters and the estimation methods that should be used (LeSage, 2008).

On the whole, whatever the methodology that is used (concentration analysis, patent citations or localized knowledge production functions), a consensus emerges around the idea of a local dimension of knowledge externalities. It would appear, however, that the diffusion of these externalities is not independent of the firms' internal characteristics and choices. A number of methods have been suggested that would enable a finer investigation of the transmission mechanisms underlying the externality phenomena and that would take the firms as actors into account more directly.

3.4 INSIDE THE BLACK BOX: THE MECHANISMS OPERATING BEHIND THE DIFFUSION OF KNOWLEDGE EXTERNALITIES

Based upon patent citations or the estimation of knowledge production functions, or even, as we shall see later on, other more specific methods, the studies concerning the geography of innovation highlight different sources and transmission modalities of knowledge externalities that justify their uneven diffusion in space. First of all, they bring to light the absorption capacities that are responsible for the asymmetry of the economic agents' capacity to benefit from knowledge flows (Section 3.4.1). We then underline the role of the interactions of agents taking part in innovative activities (Section 3.4.2) and the mobility of these agents (Section 3.4.3) that feeds this absorption capacity. The geographical question is then no longer restricted to a mere measurement of the spatial extent of the diffusion of externalities, but rather consists of defining why geography is a relevant aid for establishing effective relationships between actors.

3.4.1 Absorption Capacity

Assimilating technological knowledge that has been developed elsewhere is an expensive activity. In order to grasp technological externalities, it is in fact necessary to possess the appropriate knowledge and competences internally. The internal R&D capacity is therefore complementary to external knowledge sources. This capacity not only generates new information; it also enables the firm to improve its capacity to benefit from existing knowledge (Cohen and Levinthal, 1989). A number of empirical studies have confirmed this idea. Thus Varga's study (1998), which was applied at the aggregate territorial level, confirms the positive role of the absorption capacity of knowledge externalities for the USA. Varga noted that, through a knowledge production function, a critical mass should be reached in order to achieve a substantial local effect of the public research expenditure for the number of commercialized innovations. In the European context, Maurseth and Verspagen (1999) also observed a negative correlation between the intensity of patent citations and the productivity gap between two different regions. The greater the productivity differentials between two regions, the less likely it is that one of those regions would refer to patents registered in another region. This would tend to indicate that a sufficient quantity of internal competences is necessary in order to access the knowledge produced in neighbouring regions.

Building up a local absorption capacity also raises the question of potential externality sources and in particular concerning their intra- or intersectoral origins. Is it preferable for a region to rely upon specialization in order to facilitate knowledge exchanges, or to possess a diversified structure of the proficient competences in order to improve its absorption capacity? It would generally seem that specialization has a negative effect upon the local innovative capacity, even though the results, at this stage, remain somewhat contrasted. When considering a knowledge production function for which the innovative level of a geographical zone is explained by that zone's degree of specialization (the sector's RTA[12]), the diversity level (the RTA of connected sectors) and the degree of competition,

Audretsch and Feldman (1999) and Greunz (2004) noted that diversified zones would be more favourable to innovation. This could lead us to believe that the hypothesis for Jacobs-type externalities would be predominant. Autant-Bernard (2001) and Botazzi and Peri (2003), however, show that the technological proximity between regions increases knowledge flows by introducing a technological proximity indicator into the knowledge production function at different geographical levels. Also, studies on patent citations bear witness more to the intrasectoral nature of externalities. According to Jaffe et al. (1993) and Verspagen and Schoenmakers (2000), the probability of citing a patent is positively influenced by the technological proximity between the new and the cited patents.

It is difficult to obtain general conclusions in this field as two types of externality come into play. The question is to establish how they articulate around each other. Several results converge, notably showing that the diversity externalities are more localized than specialization externalities (Autant-Bernard and LeSage, 2011). Moreover, the differences in sectoral behaviour seem to be considerable in this area, as is shown by the study carried out for France by Massard and Riou (2002).

Finally, it should be noted that the study carried out by Duranton and Puga (2000) concerning delocalization phenomena for French firms between 1993 and 1996 may help us to interpret these results, which differ so greatly depending on the sector. Many of the de-localizations that were observed follow the pattern described by the authors in their model, i.e. they stem from a diversified area and head towards a specialized area. In terms of localization, diversified zones attract emerging activities that are still at the experimental stage (and therefore have little effect upon local growth); once they are stabilized these activities then transfer to more specialized zones, where they benefit from economies based upon specialization in order to develop. Thus the determining factors of absorption capacity appear to be dependent upon the different life-cycle phases of innovation.

Studies on the life cycle and the sectoral origin of knowledge externalities enable us to define more precisely the mechanisms that engender such externalities. What matters above all is their proximity to research activities in a number of fields and in particular during the initial phases of the innovative life cycle (Paci and Usai, 1999; Greunz, 2004). It would seem that geographical constraints diminish as technological development increases.

This information leaves the door open, however, for questions concerning how such technological spin-offs are acquired when they are more or less localized both spatially and sectorally. Answers may be found when the role of interpersonal relationships is considered. Indeed, for many authors in the geography of innovation, the localized nature of externalities is the result of the tacit dimension of knowledge. Ideas are not directly available to all; rather they are, at least partly, contained within people (Lucas, 1988). Consequently, the diffusing and absorbing of tacit knowledge seems to be determined by real human interaction.

Various studies have investigated this question by considering two main types of interaction: the fact that agents, who are close to each other, meet regularly face to face, and the relative ease with which agents who are involved in innovation are able to move both geographically and between institutions (mobility).

3.4.2 Communication Externalities Linked to Face-to-face Exchanges

Prior to working out measurements for efficient exchanges for innovation production, Charlot and Duranton (2004) concentrated on developing a methodology for isolating the externalities that are linked to communication between employees among the global effects of the local environment upon those same employees' productivity. In other words, employees do in fact have at their disposal informal and tacit knowledge. It is, however, difficult to determine the nature of the respective influences of the employees' own individual characteristics and the local environment (urbanization, employees' general level of education/training etc.) upon the capacity to enhance this knowledge through exchanges and communication. Based, notably, upon the French COI[13] survey, the authors confirm the existence of communication externalities resulting from direct interactions of employees and estimate the totality of the effects of the local environment upon urban employees at 22 per cent.

In an approach that is closer to the geography of innovation, Zucker et al. (1994) also aimed to show the importance of direct interaction in actors' capacity to develop externalities. In the case of Californian biotechnology, they show how geographical proximity is insufficient for there to be any benefits from knowledge spillovers between public and private research. Their econometric estimations demonstrate that the firms with the best performances (number of products being developed, number of products actually on the market and the growth of their employment rate) are those that are in contact (through joint publications, for instance) with university researchers within the same geographical zone. Furthermore, by making the distinction between researchers who collaborate with firms and those who are purely academic, the results show that the pure academics are of no benefit to firms. Hence it is certainly the fact of being in contact with a university that enables a firm to benefit from the activity of public research, and not merely its being located nearby. Finally, in a more recent study, Zucker and Darby (2007) continued their analysis by revealing the existence of a truly 'virtuous' circle of interactions of public and private research: private research is not the only party to benefit from such relationships given that R&D cooperation connections with firms go hand in hand with the improvement of researchers' academic productions.

In the case of France, other studies based upon researchers' co-publications also measure interpersonal relationships and enrich knowledge production functions by taking these relationships in account. The idea is the following: geographical proximity has no effect in itself other than that of making it easier to set up efficient collaborative relations between researchers. Autant-Bernard and Massard (2000) transposed this idea in the form of two hypotheses, H1: geographical proximity facilitates interaction; and H2: effective interaction induces increasing efficiency in terms of innovation. The results validate hypothesis H1 despite the fact that the geographical modalities of the collaborations vary according to the size of researchers' city of residence. Introducing co-publications into a knowledge function production model allows us next to estimate the extent to which the effect of a given zone's R&D upon the innovative capacity of another zone is influenced by the number of existing cooperative relationships between these zones. This influence appears to be positive and is greater when the interactions are local. Hence not only does geographical proximity facilitate the establishing of collaborations; it also helps to increase the externalities produced by such collaborations.

However, although face-to-face meetings in the context of R&D cooperation are an important transmission vector of knowledge, other authors consider that employee mobility is an essential vector for the transmission of spillovers.

3.4.3 Professional Mobility

Using patent citations, Almeida and Kogut (1997b) apply the methods of Jaffe et al. to the case of semiconductors in order to study regional differences in terms of spillover localization. Their hypothesis states that the main vector for the diffusion of spillovers is the interfirm mobility of employees. If the spillovers are localized, then this must be due to the existence of local networks within the labour market that geographically circumscribe such mobility.

In order to test this hypothesis, Almeida and Kogut noted patent holders' professional trajectories, using the information provided in the patents concerning the inventor engineer's name and the firm where he or she was employed. The results indicate, on the one hand, that there are important regional disparities in the degree of the labour force's interfirm mobility. These disparities coincide with the differences in terms of localization. Silicon Valley, for instance, holds record mobility within the area. It would seem, then, that the greater the professional mobility, the more knowledge is passed on from one firm to another. On the other hand, interregional mobility is low, which would explain the localized dimension of spillovers and the appearance of cumulative effects.

In order to confirm these results, Almeida and Kogut then observed whether or not the firms who hired a new patent-holding engineer are more likely to cite that engineer's patent. To this end, they assembled a new control sample, which reflected the probability of the patent concerned being cited, even if the engineer was not hired. The test results are positive: firms that hire a new engineer are more likely to cite that engineer's patent than are other firms. Thus it would seem that the adjunction of a new engineer stimulates a firm's innovative performances in the corresponding technological field. The idea appears once again in the works of Zucker et al. (1994) and Balconi et al. (2004) that the localization of externalities is the result of the individual's spatially circumscribed mobility.

On the whole, it would appear that one of the essential lessons to be learned from the studies mentioned above is that overflow effects are not uniform phenomena. They are dependent upon interpersonal exchanges and the flows of the labour force, and cannot be dissociated from individuals themselves. The existence of an absorption capacity appears to be necessary, not only in terms of previous knowledge, but also from the point of view of the diversity of mastered knowledge. It is also an integral part of the evaluation of the geographical dimension and the extent of such phenomena to take into account both their sources and the related externality transmission modalities. In fact, when technological proximity or interpersonal relationships are introduced, it appears that spillovers not only occur locally. Very real local phenomena often combine, and sometimes in a complex manner, with exchanges of knowledge from further away, based upon technological proximity and interpersonal relationships.

Improving estimation techniques is a field of study currently being developed and ought to enable us to grasp the different effects at work and evaluate their geographical dimension more precisely. In particular, we can expect improvements in spatial econometrics. Analyses should be substantially enriched as new tools, adapted to the panel and count data used especially in innovation econometrics, are developed (Anselin et al., 2004; LeSage et al., 2007).

Beyond these technological advances, however, current research has turned towards new questions. Indeed, taking into account interpersonal exchanges and professional trajectories between firms can be included in a wider area of study that highlights the impact of networks upon firms' innovative capacities. From the point of view of the geography of innovation, it is no longer merely a question of measuring the extent of geographical externalities, but rather of measuring the impact of geography as a substratum of the network structure of knowledge flows.

3.5 NETWORKS IN KNOWLEDGE PRODUCTION: NEW CHALLENGES FOR THE ANALYSIS OF INNOVATION–SPACE RELATIONSHIPS

3.5.1 Networks and the Spatial Diffusion of Knowledge

There has been an increasing interest in networks due to important changes both in the creation processes and in the diffusion of knowledge. One of the main characteristics of these changes is probably the increasing networking processes involved in the production of knowledge. The production of knowledge is less and less dependent upon firms, research centres or individual inventors, but instead relies more and more upon the exchange and circulation of information between multitudes of actors. An innovation network may be defined as the set of agents involved in innovative production and in the contacts established between agents allowing the circulation and creation of knowledge. Several studies, based upon articles, patents or R&D collaborations, show that these networks are becoming increasingly complex and are characterized by:

- *An increasing number of agents.* Based upon different indicators, several authors have concluded that there is a significant increase in the number of agents involved in innovation networks. This phenomenon is brought to the fore in the R&D collaborative networks that were studied in the pharmaceutical industry at the end of the 1970s, and then in the 1980s and 1990s (Roijakkers and Hagedoorn, 2006). Similar results may be found in Newman's study (2004), which concentrated upon co-publications, and Wagner and Leydersdorff's study (2005), which was devoted to co-patenting.
- *Increased density and complexity within networks.* In particular, intersectoral and inter-organizational collaboration has taken up more space (Powell et al., 1996; Roijakkers and Hagedoorn, 2006, for the pharmaceutical industry; Hagedoorn et al., 2006, for the computer industry).
- *A wider geographical distribution.* Wagner and Leydesdorff (2005) and Roijakkers and Hagedoorn (2006) observed that innovation networks are becoming more international. The studies carried

> out by these authors, however, still need further investigation. Thus it may well be that agents are at the same time becoming more internationalized and more concentrated within each country. Furthermore, collaborations may be more international but only connecting a limited number of the larger countries or regions.

These transformations offer new challenges for the geography of innovation. To be more precise, the fact that scientific research is increasingly carried out within the framework of a network organization may well change the spatial diffusion of knowledge. Thus Johansson and Quigley (2004) state that the emergence of agglomeration economies and the diffusion of these external economies via networks will become key factors of regional development during the twenty-first century. According to measurements taken up until now in the geography of innovation, the local dimension of knowledge externalities may simply reveal the effects of geographical proximity upon collaborative choices and thus not reflect in the least the existence of spatial externalities in the strict sense of the term. Breschi and Lissoni (2006a) thus show that the networks of interpersonal relationships, which are the main vector for knowledge flows, appear to be concentrated locally and are alone the explanation for the spatial agglomeration of innovation. So, in order to understand the determining factors of the geography of innovation, it is no longer simply the case of measuring the extent of local knowledge externalities, in the sense of the free and non-paying diffusion of knowledge, but rather it becomes necessary to understand the voluntary strategies that are implemented by those taking part in innovation in order to acquire knowledge from within the networks. We have therefore shifted from a logic concerning the diffusion of externalities to a logic concerning the accessibility of knowledge through networks (Massard and Mehier, 2009).

In order to grasp the new issues for the future geography of innovation, we therefore need to develop a better understanding of how widespread groups of scientists and innovators may form and collaborate to create and diffuse knowledge, and the specific role played by geography in these processes. A certain number of studies have been developed in the field of economics, which may help to answer these questions. A first type of study, of a theoretical nature, deals with economic models for the creation of networks. These studies employ tools from game theory to account for the strategic choices that lead to the setting up of collaborative links between actors and that may give rise to the diffusion of knowledge. Recently, some of these studies have included the geographical dimension as one of the determining factors of these choices (Section 3.5.2). A second type of study, of an empirical nature, evaluates the respective influences of the proximity created between actors and their network of relations (relational proximity) and the geographical proximity in collaborative choices (Section 3.5.3).

3.5.2 Introducing the Geographical Dimension into Economic Models of Collaborative Networks Formation

Economic models for the creation of networks deal with situations where the agents are able to establish bilateral connections with other actors in order to gain access to specific resources. The totality of these bilateral connections forms a network. Jackson and Wolinsky (1996) wrote the founding text for the related literature. The connections model that was presented by these authors has been quoted in a number of later works that have integrated the geographical dimension into the choices governing the creation of these connections.

In the connection model, each agent is initially in possession of information. When these agents are firms, the information may concern, for instance, technologies, markets or products. Establishing a link between agent *i* and agent *j* allows agent *i* access not only to the information initially held by agent *j* but also to other information to which agent *j* has access via his other connections (and vice versa for agent *j*). What is more, the further away from agent *j* in the relationship network agent *i* is, the lesser the amount of agent *j*'s initial information to which he has access will be. Finally, establishing a link between two agents has a cost that is shared by the agents involved. Recent empirical studies (Singh, 2005; Breschi and Lissoni, 2006b) suggest that Jackson and Wolinsky's model may be applied to knowledge flows between agents who are involved in innovation processes. Hence these studies show that the connections between agents are the basis for knowledge externalities and that knowledge flows from one agent to another decrease considerably when the distance within the network between these two agents increases.

Jackson and Wolinsky are interested in the networks that should emerge when agents are able to choose their links. They then have to define a new notion of equilibrium: stability by pair. A network is stable by pair if it satisfies two properties: on the one hand when two agents have no connection between them, at least one of them has not been encouraged to form the said connection; on the other hand neither agent has any interest in withdrawing from the connection in which he is involved.

Johnson and Gilles (2000) and Carayol and Roux (2008) introduced the geographical dimension into the connection model by making the costs of creating these connections dependent upon the agents' spatial localization links. For Johnson and Gilles, space is represented by a unit-length line along which the agents are situated at fixed intervals. The authors suppose that the cost of a connection between two agents increases linearly with the distance between the two agents on the line. The payment function of an agent takes the following form:

$$\pi_i(g) = \sum_{j \neq i} \delta^{d_{ij}} - c \sum_{j \neq i} g_{ij} l_{ij} \tag{3.7}$$

where δ is a (decay) parameter between 0 and 1, d_{ij} is the geodesic distance[14] between i and j in the g network, c is the cost of a link, g_{ij} is equal to 1 if i and j have formed a link and otherwise g_{ij} is equal to 0, and l_{ij} is the geographical distance between i and j on the line. The value of the information granted initially to each agent is normalized at 1. We set down $d_{ij} = \infty$ if i and j are not linked within network g.

Cayarol and Roux's model is distinct from that of Johnson and Gilles in that the agents are situated on a circle at equidistant intervals, and therefore do not initially occupy asymmetrical positions.

For reasonably large parameter intervals, and within the network equilibrium, these two models both generate 'small-world' networks, that is to say, networks characterized by connections with very high rates of proximity connections and a few long-distance connections.[15] Thus the models predict that geographical proximity should be a central determining factor for collaborative choices. The intuition behind this result is relatively simple. All things being equal, it is more in an agent's interest to create a link with another agent who is close by, rather than with one who is further away, as the initial information endowments, and consequently the value, of each agent is identical and the cost of creating a link with a closer agent is less. At the same time, in a configuration where an agent has only formed links with his neighbours, the average distance of one agent from the other is at a maximum. In this case, if the 'decay' parameter is low enough, it may be worthwhile for an agent to substitute a link with a neighbouring agent for a link with an agent who is further away, as the resulting cost excess would be more than compensated for by the possibility of benefiting from the higher earnings of indirect connections.

Furthermore, in these two models the authors show that, in network equilibrium, distant connections may be too few in view of what would be socially necessary. The logic underlying this efficiency problem is the following: when an agent creates a long-distance connection, this generates a positive externality for the agents who are nearby in the network and it may well be that no other agent has any individual interest in establishing such a link even though it is a socially efficient link (the value of a long-distance connection may be, for instance, that of escaping the 'competence traps' that are the result of insufficient open-mindedness towards the outside world of local economic agents). Moreover, it transpires that when a long-distance connection is established by an agent, other agents with whom he is connected are less inclined to create their own long-distance connections, given that they benefit indirectly from the one that has already been set up.

Both Johnson and Gilles's and Cayarol and Roux's models demonstrate the value of giving strategic foundations to the architecture of the social 'small-world' networks that were observed in the empirical studies and that consider the impact of geographical localization for the creation of collaborative connections. Furthermore, by pointing out the possible lack of links between agents who are far apart, they are able to legitimize certain devices that have been put in place by the authorities concerning innovation policies. In particular, these models are echoed by the European Union policies within the Framework Programme for Research and Technological Development (RTD FP), which consist of demanding as a criterion for the financial aid of a project that the participants be from at least three different countries. The analysis framework for both of these models, however, is too complicated for it to be possible to give sufficiently detailed results. In particular, for an intermediate degree of 'decay', it is difficult to predict what the long-distance connections will be and what proportion of the whole they will represent.

Several extensions of these studies have attempted to go beyond these limits. The first type of extension, carried out by Jackson and Rogers (2005), consists of simplifying the previous models in terms of the agents' heterogeneity. More precisely, Jackson and Rogers have constructed a model where the agents are brought together into 'islands' where the cost of the connections situated on the same island is less than that of two agents situated on different islands. This form of modelling may be particularly appropriate for the analysis of innovative collaboration networks, in situations where the actors are dispersed in different cities or in spatially distinct innovative clusters. In this case several factors may diminish the cost of collaboration between agents belonging to the same entity (or within the same island, according to the model of Jackson and Rogers): reduced transport costs in order to organize face-to-face meetings, existence of a common culture in order to facilitate communication etc. In such a context, Jackson and Rogers are able to characterize all the stable networks. They show that all these networks (as well as the efficient networks) are 'small-world' networks.

The second type of extension retains the complete heterogeneity, but deals with the creation of networks as a dynamic process. A first study, by Carayol and Roux (2009), which tends in this direction, models the formation of networks in the form of a stochastic process disrupted by the creation of links that allows us to explore the structural attributes of network equilibrium for different values of the 'decay' parameter. The authors show that for a reasonably wide interval of this parameter's value, the network equilibrium is made up of small-world configurations that are characterized at the same time by a high proportion of local connections and by a low average distance. A second study by Carayol et al. (2008) develops techniques (genetic algorithms and Monte Carlo simulations) that enable a better understanding of efficient networks and the means to determine the inefficiency of created networks. In the authors' results it appears that long-standing equilibrium networks are not dense enough and that long-distance connections may be too few. An interesting result is that distant links should be more structured around central agents. Central agents may be those who set up the most connections within a network ('degree centrality') or those who play the role of gatekeeper, that is who create the links between groups of agents who are scattered and thereby enable the diffusion of knowledge ('betweenness centrality'). Thus, when it is the same agent within a group who establishes the connections with other groups, this agent becomes central, both from a degree and a betweenness point of view. This result corroborates one of the recommendations issued by a European Commission report concerning the RTD FP (Malerba et al., 2006) that advocated favouring the development of exceptional agents, both in scientific and technological terms, as central agents within collaborative networks created by R&D projects, financed by the European Commission in the context of the RTD FP.

The previous models have several characteristics in common, which may be open to debate. In particular, they take no account of any change in the agents' knowledge during the interaction processes. Nevertheless, several authors, and in particular Nooteboom (2004), have underlined that repeated collaboration between partners reduces the cognitive distance between them. This may diminish the interest in any further future collaboration, in that each partner possesses less new knowledge to share with the other.

It is from this point of view that Cowan et al.'s (2006) model is interesting, in that it integrates the past-dependent dynamic into a network's creation process. In this model, the creation and destruction of links between firms is an ongoing process. What is more, this process is shaped by the specific, changing characteristics of firms during the collaborative process. To be precise, at each stage of the process, each firm holds a certain stock of knowledge and chooses the partner with whom they will seek to collaborate. Through these collaborations, the firms will combine their knowledge in order to create new knowledge and innovate. Each collaboration has a level of success probability. If the collaboration does succeed, then new knowledge is created that becomes input for the innovation process. Furthermore, the knowledge that has been created is added to both firms' stock of knowledge. The repetition of collaboration between two firms, however, is against their collaborative interest. In the first instance, the repetition of collaboration between two firms results in a combining of their stock of knowledge, which has a negative effect upon the innovative output from their collaboration. Second, the repetition of collaboration reduces uncertainty and renders each partner's behaviour easier to anticipate; this makes collaboration easier and increases its chances of success.

The geographical dimension is not explicitly introduced into this model. It would be possible, however, to re-examine it, taking this dimension into account. In particular, Cowan et al. consider that the fact of having collaborated during previous periods is the only factor that reduces the uncertainty concerning the failure risk of any collaboration. Geographical proximity between two agents, however, is also likely to generate confidence in the relationship. This proximity may, notably, facilitate the circulation of information concerning the reliability of potential partners or increase the possibility of sanctions in the case of disloyal behaviour. In this context, the agents should have a greater tendency to engage in relationships with agents who are nearby. Geographical proximity may then play a substitute role for technological proximity in order to ensure the success of collaborations. This result is similar to that of the empirical approaches that demonstrate the more restricted nature of inter-industrial collaboration when compared with collaboration within the same industry, which may develop at greater distances (Autant-Bernard, 2000).

In fact, the relational proximity (or social proximity) of two agents, defined as the geodesic distance between two agents within a network, and the geographical proximity are both likely to be determining factors in collaborative choices. Hence the interest in empirical studies that aim to examine whether it is relational proximity or geographical proximity that is the more significant in choices for collaboration.

3.5.3 Measuring the Respective Influences of Geographical Proximity and Relational Proximity for the Choice of Collaborative Connections

Recent studies have considered the increasing importance of the diffusion of knowledge through network collaborations in R&D and attempt to estimate the role played by geographical distance when compared to the social or relational distance between individuals.

Based upon citations as a measurement for the diffusion of knowledge between inventors, and using individual data, a first series of studies considers the effects of social and geographical proximity upon the probability of citing a patent. They conclude that the effects of social proximity are stronger than those of geographical proximity (Singh, 2005; Sorenson et al., 2006; Gomes-Casseres et al., 2006). The fact that individuals have already cooperated, or that they are only slightly distant from each other (geodesic distance), within co-invention networks, greatly increases the chances that they will cite each other as inventors.

For their part, Breschi and Lissoni (2003, 2006a) have reviewed the methodology for analysing the localization of patent citations developed by Jaffe et al. (1993) by taking into account the relationship networks established by firms via the researchers' mobility. They found that the structure of the citations that they observed is largely explained by these mobility relationships and where the geographical mobility of these 'multi-firm' inventors is rather limited, the resulting citation network reveals itself to be highly localized. Thus their conclusion is once more that geographical proximity is not a sufficient condition for access to local knowledge; this access requires an active network for the exchange of knowledge. The role of geographical proximity, and that of technological proximity, as put forward by Jaffe et al., are in fact merely revealing of the effects of another more determining variable: the social proximity between inventors, measured via the place that they hold within active exchange networks, established thanks to researchers' interfirm mobility.

The approach implemented by Maggioni et al. (2007) is different in that they use the aggregated data at the level of the European regions. Estimating a knowledge production function, they highlight the importance of spatial distance. In particular, their results show that spatial autocorrelation phenomena exceed autocorrelation phenomena that are based upon relational distance matrices, thereby upholding the idea that the regions' propensity to register patents depends clearly more upon local knowledge spillovers than upon knowledge flows resulting from long-distance collaborations. These studies, however, analyse collaborations without taking the network dimension completely into account. Co-inventions are only considered as bilateral relations between individuals, so that the position of individuals within the networks created by these collaborations is not taken into account.

Furthermore, given the proven importance of the way scientific and technological networks are structured for their innovative capacity, other authors, although they are still few, are interested in the determining factors that lead to the creation of these structures and refer to the literature on the formation of networks that we have presented here. Thus Hanaki et al. (2007) apply the co-invention data from the NBER (National Bureau of Economic Research) to the field of ICT between 1985 and 1995 to measure the effects of 'cyclic closure'[16] type networks or 'preferential attachment'[17] upon the choices for establishing new collaborations between firms. The estimations of geographical effects do not reveal any significant effects for this variable. This estimation, however, is based upon a simple measurement of the localization of the registered offices within the same county.

Also based upon the theoretical approaches that explain the microeconomic grounds for the creation of networks, Autant-Bernard et al. (2007) use a model of discrete choices for interfirm innovative cooperation; their objective is to confront the importance of spatial effects with relation to network effects. From the data that describe the cooperative projects proposed by the European Commission within the context of the 6th RTD FP in micro- and nano-technology, spatial distance and social distance variables are introduced in order to explain partner choices. The results show that firms' positions within cooperative networks that were constituted previously (during the 5th RTD FP) are determining for cooperative choices. Auto-reinforcement effects surrounding networks' central actors prevail over cooperation choices at a European level, whereas the effects of geographical proximity only appear when intranational cooperation is considered.

When compared to the many empirical analyses of the factors determining interfirm cooperation that take only pair characteristics into account, it is noticeable that there is still a limited number of empirical studies taking network effects directly into account and confronting geographical position with position within networks as determining factors for cooperation. The difficulties of collecting the systematic geo-localized data necessary to conduct this type of analysis as well as the methodological difficulties of representing R&D collaborative networks (cf. Billand et al., 2008) no doubt explain this scarcity.

3.6 CONCLUSION

Beginning with the acknowledgement of the high geographical concentration of innovative activities and the emphasis placed upon theories explaining the existence of localized knowledge externalities, the trend in the geography of innovation during the 1990s focused largely upon the empirical measurement of the spatial dimension of externalities. This research confirmed the existence of a spatial constraint for the diffusion of knowledge while at the same time showing that it was also interwoven with other complex factors for the founding of the geographical structure of innovative activities. It therefore became necessary to turn towards an analysis of the mechanisms underlying the diffusion of knowledge in space (absorption capacity, face-to-face exchanges and professional mobility).

Bringing these mechanisms to the fore in turn justifies the research angles that are directed towards understanding individual cooperative behaviour patterns in terms of innovation.

This more recent research using microeconomic cooperation or mobility data in order to trace relational graphs between the actors of science and technology and evaluate the spatial implications is still very rare. Their development in years to come should enable us to give more detailed answers to three essential issues in terms of public policies. First, they will enable us to appreciate the extent to which geographical space is able to explain R&D collaborative networks and, conversely the extent to which the spatial structure of these networks is a determining factor for their performance. Second, the actors' capacity to take part in these networks depends upon their attractiveness as partners. Building this capacity to integrate global research and technology networks therefore becomes an important issue. Consequently, exploring the implications of such demands upon localization choices and the effects of the resulting agglomeration becomes necessary for understanding the future geography of innovation. Third, and finally, another essential issue for defining local public policies is the analysis of the best practices that will allow local benefit from knowledge created by these spatially scattered teams.

NOTES

1. Cf. Puga (1999), Amiti (1998), OST (1998), Paci and Usai (1999) and Vertova (2002).
2. It should be noted that the idea of innovation considered in the studies presented here covers product innovations or potentially patentable procedures that are the result of public or private R&D activity. We are therefore essentially discussing technological innovation.
3. Source: Eurostat.
4. Cf. www.oecd.org/sti/scoreboard.
5. Cf. www.oecd.org/sti/scoreboard.
6. Cf. Baldwin and Martin (2004) for a review.
7. These externalities are known as MAR, referring to the different authors who contributed to the elaboration of this concept. These externalities, which are associated with the geographical concentration of a particular industry, are also referred to by Porter (1990). His analysis, however, differs as to the structure of a market that would be favourable to the development of such spillover effects. He believes that competition produces a positive impact upon innovation and growth. Following on from the Schumpeterian view, the MAR theory, however, is based upon the idea that local monopolies are preferable to competition, in that they allow the innovator to internalize the externalities. The results obtained by Glaeser et al. (1992) tend to confirm the positive role played by competition, i.e. Porter type of externalities.
8. The results concerning other factors for the concentration of production are not analysed here as they are of no direct interest for our study. Moreover, the ensuing debate is much vaster and the subject of a considerable amount of literature.
9. The patenting system allows for indications concerning the prerequisite knowledge

that accompanies any innovation. These indications fall into two categories: references made to scientific literature and references made to other patents. These citations, whether of articles or patents, are used to clearly establish the specific contribution of the new patent. We may therefore consider that the citations included in a new patent represent a stock of previous knowledge. The firms or universities use this stock in order to innovate. The 'public' nature of this knowledge suggests that these patent citations are a way of pinpointing technological spillovers, particularly in their geographical dimension. The works that use such data rely only on one of these two types of citation: patent citations.

10. Jaffe et al. (1993) call this the 'frequency control'. The sample of 'control patents' is organized as follows: each patent (b_i), which refers to another patent (b_c), is associated with another patent (b_j), which was registered in the same technological field as *bi* but which does not refer to the same original patent b_c. Each pair of patents (b_i, b_j) then enables us to compare the location of the control patent (b_j) with that of the original patent that was cited (b_c). If their location is the same, then the spillovers are not significantly localized.
11. Based upon a sample of almost 2000 inventors, Jaffe et al. (2000) attempted to establish whether or not citations correspond to spillovers. For this purpose, they questioned inventors about the possible contacts they may have had with the inventors who registered the original patents that they cited. It became apparent that approximately half of the citations bear no relation to knowledge flows. The economic and technological value of the patent seems to be more of a determining factor than the existence of any real connection between the inventors.
12. The revealed technological advantage (RTA) is a measurement of specialization. By noting *Pid*, the activity of a region *i* in a field *d*, it is defined as the ratio between two proportions. The first (the numerator) is internal to the region: *Pid* / Σ*d Pid* designates that part of the field *d* for all of the activities in region *i*. The second (denominator) is relative to the reference zone, generally the country: Σ*i Pid* / Σ*id Pid* designates the part of field *d* for all national activities. If the ratio of these two proportions is above 1, this signifies that the part of the field *d* in region *i* is superior to the part that this field represents on a national level. Specialization will therefore occur.
13. Organisational changes due to computerization.
14. The geodesic distance between two agents within a network is measured by the number of links making up the shortest path between these two agents within the network (it is therefore a relational distance measurement).
15. A 'small-world' network has to satisfy two properties. The first is the small diameter of the network, as well as the low average distance between the agents inside the network, given that the diameter of a network is the maximum geodesic distance between two agents of the same network. The second property is a high clustering coefficient relative to the networks generated by a random process for the creation of links; the clustering coefficient measures the frequency with which two agents who both have a connection with a third agent are themselves connected.
16. A dynamic that is based upon the idea that 'the friends of my friends are my friends' and that, within a network, leads to the fact that there is a stronger probability of establishing a connection with a partner of one's own partners.
17. This is a cumulative process that is based upon the greater attractiveness of actors who already have the most partners.

REFERENCES

Almeida, P. and B. Kogut (1997a), 'The exploration of technological diversity and the geographic localization of innovation', *Small Business Economics*, **9**, 21–31.

Almeida, P. and B. Kogut (1997b), 'Localization of knowledge and the mobility of engineers in regional networks', *Management Science*, **45**, 905–17.
Amiti, M. (1998), 'New trade theory and industrial location in the EU: a survey of evidence', *Oxford Review of Economic Policy*, **14** (2), 45–53.
Anselin, L., R. Florax and S. Rey (eds) (2004), *Advances in Spatial Econometrics*, Heidelberg: Springer Verlag.
Anselin, L., A. Varga and Z. Acs (1997), 'Local geographic spillovers between university research and high technology innovations', *Journal of Urban Economics*, **42**, 422–48.
Arrow, K.J. (1962), 'Economic welfare and the allocation of resources of invention', in R.R. Nelson (ed.), *The Rate and Direction of Inventive Activity: Economic and Social Factors*, Princeton, NJ: Princeton University Press, pp. 609–26.
Audretsch, D.B. and M.P. Feldman (1996), 'R&D spillovers and the geography of innovation and production', *The American Economic Review*, **86** (3), 630–40.
Audretsch, D.B. and M.P. Feldman (1999), 'Innovation in cities: science-based diversity, specialization, localized competition', *European Economic Review*, **43**, 409–29.
Autant-Bernard, C. (2000), *Géographie de l'Innovation et Externalités Locales de Connaissance: Une Étude sur Données Françaises*, PhD thesis, Université Jean Monnet Saint-Etienne.
Autant-Bernard, C. (2001), 'The geography of knowledge spillovers and technological proximity', *Economics of Innovation and New Technology*, **10** (4), 237–54.
Autant-Bernard, C. and J. LeSage (2011), 'Quantifying knowledge spillovers using spatial econometric tools', *Journal of Regional Science*, **51** (3), 471–96.
Autant-Bernard, C. and N. Massard (2000), 'Scientific interactions, geographic spillovers and innovation. an empirical study on the French case', paper presented at the 40th European Regional Science Association Congress, Barcelona, 29 August–1 September.
Autant-Bernard, C., N. Massard and S. Charlot (2008), 'Les déterminants géographiques de l'innovation: diffusion spatiale des connaissances et choix de localisation', in T. Madiès and J.-C. Prager (2008), *Innovation et Compétitivité des Régions*, Rapport Conseil d'Analyse Economique, La documentation française, pp. 227–66.
Autant-Bernard, C., P. Billand, D. Frachisse and N. Massard (2007), 'Social distance versus spatial distance in R&D cooperation: empirical evidence from European collaborations choices in micro and nanotechnologies', *Papers in Regional Science*, **86** (3), 495–519.
Balconi, M., S. Breschi and F. Lissoni (2004), 'Networks of inventors and the role of academia: an exploration of Italian patent data', *Research Policy*, **33** (1), 127–45.
Baldwin, R.E. and P. Martin (2004), 'Agglomeration and regional growth', in J.V. Henderson and J.F. Thisse (ed.), *Handbook of Regional and Urban Economics*, vol. 4, Amsterdam: Elsevier, pp. 2671–711.
Billand, P., D. Frachisse and N. Massard (2008), 'Affiliation network: representations and analysis', 13th Coalition Theory Network Workshop, Venice, 24–25 January.
Bottazzi, L. and G. Peri (2003), 'Innovation and spillovers in regions: evidence from European patent data', *European Economic Review*, **47** (4), 687–710.
Breschi, S. and F. Lissoni (2003), 'Mobility and social networks: localised

knowledge spillovers revisited', CESPRI Working Papers, no. 142, Università Bocconi, Milan.
Breschi, S. and F. Lissoni (2006a), 'Mobility of inventors and the geography of knowledge spillovers. New evidence on US data', paper presented at the ADRES Conference, Saint-Etienne, 14–15 September.
Breschi, S. and F. Lissoni (2006b), 'Cross-firms inventors and social networks: localised knowledge spillovers revisited', *Annales d'Economie et de Statistiques*, **79–80** (special issue from the Zvi Griliches Conference, edited by Jacques Mairesse and Manuel Trajtenberg).
Caniëls, M. (2000), *Knowledge Spillovers and Economic Growth*, Cheltenham, UK and Northampton, MA, USA: Edward Elgar.
Carayol, N. and P. Roux (2008), 'The strategic formation of inter-individual collaboration networks. Evidence from co-invention patterns', *Annales d'Economie et de Statistiques*, **87–8**, 275–301.
Carayol, N. and P. Roux (2009), 'Knowledge flows and the geography of networks. A strategic model of small worlds formation', *Journal of Economic Behavior and Organization*, **71** (2), 414–27.
Carayol, N., P. Roux and M. Yildizoglut (2008), 'Inefficiencies in a model of spatial networks with positive externalities', *Journal of Economic Behavior and Organization*, **67** (2), 495–511.
Charlot, S. and G. Duranton (2004), 'Communication externalities in cities', *Journal of Urban Economics*, **56**, 581–613.
Cohen, W. and D.A. Levinthal (1989), 'Innovation and learning: the two faces of R&D', *The Economic Journal*, **99**, 569–96.
Cowan, R., N. Jonard and J.-B. Zimmermann (2006), 'Evolving networks of inventors', *Journal of Evolutionary Economics*, **16** (1–2), 155–74.
Duranton, G. and D. Puga (2000), 'Diversity and specialisation in cities: why, where and when does it matter?', *Urban Studies*, **37** (3), 533–55.
Duranton, G. and D. Puga (2001), 'Nursery cities: urban diversity, process innovation and the life-cycle of products', *American Economic Review*, **91** (5), 1454–77.
Duranton, G. and D. Puga (2005), 'From sectoral to functional urban specialisation', *Journal of Urban Economics*, **57**, 343–70.
Feldman, M. (1994), *The Geography of Innovation*, Dordrecht: Kluwer Academic Publishers.
Feldman, M. and N. Massard (eds) (2002), *Institutions and Systems in the Geography of Innovation*, Dordrecht: Kluwer Academic Publishers.
Glaeser, E., H.D. Kallal, J.A. Scheinkman and A. Shleifer (1992), 'Growth in cities', *Journal of Political Economy*, **100** (6), 1126–52.
Gomes-Casseres, B., J. Hagedoorn and A. Jaffe (2006), 'Do alliances promote knowledge flows?', *Journal of Financial Economics*, **80** (1), 5–33.
Greunz, L. (2004), 'Industrial structure and innovation – evidence from European regions', *Journal of Evolutionary Economics*, **14** (5), 563–92.
Griliches, Z. (1979), 'Issues in assessing the contribution of research and development to productivity growth', *The Bell Journal of Economics*, **10** (1), 92–116.
Hagedoorn, J., D. Cloodt and H. van Kranenburg (2006), 'The strength of R&D Network ties in high-tech industries: a multi-dimensional analysis of tie strength on technological performance', Proceedings of the Danish Research Unit for Industrial Dynamics (DRUID) Summer Conference, Copenhagen Business School, Copenhagen, Denmark, 18–20 June, 11th Annual Meeting.

Hanaki, N., R. Nakajima and Y. Ogura (2007), 'The dynamic of R&D collaboration in the IT industry', available at: http://ssrn.com/abstract=1000103.
Jackson, M. and A. Wolinsky (1996), 'A strategic model of economic and social networks', *Journal of Economic Theory*, **71**, 44–74.
Jackson, O.J. and B.W. Rogers (2005), 'The economics of small worlds', *Journal of the European Economic Association*, **3** (2–3), 617–27.
Jacobs, J. (1969), *The Economies of Cities*, New York: Random House.
Jaffe, A.B. (1989), 'Real effects of academic research', *The American Economic Review*, **79** (5), 957–70.
Jaffe, A.B., M. Trajtenberg and M.S. Fogarty (2000), 'The meaning of patent citations', report on the NBER/Case-Western Reserve Survey of Patentees, NBER Working Paper no. W7631, National Bureau of Economic Research, Cambridge, MA.
Jaffe, A.B., M. Trajtenberg and R. Henderson (1993), 'Geographic localization of knowledge spillovers as evidenced by patent citations', *The Quarterly Journal of Economics*, **108** (3), 577–98.
Johansson, B. and J. Quigley (2004), 'Agglomeration and networks in spatial economies', *Papers of Regional Science*, **83**, 165–76.
Johnson, C. and R.P. Gilles (2000), 'Spatial social networks', *Review of Economic Design*, **5**, 273–99.
Krugman, P. (1991), *Geography and Trade*, Cambridge, MA: The MIT Press.
LeSage, J.P. (2008), 'An introduction to spatial econometrics', *Revue d'Economie Industrielle*, **123** (3), 19–44.
LeSage, J.P., M. Fischer and T. Scherngell (2007), 'Knowledge spillovers across Europe: evidence from a Poisson spatial interaction model with spatial effects', *Papers in Regional Science*, **86** (3), 393–422.
Lucas, R. (1988), 'On the mechanics of economic development', *Journal of Monetary Economics*, **22**, 3–42.
Maggioni, M., M. Nosvelli and E. Uberti (2007), 'Space vs. networks in the geography of innovation: a European analysis', *Papers in Regional Science*, **86** (3), 471–93.
Malerba, F., N. Vonortas, S. Breschi and L. Cassi (2006), *Evaluation of Progress Toward a European Research Area for Information Society Technologies*, Report for the European Commission, available at http://ec.europa.eu/dgs/information_ society/evaluation/data/pdf/studies/s2004_02/2006_cespri_final.pdf (2010-02-26).
Marshall, A. (1920 [1890]), The *Principles of Economics*, London: Macmillan.
Massard, N. and C. Mehier (2009), 'Proximity and innovation through an accessibility to knowledge lens', *Regional Studies*, **43** (1), 77–88.
Massard, N. and S. Riou (2002), 'L'impact des structures locales sur l'innovation en France: spécialisation ou diversité?', *Reveu Région et Développement*, **16**, 111–36.
Massard, N. and A. Torre (2005), 'Innovation et proximité', in B. Pecqueur and J.-B. Zimmermann (eds), *Economies de Proximité*, Paris: Hermès, pp. 155–80.
Maurseth, B. and B. Verspagen (1999), 'Knowledge spillovers in Europe and its consequences for systems of innovation', ECIS Working Paper 98–00, Eindhoven University of Technology.
Newman, M.E.J. (2004), 'Coauthorship networks and patterns of scientific collaboration', *Proceedings of the National Academy of Science of the United States of America*, **101**, 5200–205.

Nooteboom, B. (2004), *Interfirm Collaboration, Learning and Networks. An Integrated Approach*, London: Routledge.

OST (1998), *The Dynamics of S&T Activities in the EU Regions. Characterization, Cohesion and Convergence. A Quantitative Analysis*, research co-financed by OST and European Commission, in the context of the project Strategic Analysis for European S&T Policy Intelligence, TSER project 1093.

Paci, R. and S. Usai (1999), 'Externalities, knowledge spillovers and the spatial distribution of innovation', *GeoJournal*, **49** (4), 381–90.

Porter, M.E. (1990), *The Competitive Advantage of Nations*, London: Macmillan.

Powell, W.W., K.W. Koput and L. Smith-Doerr (1996), 'Inter-organizational collaboration and the locus of innovation: network of learning in biotechnology', *Administrative Science Quarterly*, **41**, 116–45.

Puga, D. (1999), 'Rise and fall of regional inequalities', *European Economic Review*, **43** (2), 303–44.

Roijakkers, N. and J. Hagedoorn (2006), 'Inter-firm R&D partnering in pharmaceutical biotechnology since 1975: trends, patterns, and networks', *Research Policy*, **33**, 1153–65.

Romer, P. (1986), 'Increasing returns and long run growth', *Journal of Political Economy*, **94**, 1002–37.

Saxenian, A.L. (1994), *Regional Advantage: Culture and Competition in Silicon Valley and Route 128*, Cambridge, MA: Harvard University Press.

Singh, J. (2005), 'Collaboration networks as determinants of knowledge diffusion patterns', *Management Science*, **51** (5), 756–70.

Sorenson, O., J.W. Rivkin and L. Fleming (2006), 'Complexity, networks and knowledge flow', *Research Policy*, **35**, 994–1017.

Varga, A. (1998), *University Research and Regional Innovation: A Spatial Econometric Analysis of Academic Technology Transfers*, Boston, MA: Kluwer Academic Publishers.

Verspagen, B. and W. Schoenmakers (2000), 'The spatial dimension of knowledge spillovers in Europe: evidence from firm patenting data', paper presented at the AEA Conference on Intellectual Property Econometrics, Alicante, 19–20 April.

Vertova, G. (2002), 'A historical investigation of the geography of innovative activities', *Structural Change and Economic Dynamics*, **13** (3), 259–83.

Wagner, C.S. (2004), *International Collaboration in Science: A New Dynamic for Knowledge Creation*, doctoral thesis, University of Amsterdam.

Wagner, C.S. and L. Leydesdorff (2005), 'Network structure, self-organisation, and the growth of international collaboration in science', *Research Policy*, **34**, 1608–18.

Zucker, L.G. and M.R. Darby (2007), 'Virtuous circles in science and commerce', *Papers in Regional Science*, **86** (3), 445–70.

Zucker, L.G., M.R. Darby and J. Armstrong (1994), 'Intellectual capital and the firm: the technology of geographically localized knowledge spillovers', NBER Working Paper Series, no. 4946, Cambridge, MA: National Bureau of Economic Research.

4. The development potential of urban migrant entrepreneurship – new opportunity seekers in the Netherlands

Mediha Sahin, Alina Todiras and Peter Nijkamp

4.1 INTRODUCTION

Entrepreneurship has been the subject of numerous debates and investigations over the last decades. It has attracted increased attention in the domain of scientific research on business administration. Likewise, the importance of entrepreneurship as a strategic tool for economic growth has been clearly recognized by politicians and policy makers. However, it was not until the mid-1970s that entrepreneurship was given due attention; up until then the dominant form of organization was mainly the large enterprise characterized by mass production and economies of scope. A dramatic shift toward smaller enterprises has occurred as a result of the joint effect of globalization and the ICT revolution, which subsequently reduced the cost of moving capital and information to low-cost locations outside Europe and North America. Carlsson (1992) explains this shift by relating it to the increase in global competition, the growth in market fragmentation and technological progress. Other factors that prompted the occurrence of flexible specialization have been the reduction of trade barriers and ample diseconomies of scale due to technological advances, increase in labour supply, change in consumer tastes, public policies promoting the small business sector, and horizontal and vertical disintegration (Carlsson, 1992; Loveman and Sengenberger, 1991; Brock and Evans, 1989). Acs (1992) has attributed an important role to the small firms in the economy; they are regarded as agents of change that, through their entrepreneurial action, generate innovative activity, stimulate industry evolution and lead to new job creation. The increase in the number of firms intensifies the competition for new ideas, while greater competition across firms facilitates the entry of new firms specializing in a particular new product niche. This also explains why the necessary complementary inputs are probably more available from small specialist niche firms than from large, vertically-integrated producers. Consequently, small firms play an important role in the emergence of new industries, such as software, biotechnology etc. as they have a relatively innovative advantage over the larger enterprises because of their inherent element of 'flexibility'.

Entrepreneurship has evolved into an imperative element in the organization of economies. It has been further fostered by deregulation and privatization processes in many Western countries Furthermore, governments have acknowledged and started promoting the role of entrepreneurship in stimulating economic growth and development. However, entrepreneurship has not emerged concurrently; North America was much ahead of Europe in 'embracing the entrepreneurial energy' and absorbing its merits (Thurik, 2009). Currently, the European Union perceives entrepreneurship as a central driver in the economy. Multiple EU programmes for building and fostering a climate in which entrepreneurial initiatives and business activities can thrive are being put in place.

Carree and Thurik (2010) present quite a comprehensive definition of entrepreneurship: 'the manifest ability and willingness of individuals, on their own, in teams, within and outside existing organizations to perceive and create new economic opportunities . . . and to introduce their ideas to the market in the face of uncertainty and other obstacles by making decisions on location, form and the use of resources and institutions'. Audretsch and Thurik (2004) argue that 'entrepreneurship has emerged as the engine of economic and social development throughout the world'. Porter (1990) realized early on that entrepreneurship is at the heart of national advantage, being a catalyst for new firm formation, innovations and market rivalry. Furthermore, some authors consider the market rivalry more conducive to knowledge externalities than local monopolies (Jacobs, 1969; Porter, 1990). Acs et al. (2005) also emphasize that there is a strong relationship between knowledge spillover and entrepreneurial activity. Therefore one way in which entrepreneurship capital generates economic growth is by knowledge spillover, when firms can appropriate some of the returns by taking advantage of the investments made externally (Cohen and Levinthal, 1989). Another way is by increasing the number of firms, which in turn augments the competition for new ideas and facilitates the entry of new firms specializing in a particular new product niche (Thurik, 2009). Entrepreneurship can also generate economic growth through promoting diversity among firms. Another important contribution could be the element of 'newness', through transformation of inventions and ideas into economically viable entities (Carree and Thurik, 2010).

Entrepreneurial action is often restrained owing to institutional and cultural forces: However, successful entrepreneurs are those who can understand, and benefit from, the local institutional regimes. In many cases this has led to the formation of distinctive business systems (Bruton et al., 2008). Furthermore, cross-cultural influences have increased the demand for variety and thus have reshaped the outlook of new firms. The latter have become the most obvious suppliers of new and specialized products (Carree and Thurik, 2010). Thurik (2009) assigns to entrepreneurs three major roles: the role of innovator; the role of perceiving profit opportunities; and the role of assuming the risk associated with uncertainty. The entrepreneurs who succeed in fulfilling these roles often develop into managerial business owners or start new ventures. Gompers et al. (2008) provide evidence that entrepreneurs with a track record of success have much higher chances of success in contrast with the first-time entrepreneurs or those who have failed. This is due to accuracy in selecting the right industry and the right time to start a venture.

A tendency over recent decades has also been the choice of migrants to become self-employed, which has led to the emergence of the term 'migrant entrepreneurship'. Kloosterman and Rath (2003) suggest that self-employed migrants play an important role in the emergence of small firms. In most of the cases they are pushed to engage in entrepreneurial activities due to restricted access to jobs and blocked opportunities for upward social mobility. Numerous studies attest that most of the entrepreneurial activity of migrants takes place in the traditional labour-intensive industries, e.g. retail, catering and hospitality, which have lower access barriers and require fewer skills (Barrett et al., 2003; Sahin et al., 2012; Baycan-Levent et al., 2009; Hermes and Leicht, 2010). Hermes and Leicht (2010) argue that a more advanced country's economic development can reflect a higher probability rate of migrant entrepreneurial activity in simple routine services. However, the self-employment rates vary more between countries than between migrants and natives (Tubergen, 2005). In the next section, we briefly describe some of the background of migrant entrepreneurship in the Netherlands.

4.2 MIGRANT ENTREPRENEURSHIP: A NEW PROMISE

In recent years, self-employment among migrant minorities has increased significantly in many countries, including the Netherlands, and migrant entrepreneurs have become the subject of growing interest. Encouraging migrants to become self-employed has been an important feature of national and local policy making in the past few years. The recent literature has documented that migrant businesses are one of the fastest-growing sectors in the Dutch economy. The entrepreneurship rate of migrants is growing far more rapidly than among natives in the Netherlands. Despite the fast growth of migrant entrepreneurship in the country, empirical information that documents socioeconomic differences in the business performance of migrant entrepreneurs is lagging far behind the rapid growth of these entrepreneurs. Previous empirical research has mainly focused on knowledge about native entrepreneurs as a strategic input for Dutch policy, education and research. Migrant entrepreneurs make a variety of contributions to the economic environment of their host and home countries. Migrant entrepreneurship (ME) provides the opportunity for, and access to, economic growth, equal opportunity and upward mobility for many of those who have traditionally been excluded from business, in particular migrant minorities. Migrants of various ethnicities who form a strong entrepreneurial group can be of great economic significance for the migrant business community, as well as for the total community, through job and opportunity creation (Rettab, 2001).

ME is also an important phenomenon for the socioeconomic development of Dutch cities. It partly solves the problem for migrant people in their quest for a job, and it may improve their economic position. There are relatively more migrant entrepreneurs compared with native entrepreneurs in the Netherlands, because many migrants prefer the independence of entrepreneurship above a poorly paid job at the bottom of the labour market. By starting up a new enterprise they hope to increase their income and climb up the social ladder. At the micro-level, migrant entrepreneurs help to satisfy a variety of migrant needs and wants for both migrant and non-migrant consumers (Super, 2005). Furthermore, at the macro-level migrant entrepreneurs, together with their enterprises, contribute to the further integration of these migrant people, and strengthen the local economy.

In our study, ME refers to business activities undertaken by migrants with a specific sociocultural and ethnic background or migrant origin. This phenomenon is distinguished from 'normal' entrepreneurship through its orientation to migrant products, to migrant market customers or to indigenous migrant business strategies (Choenni, 1997). ME is also generally regarded as an important self-organizing principle, through which migrant minorities are able to improve their weak socioeconomic position (Baycan-Levent et al., 2003). There are several reasons why migrants opt for entrepreneurship. Jenkins (1984) presents three explanatory models for migrant entrepreneurship. These are: (i) the economic opportunity model; (ii) the culture model; and (iii) the reaction model. The first of these refers to the reliance of migrant businesses on the opportunities in the local markets. The second model assumes that some cultures are more predisposed to behave entrepreneurially than others. And the third model assumes that some ethnic minorities will pursue self-employment as a reaction to hostile host societies, and blocked opportunities and social mobility due to discrimination and racism. According to Waldinger et al. (1990), migrant minority businesses are a product of the interplay of opportunity structures, groups' characteristics and strategies for adapting to the environment.

It is noteworthy that the rate of participation in entrepreneurship differs greatly among the various migrant populations (Kloosterman et al., 1998), and the degree of success in establishing their own enterprise is clearly different among various minority groups. When comparing the migrant origin of active migrant entrepreneurs from Turkish, Moroccan and Surinamese ethnic origin in the Netherlands, we can see that the biggest group is formed by Turkish entrepreneurs (Sahin et al., 2007). It is noteworthy that the tendency or ability to become self-employed differs greatly between natives and migrants; migration involves taking risks and migrants hence may be more ready to become self-employed. According to Verheul et al. (2001), migrants are considered to have an appropriate attitude or mind-set to start a business.

The focus of this chapter is on the business performance of urban migrant entrepreneurs in the Netherlands of Turkish, Moroccan and Surinamese ethnic origin, with the aim to explore and review significant differences in the business performance of these entrepreneurial migrant groups in the Netherlands. These differences will be explained in terms of their personal and business characteristics, as well as their participation in social networks, on the basis of a sample of the population in the city of Amsterdam. By applying a blend of theoretical and applied research, our study addresses the question: are there significant differences in business performance between distinct groups of migrant entrepreneurs in the services sector (notably, tax and consultancy offices) in the city of Amsterdam, and – if so – can these differences be explained by their personal and business characteristics and by their degree of participation in (in)formal network support systems?

This chapter is structured as follows; first, in section 4.2 we provide a brief overview of the migration flows from and to the Netherlands with an emphasis on the postwar immigration and its impact on Dutch society. Second, we discuss the living and working conditions of migrant groups and compare these groups in terms of their entrepreneurial behaviour. Our comparisons and evaluations are, of course, limited due to the available data. Section 4.3 provides a brief overview of the literature on migrant entrepreneurship and evaluates the development of migrant entrepreneurship in the Netherlands. We discuss some key aspects of migrant entrepreneurs in the Netherlands, including explanations of the different patterns of self-employment among migrant groups – particularly Turkish, Moroccan and Surinamese entrepreneurs – regarding their personal (e.g. age, marital status, education, traits) and business (e.g. experience, the role of the family in the business) characteristics, as well as their participation in social networks (in particular, the role of business support agencies and others in the development of their businesses). We examine the basic concepts of migrant entrepreneurship on the basis of its main characteristics and psychological, sociological, economic and demographic determinants. Section 4.4 then examines the background and the development of migrant entrepreneurship in the Netherlands and compares the three main migrant groups, i.e. Turks, Moroccans and Surinamese, in terms of their entrepreneurial behaviour. Finally, Section 4.5 concludes with a discussion on differences in the entrepreneurial behaviour and business performance of these various ethnic groups, and with recommendations for further research in this field.

4.3 MIGRATION FLOWS IN THE NETHERLANDS

In the early 1960s, the Netherlands switched from being an emigration to an immigration country. The increase in prosperity in the Netherlands reduced emigration and induced new immigration flows at the same time. Postwar immigrants can be divided into three main groups: immigrants from former colonies; those who were recruited for unskilled jobs (known as 'guest workers'); and – more recently – refugees. The socioeconomic position of migrant minorities is, in general, not comparable with that of the natives, although a clear improvement in their position is observable. Policy makers have reacted to a structural migration surplus with a restrictive immigration policy, while simultaneously aiming to improve the position of immigrants who have already arrived (Zorlu and Hartog, 2001). Zorlu and Hartog (2001) have made a very interesting study on migration flows in the Netherlands. They investigated the emigration and immigration flows in different periods. The following is based on their study of the topic of migration experiences.

The first period of an immigration surplus was from 1585 to 1670, a period known as the Golden Age in Dutch history. In fact, the percentage of immigrants was higher in the seventeenth and eighteenth centuries than it was in the 1990s (Lucassen and Penninx, 1997). In the period of the Golden Age, there was relatively great prosperity and tolerance in the Netherlands compared with the surrounding countries, which attracted many immigrants. A large number of immigrant workers, as well as religious and political refugees, moved to the Netherlands either for a short stay or to settle permanently. Lucassen and Penninx (1997) argue that the change in the share of foreigners is closely correlated with the relative prosperity of the Netherlands. The percentage of immigrants sharply decreased in the nineteenth century, while the economy stagnated. In the seventeenth and eighteenth centuries, a relatively small number of migrants left the Netherlands. In these two centuries, no more than 10 000 people emigrated to North America, while from the mid-nineteenth century to the mid-twentieth century the number of Dutch people leaving the Netherlands was higher than the number of immigrants. An overwhelmingly large part of Dutch emigrants headed for North America. After 1870 the number of emigrants increased: from 50 000 between 1890 and 1900 to 175 000 in 1930 (Lucassen and Penninx, 1997). Until 1960, the Netherlands was considered to be an emigration country, although, from time to time, immigration was larger than emigration in connection with various historical events such as wars and economic crises. During the First World War, thousands of Belgian refugees crossed the border trying to escape from the war. From 1920 to 1940, a large portion of the immigrants were Jews and other opponents of the Nazi regime from Eastern Europe, Germany and Austria. After the German invasion in 1940, many Dutch people fled to the UK.

After the Second World War, the Netherlands experienced an emigration surplus in the recovery period of the economy until the early 1960s. Since 1961, however, the annual immigration flows have exceeded emigration flows systematically, except in one year, namely 1967. From this year on, the Netherlands can be considered more of an immigration country than an emigration country. The immigration flow fluctuated highly between 37 000 and 127 000 people per annum, while the emigration flow was more stable, around 60 000 people per year since 1953. The first large immigration flow was from Indonesia, which had been a Dutch colony until December 1949. Large numbers of Eurasian repatriates who had been interned in the Japanese camps in the Dutch East Indies/Indonesia during the war returned home. The two major immigration waves occurred directly after the decolonization of Indonesia in 1949, between 1949 and 1951, and between 1952 and 1957. Another immigration stream occurred in the early 1960s after the conflict between the Netherlands and Indonesia about New Guinea. Two large immigration flows occurred after the decolonization of Surinam in 1975, and between 1979 and 1980 prior to the expiry of the transitional agreement on the mutual settlement and residence of citizens (Lucassen and Penninx,

1997). However, immigration from Surinam and the Dutch Antilles did not lead to a smooth economic integration, and these groups are still targets for economic policies. The period of overall net immigration started at the beginning of the 1960s. The flow of large numbers of 'guest workers' after that time (the 1960s) created an immigration surplus in the Netherlands. During the long postwar boom, the demand for workers for unskilled jobs increased, while the supply of unskilled Dutch workers was decreasing. The shortage of unskilled labourers was compensated by an inflow of Mediterranean workers (Hartog and Vriend, 1990). Workers were actively recruited or came spontaneously from countries like Italy, Spain, Portugal, Turkey, Greece, Morocco, Yugoslavia and Tunisia. The recruitment policy stopped during the first oil crisis, but the immigration from the recruitment countries continued as chain migration, at first in the form of family reunification throughout the 1970s, and later on in the form of family formation in the 1980s and 1990s. Between 1982 and 1983 the immigration flow stagnated and even dropped almost to the level of emigration, no doubt as a reaction to the deep recession of the Dutch economy after the second oil crisis in 1979. The increase of immigration in the second half of the 1980s was dominated by family formation/reunion of 'guest workers'. Additionally, the flow of political refugees and asylum seekers, from politically unstable areas in the world, also increased. While the chain migration from Turkey and Morocco has continued during the last two decades, the number of Southern European immigrants did not grow much after the end of formal recruitment, and even experienced a decrease. From 1958 until the early 1960s, both immigration from, and emigration to, the EU countries increased substantially. Ultimately, Surinamese, Antilleans, Turks and Moroccans became the largest migrant minority groups, and this group as a whole is gradually growing due to a combination of continuous immigration and a relatively high birth rate. Immigration streams are now increasingly dominated by political refugees and asylum seekers.

The motives for emigration were fear of unemployment, the Cold War, perceived lack of opportunities for agriculture and generally low economic expectations. In the last two centuries, the main destinations of Dutch emigration have been the specific immigration countries: Australia, Canada, New Zealand, South Africa and the USA. In the early 1950s, there was a sharp increase, accompanied by a deliberate emigration policy: subsidies for transport, counselling, guidance and bilateral international agreements about the admission of Dutch emigrants. Emigration decreased considerably after 1952 and then became relatively stable, contrary to the overall immigration pattern. Between

1946 and 1972, almost 500000 Dutch citizens emigrated mainly to Canada, the USA, Australia and New Zealand. Migration to other EU countries increased considerably between 1959 and 1967. From that time, emigration in both directions marginally decreased until 1987 and then increased again. Clearly, the migration pattern within a country is strongly influenced by its migration policy. The flow of the people is regulated with various strict rules. In the 1960s, the Netherlands recruited guest workers from other countries on a temporary basis, but when unemployment strongly increased after the early 1970s, the guest workers did not return to their homeland. Originally, the integration of the guest workers was not a policy goal, because they were only supposed to be temporary workers. The main aim was to ensure that immigrants would have sufficient opportunities to participate in Dutch society without giving up their own lifestyle and values, since this would strengthen the ties with their home country. The Netherlands became a magnet for international migration flows with its internationally high standard of living. As a reaction, the Dutch government has tightened its immigration policy after the second half of the 1980s. Labour migration had already been banned in 1973. For non-EU residents, family formation and reunion are the two main grounds of admission, subject to strict conditions. Immigrants were allowed to settle (temporarily) in the Netherlands, if and only if they were: (i) a minor family member (younger than 15 years old) or the partner of a legal resident (native Dutch or legal non-Dutch) with a paid job which provided an income above the minimum wage; (ii) students, who were mostly allowed in on the basis of bilateral agreements; (iii) labour migrants, according to the Law on Foreign Workers, who were mostly top managers and top sportsmen; (iv) political refugees, although in recent years their selection procedure has become increasingly strict.

In summary, the first group of migrants, solely males, arrived in the Netherlands in 1960. In 1966, the Dutch economy experienced an economic recession that led some immigrants to return home. In 1968 the Dutch economy began to grow again; and then the second recruitment period started and continued until 1974. In that same year, the impact of the oil crisis on the economy was severely felt. As a result, in 1974 the Dutch government took measures to restrict spontaneous migration, and official recruitment stopped. But in the 1970s, increasingly more migrant workers brought their families. In the first half of the 1980s, the net migration balance declined as a result of a combination of factors: restrictive admission policy, poor job prospects and the slowing down of family reunification. In 1985, immigration began to increase again as a result of family formation: the children of the first-generation labour migrants brought marriage partners in from their countries (Kraal and Zorlu, 1998).

After this historical overview of the migration from and to the Netherlands with an emphasis on the postwar immigration and its impact on Dutch society, we now discuss the living and working conditions of different migrant groups in the Netherlands. The labour market positions of the main groups (migrants from former colonies, guest workers and refugees) in the Netherlands are characterized by strong differences, just like their migration history.

4.4 LIVING AND WORKING CONDITIONS OF MIGRANT GROUPS IN THE NETHERLANDS

The Netherlands has shown a remarkable openness *vis-à-vis* foreigners, a situation that can clearly be observed in the history of the country. At present, the share of migrants in Dutch society is approx. 20 per cent, while the share of non-Western migrants is about 10 per cent (CBS, 2003, 2004). From the non-Western migrant population, three groups have a dominant position (namely, approx. 60 per cent), i.e. Turks, Moroccans and Surinamese. Since 1970, the number of migrants in the Netherlands has increased rapidly. Most migrants coming into the Netherlands originate from non-Western countries (Jansen et al., 2003), from Turkey, Morocco, Surinam and the Antilles (see Table 4.1(a)).

Migrant minorities are typically characterized as an urban population category (see Table 4.1(b)). In 1992, 61 per cent of the minority population lived in cities with more than 100 000 residents (Kraal and Zorlu, 1998). Forty-four per cent of the minority population lives in the four largest cities (Amsterdam, Rotterdam, the Hague, Utrecht), while 13 per cent of native Dutch people live in these cities. The determinants of concentration and segregation in cities are partly linked to the kind of migration. Turkish and Moroccan migrants came for low and unskilled employment in industry, and settled in industrial centres in or near the cities. The Surinamese and the Antilleans came to study or sought work in the service sector. All this was available in the big cities – Rotterdam, the Hague, Amsterdam and Utrecht (Kraal and Zorlu, 1998).

The migrant populations from Turkey and Morocco in the Netherlands are very similar regarding their demographic composition. They are, on average, the least well educated and most likely to be married, and most migrants from these countries consider themselves to be Muslim. The migrants from Surinam and Antilles are better educated, more familiar with the Dutch culture and language, and more often single or single

Table 4.1 Migrant groups and their destinations in the Netherlands

(a) Important migrants groups and natives in the Netherlands, in absolute figures

	Year	Turks (× 1000)	Moroccans (× 1000)	Surinamese (× 1000)	Antilleans (× 1000)	Dutch (× 1000)
Total population	2000	308.9	262.2	302.5	107.2	13 088.6
	2001	319.6	272.2	308.8	117.1	13 116.9
	2002	330.7	284.1	315.2	124.9	13 140.3
	2003	341.4	295.3	320.7	129.3	13 153.8
	2004	351.7	306.2	325.3	130.7	13 169.9
	2005	358.8	315.8	329.4	130.5	13 182.9
	2006	364.6	323.3	332.0	120.4	13 184.1

(b) Share of main migrant groups in the four big cities in the Netherlands (%)

Main migrant groups	The Netherlands	Amsterdam	Rotterdam	The Hague	Utrecht
Moroccans	1.04	8.8	6.3	5.3	8.9
Turks	1.30	5.0	7.5	6.6	4.4
Surinamese	0.98	9.5	8.7	9.6	3.0
Antilleans	0.60	1.5	3.3	2.3	0.7
Others	2.40	9.5	9.3	8.3	4.0
Total of migrants	6.32	34.3	35.1	32.1	21.0
Total of natives	93.68	65.7	64.9	67.9	79.0
Total	100.0	100.0	100.0	100.0	100.0

Sources: CBS (2004, 2006).

parents. All migrant populations have in common that they are relatively young compared with the native Dutch population (Jansen et al., 2003). Migrants from Surinam and the Antilles also have similar demographic characteristics. Their age distribution is similar to the age distribution of migrants from Turkey and Morocco.

Regarding the labour-force participation rate of women and the share of married couples in the total number of households, migrants from these West Indian countries have much in common with the native Dutch population (Jansen et al., 2003). Migrant minorities face similar problems when it comes to labour market participation and educational performance. The labour market position of many migrant workers is weak because of their low educational level and lack of Dutch language skills. In terms of education, the migrant minorities have a number of serious problems. A high percentage of people (between 15 and 24 years) leave secondary school without any qualifications. There is a relatively low level of participation of Turks in higher education. As most Turks and Moroccans belong to the lowest socioeconomic category, ethnic origin is so closely intertwined with social class that it is not really possible to differentiate between the two. However, education is the prime factor for the socioeconomic position of minorities in the Netherlands, particularly for the second-generation minorities (Avci, 2006).

In Table 4.2, we can also see that the educational level is lowest for migrant groups from Turkey and Morocco. In contrast, migrants from Surinam and the Antilles have, on average, higher educational levels, but not yet quite as high as those of the native population. In addition, we can also see in more detail that the percentage of people with a university degree or professional qualification has decreased for each group. Nevertheless, although there has been a general decrease at this level, the percentage of people with a Bachelor and Master of Science University degree has now begun to increase for each group. This may be caused by the recent introduction of a new system of higher education. With respect to education level, the differences in gender are rather small for the Turkish population. The education rate at different levels is much lower for both sexes in that group compared with the other groups. Turkish male and female migrants have an almost similar rate for the pre-university or professional education level. For Moroccan female migrants, this rate is in general relatively much higher in comparison with Turkish female and Moroccan male migrants. When we look at the higher education level for this group of female Moroccans, we can see that the difference between gender and education level becomes much smaller. In terms of education level, the Surinamese and the Antillean migrants are comparable with the native Dutch population. The differences in gender regarding the education level are also similar among these groups.

Within the migrant minority groups, the Turks and Moroccans share some similarities, but they both show some differences compared with the Surinamese and Antilleans. The Surinamese and the Antilleans also share some similarities. The various distinctions between the first group and the second group have several causes. Three major distinctions can be made between the group of Surinamese and Antilleans and the group of Turks and Moroccans. First, the Surinamese and Antilleans were a postcolonial migrant group, whereas the Turks and Moroccans arrived in the Netherlands as 'guest workers'. The latter were mainly driven by economic motives. Surinamese migration was more sociopolitically motivated, as it was strongly linked to Surinamese independence in 1975 (Van Amersfoort, 1987). A second difference was the degree of transnationality of the migration patterns. Turkish and Moroccan migration was highly transnational: large groups of Turks and Moroccans settled in various Western European countries, and links soon emerged between

Table 4.2 Education level of main migrant groups[1] in the Netherlands in absolute numbers and percentages

Educational level		Turks			Moroccans		
		t	m	f	t	m	f
University of professional education	2000–2001	**330**[2]	180	150	**400**	180	220
	%	***75***	*77*	*73*	*83*	*80*	*86*
	2001–2002	**380**	180	200	**440**	200	240
	%	***86***	*78*	*74*	*79*	*77*	*80*
	2002–2003	**440**	200	240	**500**	220	280
	%	***73***	*73*	*74*	*77*	*72*	*79*
	2003–2004	**550**	250	300	**560**	250	310
	%	***69***	*68*	*69*	*75*	*71*	*78*
	2004–2005	**490**	230	260	**580**	240	340
	%	***63***	*63*	*63*	***68***	*66*	*70*
University (Old Master)	2000–2001	**110**	55	55	**80**	45	35
	%	***25***	*23*	*27*	***17***	*20*	*14*
	2001–2002	**120**	50	70	**120**	60	60
	%	***24***	*22*	*26*	***21***	*23*	*20*
	2002–2003	**130**	60	70	**110**	45	65
	%	***22***	*22*	*22*	***17***	*15*	*18*
	2003–2004	**160**	70	90	**100**	50	50
	%	***20***	*19*	*21*	***13***	*14*	*13*
	2004–2005	**110**	55	55	**130**	50	80
	%	**14**	15	13	15	14	16
University Bachelor[3]	2000–2001						
	%						
	2001–2002						
	%						
	2002–2003	**20**	10	10	**20**	10	10
	%	3	4	3	3	3	3
	2003–2004	**60**	30	30	**60**	30	30
	%	***8***	*8*	*7*	***8***	*9*	*8*
	2004–2005	**120**	50	70	**90**	40	50
	%	***15***	*14*	*17*	***11***	*11*	*10*
Master of Sciences	2000–2001						
	%						
	2001–2002						
	%						
	2002–2003	**10**	5	5	**10**	10	0
	%	***2***	*2*	*2*	***2***	*3*	*0*
	2003–2004	**30**	15	15	**30**	20	10
	%	***4***	*4*	*3*	***4***	*6*	*3*
	2004–2005	**60**	30	30	**50**	35	15
	%	***8***	*8*	*7*	***6***	*10*	*3*

Notes:

1. The share of migrants per education level and year in the total of the population category concerned, t = total; m = male; f = female.
2. Total absolute numbers shown in bold: percentages shown in italic.
3. No migrant figures for 2000–2001, 2001–2002 for university Bachelor and Master of Sciences.

Surinamese			Antilleans			Dutch		
t	m	f	t	m	f	t	m	f
600	230	370	**370**	180	190	**35770**	15950	19830
70	*68*	*74*	*71*	*72*	*70*	*70*	*68*	*72*
610	235	375	**420**	160	260	**36250**	16070	20190
73	*72*	*74*	*72*	*67*	*10*	*69*	*67*	*70*
660	245	425	**480**	190	290	**36320**	16010	20300
69	*66*	*70*	*70*	*72*	*68*	*67*	*64*	*69*
700	290	410	**520**	190	330	**36290**	16210	20070
65	*64*	*65*	*67*	*61*	*70*	*63*	*61*	*64*
820	290	530	**550**	220	330	**35160**	15820	19930
50	*60*	*60*	*60*	*63*	*59*	*56*	*55*	*57*
240	110	130	**150**	70	80	**15390**	7580	7810
29	*32*	*26*	*29*	*28*	*27*	*30*	*32*	*28*
230	90	130	**160**	80	80	**15960**	7760	8200
27	*28*	*26*	*28*	*33*	*24*	*31*	*33*	*29*
250	90	170	**170**	50	120	**15120**	7010	8110
26	*24*	*28*	*25*	*19*	*28*	*28*	*28*	*28*
230	80	150	**190**	80	110	**14920**	6650	8270
21	*18*	*24*	*24*	*26*	*23*	*16*	*25*	*26*
260	80	180	**170**	50	120	**14020**	6200	7820
19	17	20	19	14	21	22	22	22
						70	30	40
						10	10	10
						60	30	40
						10	10	10
40	30	10	**30**	20	10	**1560**	990	570
4	8	2	4	8	2	3	4	*2*
100	50	50	**50**	30	20	**4330**	2190	2140
9	*11*	*8*	*6*	*10*	*4*	*7*	*8*	*7*
200	80	120	**120**	40	80	**9320**	3990	5430
15	*17*	*14*	*13*	*11*	*14*	*15*	*14*	*15*
10	5	5	**10**	5	5	**1180**	890	290
1	*1*	*1*	*14*	*2*	*1*	*2*	*4*	*1*
50	30	20	**20**	10	10	**2260**	1430	830
5	*7*	*6*	*3*	*3*	*2*	*4*	*5*	*3*
80	30	50	**70**	40	30	**4510**	2560	1960
6	*6*	*9*	*8*	*11*	*5*	*7*	*9*	*6*

Source: CBS (2006).

these different Turkish and Moroccan communities (Ostergaard-Nielsen, 2000). In contrast, most Surinamese and Antillean migrants settled in the Netherlands. They maintained no transnational ties other than with their home countries. The third difference is the historical relationship between the Netherlands and the migrants' country of origin. Surinam had been a Dutch colony for centuries until 1975. The Antilles had also been a Dutch colony. Turkey and Morocco had no particular historical ties with the Netherlands. Before 1960 there was just a small group of Surinamese, and virtually no Turks and Moroccans in the Netherlands. This changed as large numbers of Surinamese and Antillean and Turkish and Moroccan migrants arrived in the country in the decades after 1960 (Vermeulen, 2005).

The labour market position of migrants also varies across migrant minority groups, and is related to their migration history. There is a significant difference among the various migrant groups. Zorlu (2002) has made an extensive study of the labour market position of migrant minority groups in the Netherlands. He investigated their participation, unemployment rates and earnings. Immigrants from the former colonies often speak the Dutch language before they arrive. They are also more familiar with Dutch society. However, we still observe significant differences within this category. The position of some groups, like the Indonesians, has strongly improved, while the Surinamese and the Antilleans have a less favourable position, even though some improvement is also noticeable. Immigrants who initially arrived as guest workers also strongly differ in terms of their social status in the Netherlands. The South Europeans – Italians, Spanish, Portuguese, Greeks, and Yugoslavs and their descendants – have improved their position significantly, while Turks and Moroccans still occupy an unfavourable position (Lucassen and Penninx, 1997; van Ours and Veenman, 1999). Related to these differences, policy attention and research concentrate mainly on the Moroccans, Turks, Surinamese and Antilleans. These migrant groups often find themselves in marginal economic positions. In the Netherlands, the low qualification level of migrant minorities causes them to have disadvantages in job level, participation level and earnings, in addition to unemployment. Migrants' low-level jobs can be explained by their personal characteristics such as sex, family background and experience. However, a majority of the labour force among the migrant groups have succeeded in becoming part of the economic life of the city in paid employment.

With a few exceptions, migrant groups belong in general to the lower socioeconomic segment of European cities, mainly as a result of their lack of education and skills. When they have the opportunity to work, this has occurred more often in the less attractive segments of the labour market

(Rath, 1998). Most of the migrant workers are in the service sector, in particular in health care and in other business service sectors. This largely applies to Surinamese and Antillean foreign workers. The other major migrant groups are more active in industry, trade and catering services, because of their personal characteristics (e.g. age, gender, lack of Dutch language), educational qualifications, discrimination and absence of relevant economic networks outside these branches (Rath, 1998). But the position of people working for the government or in education among the Surinamese and Antillean groups is the same as that of the indigenous workers (Berdowski, 1994). According to Zorlu (2002), migrant minorities from Turkey and Morocco have the worst labour market position. The Surinamese and the Antilleans have a relatively better labour market position than the Turks and the Moroccans. The Surinamese and the Antilleans have a common history with Dutch people, and people from this group often speak Dutch as their mother tongue. Additionally, women from this group have an exceptional labour market performance, even better than Dutch women. Surinamese and Antillean men have higher participation and employment rates but they suffer a high level of unemployment (Zorlu, 2002). Turks and Moroccans have comparable participation and employment rates. Surinamese women have the highest participation and employment rates. The employment and participation rates of Dutch women are similar. Moroccan and Turkish women have the lowest participation and employment rates and the highest unemployment rates.

In general, migrant minority groups suffer from relatively higher unemployment rates. The unemployment rate among ethnic minorities is three times higher than that of native Dutch people (see Figure 4.1). The participation rate is very low among two minority groups, namely Turks and Moroccans, who have the most unfavourable position in the labour market. The labour market position of these minorities remains vulnerable because a relatively large proportion of them is employed in industry and low-paid jobs. The unfavourable labour market position of minorities results in a low household income. However, not all ethnic minority groups have the same unfavourable labour market position. Surinamese and Antillean people are less frequently unemployed than Turks and Moroccans. Moreover, the distribution of employed Surinamese and Antilleans over different sectors shows more similarities to that of Dutch people. The household composition of migrant groups also tends to differ with respect to gender categories. Working women live less often with a partner and child, compared with working men. The latter are more often with a partner but childless, or are just single. Differences in household composition are more striking among migrant groups within gender

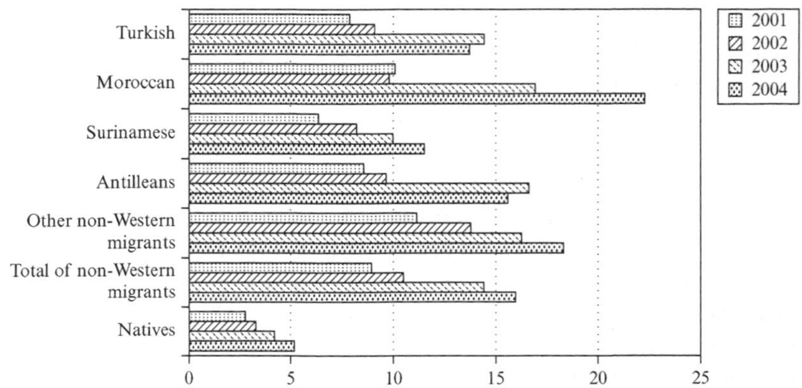

Source: Annual Report Integration 2005.

Figure 4.1 Unemployment among migrant groups in relative figures

categories. Surinamese and Antillean men are less often in a household type characterized by a partner and children, and more often in a household type characterized by a partner and without children, while Turkish and Moroccan men are more often with a partner and children, and less often with a partner and without children. Considering the household income, the higher percentage of Surinamese, Antilleans, Turks and Moroccans in the lowest income category is notable, as is the low percentage of Surinamese and Antillean women and Turkish and Moroccan men in the highest income category.

4.5 DEVELOPMENT OF MIGRANT ENTREPRENEURSHIP IN THE NETHERLANDS

In recent years, entrepreneurship has increased among people of different migrant minority groups in the Netherlands. One out of five new businesses in the Netherlands is set up by a migrant entrepreneur. Migrant minorities have started their own small firms in response to their declining opportunities in the regular labour market, in sectors where the production is labour intensive, the profit margin is low and little start-up capital is required. Their businesses rely mainly on family labour and the labour force of their own ethnic community. They have often started their own shops, oriented mainly to their own migrant group, although supermarkets have increasingly gained ground from small shops.

For example, in 2005 over 80000 people started an enterprise in the

Netherlands. This is approx. 10 000 more than in 2004, which is a growth of 15 per cent. In the Netherlands, between 1989 and 1999 the number of migrant businesses grew relatively more than that of native businesses (Tillaart, 2001). Between 1986 and 2000, the number of migrant enterprises more than tripled from 11 500 to 36 461 (Tillaart, 2001; Maas, 2004). In 2000 there were 36 461 economically-active migrant enterprises within the Netherlands. The number of starting migrant entrepreneurs has strongly increased since the beginning of 2004. In 2003, there were 10 700 migrant entrepreneurs, in 2004, 12 800 and in 2005, this was 14 900. This was an increase of almost 40 per cent in the space of two years. Moreover, this concerns persons who were not born in the Netherlands. Of the 14 900 starting migrant entrepreneurs, 4600 belong to the traditional large migrant group from Morocco, Turkey, Surinam, the Antilles and Aruba (KvK, 2006).

The big cities in the Netherlands have a rich variety of migrant entrepreneurs. A large part of migrant enterprises and entrepreneurs are situated in the four big cities: Amsterdam, Rotterdam, the Hague and Utrecht. For a long time these cities were the place of settlement for major migrant groups of different national and cultural origin. Jewish people were a driving force, but not the only entrepreneurial group in the cities (Lucassen and Penninx, 1997); other examples of early entrepreneurial groups were Belgian manufacturers, German bakeries and breweries, and Italian plaster sculpture sellers (Henkes, 1995; Miellet, 1987). In 2006, the city of Amsterdam had approximately 6776 migrant enterprises and 8198 migrant entrepreneurs. It can be stated that almost 19 per cent of all the migrant enterprises within the Netherlands are located in Amsterdam (GEM, 2004). The number of enterprises of first-generation migrants has tripled countrywide over the last 15 years within the Netherlands. In 1986, the Netherlands had 11 500 migrant enterprises, while in 2000 this number had increased to 36 461. Clearly, in reality the number of migrant enterprises is much more than the stated 36 461, because these figures exclusively represent enterprises of the first generation of immigrants. In Amsterdam, the share of migrant enterprises in the total number within the Netherlands in 2000 was 18.6 per cent. This figure is clearly different when compared with the other big cities in the Netherlands: Rotterdam 10.5 per cent, the Hague 9.7 per cent and Utrecht 2.7 per cent. Figure 4.2 shows the share of migrant enterprises distributed among the big four cities, Utrecht, Amsterdam, Rotterdam and the Hague, within the Netherlands (GEM, 2004).

The migrant enterprises in the Netherlands are much smaller compared with native Dutch enterprises. More than half (55 per cent) of the migrant enterprises are a single-person business. About 39 per cent of migrant enterprises have two to four employees. Only 1 per cent of the

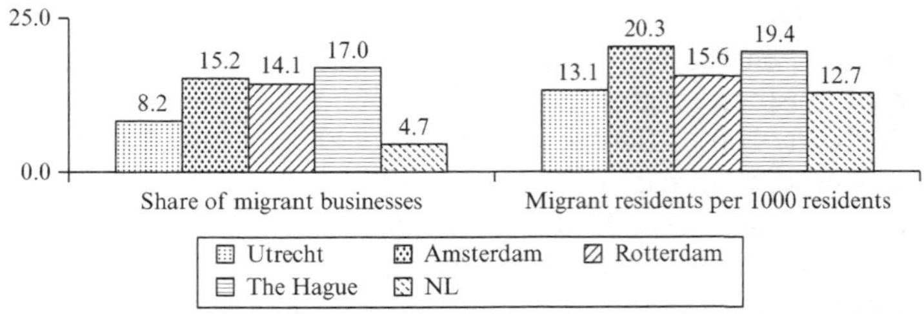

Source: Van den Tillaart (2001).

Figure 4.2 Share of migrant enterprises in four big cities in the Netherlands

migrant enterprises have nine or more employees. Migrant enterprises are thus often registered as a one-man business, because two-thirds of migrant enterprises have this legal form. More than a quarter of these enterprises (29 per cent) are 'partnerships'. Only 3 per cent are private companies (Tillaart, 2001; GEM, 2004). The number of enterprises and the number of entrepreneurs have developed significantly differently. In private businesses the number of ventures over the period 1987–2000 grew by an average of 2.8 per cent per year, whereas the number of entrepreneurs increased by at least 4.2 per cent per year. As already mentioned, the number of entrepreneurs in private businesses grew at a much greater rate than the number of enterprises. The number of entrepreneurs by enterprise has therefore increased. More entrepreneurs are now working in teams (partnerships) than in the past, which means that the number of entrepreneurs by enterprise has increased. The number of entrepreneurs by enterprise does not have to be really changed. The chances of survival for starting migrant enterprises are lower compared with native Dutch enterprises. The main cause of this phenomenon is the greater chance that starting companies will fail during the first year. The number of starting migrant entrepreneurs has risen year-by-year between 1989 and 1999. In 1989, just 2500 migrant entrepreneurs set up in the Netherlands, while in 1999 this number reached 6500. There are now 78 900 migrant entrepreneurs registered within the chambers of commerce, of whom 43 926 are actively involved in an existing and economically-active enterprise.

The rate of participation in entrepreneurship differs greatly between the various migrant populations (Kloosterman et al., 1998). Success in establishing their own enterprise differs among the various minority groups. Frequently, more Turks and Italians are entrepreneurs than Surinamese, Moroccans and other Southern Europeans. The degree of entrepreneurship is very high within some other small minority groups, in particular

Chinese, Egyptians, Pakistanis, Indians (Choenni, 1997). In general, minority business is unequally distributed over sectors. Firms of ethnic minorities are overrepresented in such sectors as restaurants, snack bars, retail trade and wholesale. When comparing the migrant origin of these active migrant entrepreneurs, who are mainly entrepreneurs involved in an existing and economically active enterprise, we can see that the biggest country groups are: Turkey: 9047; Suriname: 6439; China/Hong-Kong: 5130; Morocco: 3424; Egypt: 2037; Dutch Antilles/Aruba: 1615; Poland: 1385. It should be noted that a great majority of migrant entrepreneurs go bankrupt within three years, because of lack of training and incompetence.

When referring to migrant entrepreneurs, it is important to distinguish between first- and second-generation migrants, since they tend to follow a different path. The first group comprises those migrants who have been directly recruited for employment reasons, most often for low-skilled jobs. The second generation is formed by the children of migrants who were born in the host countries and generally have a better educational attainment. This last group can be considered more advantaged because of higher qualifications, and a better knowledge of the host-country language and the labour market, and thus are more selective in choosing and finding a job. First-generation migrants are likely to most often choose to become self-employed in the traditional sectors, characterized by fierce competition, low profits and a low survival rate. It is commonly known that the hotel and catering industry usually attracts a great number of migrant entrepreneurs. More than a quarter (26 per cent) of the existing and economically-active first-generation migrant enterprises are involved with the hotel and catering industry. It can, therefore, be stated that the hotel and catering industry is the most prominent sector of migrant enterprise chosen by first-generation entrepreneurs. In 2000, of all the 36461 migrant enterprises within the Netherlands, 31 per cent is found in the wholesale trade and retail industry, 27 per cent in business and personal services, and 26 per cent in the hotel and catering industry.

The number of first-generation migrant entrepreneurs tripled over the period 1986–2000, from 14450 entrepreneurs in 1986 to almost 44000 in 2000. The total number of entrepreneurs in the Netherlands also rose in the same period, but this growth is less compared with that of the migrant entrepreneur in particular. The total number of entrepreneurs rose from 460000 in 1986 to 730000 in 2000. In 1986, the 14450 migrant entrepreneurs managed 11500 enterprises. By 2000, the 43926 migrant entrepreneurs accounted for 36461 enterprises. Thus we can conclude that the number of migrant enterprises more than tripled over this period (GEM, 2004). In 2000 there was a total of 44000 first-generation migrant entrepreneurs active within the Netherlands. At the beginning of 2001 there were more than 4800 active second-generation migrant entrepreneurs – entrepreneurs who were either born in the Netherlands or with at least one parent born in a foreign country. Thus the total number of migrant entrepreneurs was roughly 49 000 in 2000 (GEM, 2004).

In Table 4.3, we can see that, during the last decade, the proportion of first- and second-generation entrepreneurs has risen steadily in the Netherlands. We can also conclude that the first-generation migrants are far more entrepreneurial than those of the second-generation. Among the Turkish and Moroccan migrant groups it can be seen that men are relatively more entrepreneurial. In the other two major groups of migrants from Surinam and the Dutch Antilles entrepreneurship is more or less evenly distributed among males and females. When considering the second-generation migrants from the Turkish and Moroccan groups, it can be seen that these are relatively more male than female entrepreneurs. In the Surinamese and Antillean groups it can be seen that second-generation women are more entrepreneurial than the men. The net gender effect is very strong for the Surinamese population in the Netherlands. The labour force participation rate in general is relatively high for female migrants from Surinam. However, besides the relatively high labour force participation rate, there is still a relatively low entrepreneurship rate for female Surinamese migrants compared with that of the native female Dutch population. On the other hand, the entrepreneurship rate for female Surinamese are still somewhat higher than it is for female Turkish and Moroccan migrants. Female migrants from Turkey and Morocco are far less entrepreneurial than, for instance, the native Dutch females. This is probably related to cultural and/or religious differences. Besides entrepreneurship rates, labour force participation rates for these two groups of female migrants are also much lower than those of native Dutch women. The combination of a high labour force participation rate and a low rate of entrepreneurship for female Surinamese migrants may be related to the relatively high share of single-parent families in this migrant group.

In 2005, almost one out of three (32 per cent) starting entrepreneurs is female. The share of female entrepreneurs among starting entrepreneurs has been increasing annually. For example, the year 2005 shows a clear growth in the proportion of female entrepreneurs compared with the previous year 2004 (31 per cent). In 2000 there were 25 per cent female entrepreneurs. In absolute numbers we can speak of 25 000 women who started an enterprise in 2005. The largest number of female starters can be found in personal services (6700), *inter alia* beauty care (1530), hair care/hairdressing (1410) and foot care/pedicure (720). There are also many female starters active within the retail industry (5600). The biggest category within this industry is mail-order firms, with approximately 1000 starting women. This is double the amount compared with 2004. This usually refers to virtual stores, for which the Internet is the most important sales channel. Furthermore, 15 per cent of all the female starters in 2004 were born outside the Netherlands.

These branches are also in the top five branches with the highest share of female starters. The percentage of women in the building industry is 3 per cent, which is also the branch with the lowest share of female starters. The percentage of starting female entrepreneurs born in Morocco has increased from 10 per cent in 2000 to 15 per cent in 2004. In addition, the number of entrepreneurs born in the Dutch Antilles has increased significantly. Women often work part-time, because they have to take care of their family. A total of 32 per cent of the women started their own business because of the need to combine childcare and work. Therefore many female entrepreneurs cannot stimulate the growth of their business. Another reason why they do not grow is that women tend to take fewer risks than male entrepreneurs. They start with less capital and growth is less important for women. Having their own enterprise is seen as a pleasant completion of the worker's life. But women do take entrepreneurship seriously and prepare themselves better than men do.

Migrant entrepreneurs have some distinct features. Migrant enterprises are usually found at the bottom of the market, where less financial capital and specific knowledge is required and entry barriers are thus relatively lower (Rath and Kloosterman, 1998). These markets are characterized by strong competition, mostly from co-migrants and based on price rather than quality, and the entrepreneurs often have to accept small profit margins, while relatively many are forced to close after only a short time (Rettab, 2001; Maas, 2004). In the Netherlands, approximately 60 per cent of all migrant entrepreneurs are found in the more traditional sectors such as wholesale, retail and the catering industry (Tillaart, 2001).

Furthermore, they make use of their social networks to acquire employees, informal credit and information, and also in the products that they offer they are often primarily targeting their own migrant community (Choenni, 1997; Tillaart and Poutsma, 1998). In particular, family and migrant networks are deemed a crucial part of entrepreneurial success among migrants (van Delft et al., 2000).

While native entrepreneurs within the Netherlands usually acquire their starting capital from the bank, migrant entrepreneurs usually obtain this starting capital from their family, i.e. parents, brothers, sisters, uncles and aunts. Family members often invest in the business; therefore it is also in the interest of the family to make the business a success. Also personal money from the entrepreneur him/herself is a widely used financial source. It is still common that migrant people can less easily obtain a loan from

Table 4.3 Distribution of the main group of migrant entrepreneurs in the Netherlands, in absolute and relative figures

Year		Turks (× 1000)			Moroccans (× 1000)			Surinamese (× 1000)			Antilleans (× 1000)		
		t	m	f	t	m	f	t	m	f	t	m	f
First generation entrepreneurs	1999	7.2	5.9	1.3	2.5	2.2	0.3	5.1	3.5	1.6	1.1	0.7	0.4
	%	*91*	*92*	*87*	*89*	*92*	*75*	*80*	*80*	*80*	*70*	*70*	*80*
	2000	8.2	6.8	1.4	3.0	2.6	0.4	5.6	3.9	1.7	1.2	0.8	0.4
	%	*88*	*89*	*82*	*88*	*90*	*80*	*79*	*80*	*77*	*67*	*67*	*67*
	2001	9.6	8.0	1.6	3.5	3.1	0.4	6.2	4.4	1.8	1.4	1.0	0.4
	%	*87*	*88*	*84*	*88*	*89*	*80*	*79*	*81*	*75*	*71*	*71*	*67*
	2002	9.9	8.3	1.6	3.7	3.3	0.4	6.2	4.3	1.9	1.4	0.9	0.5
	%	*86*	*87*	*84*	*88*	*89*	*80*	*78*	*78*	*76*	*64*	*64*	*67*
	2003	10.2	8.6	1.6	3.9	3.4	0.5	6.3	4.3	2.0	1.5	1.0	0.5
	%	*86*	*87*	*80*	*89*	*89*	*83*	*79*	*78*	*80*	*71*	*71*	*71*
Second generation entrepreneurs	1999	0.8	0.6	0.2	0.3	0.2	0.1	1.2	0.8	0.4	0.5	0.3	0.2
	%	*10*	*9*	*13*	*11*	*8*	*25*	*19*	*19*	*20*	*33*	*30*	*40*
	2000	1.0	0.8	0.2	0.4	0.3	0.1	1.4	0.9	0.5	0.6	0.4	0.2
	%	*11*	*11*	*12*	*12*	*10*	*20*	*20*	*19*	*23*	*33*	*33*	*33*
	2001	1.3	1.0	0.3	0.4	0.3	0.1	1.6	1.1	0.5	0.6	0.4	0.2
	%	*12*	*11*	*16*	*10*	*9*	*20*	*21*	*20*	*21*	*30*	*29*	*33*

	2002	1.5	1.2	0.3	0.5	0.4	0.1	1.8	1.2	0.6	0.7	0.5	0.2
	%	*13*	*13*	*16*	*12*	*11*	*20*	*22*	*22*	*24*	*33*	*36*	*29*
	2003	1.7	1.3	0.4	0.5	0.4	0.1	1.8	1.2	0.6	0.7	0.5	0.2
	%	*14*	*13*	*20*	*11*	*11*	*17*	*23*	*22*	*24*	*33*	*35*	*29*
Total of entrepreneurs	1999	7.9	6.4	1.5	2.8	2.4	0.4	6.4	4.4	2.0	1.5	1.0	0.5
	2000	9.3	7.6	1.7	3.4	2.9	0.5	7.1	4.9	2.2	1.8	1.2	0.6
	2001	11.0	9.1	1.9	4.0	3.5	0.5	7.8	5.4	2.4	2.0	1.4	0.6
	2002	11.5	9.5	1.9	4.2	3.7	0.5	8.0	5.5	2.5	2.1	1.4	0.7
	2003	11.9	9.9	2.0	4.4	3.8	0.6	8.0	5.5	2.5	2.1	1.4	0.7

Note: Percentages mean: the share of migrant entrepreneurs of a generation cohort in the total of migrant entrepreneurs of the total population of the category concerned.

Source: CBS (2006).

the bank in comparison with the native Dutch. Successful Turkish entrepreneurs within the Netherlands have sometimes also succeeded on their own or with help from their family and friends.

Migrant enterprises are less equally spread across the population in comparison with other enterprises. One can come across them more in urban areas, particularly in the western part of the country, where one can also find a bigger clustering of migrant populations. It appears that migrant enterprises provide a better understanding of the needs and wants of their 'own group'. In this connection, family bonds and informal networks also play an important role as well as in financial and personal aspects. Many enterprises have therefore developed a nurturing structure, which is specifically aimed at their 'own group'; the 'migrant enclave'. This implies the danger of having a biased approach to the market, whereby one is likely to overlook other market niches. Usually, migrant entrepreneurs find a niche in their immigrant community, and start up in a well-defined migrant market, so as to provide typical services and products. An enclave economy can then temporarily positively affect the perspective of migrant entrepreneurs. Immigrants of various ethnicities who form a strong entrepreneurial group can be of great significance for the migrant business community, through job and opportunity creation. So, besides having co-migrant clients, the migrant entrepreneur is close to his/her own migrant group when it comes to the workforce, business financing or even informal networks for information gathering. Migrant entrepreneurs are often literally close to each other in the case of geographical clustering, since many migrant entrepreneurs start their enterprises in areas where a large population with the same migrant background is already living.

Migrant entrepreneurs may differ in motivation. Scholars like Brush (1992), Buttner and Moore (1997), Fagenson (1993), Fischer et al. (1993) and Baycan-Levent et al. (2003) have investigated the individual characteristics of migrant entrepreneurs, such as their demographic background, motivations, educational and occupational experience as entrepreneurs etc. These studies show that, although there are some similarities in migrants' demographic and educational characteristics, and the problems they have to cope with, there are also some differences in educational background, work experience, skills, business goals and management styles. The most important personal characteristics that explain why migrants become entrepreneurs are mentioned in many studies as: their lower education level, their less favoured position as a result of low education and lack of skills, and high level of unemployment. The existence of migrant and social networks also plays a major role in their motivation. The studies show that most migrant enterprises belong to the services sector, are small and relatively young, and mainly have family ownership as their legal form. The common problems of migrant entrepreneurs are: administrative and regulatory barriers, lack of capital and credit, lack of knowledge, language deficiencies, lack of education, lack of management skills, constraints on access to formal business networks and migrant discrimination (Baycan-Levent et al., 2003).

When comparing the motivation differences of the younger generation entrepreneurs with the earlier generation, we can see some differences. Masurel et al. (2004) investigated the motivational differences between first-generation and second-generation migrant entrepreneurs. They show that the former have usually chosen to become entrepreneurs because of discrimination in the workplace, problems with the transferability of diplomas and in order to obtain status. The latter have usually chosen to become entrepreneurs because of blocked promotion in previous jobs. It is thus plausible that first-generation entrepreneurs are usually driven by push factors. In this sense we can speak of 'captive entrepreneurship'. In contrast, the second-generation entrepreneurs choose self-employment more voluntarily; they are more assertive and see entrepreneurship as a viable alternative to being stuck in an unfavourable position in their former employment.

The exact motivation for migrant female entrepreneurs is still somewhat unexplored in the Netherlands, maybe because the share of female entrepreneurs is still lower than that of men. This rate is even lower when considering migrant females. When comparing the female labour force participation rates of Turkish and Moroccan immigrants, it can be seen that this is much lower than that of the native Dutch women. This is probably related to cultural and/or religious differences. But when looking at Surinamese and Antillean immigrants, it can be seen that these migrant groups have a high labour force participation rate among females. But still their entrepreneurship rates are very low. In general, women choose self-employment over a business career in the paid sector when they are older, less educated, have under-age children and have parents who are self-employed themselves. When women are younger and more educated but have children, they choose self-employment as a way to circumvent unemployment.

Although migrant groups are not uniform and display a great variation in motives, attitudes and behaviour, migrant enterprises and migrant entrepreneurs also have some similar characteristics (CEEDR, 2000; Deakins, 1999; Kloosterman et al., 1998; Lee et al., 1997; Masurel et al., 2002; Ram, 1994). Baycan-Levent et al. (2003) have made an in-depth study of entrepreneurship diversities. They investigated migrant differences in enterprises and entrepreneurs' characteristics between male and female natives and non-natives. The following comparisons are based on their findings on the topic of migrant entrepreneurship. Migrant and native entrepreneurs differ in: (i) personal characteristics (migrant entrepreneurs are younger than their native counterparts); (ii) experience (migrant entrepreneurs have less formal or enterprise-related education or prior work experience than natives, and they have less entrepreneurial or management experience than natives); (iii) sector preferences and fields of interest (migrant entrepreneurs are less likely to own enterprises in goods-producing industries than native entrepreneurs); (iv) enterprise features (migrant minority-owned enterprises are somewhat smaller and somewhat younger than native-owned enterprises); (v) networks (migrant entrepreneurs use fewer formal business support organizations than natives); (vi) management styles (migrant entrepreneurs have specific management methods and enterprise structures); and (vii) training (migrant minorities tend to prefer less formal, experienced-based training, to learn from their community-based informal networks, and to be helped or mentored by this network).

There are differences between different generations, but also between the genders. Like second-generation migrant entrepreneurs, migrant female entrepreneurs – they also constitute second-generation migrant entrepreneurs – are more influenced by pull factors. Their motivation stems from their education level and work experience. They have a dual character, migrant and female, whereby sometimes their migrant characteristics dominate their behaviour, and sometimes their female characteristics have more influence on their attitudes (Baycan-Levent et al., 2003). As observed generally in migrant enterprises, most of the migrant female enterprises belong to the services sector and they are small and relatively young. The existence of migrant and social networks also plays a major role in motivating females towards entrepreneurship, just as it does for their male counterparts. Besides these similarities in the characteristics of migrant male and female entrepreneurs, there are also some gender-based differences between them (Baycan-Levent et al., 2006). In general, gender-based differences in entrepreneurship are to be found in the migrants' educational background, work experience and skills, business goals and management styles and personal value systems (see, e.g., Brush, 1992; Fagenson, 1993; Fischer et al., 1993; Verheul et al., 2001). These differences are also observed in migrant female entrepreneurship. In particular, a better education level and a stronger orientation to the service sector are the most prominent features of gender-based differences in migrant entrepreneurship. The difference in entrepreneurial attitude and behaviour among the different groups and between different migrant populations in the Netherlands can have many causes. The different determinants of entrepreneurship, which combine various factors into an eclectic framework, have been defined by Verheul et al. (2001) as follows: (i) psychological determinants; focus on motives and character traits; (ii) sociological determinants; focus on the collective background of entrepreneurs; (iii) economic determinants; focus on the impact of the economic climate and technological development; (iv) demographic determinants; focus on the impact of demographic composition on entrepreneurship (Sahin et al., 2007). It is possible that for certain migrant groups some aspects of these four determinants will have more significance, which will increase the chances of an individual having a propensity for entrepreneurial behaviour. For instance, within the economic determinants it can be said that whenever high unemployment rates and low average incomes are highly applicable to a certain migrant group, this group will contain more individuals who are 'pushed' towards entrepreneurship in order to escape from unemployment. In this case, many aspects of these four determinants may be relevant, and this can explain the cause of strong or weak entrepreneurial behaviour.

In the Netherlands, the migrant minorities who originate from Turkey and Morocco tend to have more similar characteristics in comparison with other migrant minorities within the Netherlands. In this case we can speak of similar migration background and experience, religion, or language deficiencies (in comparison with, for example, immigrants from Surinam and the Dutch Antilles). Yet the entrepreneurship rates between these two groups are highly different. Our explanation is related to the cultural background of the immigrants. Whereas many first-generation immigrants from Turkey already had an entrepreneurial background in their country of birth, immigrants from Morocco showed considerable lower entrepreneurial rates. Therefore the later generations already come from families with an entrepreneurial background, which may explain the difference in motivation and orientation.

Besides the migrant network and support, the success of migrant entrepreneurs depends on their personality and work discipline; and on their attitude to be ambitious, patient, obstinate or self-confident. Other reasons for success could be: to work hard and conscientiously and to have good relationships with clients. To like the job and to do a good job, and to be supported by spouse and family members may all explain the success of migrant entrepreneurs (Baycan-Levent et al., 2003).

As can be seen in Table 4.4, Antilleans and Surinamese entrepreneurs appear to be very successful, with the first-generation's profit rate being very close to that of the second-generation. On the other hand, the profit of first-generation Turkish and Moroccan entrepreneurs is much higher than that of the second generation. Even though the Surinamese and Antillean groups are much smaller than the other two groups, they have

Table 4.4 Profit profiles of migrant entrepreneurs in the Netherlands (in absolute figures in €)

Year		Turks (× 1000)	Moroccans (× 1000)	Surinamese (× 1000)	Antilleans (× 1000)
Profit of first-generation entrepreneurs	1999	18.0	15.5	19.2	22.0
	2000	21.0	19.4	21.4	22.3
	2001	19.3	17.2	21.4	21.8
	2002	19.2	18.0	22.9	24.1
	2003	18.0	17.0	21.9	23.1
Profit of second-generation entrepreneurs	1999	13.9	12.2	21.2	18.8
	2000	14.9	15.7	23.0	19.4
	2001	14.0	12.7	20.9	19.7
	2002	13.8	15.2	22.2	22.2
	2003	12.8	12.6	20.7	22.1
Profit of total entrepreneurs	1999	17.6	15.2	19.6	21.0
	2000	20.3	19	21.7	21.3
	2001	18.7	16.7	21.3	21.1
	2002	18.5	17.6	22.7	23.4
	2003	17.2	16.4	21.6	22.7

Source: CBS (2006).

a higher profit profile. This may be explained by the difference in their entrepreneurial behaviour. There are clearly differences in the profits of first- and second-generation migrant entrepreneurs from the four main groups in the Netherlands.

4.6 POLICY AND RESEARCH CONCLUSIONS

Entrepreneurship is a major driver of innovation, competitiveness and growth. Due to the strong presence of entrepreneurship in key sectors such as services and knowledge-based activities, smaller enterprises and entrepreneurs today play a central role in the economy. A positive and robust correlation between entrepreneurship and economic performance has sometimes been found in terms of growth, firm survival, innovation, employment creation, technological change, productivity increases and exports (Audretsch, 2002). But entrepreneurship brings more than that to the Netherlands and other societies. It is also a vehicle for personal development, and can create social cohesion when the opportunity of setting up one's own business is offered to everybody, regardless of background or location.

Since the mid-1980s the policy of nearly all member countries of the OECD has to a large extent been aimed at reducing the level of unemployment. Part of this policy involves improving the entrepreneurial climate. This is because entrepreneurship is a major factor in the national economy. In the Netherlands, entrepreneurship is also considered to be of vital importance for the positive development of economic growth and employment (Tillaart, 2001). The significance of entrepreneurship arises from the various socioeconomic aspects that are recognized at both the national and international level. In the Netherlands, the policy relevance of entrepreneurship in general has been fully recognized (Wolters, 2001).

The growth of the SME sector is important for the public policy agendas of governments like the Netherlands that are seeking to optimize the employment opportunities associated with the SME sector. Underperforming SME firms lead to many social costs – costs that include reduced earnings for proprietors, potential job loss for staff and financial hardship for suppliers, as well as a reduction in the average per capita spending power of the community in which the failed or underperforming business is based. Based on evidence that entrepreneurs are a heterogeneous group with different backgrounds, experience, motivations, behaviour and needs, and that certain demographic segments of society are underrepresented in business ownership, the governments in the USA, Canada, Australia, and to some extent, Sweden, Finland, the Netherlands, the UK, Spain, Ireland and Taiwan, have targeted special groups for greater attention. The most prevalent target group consisted of young entrepreneurs, followed by women, migrant minorities, immigrants, Aboriginals, the unemployed, new graduates, veterans, people with disabilities and fast-growth technology entrepreneurs. Countries differ on which target groups have priority, the degree of support and the rationale for their interventions. These factors will depend on the demographic make-up of a country's population, labour force and business owners, and what gaps need to be addressed. There are segments of the population who are underrepresented in the business ownership statistics, owing to a lack of awareness and information, a lack of confidence and know-how, a lack of access to resources, and groups who face other societal and economic barriers.

4.7 RETROSPECT AND PROSPECT

The Netherlands did not perceive itself as an immigration country after the Second World War and emigration was stimulated. The erroneous belief that immigrants would only stay temporarily led to a double policy. Originally, a certain integration and functioning in society was demanded for as long as immigrants stayed. But after 1980, the government decided that it was necessary to introduce a minority policy to integrate minorities while also maintaining their cultural identity. The new category of 'minorities' was a policy category: target groups of the minority policies were socially and economically disadvantaged and were ethnically and culturally different. The minority policies were aimed at reducing disadvantages, especially in the domains of labour, education and housing. Later on, the emphasis shifted from 'minority policy' towards 'integration policy' (Kraal and Zorlu, 1998).

In the past decade, the number of entrepreneurs has increased among people of different migrant minority groups in the Netherlands. Entrepreneurship can be a way to improve the economic position of migrants. The rise of migrant entrepreneurship, in general, appears to have had a favourable effect on the economy of the Netherlands. During the economic decline of recent years, the presence of migrant entrepreneurs has been one of the important factors that has kept the urban economy going. The labour market positions of the main groups (migrants from former colonies, guest workers and refugees) in the Netherlands are characterized by strong differences, just like their migration history.

The unemployment rate among ethnic minorities is, on average, three times higher than that of the native Dutch people. The participation rate is considerably low among two minority groups, namely Turks and Moroccans, who have the most unfavourable position in the labour market. The labour market position of these minorities remains vulnerable because quite a large proportion of them are employed in industry and low-paid jobs. The unfavourable labour market position of minorities results in a low household income.

Clearly, migrant entrepreneurs deserve more attention. In order to succeed in the current business climate, it is essential that businesses recognize that customers all over the world have a choice and consumers have to be targeted for their business. Working with migrant minority businesses offers the opportunity to meet this goal. Small and medium-sized enterprises play a significant role in the urban economies of most countries. Each and every successful self-employed migrant or minority business contributes to improved social and economic integration. A growing migrant economy creates a virtuous circle: business success gives rise to a distinctive motivational structure, breeding a community-wide orientation towards entrepreneurship.

The migrant entrepreneur struggles with some bottlenecks. There is a lack of professionalism, they often have serious problems, they do not join networks, and they have insufficient access to services for migrant entrepreneurs. Therefore it is important to increase ME, but apart from the quantitative aspect it is also necessary to improve the quality of these entrepreneurs. Migrant entrepreneurs particularly deserve more attention, since this group not only has to deal with the common problems of entrepreneurship, but also with the specific problems that occur among these group members. First, communication is an important aspect that needs attention. One of the main problems is the distant, impersonal approach by the various official organizations and the overload of information sent via letters and on the Internet. This type of communication is not effective among migrant entrepreneurs, since they prefer the personal approach. Second, the fact that most migrant entrepreneurs are uninformed and have a limited network is a main barrier. Most of the time they are unaware of the legal rules and the facilities that are provided. Rarely do they have a business plan, which often causes an unprepared start. In this connection, developing role models would help. Finally, lack of open contact between migrant entrepreneurs and consulting organizations such as business associations, chambers of commerce, and native entrepreneurs is a problem as well. An important consequence is that migrant entrepreneurs do not make use of the information/support/assistance possibilities.

Policy measures on migrant entrepreneurship could be important, as the potential gains of immigration could be the revitalization of labour markets, growth generation and an increase in the use of unskilled labour. However, regardless of these potential gains from migration, the current situation is that migration policies are becoming stricter in Europe. Because the benefits of immigration are reliant on the skill levels of migrants, policy might focus on determining the optimal composition of skill levels of migrants and not on the question of the maximum permissible level of immigrants.

REFERENCES

Acs, Z.J. (1992), 'Small business economics: a global perspective', *Challenge*, **35**, 38–44.

Acs, Z.J., D.B. Audretsch, P. Braunerhjelm and B. Carlsson (2005), 'The knowledge spillover theory of entrepreneurship', *Small Business Economics*, **32** (1), 15–30.

Amersfoort, van H. (1987), 'Van Willem Kegge tot Ruud Gullit: de Surinaamse Migratie naar Nederland: Realiteit, Beeldvorming en Beleid', *Tijdschrift voor Geschiedenis*, **100** (3), 475–490.

Audretsch, D.B. (2002), 'Entrepreneurship: a survey of the literature', prepared for the European Commission, Enterprise Directorate General, Brussels, July.

Audretsch, D.B. and R. Thurik (2004), 'The model of the entrepreneurial economy', *International Journal of Entrepreneurship Education*, **2** (2), 143–66.

Avci, G. (2006), 'Comparing integration policies and outcomes: Turks in the Netherlands and Germany', *Turkish Studies*, **7** (1), 67–84.
Barrett, G., T. Jones and D. McEvoy (2003), 'United Kingdom: severely constrained entrepreneurialism', in R. Kloosterman and J. Rath (eds), *Immigrant Entrepreneurs: Venturing Abroad in the Age of Globalization*, Oxford: Berg, pp. 101–22.
Baycan-Levent, T., E. Masurel and P. Nijkamp (2003), 'Diversity in entrepreneurship: migrant and female roles in urban economic life', *International Journal of Social Economics*, **30**, 1131–61.
Baycan-Levent, T., E. Masurel and P. Nijkamp (2006), 'Gender differences in ethnic entrepreneurship', *International Journal of Entrepreneurship and Innovation Management*, **6** (3), 173–90.
Baycan-Levent, T., P. Nijkamp and M. Sahin (2009), 'The urban growth potential of second-generation migrant entrepreneurs', Tinbergen Institute Discussion Paper, TI 2009–026/3, Tinbergen.
Berdowski, Z. (1994), *Ouderen in Amsterdam 1993*, Amsterdam: Koordinatie Kommissie Onderzoek van de Gemeente Amsterdam.
Brock, W.A. and D.S. Evans (1989), 'Small business economics', *Small Business Economics*, **1** (1), 7–20.
Brush, C.G. (1992), 'Research on women business owners: past trends, a new perspective and future directions', *Entrepreneurship Theory and Practice*, **17** (4), 5–30.
Bruton, G.D., D. Ahlstrom and K. Obloj (2008), 'Entrepreneurship in emerging economies: where we are today and where should the research go in the future', *Entrepreneurship Theory and Practice*, **32** (1), 1–14.
Buttner, E.H. and D.P. Moore (1997), 'Women's organizational exodus to entrepreneurship: self-reported motivations and correlates with success', *Journal of Small Business Management*, **35** (1), 34–46.
Carlsson, B. (1992), 'The rise of small business: causes and consequences', in W.J. Adams (ed.), *Singular Europe: Economy and Policy of the European Community after 1992*, Ann Arbor, MI: University of Michigan Press, pp. 145–69.
Carree, M.A. and A.R. Thurik (1999), 'Industrial structure and economic growth', in D.B. Audretsch and A.R. Thurik (eds), *Innovation, Industry Evolution and Employment*, Cambridge: Cambridge University Press, pp. 86–110.
Carree, M.A. and A.R. Thurik (2010), 'The impact of entrepreneurship on economic growth', in D.B. Audretsch and Z.J. Acs (eds), *Handbook of Entrepreneurship Research*, Berlin: Spring Verlag, pp. 557–94.
CBS (Central Bureau of Statistics) (2003, 2004, 2006), *Allochtonen in Nederland 2003*, Voorburg.
CEEDR (2000), *Young Entrepreneurs, Women Entrepreneurs, Ethnic Minority Entrepreneurs and Co-Entrepreneurs in the European Union and Central and Eastern Europe*, Final Report to the European Commission, DG Enterprise, Centre for Enterprise and Economic Development Research (CEEDR) Middlesex University Business School, UK.
Centraal Bureau voor de Statistiek (CBS) (2005), *Annual Report Integration*, http://www.cbs.nl.
Choenni, A. (1997), *Veelsoortig Assortiment. Allochtoon Ondernemerschap in Amsterdam als incorporatietraject 1965–1995*, PhD dissertation. Amsterdam: University of Amsterdam.
Cohen, W. and D. Levinthal (1989), 'Innovation and learning: the two faces of R&D', *Economic Journal*, **99** (3), 569–96.

Cormack, J. and J. Niessen (2002), *Supplier Diversity, the Case of Immigrant and Ethnic Minority Enterprises*, Background paper prepared for the Transatlantic Round Table on Supplier Diversity, Brussels.
Deakins, D. (1999), *Entrepreneurship and Small Firms*, 2nd edn, London: McGraw-Hill.
Delft, van H.C. Gorter and P. Nijkamp (2000), 'In search of migrant entrepreneurship opportunities in the city: a comparative policy study', *Environment and Planning C: Government and Policy*, **18**, 429–51.
Fagenson, E.A. (1993), 'Personal value systems of men and women entrepreneurs versus managers', *Journal of Business Venturing*, **8**, 409–30.
Fischer, E.M., A.R. Reuber and L.S. Dyke (1993), 'A theoretical overview and extension of research on sex, gender, and entrepreneurship', *Journal of Business Venturing*, **8** (2), 151–68.
Global Entrepreneurship Monitor (GEM) (2004), *GEM 2003 Executive Report*.
Gompers, P., A. Kovner, J. Lerner and D. Scharfstein (2008), 'Performance persistence in entrepreneurship', Harvard Business School Working Paper, 09-028.
Hartog, J. and N. Vriend (1990), 'Young Mediterraneans in the Dutch labour market: a comparative analysis of allocation and earnings', *Oxford Economic Papers*, **42**, 379–401.
Henkes, B. (1995), *Heimat in Holland, Duitse Dienstmeisjes, 1920–1950*, Amsterdam; Babylon-De Geus.
Hermes, K. and R. Leicht (2010), 'Scope and characteristics of immigrant entrepreneurship in Europe: a cross-national comparison of European countries', Working Paper, Department of Environment and Geography, Australia. Institute for Small Business Research, Germany.
Jacobs, J. (1969), *The Economy of Cities*, New York: Random House.
Jansen, M., J. de Kok, J. Spronsen and S. Willemsen (2003), *Immigrant Entrepreneurship in the Netherlands – Demographic Determinants of Entrepreneurship of Immigrants from Non-Western Countries – Scales*, Zoetermeer.
Jenkins, S.P. (1984), 'Winners and losers: a portrait of the UK income distribution of Swansea Department of Economics', Discussion Paper, No. 94–97.
Kamer van Koophandel (KvK) (2006), *www.kvk.nl*.
Kloosterman, R. and J. Rath (2003), *Immigrant Entrepreneurs. Venturing Abroad in the Age of Globalization*, Oxford and New York: Berg.
Kloosterman, R., J. van der Leun and J. Rath (1998), 'Across the border: immigrants' economic opportunities, social capital and informal business activities', *Journal of Migrant and Migration Studies*, **4**, 249–68.
Kraal, K. and A. Zorlu (1998), *City Template Amsterdam. Basic Information on Ethnic Minorities and Their Participation*, Report According to the Grid for City Templates of the MPMC project, Amsterdam: IMES.
Lee, Y., T. Cameroen, P. Schaeffer and C.G. Schmidt (1997), 'Migrant minority small business: a comparative analysis of restaurants in Denver', *Urban Geography*, **18**, 591–621.
Loveman, G. and W. Sengenberger (1991), 'The re-emergence of small-scale production: an international comparison', *Small Business Economics*, **3**, 1–37.
Lucassen, L. and R. Penninx (1997), *Newcomers. Immigrants and their Descendants in the Netherlands 1550–1995*, Amsterdam: Het Spinhuis (published originally in Dutch in 1994: *Nieuwkomers, Nakomelingen, Nederlanders*).

Maas, M. (2004), 'Filipino entrepreneurship in the Netherlands, male and female business activity compared', Working Paper, GAP, Research Team Governance and Places, Nijmegen.

Masurel, E., P. Nijkamp and G. Vindigni (2004), 'Breeding places for ethnic entrepreneurs: a comparative marketing approach', *Entrepreneurship and Regional Development*, **16**, 77–86.

Masurel, E., P. Nijkamp, M. Tastan and G. Vindigni (2002), 'Motivations and performance conditions for migrant entrepreneurship', *Growth & Change*, **33**, 238–60.

Miellet, R.L. (1987), 'Immigratie van Katholieke Westfalers en de Modernisering van de Nederlandse Detailhandel', *Tijdschrift voor Geschiedenis*, **100**, 374–93.

Ostergaard-Nielsen, E. (2000), 'Trans-state loyalities and politics of Turks and Kurds in Western Europe', *SAIS Review*, **20**, 23–38.

Ours, J.C. van and J. Veenman (1999), 'The Netherlands: old emigrants – young immigration country', Discussion Paper 80, Bonn: IZA.

Porter, M.E. (1990), *The Comparative Advantage of Nations*, New York: Free Press.

Ram, M. (1994), *Managing to Survive: Working Lives in Small Firms*, Oxford: Blackwell.

Rath, J. (1998), 'Een Etnische Stoelendans in Mokum. Over de Economische Incorporatie van Immigranten en hun Nakomelingen in Amsterdam', in A. Gevers (ed.), *Uit de Zevende. 50 Jaar Sociaal-Culturele Wetenschappen aan de Universiteit van Amsterdam*, Amsterdam: Het Spinhuis, pp. 235–49.

Rath, J. and R. Kloosterman (eds) (1998), *Rijp en Groen. Het Zelfstandig Ondernemerschap van Immigranten in Nederland*, Amsterdam: Het Spinhuis.

Rettab, B. (2001), *The Emergence of Migrant Entrepreneurship – A Conceptual Framework*, EIM/Business and Policy Research, Zoetermeer.

Sahin, M., P. Nijkamp and T. Baycan-Levent (2007), 'Migrant entrepreneurship from the perspective of cultural diversity', in Léo-Paul Dana (ed.), *Handbook of Research on Ethnic Minority Entrepreneurship: A Co-evolutionary View on Resource Management*, Cheltenham, UK and Northampton, MA, USA: Edward Elgar Publishing, pp. 99–113.

Sahin, M., A. Todiras and P. Nijkamp (2012, forthcoming), 'An explanatory model for the economic performance of migrant entrepreneurs in the high-tech sector', in P. Nijkamp, J. Poot and M. Sahin (eds), *Migration Impact Assessment: New Horizons*, Cheltenham, UK and Northampton, MA, USA: Edward Elgar Publishing.

Super, I. (2005), *Country of Origin as a Source of Opportunity*, Master's thesis, RSM Erasmus University, Rotterdam.

Thurik, A.R. (2009), 'Entreprenomics: entrepreneurship, economic growth and policy', in Z.J. Acs, D.B. Audretsch and R. Strom (eds), *Entrepreneurship, Growth, and Public Policy*, Cambridge: Cambridge University Press, pp. 219–49.

Tillaart, H. van den (2001), *Monitor Etnisch Ondernemerschap: Zelfstandig Ondernemerschap van Etnische Minderheden in Nederland in de Periode 1990–2000*, [Monitor Ethnic Entrepreneurship: Independent Entrepreneurship of Ethnic Minorities in the Netherlands from 1990–2000], Nijmegen: ITS, p. 11.

Tillaart, H. van den and E. Poutsma (1998), *Een Factor van Betekenis: Zelfstandig Ondernemerschap van Allochtonen in Nederland*, Instituut voor Toegepaste Sociale Wetenschappen, Nijmegen.

Tubergen, F. van (2005), 'Self-employment of immigrants: a cross-national study of 17 Western societies', *Social Forces*, **84** (2), 709–32.

Verheul, I., S. Wennekers, D. Audretsch and R. Thurik (2001), *An Eclectic Theory of Entrepreneurship: Policies, Institutions and Culture*, Research Report 0012, Zoetermeer: EIM.

Vermeulen, F. (2005), 'Organisational patterns: Surinamese and Turkish associations in Amsterdam, 1960–1990', *Journal of Ethnic and Migration Studies*, **31** (5), 951–73.

Waldinger, R.D., H.E. Aldrich, R. Ward and J. Blaschke (1990), *Migrant Entrepreneurs: Immigrant Business in Industrial Societies*, Newbury Park, CA: Sage Publications.

Wolters, T. (2001), *Nascent Entrepreneurship in the Netherlands: A Glimpse behind the Scenes of Business Start-ups*, Zoetermeer: EIM.

Zorlu, A. (2002), *Ethnic and Gender Wage Differentials; An Exploration of LOONWIJZERS 2001/2002*, AIAS Research Report 13, Universiteit van Amsterdam.

Zorlu, A. and J. Hartog (2001), 'Migration and immigrants: the case of the Netherlands', prepared for Migration Policy and The Economy: International Experiences, Munchen: Hans Seidel Stiftung.

5. Innovation in low- and medium-technology manufacturing – the role of networks and non-R&D inputs

Juan Julio Gutierrez

This chapter explores the determinants of three innovation outputs in low- and medium-technology (LMT) manufacturing establishments located in a group of four lower-middle-income countries (El Salvador, Guatemala, Honduras and Nicaragua) participants in the Central American Free Trade Agreement with the USA. Two outputs were laid out in Schumpeter's five-category typology (1934): (a) new products; and (b) new production processes. The third one, (c) improvements in existing products, is drawn from Kline and Rosenberg's (1986) insight that innovation implies not only the creation of completely new products or processes but incremental changes in product performance that may later have major technological and economic effects. The theoretical base for identifying the determinants of innovation outputs stems from two bodies of literature. First, innovation is dependent on the establishment's network of relationships, both internal and external. The internal network is equated to intrafirm cooperation, which encompasses the relationship of foreign-owned establishments with their headquarters. The external network is divided between inter-establishment/firm relationships and institutional interactions (Zanfei, 2000). Second, as Kline and Rosenberg (1986) identified, other innovation inputs are: (a) adaptation and development within the establishment; (b) acquisition of machinery and equipment; and (c) human capital. The previous analytical framework is then applied to a cross-country establishment-level database of LMT manufacturing industries in Central America. The results support the idea that external networks, mainly interaction with universities and with local clients, and purchasing of foreign licences constitute a mechanism for generating product innovations in LMT sectors. However, foreign ownership is not significant for explaining innovation outputs, which could mention enclave characteristics of foreign-owned establishments. On the input side, the results are robust across innovation outputs on: (1) machinery and equipment acquisition, since new technology is embodied in capital goods; (2) adaptation and development within the establishment where learning by doing is an integral component for gaining incremental progress in LMT industries; and (3) hiring of new personnel helps to absorb, use and adapt new technology as it is assumed that know-how is embodied in technical personnel.

5.1 INTRODUCTION

The purpose of this chapter is to investigate: (a) the role of networks, both internal and external to the firm in its innovation process; and (b) the influence of other innovation inputs besides R&D expenditures, specifically for manufacturing sectors that are considered as low and medium technology, according to their relatively low R&D intensity (OECD, 2005). Innovation is a firm-based process, although it is greatly influenced by interactive learning, which is in turn shaped by the relationships the firm has and the institutional set-up it is immersed in.

Much of the recent research on innovation is focused on trying to understand how product and process innovation come about. New products expand the firm's markets and, in many cases, enhance productivity as the average cost of production diminishes. New processes enhance efficiency as the way to manufacture is streamlined. This view is compatible with the first two types of Schumpeter's five-category typology (1934) of innovation outputs: (a) new products; (b) new production processes; (c) new markets; (d) new sources of raw materials; and (e) new forms of organization.

The chapter analyses the drivers of innovative outputs within a lower-middle-income developing-country context. In the developing world the presence of LMT sectors is pervasive; the importance of these sectors is reflected in the countries' economic structure in terms of employment and value added. Firms in high-technology sectors, common in high-income economies, tend to generate a relatively marginal percentage on both categories. The analysis is performed for establishments located in four Central American countries (El Salvador, Honduras, Nicaragua, Guatemala) in 2002.

Access to foreign technology within the firm's internal network (intrafirm cooperation) is one driver of innovation output generation. Frequently intrafirm relationships happen within a foreign direct investment (FDI) type of relation among headquarters and subsidiaries located in host economies, generally in low-cost countries. However, foreign technology can also be accessed through external networking (interfirm networking), by subcontracting and licensing. Further, external interfirm networking also encompasses relationships with suppliers and clients, but also interactions with local as well as non-local institutions, such as universities and chambers of commerce and other trade associations (Zanfei, 2000). Finally, the last drivers are innovation inputs, considering efforts in technology adoption and adaptation, but also including non-R&D inputs to innovation such as acquisition of machinery and equipment and training (Kline and Rosenberg, 1986). Also, the chapter explores significant differences in innovation by manufacturing sector and firm size.

The chapter is presented in six sections. Section 5.2 explores the role of internal and external networks in generating innovation outputs, elaborating on both the intrafirm network, the potential spillovers from foreign direct investment (FDI), and the interfirm and institutional networks. Section 5.3 explains the role of non-R&D innovation inputs with special emphasis on LMT industries,[1] which in many cases have null or marginal R&D expenditures; therefore some inputs come from, for example, their interaction with high-technology industries. Section 5.4 presents a model of the drivers of innovation output and describes the establishment-level data used for the analysis. Section 5.5 tests the model and presents the results, which suggest that FDI does not represent a source of innovation, non-R&D inputs are strong determinants of innovation outputs, and external network variables are important for product innovation, specifically access to foreign licences, feedback from users and relationships with universities. For process innovation the institutional variable chambers of commerce seem to influence innovation positively. Finally, Section 5.6 offers some observations on the public policy implications of the results.

5.2 INTERNAL AND EXTERNAL NETWORKS IN INNOVATION PROCESS GENERATION

Companies have recently transitioned towards a new organizational mode defined as a 'double network' (Zanfei, 2000). On one hand, the internal network for foreign-owned establishments could function as a link between different units of the same firm, for instance as vertical and unidirectional knowledge transfer from headquarters to local subsidiaries. However, the knowledge spillovers to other firms outside the company are uncertain, as described in the following section. The potential for knowledge spillovers is related to the type of FDI and the level of human capital in the host country. FDI in high-technology industries is more likely to generate knowledge-intensive spillovers (Acs et al., 2005). This chapter tries to clarify if knowledge spillovers emanating from the headquarters actually promote the production of innovative outputs in the local subsidiaries within LMT sectors. On the other hand, subsidiaries develop external networks with other firms and institutions to gain access to local sources of information and application abilities (Zanfei, 2000). Locally owned firms also benefit from both interfirm and institutional external networks.

5.2.1 Internal Networks and Potential Spillover Effects

It has been argued that access to foreign technology reduces the information 'gap' on business ideas, products and processes faced by innovators, especially small and medium-sized entrepreneurial firms (Kauffman Foundation, 2007). Foreign technology may also produce spillovers to the rest of local firms; Blomström and Kokko (1998) describe the scenarios by which these spillovers enhance economic growth:

> Spillovers may take place when local firms improve their efficiency by copying technologies of foreign affiliates operating in the local market either based on observation or by hiring workers trained by the affiliates. Another kind of spillover occurs if multinational entry leads to more severe competition in the host country market and forces local firms to use their existing resources more efficiently or to search for new technologies. (Smarzynska, 2002, p. 5)

As a matter of fact, markets can be inefficient and market failures can be the norm and not the exception in many institutional contexts. The presence of positive externalities or spillovers is a main justification for FDI attraction policies.

Positive externalities are also known as spillovers and can be classified as:

- *Pecuniary externalities* Multinational Enterprises' (MNEs') presence can generate demand for investments in goods whose production is characterized by economies of scale. For example, it could lead to the development of input supplier industries, also providing better-quality inputs at lower prices to local firms. But growing demand can also raise the price of local factors of production (e.g. labour).
- *Technological externalities* Besides market transactions, there are transfers taking place that do not benefit the MNE directly. For example, local assemblers could learn much more about the technology of the components they assemble than MNEs wish them to. That is the case with Japan's and Korea's early developing stages, with the use of reverse engineering.

- *Procompetitive effects* MNEs may increase competition in domestic markets. This may force local firms to increase efficiency. But reduction of market share can lead local firms away from the minimum efficient scale, forcing less efficient firms to exit. However, when MNEs are export oriented, the competition for the domestic market does not take place.

However, empirical analysis based on firm-level panel data, which examines whether the productivity of domestic firms is correlated with the extent of foreign presence in their sector or region, casts doubt on the existence of spillovers from FDI in developing countries (Smarzynska, 2002; Alfaro and Rodriguez-Clare, 2004).[2] Although the picture is more optimistic in the case of industrialized countries, a recent paper by Haskel et al. (2002) provides convincing evidence of positive FDI spillovers in the UK.

Rodriguez-Clare (1996) finds that linkage or spillover effects of foreign companies on host countries are more likely to be positive when the good or service produced by foreign companies uses intermediate inputs intensively, when there are large costs of communication between headquarters and the local plant, and when host and home countries are not too different in terms of the variety of intermediate goods produced. Moreover, if these conditions are reversed, MNEs could have a negative effect on the developing economy through creation of enclaves with little connection to the domestic economy.

Therefore the existence of FDI spillovers in the same sector seems dubious, and to have spillovers across sectors there is a need for links between foreign firms and their local suppliers (backward linkages). Such spillovers can operate through: (i) direct knowledge transfer from foreign customers to local suppliers; (ii) more demanding requirements regarding product quality and on-time delivery introduced by MNEs, which provide incentives to domestic suppliers to upgrade their production management or technology; (iii) indirect knowledge transfer through labour turnover; (iv) increased demand for intermediate products due to MNE entry, which allows local suppliers to reap the benefits of scale economies; (v) competition effects, by which MNEs acquiring domestic firms may choose to source intermediates abroad, thus breaking existing supplier–customer relationships and increasing competition in the intermediate products market (Smarzynska, 2002).

Altenburg (2000), among other authors, finds that linkages between foreign firms and local suppliers are stronger if foreign affiliates are domestic-market-oriented and thus tend to purchase more locally than export-oriented foreign firms. Second, it has also been argued that affiliates established through mergers and acquisitions or joint ventures are likely to source more locally than those that are built from scratch (i.e. greenfield projects). While the latter have to take time and effort to develop local linkages, the former can take advantage of the supplier relationships established by the acquired firm or their local partner (UNCTAD, 2001).

So a question remains about what the role of host countries and local firms is (both foreign subsidiaries and locally owned). Is their role almost exclusively in the adoption and diffusion of a centrally created technology (i.e. by foreign companies)?

5.2.2 External Interfirm and Institutional Networks

Interfirm external networks encompass other channels to access foreign technology besides foreign ownership; technology transfer occurs through market transactions deliberately negotiated between parties (Barba Navaretti and Venables, 2004). Transfers may take the form of licensing agreements or be part of a package of upgrading efforts associated with the supply of inputs (i.e. subcontracting). However, according to Acs et al. (2005), foreign firms may have concerns about piracy of intellectual property, reverse engineering of goods and also differing production qualities of branded goods, making the upgrading characteristic of subcontracting dubious.

Other forms of firm interaction within the external network go beyond market channels. According to Hirsch-Kreinsen (2006), well-adjusted and intensively cooperative interfirm relations also occur in LMT sectors. First, client firms may play an important role, triggering customer-oriented product innovations and also process innovations such as the corresponding layout of storage and logistics systems. This could be especially true in LMT sectors because they have been characterized as buyer-driven. Second, the suppliers of material and product components can play a relevant role in product development. Suppliers can give impulses for the further development of low-tech products due to their special knowledge of materials, production possibilities etc.

Innovation is a firm-based process, although it is greatly influenced by interactive learning, which is in turn shaped by the economic structure and the institutional set-up. Our theoretical framework accounts for the external network of interfirm relations. Nevertheless, the national innovation systems literature (Lundvall, 1992) points out that successful innovations can also be generated by a close collaboration of different organizations such as universities, trade associations and chambers of commerce. In high-technology sectors it is more often that the link between universities and firms takes the form of highly formalized R&D contracts (Halpern,

2007). In LMT sectors, the link between universities and firms might take the form of consultancies and/or offices of technology transfer. Trade associations and chambers of commerce are spaces where informal communications between members, often from the same sector, take place. Nevertheless, there can be more systematized ways for knowledge exchange, e.g. through workshops and training sessions.

The framework for analysing the drivers of innovative output in terms of the channels for technology transfer has been presented. Now the investigation turns to consider what inputs are needed to generate the innovative outputs, focusing on those prevalent in LMT manufacturing firms.

5.3 NON-R&D INNOVATIVE INPUTS IN LMT INDUSTRIES

In manufacturing sectors learning by doing is an integral component for gaining incremental innovation; therefore the separation of R&D facilities from the manufacturing plant is ineffective (Kelley et al., 2004). Specifically, in LMT industries many of the innovations and adoption of related activities operate in practical and pragmatic ways by doing and using (von Tunzelmann and Acha, 2005).

The importance of LMT industries within the manufacturing sector is greater in developing countries than in developed ones, in terms of both value added and employment generation. Moreover, in developing countries firms are very likely to lack the budget to perform R&D or few firms categorize any expenditure as R&D (Recanatini et al., 2000), and thus adoption and adaptation by doing and using are major inputs to the generation of innovative outputs.

Yet LMT manufacturing firms are a vehicle for spreading and implementing technologies embodied in equipment and capital goods and basic materials, which require traditional R&D expenditures. LMT firms generate innovative outputs by using new machinery and equipment. Therefore LMT sectors could serve as carrier industries for diffusing the gains of new technologies and for incorporating advances in the production of the products they yield as well as providing feedback to tune up products and processes.

For example, wearing apparel and fur production (ISIC 18) can benefit from the use of inputs generated by advanced technology industries such as computer and advanced instrumentation manufacturing (ISIC 30), which are used to design durable water-repellent finishes in textiles or to test windproof fleece. In that sense, innovation in industries regarded as LMT could be fostered by increasing their interaction with advanced technology inputs. There is a complementarity between LMT and high-technology manufacturing because most products from the latter are producer goods (i.e. inputs into traditional production), not consumer goods (Kelley et al., 2004).

Local firms, both foreign and locally owned, are more likely to use high-technology inputs if the market for the final product is global. In this case, local suppliers may not be able to satisfy the demand of high-technology inputs because of higher quality requirements or constraints imposed by the parent company etc. (Smarzynska, 2002).

5.4 DATA AND MODEL FOR THE DRIVERS OF INNOVATIVE OUTPUT

5.4.1 Data

The study uses a cross-country database at the establishment level for four Central American countries, the World Bank Investment Climate Survey (ICS). The survey data were collected in 2003 and refer to information from 2000 to 2002 (See Appendix 5A.2 for parts of the questionnaire used). The sample contains a total of 1771 observations of manufacturing establishments legally registered in four countries (El Salvador, 465 obs; Guatemala, 431 obs; Honduras, 439 obs; Nicaragua, 436 obs). The four countries studied are participants in the Central American Free Trade Agreement with the USA (CAFTA), allowing them to enjoy tariff-free exports for certain line items.[3] Table 5.1 confirms that foreign firms in the textile and garment sectors have mostly used the provisions of the Free Trade Agreement to install factories in Central America to supply the US market (Gereffi, 1999).

The sample of 1771 observations was drawn from industrial registers in the four countries and encompasses establishments from seven LMT manufacturing sectors (see Table 5.1 and note 4 for detailed list). The ICS database is moderately disaggregated. The industry sectors are defined at the 2-digit International Standard Industrial Classification (ISIC) level.

An establishment is a single physical location where business is conducted or where services or industrial operations are performed. A firm may have one or many establishments. For example, a firm that produces beverages can have many bottling and distribution establishments as well as the establishment where the beverages are made. For the purposes of the ICS, an establishment makes its own financial decisions and has accounts separate from those of the firm. An establishment should have its own managerial oversight and control its payroll (World Bank, 2007).

Table 5.1 Descriptive statistics of establishment sector and size

Sector	Establishment size									Foreign owned %
		Micro/small		Medium		Large		Total		
	ISIC	No. of establishments	%	No. of establishments	%	No. of establishments	%	No. of establishments	%	
Textiles	17	33	47	14	20	23	33	70	4	23
Wearing apparel and fur	18	170	48	50	14	136	38	356	20	23
Chemicals and chemical products	24	96	45	59	28	56	27	211	12	13
Food products and beverages	15	222	54	90	22	96	24	408	23	10
Wood & products of wood & cork, excl. furniture	20	200	74	48	18	21	8	269	15	6
Leather and articles; footwear	19	55	80	8	12	6	9	69	4	4
Other non-metallic mineral products	26	162	80	26	13	15	7	203	11	2
Rubber and plastic products	25									
Metal products	28	125	68	46	25	14	8	185	10	9
Total		1063	60	341	19	367	21	1771	100	12

Note: Firm size: micro/small: 1–25 permanent workers (hired for at least a year); medium: 26–75 permanent workers, large: more than 75 workers. We follow Fajnzylber and Fernandez (2006) for breakdown of firm size, acknowledging that the US classification by number of workers is not appropriate to capture the smaller firm scale in developing countries (i.e. the Small Business Administration defines as small firms those with 500 or fewer employees).

Source: World Bank ICS – author's calculations.

The ICS is targeted to a particular set of firms: manufacturing establishments with five or more full-time employees, located in major urban centres. As a matter of fact, 98 per cent of the establishments in our sample fulfil this characteristic. Full-time employees are those who work up to eight or more hours per day. Finally, the ICS was administered by face-to-face interviews with managing directors, accountants, human resource managers and other relevant company staff.

The distribution of establishments by size (see Table 5.1) is consistent with what has been observed in developing countries, the so-called 'missing middle' phenomenon. There are some large firms and many small firms, but relatively few middle-sized firms, which are common in industrialized countries (Recanatini et al., 2000). For the USA, Axtell shows that the firms' size distribution follows the Zipf law (Axtell, 2001). If the Zipf law were also applied to our sample, the medium size category would reach a proportion higher than 19 per cent. Some believe an explanation of this phenomenon lies in the presence of a small market, which has also been suggested as a barrier to technological change.

However, the information is not in the form of panel data, which poses some weakness to the study: (a) no research could be done on the effects of policy interventions and the process of industry evolution; (b) attrition bias may arise when firms disappear (exit) because of mergers, acquisitions, consolidation or bankruptcy, or when a firm is included in the sample only if it survives up to the point of interview. Without accounting for attrition, the sole reliance on surviving firms will inevitably bias, usually upward, performance measurements (i.e. production of innovation outputs).

5.4.2 The Model

Model specification

The ICS has a set of questions that allow the elucidation between innovative and non-innovative establishments, so the innovation function specification has a binary variable accounting for the propensity to innovate. In fact, three different regressions are performed for each of the three innovation outputs described above. A logistic regression technique is appropriate to accommodate the dichotomous characteristic of the dependent variable and its results are easier to interpret than those of other dichotomous regression techniques (e.g. probit).[4] The logistic regression equation is:[5]

IOi = β1 + β2 (Internal network (intrafirm) variables [*IN*]) + β4 (External network (interfirm and institutional) variables [*EN*]) + β5 (Innovation

Table 5.2 Establishments producing innovative outputs

Type of innovation	No. of establishments	%
1. New products	935	52.8
2. New production processes	1423	80.4
3. Improvements in existing products	862	48.7

Source: World Bank ICS – author's calculations.

inputs [*II*]) + β6 (Establishment size *i*) + β7 (Sector *j*) + β8 (Country *k*) + ε (5.1)

Control variables

We use the common control variables found in the innovation literature (see, e.g., firm size dummies, sector dummies and country dummies to isolate the effect of scale, industry characteristics and country characteristics, respectively).

- Firm size:[6] micro/small: 1–25 permanent workers (hired for at least a year), medium: 26–75 permanent workers, large: more than 75 workers.
- Industry sector.[7]
- Country: El Salvador, Honduras (contrast variable), Nicaragua, Guatemala.

Dependent variables: innovative outputs (*IO*) (see Appendix 5A.1 for variable operationalization)

Following the Schumpeterian typology, innovation outputs take the form of: (a) new products; (b) new production processes; and, additionally, (c) improvements in existing products. The rationale behind this last innovation output is based on Kline and Rosenberg's (1986) insight that innovation implies not only the creation of completely new products or processes but incremental changes in product performance, which may (over a long period) have major technological and economic implications. The ICS obtains information for these three innovation outputs by asking if the establishment (plant) had initiated any of the three types of output innovations in the previous two years; therefore each is a dichotomous variable where 0 = 'did not initiate the activity' and 1 = 'initiated the activity'. As we can see in Table 5.2, the results of the ICS suggest that a substantial proportion of LMT establishments produce innovative outputs. About half of the establishments

Table 5.3 Innovation output combinations

Innovation output combination	No. of establishments	%
No innovation	206	11.6
Product innovation	68	3.8
Process innovation	299	16.9
Incremental product innovation	49	2.8
Product & process innovation	336	19.0
Product & incremental product innovation	25	1.4
Process & incremental product innovation	282	15.9
Prod. & process & incremental product innovation	506	28.6
Total	1771	100.0

Source: World Bank ICS – author's calculations.

had produced new products or significantly improved existing ones. Moreover, 80 per cent of surveyed establishments reported that they developed new production processes.

The information gathered by the ICS can be contrasted with, for example, data from the European Union's Community Innovation Surveys (CIS-3), which show that 47 per cent of surveyed manufacturing firms in Germany had made product innovations between 1998 and 2000, compared to an EU average of 35 per cent among 16 countries. Process innovation was achieved by an average of 31 per cent of surveyed manufacturing European firms. Since the answers in both cases are self-reported, a key question, not part of this study, is how innovative are the innovation outputs.

Establishments engaged in innovation activities can develop more than one innovation output. Table 5.3 shows that the bigger proportion of establishments (29 per cent) had developed the three types of innovation output at the same time. At the same time, one type of innovation does not happen alone; 36 per cent of establishments produced innovation outputs in some combination pair. Only process innovation seems to be accomplished in isolation by a relatively large proportion of establishments (16 per cent).

Independent variables

A. Internal networks (intrafirm cooperation variables, *IN*): the establishment is considered under foreign ownership if foreign capital is 10 per cent or greater, which will be an indication of FDI. This is the same cutoff used by Smarzynska (2002). A firm is also considered under foreign ownership if the establishment's main channel to acquire technology comes from the headquarters, which would be the case of an MNE subsidiary. Therefore the variable *forown* is binary and equal to 1 if it satisfies any of the two previous conditions, and equal to 0 otherwise.

B. External network (interfirm networking variables, *EN*): Barba Navaretti and Venables (2004) suggest that market channels employed by any domestic firm to access foreign technology could be through market transactions in the form of subcontracting and licensing. This is measured as a dummy variable equal to 1 if the establishment's main channel for acquiring new technology was purchasing a foreign licence (*forlic*). Also, a dichotomous variable is created if the establishment's sales to MNEs are greater than 10 per cent, which would be an indication of subcontracting (*forsubcont*).

Yet interfirm networking also encompasses relationships between the establishment and: (a) suppliers of equipment (*locsuppl*); (b) clients (*locclient*) as well a local market channel; and (c) licensing from other domestic firms (*loclic*). The dummy value is equal to 1 if the interaction implied a major channel for technology acquisition.

Finally, two measures identifying the institutional network (Zanfei, 2000) are created. Those are the relationships between the establishment and institutions such as universities and public institutions (*locuniv*) and local chambers of commerce / trade associations (*locchamb*).

C. Innovation input variables (*II*): for a sizeable proportion of LMT firms (especially in developing countries), adoption and adaptation of new technologies are primary channels for innovation rather than classical expenditures in R&D. If the establishment had developed and adapted technology (*D&A*), it is an input for generating innovative outputs. Therefore the dummy has a value of 1, and 0 otherwise. Non-R&D inputs to innovation are also considered (Kline and Rosenberg, 1986), assuming that newer equipment represents a higher level of technology, and that technological know-how is embodied in technical personnel. If machinery and equipment acquisition (*newequip*) and hiring of human capital (*humanK*) are channels for new technology incorporation, the dummies take the value of 1, and 0 if not.

The establishments surveyed in the ICS had made relatively more use of machinery and equipment acquisition as the primary channel of technological change (Table 5.4). On the other hand, a smaller proportion of establishments had used both internal intrafirm and external networks as innovation inputs.

Table 5.4 Channels to introduce innovations

A. INTERNAL NETWORKS	Variable name		
Intrafirm cooperation variables			
1. foreign ownership	*forown*	No. of establishments	204
		%	12
B. EXTERNAL NETWORK			
Interfirm variables			
2. subcontracting	*forsubcont*	No. of establishments	170
		%	10
3. foreign licence	*forlic*	No. of establishments	46
		%	3
4. suppliers of equipment	*locsuppl*	No. of establishments	200
		%	11
5. local licence	*loclic*	No. of establishments	18
		%	1
6. clients	*locclien*	No. of establishments	128
		%	7
Institutional networking variables			
7. universities and public institutions	*locuniv*	No. of establishments	45
		%	3
8. chambers of commerce	*locchamb*	No. of establishments	67
		%	4
C. INNOVATION INPUT VARIABLES			
9. machinery and equipment acquisition	*newequip*	No. of establishments	942
		%	53
10. human capital hiring	*humanK*	No. of establishments	654
		%	37
11. development and adaptation	*D&A*	No. of establishments	523
		%	30

Source: World Bank ICS – author's calculations.

5.5 RESULTS OF THE MODEL TEST

5.5.1 Internal (Intrafirm) Networks

The presence of foreign ownership (*forown*), the intrafirm channel for technological change, is not a mechanism to foster innovation within the establishment on any of the three innovation outputs considered. In other words, there is not a foreign premium in terms of generation of innovation outputs. Though not part of this chapter, these results may also support findings in the literature review provided by Alfaro and Rodriguez-Clare (2004), who describe the lack of FDI spillovers within the same sector. If spillovers are to happen, they are more likely to be vertical rather than horizontal in nature. For example, foreign ownership may have positive spillovers in local suppliers through backward linkages (Smarzynska, 2002).

5.5.2 External Networks

- *Interfirm network* (*foreign*) Establishments with access to foreign technology through interfirm licensing (*forlicen*) have odds that are twice as high for the development of new products or for improvement of existing products than those that do not have access to this technology. Although only 3 per cent of the surveyed firms purchased a foreign licence, the impact on innovative outputs is quite significant. The other market channel for access to foreign technology was subcontracting; the results contradict the idea that foreign firms purchasing locally intermediate inputs and services would foster innovation through a package of upgrading efforts associated with the supply of inputs (Barba Navaretti and Venables, 2004; Smarzynska, 2002).
- *Interfirm network* (*local*) The establishments' relationships with other firms prove vital to developing improvements on existing products. Establishments that acquired technology through cooperation with suppliers of machinery and equipment (*locsuppl*), collaboration with client firms (*locclient*) and local licensing (*loclic*) show odds 1.5 times higher of improving existing products than those establishments that lacked those interactions. Additionally, the odds of creating new products are 1.8 times larger for establishments that obtain technology through interactions with clients (*locclient*).
- *Institutional networks* The model results suggest that establishments with relationships with universities and public institutions (*locuniv*) have greater odds of creating new products and improvements of existing products than those establishments without those interactions. Although the specific nature of the interaction activity has not been elucidated, it well may be that training provision and consulting are ways that universities and institutions foster innovation in local plants. Additionally, the third type of innovation output, a new production process, is more likely if the establishment has acquired its technology from interacting with local chambers of commerce (*locchamb*). The collaboration and learning from peers seems to be vital in the course of devising new production processes.
- *Innovation inputs* The most consistent and important drivers for all three innovation outputs are the inputs described by Kline and

Rosenberg (1986). As Table 5.4 shows, establishments that are engaged in development and adoption of technology (*D&A*), hiring new personnel (*humanK*), and acquiring new machinery and equipment (*newequip*) show higher odds for the development of innovative outputs. The result stresses the importance of non-R&D inputs in the generation of innovation, especially in LMT industries. Moreover, in developing countries, adoption and adaptation of new technologies within the establishment are primary channels for innovation rather than classical expenditures in R&D. The hiring of new personnel (*humanK*) helps to absorb, use and adapt new technology and it is assumed that technological know-how is embodied in technical personnel (Griliches, 1969; Nelson and Phelps, 1966). Finally, the acquisition of new machinery and equipment (*newequip*) embodies technological progress and represents a higher level of technology.

- *Sector* (A) For the generation of new products, out of seven manufacturing sectors, two had statistically significant results. Establishments of garment and fur manufacturing (ISIC 18) and non-metal product manufacturing (ISIC 26) show odds that are 0.7 and 0.6 of those establishments devoted to metal product (ISIC 28) manufacturing. This result is particularly noticeable since almost a quarter of establishments in the wearing apparel and fur sector are foreign owned and a large fraction are large establishments (38 per cent, see Table 5.1). As a conclusion, innovation within the wearing apparel and fur sector at the local level is not fostered by a high presence of foreign-owned establishments, which is associated with larger establishment size. These results are similar to those of Smarzynska (2002) and Alfaro and Rodriguez-Clare (2004), who do not find evidence of spillovers from foreign ownership in local establishments within the same sector. (B) Textile (ISIC 17) establishments show odds 1.9 times higher than those of metal manufacturing establishments to generate improvements in existing products. The characteristics of the textile manufacturing are similar to those of the garment and fur manufacturing sector (ISIC 18). The presence of foreign ownership is as high as in the garment manufacturing sector, 23 per cent, and the fraction of large firms is large too (33 per cent; see Table 5.1). On the contrary, the odds of making improvements in existing products for leather and articles; footwear (ISIC 19) establishments is 4.4 times larger than for those establishments engaged in metal products manufacturing, although the importance of foreign ownership and large firms is low. Foreign ownership in the leather and footwear manufacturing sector only amounts to 4 per cent of the establishments, and micro and small establishments dominate

Table 5.5 Model results

		(a) New products	(b) New production processes	(c) Improvements in existing products
A. INTERNAL NETWORKS – INTRAFIRM COOPERATION VARIABLES				
Forown	Odds ratio	0.77	1.20	0.96
	Z-statistic	−1.53	−0.78	−0.24
B. EXTERNAL NETWORK				
B1. INTERFIRM VARIABLES				
Forsubcont	Odds ratio	1.00	1.30	1.30
	Z-statistic	−0.01	−1.10	−1.50
Forlicen	Odds ratio	**2.07**	2.31	**2.02**
	Z-statistic	2.14*	−1.56	2.09*
Locsuppl	Odds ratio	0.97	0.94	**1.48**
	Z-statistic	−0.17	−0.32	2.44**
Loclic	Odds ratio	1.29	0.91	**3.02**
	Z-statistic	−0.49	−0.15	1.90*
Locclient	Odds ratio	**1.81**	1.43	**1.53**
	Z-statistic	2.93**	−1.26	2.15*
B2. INSTITUTIONAL NETWORKING VARIABLES				
Locuniv	Odds ratio	**2.42**	2.17	**3.72**
	Z-statistic	2.51**	−1.44	3.62**
Locchamb	Odds ratio	1.19	**2.69**	0.86
	Z-statistic	−0.66	2.09*	−0.57
C. INNOVATION INPUT VARIABLES				
Newequip	Odds ratio	**2.15**	**1.84**	**2.47**
	Z-statistic	7.13**	4.39**	8.24**
humanK	Odds ratio	**1.51**	**1.95**	**1.31**
	Z-statistic	3.80**	4.40**	2.41**
D&A	Odds ratio	**1.24**	**1.61**	**2.19**
	Z-statistic	1.84*	2.87**	6.69**
ESTABLISHMENT SIZE				
Micro–small size	Odds ratio	0.82	1.16	0.95
	Z-statistic	−1.29	−0.76	−0.35
Medium size	Odds ratio	0.93	1.37	0.94
	Z-statistic	−0.45	−1.42	−0.36
ESTABLISHMENT SECTOR				
ISIC 18				
Wearing apparel and fur	Odds ratio	**0.70**	1.03	0.92
	Z-statistic	1.79*	−0.10	−0.40
ISIC 15				
Food products and beverages	Odds ratio	0.77	0.83	0.78
	Z-statistic	−1.39	−0.80	−1.28

Table 5.5 (continued)

		(a) New products	(b) New production processes	(c) Improvements in existing products
ESTABLISHMENT SECTOR				
ISIC 24				
Chemicals and chemical products	Odds ratio	1.18	1.14	1.03
	Z-statistic	−0.74	−0.48	−0.14
ISIC 20				
Wood & products of wood & cork, excl. furniture	Odds ratio	0.79	1.08	0.92
	Z-statistic	−1.18	−0.30	−0.38
ISIC 19				
Leather and articles; footwear	Odds ratio	1.16	**4.41**	1.47
	Z-statistic	−0.51	2.91**	−1.27
ISIC 25–26				
Other non-metallic mineral prod.	Odds ratio	**0.58**	**0.61**	**0.61**
	Z-statistic	2.51**	1.98*	2.20*
ISIC 17				
Textiles	Odds ratio	0.74	0.98	**1.88**
	Z-statistic	−1.03	−0.06	2.01*
Country dummies		Y	Y	Y
Constant	Odds ratio	0.81	1.79	0.41
	Z-statistic	−0.93	2.08*	3.76**
Observations		1771	1771	1771

Notes:
* Significant at 5% level.
** Significant at 1% level.

the sector, totalling 80 per cent of the establishments. Finally, establishments in the non-metallic production (ISIC 26) sector show odds that are 0.6 of the odds of metal product (ISIC 28) manufacturing establishments. The metallic sector excludes machinery and equipment, and it manufactures relatively non-complex products such as parts, containers and structures, usually with a static, immovable function. Also, there is a large presence of micro and small firms in this sector (68 per cent) and only 9 per cent of the establishments are foreign owned (Table 5.1). In summary, innovation does not happen homogeneously across all manufacturing sectors; more importantly the relationship with foreign firms does not guarantee innovation output generation at the establishment level.

- *Establishment size* The odds ratios related to firm size are found to be not significant (see Table 5.5).

5.6 CONCLUSIONS AND POTENTIAL FUTURE RESEARCH

First, the results suggest that there might not be a case to enact FDI attraction policies in the four countries studied. As the analyses show, ownership, either foreign or local, is not significant in generating innovation outputs. Some LMT manufacturing sectors with major relationships with foreign capital and with a big proportion of large establishments are not necessarily more innovative (e.g. garments). On the contrary, the textile-manufacturing sector has similar characteristics, but incremental product innovation seems to be more likely. It might be the case that technology brought by FDI is not fully appropriated by the subsidiaries but nevertheless it spreads to other forms in the economy. A more detailed study on spillovers is needed.

Second, despite the unclear role of foreign ownership in innovation, the results suggest that when local firms master foreign technology using licensing, product innovation is more likely to occur. This is a market channel that proved to be essential in the catching-up process of East Asian economies (Matthews, 2001).

Third, for LMT manufacturing sectors in the four countries studied, external networks in the form of interfirm relationships as well as institutional relationships are found to be important in the production of innovation outputs. Specifically the relationships with clients are relevant for product innovation (both incremental and new products). This is especially true for industries where innovation is buyer driven and user–producer interaction is key. Policies directed to facilitate the contact of potential buyers (e.g. big department stores) and firms might induce product innovation, in the form of new designs and use of new materials. Also, it seems that the venue that allows for entrepreneurs' interaction in the form of chambers of commerce may foster process innovation. More research is needed to elucidate if it is the informal communications and/or the systematic knowledge transfer through workshops and training that enhances innovation. In general, potential policies to foster coordination between the institutional network and firms (establishments) as well as enhance adoption and accelerate diffusion of foreign technology that would increase innovation of local firms are desirable.

Finally, results on innovation inputs stress the importance not only of adaptation and development within the firm in generating innovative outputs, but also the value of machinery and acquisition equipment and contracting new human capital. This is more relevant in the case of LMT manufacturing industries where learning by doing is an integral component for gaining incremental innovation. A key issue is to see which type of employee profile enhances innovation in these industries – professionals, skilled workers or administrative staff.

Moreover, it is vital to make clear the degree of innovativeness of these outputs; they can be new to the market or just to the firm, or local, regional or global. The self-reporting nature of the answers may make this difficult, but the connection of the responses with productivity metrics may bring light to bear on this issue.

ACKNOWLEDGEMENTS

For their comments I thank Zoltan Acs, Roger Stough, three anonymous referees and the participants at the Third Annual Conference: Research at Mason in Entrepreneurship, Fairfax, VA, and the 10th Uddevalla Conference, Sweden. For access to the Investment Climate Survey database I am grateful to Pablo Fajnzylber of the World Bank.

NOTES

1. According to OECD categories, the industrial sectors can be classified as follows: high-technology sectors (high-tech) with an R&D intensity of more than 5 per cent, sectors with complex technology (medium-high-tech) with an R&D intensity between 3 and 5 per cent. Industries that are not research intensive (medium-low-tech and low-tech) have R&D intensity below 3 per cent.
2. Haddad and Harrison (1993) on Morocco; Aitken and Harrison (1999) on Venezuela, and Djankov and Hoekman (2000) on the Czech Republic.
3. At the time when the survey was administered, the four countries were participants of a previous free trade agreement with the USA, the Caribbean Basin Trade Partnership Act (CBTPA). In 2004 the CBTPA was phased out and replaced with the CAFTA.
4. To check for multicollinearity among the independent variables, the variance inflation factor was calculated. The results for all variables were lower than 4; therefore multicollinearity is not a potential problem.
5. Number of independent variables: a rule of thumb is that there should be no more than one independent for each ten cases in the sample. In applying this rule of thumb, keep in mind that if there are categorical independents, such as dichotomies, the number of cases should be considered to be the lesser of the groups (e.g. in a dichotomy with 480 '0s' and 20 '1s', effective size would be 20), and by the 1:10 rule of thumb, the number of independents should be the smaller group size divided by 10 (in the example, 20/10 = 2 independents maximum). http://www2.chass.ncsu.edu/garson/PA765/logistic.htm#indeps.
6. Firm sizes: micro/small, medium. Contrast dummy: large firm.
7. Sectors: Beverage and food, Textiles, Garment manufacturing, Furniture and wood, Paper and printing, Chemicals, rubber and plastics, Non-metallic products, Shoe manufacturing and leather. Contrast dummy: Metallic products.

REFERENCES

Acs, Z., C. O'Gorman, L. Szerb and S. Tejersen (2005), 'Could the Irish miracle be repeated in Hungary?', Discussion Papers on Entrepreneurship, Growth and Public Policy, Max Plank Institute. Available: http://ideas.repec.org/p/esi/egpdis/ 2005-33.html. Accessed 10 October 2006.

Aitken, B.J. and A.E. Harrison (1999), 'Do domestic firms benefit from direct foreign investment? Evidence from Venezuela', *American Economic Review*, **89**, 605–18.

Alfaro, L. and A. Rodriguez-Clare (2004), 'Multinationals and linkages: an empirical investigation', *Economia* (Journal of LACEA), **4** (2), available at http://www.econ.psu.edu/~aur10/Papers/MultinationalsandLinkages-January-2004.pdf. Accessed 4 November 2006.

Altenburg, T. (2000), 'Linkages and spillovers between transnational corporations and small and medium-sized enterprises in developing countries: opportunities and best policies', in UNCTAD, *TNC–SME Linkages for Development: Issues – Experiences – Best Practices*, New York and Geneva: United Nations, pp. 3–61.

Axtell, R. (2001), 'Zipf distribution of US firm sizes', *Science*, **293**, 7 September.

Barba Navaretti, G. and A. Venables (2004), *Multinational Firms in the World Economy*, Princeton, NJ: Princeton University Press.

Blomström, M. and A. Kokko (1998), 'Multinational corporations and spillovers', *Journal of Economic Surveys*, **12** (2), 1–31.

Djankov, S. and B. Hoekman (2000), 'Foreign investment and productivity growth in Czech enterprises', *World Bank Economic Review*, **14**, 49–64.

Fajnzylber, P. and A. Fernandez (2006), 'International economic activities and the demand for skilled labor: evidence from Brazil and China', Policy Research Working Paper, Series 3426, The World Bank.

Gereffi, G. (1999), 'International trade and industrial upgrading in the apparel commodity chain', *Journal of International Economics*, **48**, 37–70.

Griliches, Z. (1969), 'Capital skill complementarity', *The Review of Economics and Statistics*, **51** (4), 465–8.

Haddad, M. and A. Harrison (1993), 'Are there positive spillovers from direct foreign investment? Evidence from panel data for Morocco', *Journal of Development Economics*, **42**, 51–74.

Halpern, L. (2007), *Literature Survey on the Links Between Innovation, Competition, Competitiveness, Entry & Exit, Firm Survival and Growth*, MICRO-DYN, EU Sixth Framework Programme.

Haskel, J., S. Pereira and M. Slaughter (2002), 'Does inward foreign direct investment boost the productivity of domestic firms?', NBER Working Paper, 8724.

Hirsch-Kreinsen, H. (2006), 'Low-technology: a forgotten sector in innovation policy', paper presented at the International ProACT Conference, Tampere, Finland.

Kauffman Foundation (2007), 'A roadmap to an entrepreneurial economy. A research and policy guide', Version 1.0, 27 February, available http://www.kauffman.org/pdf/Entrepreneurial_Roadmap_web.pdf, accessed 2 April 2007.

Kelley, C., M. Wang, G. Bitko, M. Chase, A. Kofner, J. Lowell, J. Mulvenon, D. Ortiz and K. Pollpetter (2004), *High-technology Manufacturing and US Competitiveness*, Washington: RAND Corporation.

Kline, S. and N. Rosenberg (1986), 'An overview to innovation', in R. Landau (ed.), *The Positive Sum Strategy: Harnessing Technology for Economic Growth*, Washington: National Academy Press, pp. 275–305.

Lundvall, B. (1992), *National Systems of Innovation. Towards a Theory of Innovation and Interactive Learning*, London: Pinter Publishers.

Matthews, J. (2001), 'National systems of economic learning: the case of technology diffusion management in East Asia', *International Journal of Technology Management*, **22** (5/6), 455–79.

Nelson, R. and E. Phelps (1966), 'Investments in humans, technology and economic growth', *Journal of Economic Theory*, March, 69–75.

OECD (2005), 'Science, Technology and Industry Scoreboard 2005', Paris: OECD Science.

Recanatini, F., S. Wallsten and L. Xu (2000), 'Surveying surveys and questioning questions – learning from the World Bank experience', Policy Research Working Paper, 2307, The World Bank.

Rodriguez-Clare, A. (1996), 'Multinationals, linkages, and economic development', *American Economic Review*, **86** (4), 852–73.

Schumpeter, J.A. (1934 [1912]), *Theorie der Wirtschaftlichen Entwicklung*, Leipzig: Duncker & Humblot. English translation (1934): *The Theory of Economic Development*, Cambridge, MA: Harvard University Press.

Smarzynska, B. (2002), 'Does foreign direct investment increase the productivity of domestic firms? In search of spillovers through backward linkages', Policy Research Working Paper Series, 2923, The World Bank.

UNCTAD (2001), *World Investment Report. Promoting Linkages*, New York and Geneva: United Nations.

von Tunzelmann, N. and V. Acha (2005), 'Innovation in "low-tech" industries', in J. Fagerberg, D. Mowery and R. Nelson (eds), *The Oxford Handbook of Innovation*, Oxford: Oxford University Press, pp. 407–32.

World Bank (2007), 'World Bank's enterprise survey – how to implement the survey', http://www.enterprisesurveys.org/documents/Implementation_note.pdf.

Zanfei, A. (2000), 'Transnational firms and the changing organization of innovation', *Cambridge Journal of Economics*, **24**, 515–42.

APPENDIX 5A.1 DEFINITIONS OF VARIABLES

A. Firm size		
Micro/small	1–25 permanent workers	
Medium	26–75 permanent workers	
B. Firm sector		ISIC 3*
Confecc	Wearing apparel and fur	18
Bebalim	Food products and beverages	15
Qcpl	Chemicals and chemical products	24
Furnwood	Wood & products of wood & cork, excl. furniture	20
Leashoe	Leather and articles; footwear	19
Non-metal	Other non-metallic mineral products; Rubber and plastic products	26 25
Textile	Textiles	17
C. Internal (interfirm) networking		
Forown	10% or more of foreign capital main technol. channel = technology from headquarters	
D. External networking (intrafirm) foreign		
Forlicen	main technology channel = foreign licences	
Forsubcont	percentage of sales to MNCs >10%	
E. External networking (intrafirm) local		
Locsuppl	main technology channel = cooperation with local suppliers of machinery and equipment	
Locclient	main technol. channel = cooperation with client firms	
Loclic	main technology channel = licensing from local firms	
F. External networking – institutional local		
Locuniv	main technology channel = universities or public institutions	
Locchamb	main technology channel = from chamber of commerce	
G. Innovation inputs		
D&A	main technology channel = developing/adapting technology within the firm	
Newequip	main technology channel = acquiring new machinery / equipment	
humanK	main technology channel = hiring new personnel or consultants	

Note: * Industrial Standard International Classification.

Source: http://www.oecd.org/dataoecd/14/28/1936170.htm.

APPENDIX 5A.2 ICS QUESTIONNAIRE

Selected parts of Survey Questionnaire. Answers given by the establishment manager.

Banco Mundial **CID/ Gallup Latinoamérica**
Estudio empresarial **June 2003**

SECTION I. GENERAL INFORMATION

1.3 What percentage of your firm is owned by?........(total must sum 100)

a. Domestic Private Sector..%
b. Foreign Private Sector..%
c. Government/State..%
d. Other (Specify)..

Total: 100 %

1.9. How many persons in total work currently in this establishment (including managers, permanent workers, temporaries, part-time and subcontracted workers)?________________

a. Of these, how many are subcontracted?__________ (total of subcontracted workers)
b. And, how many are part-time/special contract workers?______ (total part-time workers/special contract)

SECTION II. MARKETS AND RELATIONS WITH CLIENTS

II.9. Approximately what percentage of your total sales are to. . .? **(total must sum 100)**

1. Exports (direct and indirect)%..%
   (must be equal to the sum of II.1.b.2 and II.1.b.3)
2. Central Government or state owned/ controlled enterprises.............%
3. Multinationals located in your country...%
4. Firms from the same group: your parent company or affiliated subsidiaries...%
5. Large domestic firms
   (those with approximately 150 plus workers)..................................%
6. Other domestic firms (those with less than 150 workers)..................%
7. Others: includes individuals...%

SECTION IX. CAPACITY, TECHNOLOGY AND INNOVATION

IX.9. **Card 22**: Over the last two years, has your company undertaken any of the following initiatives? Yes. . .1 No. . .2

1. Developed a major new product line.
2. Upgraded an existing product line.
3. Introduced new technology that has substantially changed the way that the main product is produced.
4. Discontinued at least one product (not production) line.
5. Opened a new plant.
6. Closed at least one existing plant or outlet.
7. Agreed a new joint venture with foreign partner.
8. Obtained a new licensing agreement.

IX.10. **Card 23**: What were the leading ways in which your establishment acquired technological innovations in the last three years (since 2000)? Please identify which of the following is (read 1 through 12). . .:
(use code –5 if you did not introduce innovations)
(1st more important) (2nd more important) (3rd more important)

1. Embodied in new machinery or equipment
2. By hiring key personnel
3. Licensing or turnkey operations from international sources
4. Licensing or turnkey operations from domestic sources
5. Developed or adapted within the establishment locally
6. Transferred from parent company
7. Developed in cooperation with client firms
8. Developed with equipment or machinery suppliers
9. From a business or industry association
10. Trade Fairs and/or Study Tours
11. Consultants
12. From universities, public institutions

6. Endogenous factors in regional performance: a review of research in Australia

Robert J. Stimson

There is an increasing interest in the role of endogenous factors in regional development. The literature places emphasis on factors such as regional industrial structure and diversification/specialization, human capital, population size and growth, leadership and institutional arrangements, in addition to the traditional concerns with regional resource endowments. The chapter reviews evidence from research in Australia on the role some endogenous factors play in differentiating regional performance in mainly non-metro settings.

6.1 EVOLVING APPROACHES TO REGIONAL ECONOMIC GROWTH

Understanding the nature and potential causes of spatial variation in regional economic performance is important in the context of developing and implementing regional policy. There has been an evolution in regional economic development literature from neoclassical theory based on the Solow (1956) model through to the 'new growth theory' (see Romer, 1986, 1990; Barro, 1990; Arthur, 1994), and a shift in emphasis from the importance of regional comparative advantage to regional competitive advantage and – more recently – collaborative advantage as regional economic development analysts have focused more and more on endogenous factors and processes in regional development and growth (see Johansson et al., 2001; Stimson, Stough and Roberts, 2006).

Neoclassical economic theory argued that there was a tendency for different units to converge over time because of assumed long-run diminishing returns to capital. However, the extent to which convergence occurs is important as it provides an indication of how different groups of people or regions are changing and growing relative to each other, and what might be influencing growth rates and levels of regional performance. Theory also suggested that regional growth derived from regional specialization based on comparative advantage, with stability achieved by spreading risk across a range of economic activities. But human capital development has many dimensions (White, 1987), with education and skills development performing both an integrative and an economic function in society.

There is, however, much debate on the issue of industrial diversification as against specialization, on the nature of regional growth and decline in industry sectors and also on the power of urban scale and agglomeration, particularly for industries such as advanced producer services (Kaufman, 1993; Lande, 1994; Gordon and McCann, 2000; Taylor et al., 2002; Bureau of Transport and Regional Economics, 2004a). While considerable support exists for the notion that industrial diversity and scale enhance regional development, it is also argued that diversity *per se* does not necessarily ensure better performance but might work to insulate a regional economy from exogenous shock effects. Striving for diversity as a regional economic development strategy might reflect a preference for slow and steady growth over a boom and bust economy so that policies should encourage stabilizing industries rather than having stable industries.

Duranton and Puga (2000) identified five 'stylized facts' concerning industry diversity and specialization, noting that: (i) specialized and diversified cities coexist; (ii) larger cities tend to be more diversified while cities of similar specialization are of similar size; (iii) individual city-size rankings and specializations tend to be stable over time; (iv) individual city growth relates to specialization and diversity and relative location; and (v) high rates of firm turnover exist, with most innovations taking place in particularly diversified cities where most new firms are created, and most relocations of firms are from diversified to specialized cities.

The importance of diversity as an attractor of 'new economy' activities (and in particular the innovative industry sectors) has been demonstrated by Henderson et al. (1995), who point out that a history of specialization does seem to matter for the more mature industry sectors. A region's industry structure output can differ greatly from its employment because of a whole set of factors, including its resource endowments and industry sector capital, and labour intensiveness and productivity. But there might be specific situational settings where that may not hold true.

In the contemporary era of globalization and the increasingly competitive environment in which both nations and their regions operate, human capital has assumed increasing significance as an endogenous factor in regional economic development. That has been addressed in OECD reports (1998; 2001a, 2001b, 2001c). But human capital development has many dimensions (White, 1987), with education and skills development both an integrative function and an economic function in society. Higher levels of education and skills have benefits, including higher employability, increased earnings and higher job quality. Many have argued that policies to enhance human capital development, have been important contributors to regional economic development helping regions to keep pace with the skills-intensive nature of the 'new economy' (Quiggin, 1999; OECD, 1998, 2001b; Hanushek and Kimko, 2000; Goetz and Rupasingha, 2001). However, 'the links between education, labour quality and productivity are complex' (Bureau of Transport and Regional Economics, 2004b, p. 1).

In Australia it has been suggested that the combined effects of the distribution of a region's economic activity across industry sectors, the mix of occupations, levels of human capital and the skills mix of jobs all influence the level and distribution of income in a region, the resilience of its economy and its ability to grow over time (Bureau of Transport and Regional Economics, 2004a, p. ix).

This chapter reviews evidence from Australian studies on the role endogenous factors might play in accounting for spatial variations in regional performance, in particular in non-metro settings.

6.2 SETTING THE CONTEXT

Australia is a large continent with diverse physical and economic landscapes. It is characterized by a high degree of urbanization, with about 70 per cent of the nation's 22 million people living in just five mega-metropolitan regions where an increasing share of economic activity is concentrated, especially in the services sectors. Much of the nation is largely uninhabited desert, with settlement being confined mainly to coastal areas and within the agricultural heartland that extends a few hundred kilometres inland. There is not a well-developed urban hierarchy, with the urban system deviating markedly from the theoretical distribution of the urban centres according to the rank-size rule. Across the non-metropolitan regions there is considerable economic diversity, reflecting the regional variations in the resource base of the national economy, especially in the agricultural, pastoral and mining sectors, as well as tourism.

A study by O'Connor et al. (2001) of Australia's changing economic geography up to the mid-1990s demonstrated how multiple social and economic divides had emerged, both within the metropolitan cities and across the nation's non-metropolitan regions. Divides have also been identified in other studies (such as Baum et al., 1999; Baum et al., 2006). Spatial mismatches are evident in regional shares of population and population change, and in shares of investment in economic activity. The research by O'Connor et al. (2001) raised a series of challenging implications for people-based and for place-based policy in addressing spatial disparities and the infrastructure needs of those segments and places in the space economy that are significant contributors to national wealth and competitiveness.

In the Australian context in particular, a region's industry structure, its occupation mix and its human capital structure are affected not only by the size of the region's economy and its resource endowments, but also by its level of remoteness in the context of the nation's settlement system. Understanding the dynamics underlying the spatial differences that exist in the economic development and performance of Australia's regions is a complex task, and has been approached from a number of perspectives by researchers. Many studies have investigated regional differentials in, and the interrelationships of, regional population size and growth, employment changes, structural shifts in industry employment, income levels, resource endowments and the locational characteristics of regions. However, relatively few studies have incorporated an explicit focus on the nature of occupational structure, occupational status, and education qualifications and skills, all of which are important components in the consideration of human capital differentials in regional development and performance. Research by economists, regional scientists and geographers has identified a range of factors influencing patterns of regional development and performance. But the specific conclusions reached and the relationships identified are not necessarily consistent because of the different focus of the studies and their different methodologies, variations in the spatial units of analysis used, and the different time periods analysed.

The sections that follow provide an overview of the findings from some of the research conducted in Australia that sheds light on the role of endogenous factors in differentials in regional performance, including some in which the author has been involved.

6.3 AN OVERVIEW OF RESEARCH ON REGIONAL DEVELOPMENT AND PERFORMANCE IN AUSTRALIA

6.3.1 A Focus on Regional Industrial Structure

Like many other advanced economies, Australia has experienced structural shifts over time to become less and less dependent first on agriculture and then on manufacturing, and for work to become more and more dependent on the services sectors. But the national patterns of structural change are reflected uniformly neither across the nation's six states and the territories, nor across the regions within them.

Aggregate-level analysis

At a highly aggregated level of scale, the Bureau of Transport and Regional Economics (2004a, pp. 10–12) has analysed changes over time in employment shares of industry sectors over the decade 1991–2001. A mixed pattern of performance across the states and territories was revealed, with the highest rate of employment growth in Queensland, closely followed by Western Australia and the Northern Territory, while in Tasmania and South Australia growth was relatively slow but positive. There was strong growth in business services across all states and territories. Growth was particularly strong in food retailing in Queensland and Tasmania; a modest fall in employment shares occurred in personal and household goods retailing in all states and territories. There was strong growth in the share of petroleum, coal, chemical and associated product manufacturing in Victoria and South Australia; in the share of construction in Western Australia and Victoria; and growth in all states and territories in property services. The community services sector grew strongly, as did employment shares in libraries, museums and arts; personal services; and accommodation, cafes and restaurants (except in the Northern Territory). But in all states and territories there was a decline in employment shares in agriculture; there was a considerable decline in employment shares in metal ore mining in the Northern Territory and Western Australia;[1] and employment shares in finance and insurance declined in all states and territories. There was an increase in employment shares in government administration and defence industries in the Northern Territory, but declines in all the other states and in the Australian Capital Territory, particularly Victoria.

A degree of commonality was evident across the states and territories in some of the trends in industry structure shifts over the decade 1991 to 2001, but at the same time some industries in some of the states and territories experienced either greater growth or greater decline than in others. But an important finding from the Bureau of Transport and Regional Economics (2004a) research was there was *not* an overall pattern of convergence across the industry sectors, which reflected not only broad historic regional specialization at the aggregate level of scale, but also broad regional differentials in the adjustments state and territory economies were making *vis-à-vis* national trends.

The Bureau of Transport and Regional Economics (2004a, p. 12) also used location quotient (LQ) analysis of industry sector employment shares relative to their national employment shares over the decade 1991 to 2001 to demonstrate that states and territories did have distinctive patterns of specialization. And the study also used the Australian Remoteness Classes spatial framework to analyse the relative importance of industries by employment across Australia at the 2001 census. The research showed that retail trade was the largest employment sector in the major cities and inner regional parts of Australia, but it was surpassed by agriculture, forestry and fishing in the outer regional and remote and very remote regions. The relative importance of employment in agriculture, forestry and fishing; mining; and accommodation, cafés and restaurants increased with remoteness. The importance of employment in manufacturing; wholesale trade; cultural and recreational services; finance and insurance: property and business services; and communication services declined with increasing remoteness, with the last three of those industry sectors being important employment sectors employment in the major cities. The importance of employment in electricity, gas and water supply; retail trade; health and community services; education; and construction peaked in inner regional parts of Australia. Government administration and defence employment peaked in the remote and very remote regions, reflecting the participation of indigenous persons in the Commonwealth Government's Community Development Employment Programme (CDEP). Business services were most important in the major cities, and education was the most important source of employment in the inner regional area. Agriculture was the most important source of employment in outer regional areas and in the remote and very remote regions of Australia.

The Bureau of Transport and Regional Economics (2004a) research showed that over the decade 1991–2001 the strongest growth in total employment was found in inner regional Australia (20 per cent), followed by the major cities class (18 per cent), outer regional (10 per cent), and the remote and very remote Australia classes (1 per cent); business services grew strongly across remoteness classes, but, not surprisingly, was strongest in the major cities. The inner regional Australia class experienced very strong growth in food retailing, while community services growth was particularly strong in the inner regional and outer regional areas. Construction trade services and accommodation, cafés and restaurants employment grew across all remoteness classes; government administration employment had the highest growth in remote and very remote regions (because of CDEP); and agriculture declined in the inner regional, outer regional, remote and very remote regions, while remaining unchanged in the major cities. And the share of employment in finance and insurance declined significantly in all the remoteness classes. As expected, the LQ analysis showed that the patterns of specialization of employment in industry sectors varied considerably according to the centrality and remoteness classes.

Disaggregating the level of analysis

At a more disaggregated level, research findings indicate that the extent of diversification/specialization in employment across industry sectors in Australia is indicative of the degree to which a local labour market provides job opportunities for a wider range or a more restricted range of occupation and education skill levels. In this context, regional industry structure trends and patterns may be analysed in many ways. For example, the focus can be on industry sectors to determine either: (i) the degree of diversity or specialization in the distribution of employment across industry sectors in regions at a point in time, and how, over time, a region's industry structure may have diversified or become more specialized; or (ii) the extent to which an industry is dispersed across a nation's regions. In context (i), where the focus is on the region, it is also possible to identify those industry sectors in which a region tends to specialize and in which there is an above 'average' share of employment in an industry sector relative to the national picture. Both considerations are important in developing an understanding of trends and patterns of regional industry structure.

It is commonly hypothesized in the regional science literature that the larger a regional economy, the more diverse will be its industry sector employment opportunities, while often smaller places and places with a specific comparative advantage for particular types of economic production – which may reflect the region's particular resource endowments – have more restricted employment opportunities as their regional economies are characterized by a higher degree of industry specialization. Industry sector employment structure does seem to be a significant factor in explaining regional differences in economic growth.

The Bureau of Transport and Regional Economics (2004a) research revealed that considerable variations exist in the industry structure across the 425 labour market regions (LMRs) into which the Bureau divided Australia, as well as in the shifts occurring over time in the industrial structure of LMRs. Research by the Productivity Commission (2003) showed that often structural change is essential for regions to take full advantage of new opportunities for growth, even though it can impose costs and disadvantage for some groups in a community. The Bureau of Transport and Regional Economics (2004a, p. 18) analysis of LMRs revealed that while agriculture employed only 3.5 per cent of workers nationally in 2001, it was the dominant industry employer in 276 LMRs, and it was either the second- or third-largest employer in a further 52 LMRs. A number of other industry sectors also were the dominant employment source in between 20 and 30 LMRs, including government administration; metal ore mining; education; health services; and accommodation, cafés and restaurants. Education was among the top three employing industries in more than 70 per cent of the LMRs. And despite its increasing prominence in the national economy, business services was the major employing industry in 2001 in just five LMRs, all being centred on five capital cities (Sydney, Melbourne, Brisbane, Perth and Darwin).

Using the 'coefficient of industry (employment) localization'[2] to measure the extent to which an industry sector had dispersed across LMRs at the 2001 census, the Bureau of Transport and Regional Economics (2004a) study showed that the most localized (68 per cent) were primary industries – coal mining; commercial fishing; agriculture; forestry and logging. Outside the primary industries, sectors with highest degree of localization were defence and rail transport (43 per cent). Service industries had a very low degree of localization, with almost all having coefficients of 7 per cent or less. Manufacturing employment was more localized than the services sector industries, but it was less localized than the primary industries. Manufacturing industry coefficients ranged between 16 and 32 per cent. Over the decade 1991 to 2001 employment had become much less localized for a number of industries, including: manufacturing; services to agriculture, hunting and trapping; libraries, museums and the arts; forestry and logging; property services; and metal ore mining. But there was a marked increase in localization for rail transport and defence.

Other research focused on the differential performance of urban centres and localities (UCLs) across Australia. Stimson, Baum et al. (2004) used 2001 census data to compute an industry specialization/diversification index across 17 industry sectors (at the 2-digit level of the Standard Industry Classification). The national benchmark index was 35.21, indicating a relatively diverse mix of employment opportunities across industries. Stimson, Baum et al. (2004) report that there were relatively small variations between the capital cities of the states and territories in industry specialization/diversification, while in general the non-metropolitan regional UCLs had slightly higher levels of specialization. However, there were extremely wide variations across Australia in the degree to which UCLs had diversified or specialized industry structures.

In an investigation of the concentration and dispersion of employment in industry sectors, the Bureau of Transport and Regional Economics (2004a, pp. 21–3) calculated LQs in 2001 for its LMR geography. That disaggregated level of spatial analysis identified likely patterns of regional-level comparative advantage. Such analysis is important, but for many of the LMRs, a particular industry for which a region had a large LQ might, in fact, be based on a very small total employment. The research revealed agriculture as the most frequently featured industry as the top specialization in 112 of the LMRs, and it was one of the top three industry specializations for almost two-thirds of the LMRs. Other primary industries also featured frequently among the top three specializations, especially commercial fishing, forestry and logging, metal ore mining, and services to agriculture, hunting and trapping. There were a variety of economic activities where regions specialized beyond the primary industries, with only seven out of 53 industries not featuring among the top three specializations for at least one LMR.

The Bureau of Transport and Regional Economics (2004a) research also found that the larger the regional economy (measured by persons employed), the more likely it would be for regional employment specialization to exist in the finance and insurance and in business services. But other industry specializations were less closely tied to region size.

However, it was evident that the majority of Australia's LMRs were highly specialized in one or more primary industries for employment. Not surprisingly, regions underspecialized in primary industry employment tended to be centred on the capital cities and major coastal centres. There were LMRs in the far northern and central parts of Australia, with an underrepresentation of primary industry employment, mainly regions concentrating on mining and tourism. Regions with more than half of their employment in primary industries were especially geographically concentrated in inland south-west and mid-west Western Australia and inland Queensland.

Regional specializations of employment concentration appeared to change relatively slowly over time, although over the decade 1991 to 2001 the number of LMRs where government administration was one of the top three industry specializations (probably due to CDEP) did increase, and there was a decline in the number of regions specializing in rail transport and in 'other services'. Regional dependence on manufacturing specialization had generally declined, which was in line with the fall in employment and increased productivity in manufacturing as identified in research by the Productivity Commission (2003).

Industrial diversity and size of a regional economy

Research by Stimson, Baum et al. (2004) specifically investigated relationships between the urban hierarchy effect and industrial employment specialization/diversification across UCLs in the states and territories. Correlation analysis was used to investigate the relationship between the scores of UCLs on that index and the log of their population in 2001. As expected, there was a negative correlation, confirming the well-established hypothesis that industrial diversification is associated with urban size. However, the correlation coefficients were not particularly high, ranging from only –0.24 in Queensland and –0.27 in New South Wales, the most populous state with a relatively well-developed urban hierarchy, to a high of –0.37 in both the Northern Territory and Tasmania, with small populations.

The Bureau of Transport and Regional Economics (2004a) analysis of its LMRs explicitly examined the relationship between industrial employment diversification and the size of the regional economy for LMRs. It showed that the larger a region's economy,[3] the more likely it was to have a diversified industrial base. A total of 156 LMRs with more than 3000 employed persons had a diversity index below 85 per cent.[4]

Regional diversity and unemployment

Research by Trendle and Shorney (2003) investigated the relationship between regional industry diversity and unemployment in the State of Queensland. Using data from the 1996 and 2001 censuses, along with small area labour market data and Australian Tax Office data,[5] the study investigated a number of hypothesized relationships, including those between: (i) the level of regional diversification and a region's employment growth and the instability of that growth; (ii) regional diversity and regional unemployment rates and the instability of that rate; and (iii) the diversity of a regional economy and the stability of regional income. The researchers tested for spatial dependence. Simple and rank correlation coefficients measure those relationships, and linear regression analysis, using the Chow test for structural break, investigated the relationship between regional unemployment and regional diversity.

The research findings supported the hypothesis that industrial diversity had a significant influence on regional economic performance, and the relationship between diversity and regional instability and that between diversity and regional employment growth were as hypothesized in the regional economic development literature. But the results did not support the hypothesis that regional industrial diversity has a significant influence on regional per capita income.

Trendle and Shorney (2003) suggested that the relationship between the unemployment rate and industrial diversity might be more complex than proposed in the literature. The evidence from their analysis of Queensland LGAs suggested that industrial diversity varies according to the size of the regional labour force. They also used a Moran scatter plot to test for the stability of regional unemployment rates. The results suggested that the spatial diversity of LGAs sharing similar unemployment was not significant, and that variations in regional unemployment did not occur randomly over the state's space economy. A series of maps was produced to identify groupings of LGAs that have significant unemployment rates, unemployment instability, employment instability, employment growth and income instability. That work built on previous analyses by Trendle (1999, 2002), where he modelled regional diversification using a portfolio framework to investigate regional variations in unemployment rates across Queensland's LGAs using OLS (ordinary least squares) analysis.

Is Australia's regional industry structure diversifying?

From the foregoing discussion, an important question to address is whether Australia's regional industry structure is diversifying. The evidence is variable.

Bradley and Gans (1998) and Hogan et al. (1999), among others, have noted that Australia's regions are becoming more industrially diverse. But those studies have tended to be conducted at the highly aggregated level of statistical divisions (SDs). At a more disaggregated level of scale, the Bureau of Transport and Regional Economics (2004a) calculated a structural change index (SCI) for its LMRs to estimate the degree of change in industry structural employment over the two successive inter-censal periods, 1991–96 and 1996–2001, and as well for the decade 1991 to 2001.[6] For Australia as a whole, the SCI for the decade 1991 to 2001 was 12 per cent, meaning that 'to restore the employment mix in existence in 1991, 12 per cent of employed persons in 2001 would have to change industries' (p. 28). The structural change was much greater for the inter-censal period 1991–96 than it was for the period 1996–2001, while employment growth was stronger for the 1996–2001 component of that decade.

The Bureau of Transport and Regional Economics (2004a) also computed an industrial diversity index for its LMRs, noting that 'nationally, the diversity index has fallen from 96.2 per cent in 1991 to 95.6 per cent in 2001, indicating a small overall decline in industrial diversity' (p. 26). However, the study showed how:

> many more regions experienced an increase in industrial diversity, than experienced a decline. . . . [That] . . . seeming contradiction is due to the fact that, of Australia's capital cities, only Darwin experienced an increase in industrial diversity. For example, Sydney's diversity index decreased from 96.2 per cent to 95.2 per cent, meaning employment became rather less evenly distributed across industries over the decade. Between 1991 and 2001, the industry structure of employment has become less diversified for Australia's major cities, while other regions (on the whole) have become more industrially diverse. (Ibid.)

The Bureau of Transport and Regional Economics (2004a) analysis of structural change in industry employment across LMRs highlighted a number of significant dimensions of regional variation in industry sector employment growth and decline over the decade 1991–2001. The complexity of change occurring across Australia's regions did seem to be taking on new dimensions as some areas experienced increases in industrial diversity while others experienced a decrease in industrial diversity. The SCI analysis showed that all the LMRs had experienced some degree of structural change over the decade 1991–2001, with 75 per cent of regions having an SCI of between 10 and 20 per cent. But change was greatest in the remote regions that lack industrial diversity, and in general the larger regions – and especially those centred on the capital cities – had experienced relatively little change.

Those research findings seem to suggest that new dynamics were occurring across Australia's space economy. An earlier study of structural change in Australia for the period 1961 to 1976 (Department of Home Affairs and the Environment, 1982) – before the onset of the end of the period of post-World War II boom and the beginning of the late twentieth century era of globalization, deregulation and economic restructuring – had found that the large cities underwent less change than the smaller cities. More recently the Productivity Commission (1998) found that smaller regions were experiencing the greatest rates of structural change. The Bureau of Transport and Regional Economics (2004a) research findings might lead one to question that simple dichotomy, and the findings of its research suggest that a more complex picture might exist of regional patterns of industry structural change.

6.3.2 A Focus on Regional Population and Employment Growth

Numerous studies have focused on the relationship between regional population and employment growth in Australia. For example, Bradley and Gans (1998) used regression analysis of population and labour force growth in Australia's cities to demonstrate that labour force growth over the period 1981–91 was positively correlated with a city's previous growth and its level of industrial diversity, and that labour force growth was negatively related to the initial size of the city and to government employment share.

In another study, Garnaut et al. (2001) investigated regional influences on employment and population growth, finding that metropolitan and coastal regions experienced stronger population and employment growth than inland and remote regions over the decade 1986–96. Growth in inland and remote regions was strongest in and around the largest towns. Incomes were high in remote regions, reflecting fast employment growth in the mining and welfare sectors and the need to pay high wages to recruit workers to regions seen to have low amenity.

In yet a further study, Lawson and Dwyer (2002) used regression analysis of employment growth across 637 regions for the decade 1986–96 to show that regions were more likely to experience employment growth if they had high employment in accommodation, cafés and restaurants or high industrial diversity at the beginning of the decade. Regions experiencing strong structural change were also more likely to have had employment growth. Less significant factors associated with the likelihood of a region experiencing employment growth included a region having a coastal location and a high employment share in property and business services. Relatively remote regions and regions with high concentrations of employment in the electricity, gas and water supply sector were less likely to experience employment growth.

6.3.3 A Focus on Human Capital

Research by the Bureau of Transport and Regional Economics (2004b, pp. 23–6) suggests that a good guide to a region's performance is the quality of its labour market. Thus the level of education, skills and qualifications of a region's population is an important consideration. In recent years, there has been a great deal of interest among researchers in Australia on the nature of regional variations in these and other aspects of human capital.

Aggregate analysis of education and skills

There is conflicting evidence on the correlation between regional education and skills and employment growth. A rise in qualification levels has been occurring in general in Australia, but that has not necessarily been reflected in shifts in occupation shares.

At the aggregate level of the states and territories, the Bureau of Transport and Regional Economics (2004b, pp. 17–18) investigated patterns of change in education and occupation levels over the decade 1991 to 2001. It showed that the highest qualification and occupation levels were in the Australian Capital Territory and the States of Victoria and New South Wales (the most populous states), while Tasmania and Queensland recorded the lowest proportions of highly skilled people at the 2001 census. Queensland, the Northern Territory and Tasmania had the lowest levels of workers with high-status occupations. South Australia had a similar education structure to Queensland, but an occupation structure a little more balanced towards the higher professions. Western Australia and the Northern Territory had the highest proportions of skilled vocational workers. Queensland, Western Australia and New South Wales had education growth rates above the national average, while South Australia,

Victoria, the Australian Capital Territory and Queensland had growth rates above the average in the highest-status occupations. Queensland, Tasmania and the Northern Territory had achieved shares of the highest educational category closer to the national average, while in South Australia and Western Australia the shares of those people diverged more from the national average by the end of the decade. The distribution of skilled workers and professionals across the states and territories showed a decline of skilled trade workers across most states, with growth only in Western Australia, Queensland and the Northern Territory. All the states and territories had increased their number of professionals in teaching, health and computing, with Western Australia and Queensland leading, and those two states also had an increase in building engineers.

It is common for the big cities to have the highest concentrations of jobs requiring high levels of skills and for there to be marked metropolitan/non-metropolitan differences in levels of qualifications. Thus it was not surprising to see large differences in the incidence of the education and occupation levels shares across the remoteness structure of regions in Australia. The Bureau of Transport and Regional Economics (2004b p. 23) concluded that:

> The majority of the remoteness classes showed some evidence of equalising results within their remoteness category for both education and occupation outcomes. In particular, regions within the major cities, inner regional and very remote classes demonstrated a tendency to equalise outcomes over 1991 to 2001.

Disaggregated analysis: patterns of derived indices of human capital performance across the settlement system

Stimson, Baum et al. (2004) analysed the degree of variation existing in levels of human capital across UCLs in Australia's states and territories. Using a principal components analysis of 2001 census data on the distribution of levels of educational attainment in UCLs, three human capital indices were derived relating to: (i) university-qualified people and post-secondary participation in university education; (ii) technical qualified people and post-secondary participation in technical education; and (iii) people with no qualifications other than basic schooling.

The national benchmark score on the Stimson, Baum et al. (2004) human capital university index was 28.55. However, the range of scores of UCLs on that index varied greatly, especially across the urban systems of Victoria and New South Wales, the two most populous states with the most developed urban hierarchies. Queensland also had a wide range in UCL scores. Among the metropolitan cities, Sydney, Canberra, Melbourne, Brisbane and Perth had the highest average scores, while

Hobart and Adelaide had markedly lower scores. On average, regional UCLs in Victoria had the highest, and regional UCLs in the Northern Territory and Tasmania had the lowest, scores. When mapped, the overall spatial pattern of UCL performance on the human capital university index revealed a marked concentration of UCLs with low scores across inland areas and remote parts of Australia. Many of those places were small towns and indigenous settlements. But also some of the rapidly growing coastal towns in 'sun-belt' locations were poor performers. The larger towns in the wheat–sheep belt, some of the large towns along the coast, and the remotely located mining towns had the highest scores on the index.

The national benchmark level for the Stimson, Baum et al. (2004) human capital technical index was 34.52. In contrast to the patterns for the human capital university index, in general regional UCLs tended to do much better on the human capital technical index. Among the metropolitan cities Hobart had, on average, the highest score, followed by Perth, Sydney, Canberra and Melbourne, and Darwin had the lowest score. On average, regional UCLs in New South Wales had the highest scores, followed by Tasmania, South Australia and Western Australia, and regional UCLs in the Northern Territory on average had the lowest scores. New South Wales and Queensland had the highest range in the distribution of UCL scores. In the Northern Territory, the overall level of scores of regional UCLs was much lower than in any of the states, reflecting the high preponderance of remote, small indigenous settlements in the Northern Territory. The striking contrast in the pattern of index scores on the human capital technical index compared with that for the human capital university index score was that the incidence of high scores on the former was much more common across the towns of the wheat–sheep belt and along the coastal areas, and the remote mining towns and many of the old industrial towns (such as those in South Australia's 'iron triangle' region) have high scores. Those UCLs with the lowest scores on the human capital technical index were many of the smaller inland towns and the remote, small indigenous settlements, and some of the large regional centres that scored highly on the human capital university index.

The national benchmark score on the human capital no qualifications index was 55.80. Stimson, Baum et al. (2004) noted that in many ways the pattern of UCL scores on this index was the opposite of the pattern for the other two derived human capital indices just discussed. Of the metropolitan cities, Hobart and Adelaide on average had the highest scores on the index, well above the national benchmark score. The regional UCLs in the Northern Territory, Tasmania, Queensland and New South Wales on average had high scores. Both Queensland and the Northern Territory had a large range in UCL scores, while New South Wales and Victoria had a lower incidence of regional UCLs with high scores. Both South Australia and Tasmania tended to have a lesser incidence of regional UCLs with low scores, reflecting a better human capital performance. Queensland, South Australia and the Northern Territory – all with a relatively high preponderance of small and remote indigenous settlements – had a relatively high proportion of places with high scores. The pattern across Australia of UCL scores on the human capital, no qualifications index showed that the better-performing places tended to be concentrated in the inland wheat–sheep belt and in many of the other agricultural regions, and as well in some of the coastal service and tourism towns. The poorer-performing places were widely spread across the smaller towns of the inland farming and pastoral regions, parts of the coastal regions, and the small and remote indigenous settlements.

Human capital across labour market regions

Research by the Bureau of Transport and Regional Economics (2004b) using its LMR geography revealed that LMRs in inland areas – and in particular in the remote locations – had the lowest proportions of highly educated people, and that was especially evident in Queensland and South Australia. This was also the case to an extent in the remote areas of Western Australia and the Northern Territory, but there were some LMRs that had above average proportions of highly qualified people, in particular associated with the mining, health, education, and community services sectors. The pattern of distribution of tertiary qualified people across LMRs showed that it was predominantly the east coast regions and the capital cities that had the highest concentrations. The research also identified those non-capital city LMRs with the most highly qualified people in each industry sector. The analysis revealed that

> many regions lack workers with higher formal qualifications across a range of local industries. However, some non-capital regions are clearly demonstrating high levels of highly educated workers across a variety of local industries. (p. 26)

Some of those regions have been described by Salt (2001) as 'sea-change' towns, places that had been attracting in-migrants from the capital cities, often to retire. Some of them were displaying high levels of knowledge-based economic activity and had a university.

The UCL based study by Stimson, Baum et al. (2004) also showed that it was the coastal and the inland towns that are large regional service centres with a university campus that had the highest levels of incidence of people with high levels of human capital outside the metropolitan cities.

Regional population size, the settlement hierarchy effect and human capital
The analysis by the Bureau of Transport and Regional Economics (2004b) of the education, skills and qualifications performance of its LMRs revealed that LMRs with a greater number of employed people also were likely to have higher shares of tertiary qualified people. In general, LMRs in remote and inland locations tended to have relatively low shares of highly educated and skilled people. And the Stimson, Baum et al. (2004) research certainly showed that there was a marked regional pattern to the distribution of UCL scores on the human capital indices and on the occupation and skills diversification indices.

However, as the Bureau of Transport and Regional Economics (2004b, p. 29) study pointed out, some of the LMRs in the sparsely populated areas of Australia – including many of the mining towns – did have high shares of tertiary qualified people, and some of the 'sea-change' coastal towns in the 'sun-belt' areas with lifestyle advantages had also attracted relatively high shares of university qualified people.

Stimson, Baum et al. (2004) conducted a correlation analysis for each of the states and the Northern Territory to measure the nature of the relationship between UCL scores on: (i) the three human capital indices – university, technical and no qualifications – that have been discussed above; (ii) an industry, occupation and skills specialization/diversification index compiled by those researchers; and (iii) the log of population of UCLs. In that way the urban hierarchy effects could be ascertained. From that analysis it was evident that, on the one hand, there was a positive correlation between the population size of UCLs and their performance on the human capital university and the human capital technical indices, but that the positive relationship was stronger for the university human capital index. Conversely, there was a negative correlation between population size of UCLs and their performance on the human capital no qualifications index. Those findings indicated that larger urban places did better in terms of regional human capital performance. But what the correlation coefficients did show was that that relationship was not particularly strong in a statistical sense, except in the Northern Territory, which was alone among the states in having a correlation coefficient in excess of ± 0.40 for any of those relationships.

Those results of the Stimson, Baum et al. (2004) research, along with some of the findings from the Bureau of Transport and Regional Economics (2004b) research, suggested regional size or position up or down the urban hierarchy did matter *vis-à-vis* the human capital performance of a place. But there were some UCLs down the urban hierarchy that performed well on the human capital dimensions. The Stimson, Baum et al. (2004) analysis also revealed a negative correlation between the size of the population of a UCL, but again the correlation was not particularly high. Similarly there was a negative correlation between the population size of UCLs and their scores on the skills specialization/diversification index.

The Stimson, Baum et al. (2004) research also showed that both diversity of occupational opportunity and diversity of employment for local populations with a wide mix of skills were more likely to be found in larger places up the urban hierarchy. But the results of the correlation analysis suggested that a degree of both occupation and skills diversification could be found in some smaller places further down the urban hierarchy.

Modelling the relationship between education and skills and regional performance

Several studies have modelled the relationship between aspects of human capital and regional performance across Australia. For example, Lawson and Dwyer (2002) used a binomial logit model, discovering that there was no significant correlation between education levels and regional employment growth. However, a complementary regression suggested that a higher proportion of skilled people would be associated with higher rates of regional growth in employment. Regions with low education and skills had stronger rates of out-migration, which may be a reflection of skilled workers being more likely to leave less-educated regions because of diminishing employment opportunities. But the researchers were unable to find a significant correlation between in-migration and education and skills levels.

Draca et al. (2003) conducted a cross-sectional analysis of the relationship between education, skills and qualifications and the economic performance of five mainland states of Australia. The results showed that differences in education, skills and qualifications might explain between 10 and 20 per cent of the variation in gross state product (GSP) per capita for Victoria, Queensland and South Australia. High skill qualifications and job were important but did not have to dominate the labour force to achieve economic performance.

Another study by Garnett and Lewis (2000) suggested that 'an examination of rural education levels, and changes over time, is an important aspect of any analysis of labour markets' (p. 168). This was particularly so in rural and regional areas. The researchers pointed out that while the proportion of people holding a degree in rural and regional areas was lower than it was in the metropolitan cities, the gap narrowed between 1991 and 1996, even though it still stood at 19.2 per cent for the major urban areas compared to 8.5 per cent in rural localities and 10.9 per cent in the rural balance regions. That finding was not surprising as many rural occupations are not in professional fields, and thus do not offer the returns to investment in human capital that is the case in the big cities and larger regional centres. The out-migration of people from rural communities to larger towns and to the big cities is due to a number of factors that have been operating for a long time, but it has been exacerbated by low terms of trade for farmers and a decline in rural services such as banking, health and education in the smaller urban centres and localities.

Garnett and Lewis (2000) referred to research that revealed how 'it has long been recognized that rural [and regional] education facilities are worse than those available in metropolitan areas, and participation rates are also lower' (p. 167). That has been demonstrated in work by Harrison (1997), while research by Norris and Wooden (1996) had suggested that the difference in quality and levels of formal education might partially explain why people are migrating out of rural and regional Australia, and especially from smaller communities. And it might help explain why it is that, in general, unemployment rates are higher in rural and regional areas than they are in the metropolitan cities.

A focus on regional variations in income

The level of human capital is also reflected in part in the level of regional income. Research by the National Centre for Social and Economic Modelling (NATSEM) investigating differences in regional performance (Lloyd et al., 2000) revealed that a 'hollowing out' had occurred in the income distribution of average household incomes across all regions in Australia between 1991 and 1996. That research revealed that four-fifths of households living in the large metropolitan cities and the largest regional towns had about twice as many high-income households and a much smaller population of low-income households. The populations of both high- and low-income households had in fact increased across all regions. The regional cities and towns had experienced a similar fall to that in the big cities in the proportion of middle-income households. But the largest change was apparent in the rural towns, where low-income households increased substantially while the proportion of high-income households increased only marginally.

Lloyd et al. (2000, p. 290) referred to a 'widening income gap' between those living in affluent areas and those living in the middle-ranked areas, with those at the bottom appearing to having fared somewhat better than those in the middle of the income distribution.

A focus on technology-based development

The Bureau of Transport and Regional Economics (2004a) claims that 'technology and knowledge-based industries are of greatest importance to Australia's largest cities and university towns' (p. 19). Its research analysing trends over the decade 1991–2001 in the shares of employment in technology- and knowledge-intensive industries found that those shares declined as remoteness increased; the share was highest for the major cities remoteness structure class (40 per cent); the shares dropped to 32 per cent for the inner regional class, 26 per cent for the outer regional, and 22 per cent for the remote and the very remote Australia classes.

Using its LMR geography, the Bureau's research showed that the LMRs centred on three of the capital cities – Sydney, Melbourne and Adelaide – all had 41 per cent shares of employment in technology-based industries, while the LMR centred on the inland regional city of Armidale in New South Wales – home to the University of New England – had a 40 per cent employment share. Other LMRs with employment shares in technology- and knowledge-based industries above the national average of 37 per cent were those centred on the capital cities of Queensland and Western Australia – Brisbane and Perth – and the regional cities of Orange, Ballarat and Geelong, all with universities.

In their analysis of community opportunity and vulnerability in regional cities and towns across Australia, Stimson, Baum et al. (2004) identified a cluster of larger regional towns that formed one of their 'opportunity' clusters where the presence of a university enhanced the way that those places coped with socioeconomic change over the decade 1991–2001.

6.3.4 Relationships Between Regional Growth, Industry Structure, Human Capital, and Qualification and Occupation Levels

Some research in Australia has focused more specifically on the overall relationships between regional growth, industry structure and human capital (where the focus has been on qualification and occupation levels). But relatively little of that research has been conducted below the aggregate level of the six states and territories or the 56 statistical divisions (SD) across the nation.

Forecasting regional growth at an aggregate level

In a study based on SDs, Adams (2002) predicted that, over the period 1996/97–2007/08, all regions would grow and that growth rates were expected to converge or become more similar. It predicted that the level of average growth in real value added would range from a top of 4.7 per cent per annum growth in Perth SD (the capital city of Western Australia) to a low of 1.82 per annum growth in the Eyre SD in regional South Australia. The analysis told how 'mining and agricultural concentrations explain the extreme rankings of several regions' (p. 12). That included the goldfields, wheat-belt and mid-west in Western Australia, where relatively poor growth was forecast. But a presence of mining did not necessarily prevent a region from doing well or poorly. Likewise the absence of agriculture did not prevent a region from having a relatively low forecast, and nor did it ensure strong growth.

Beer (2002) used the Adams (2002) analysis to argue that there were five key determinants of the likely growth rates of SDs across Australia, namely: (i) local-level demand, whereby regions in states with strong growth prospects –Western Australia and Queensland – were more likely to grow strongly due to the growth impulses of those states; (ii) diversity of the production base, whereby regions with more diverse and more multi-tiered economies have better prospects because they are not reliant on one or two industries; (iii) identification and use of natural advantages for the benefit of the region, which embraced both locational advantages (such as access to major markets) and the use of resources (such as good water supplies and an attractive environment); (iv) efficient and sustainable use of natural resources, which was a key determinant of growth prospects, with unsustainable use of resources inhibiting growth; and (v) willingness of regions and their leaders to adjust to technological and other external changes, which greatly influences their rate of growth.

Disaggregating the analysis

Analysis of regional growth at a more disaggregated scale by the Bureau of Transport and Regional Economics (2004a, 2004b) used four approaches to look at the effects of: (i) national shifts in employment on regional growth; (ii) initial industry structure on regional growth; (iii) industrial diversity; and (iv) the level of education, skills and qualifications. One explanation of differences in regional employment growth proposed was that some strongly performing regions are more specialized in rapidly growing industry sectors like mining.

Shift-share analysis was used to shed light on that proposition through an investigation of the national shift component of employment change by industry sectors in LMRs over the decade 1996–2001. The modelling showed that:

> actual regional employment growth rates were much more widely dispersed than the hypothetical growth rates . . . [i.e. those derived from the national component of the shift-share analysis] . . . [But] . . . despite this, the actual and hypothetical employment growth rates were positively correlated, and the relationship was statistically significant. About 20 per cent of variation in employment growth rates across regions could be explained by the industry structure of regional employment in 1991, and subsequent national growth trends by industry. (p. 33)

That finding of 20 per cent was much below the 38 per cent found in an earlier study by the Productivity Commission (1998) for the period 1981–96, but the difference might have been due to the use of the smaller size of the LMRs in the Bureau's study compared to the large statistical subdivisions used in the Productivity Commission's analysis. However, the results also confirmed the proposition that more recent change in growth rates for industry sector employment varies more across regions because of endogenous factors.

The Bureau of Transport and Regional Economics (2004a, 2004b) research also investigated regional patterns of growth using growth in real tax income between 1990–91 and 1999–2000 as a proxy for economic growth. Part of that analysis grouped LMRs into quintiles based on their rate of growth in total real taxable income. The research highlighted differentials in the initial 1991 industry structure of LMRs across income growth quintiles, and those differentials exceed employment growth in all but the first income quintile, with the lowest two income quintiles income growth accounting for a relatively small share of employment growth.

In addition, the Bureau of Transport and Regional Economics (2004a, 2004b) used multivariate regression analysis of LMR income growth, 1990–91–1999–2000 to show that – after controlling for state/territory, size of regional economy, mean income and educational qualifications – the 1991 ANZSIC division industry sector employment shares were a statistically significant grouping of variables explaining regional variation in income growth. The model explained 42 per cent of the variation in income growth rates across LMRs, demonstrating that industry-intensive variables were significant predictors of income instability.

To test in the Australian context the applicability of Kaufman's (1993) finding in the USA that a diverse employment base creates stability and buffers the economic performance of a region against the effects of an economic shock, the Bureau of Transport and Regional Economics (2004a) researchers attempted the difficult task of isolating the relationship between industrial diversity and economic growth/stability. That analysis, using the LMR geography, provided evidence of a strong and statistically significant association between industrial diversification and income instability (with $r = -0.61$). LMRs with a low level of industrial diversity in 1991 tended to have relatively unstable incomes between 1990–91 and 1999–2000. The relationship between industrial diversity and total real taxable income was weaker ($r = +0.26$). But, in accordance with the proposition that more diverse regional economies tended to experience higher growth, the bivariate correlation between industrial diversity and income growth was present because the size of a regional economy is closely related to both industrial diversity and income growth.

Thus the Bureau of Transport and Regional Economics (2004a) also conducted a multivariate regression analysis of income growth – and, separately, instability – against the 1991 industrial diversification index, controlling for state/territory size of the regional economy, average income, Bachelor degree qualifications, and ANZSIC division employment shares of LMRs in 1991. The results indicated that the 'initial level of industrial diversity was a statistically significant explanatory of variation on income growth across regions' (p. 40).

Those results were consistent with Kaufman's (1993) findings in the USA, thus supporting the notion that industrial diversity is 'closely related to stability of economic performance, rather than to economic growth *per se*' (Bureau of Transport and Regional Economics, 2004a, p. 40).

In addition, the Bureau of Transport and Regional Economics (2004b, pp. 33–4) also examined the relationship between education and occupation levels and economic growth across LMRs and growth in total real taxable income between 1990–91 and 1999–2000. It found that for all five quintiles of income growth for the LMRs there was a link between high shares of tertiary qualified people and high-income growth, with income decline and minimal change being associated with relatively low 1991 shares of people with a Bachelor or higher degree qualifications for all regions, whether agricultural or regional. High shares of intermediary and elementary workers were associated with income decline in both agricultural and non-agricultural regions.

6.4 TYPOLOGIES OF REGIONAL URBAN CENTRE PERFORMANCE

Over the years, a number of studies conducted in Australia have developed typologies of regional performance for the nation's regional urban centres.

6.4.1 Functional Specialization Typologies

Undertaken using data before the post-1970s era of dramatic economic restructuring and deregulation in response to the need for Australia to undergo significant economic restructuring to improve its competitiveness internationally, early work by the then Commonwealth Department of Home Affairs and Environment (1982) developed a set of urban socio-economic and environmental indicators for urban areas in Australia for the 1970s. Urban centres specializing in manufacturing, electricity and transport showed higher than average income levels.

More recently a study of structural industry and employment change over the decade 1981–96 undertaken by the Productivity Commission (1998), found no systematic relationship between structural change and regional employment growth across Australia's statistical subdivisions. But a high degree of structural change did not mean a low or negative regional employment growth, with 38 per cent of the variability in actual employment growth in regions being explained by the national shift component in industry sector employment.

Focusing on the changing economic roles of cities and towns across the national settlement system, research by Beer (1999) and Beer and Maude (1995) developed a functional classification of regional cities and towns from 1961 to 1996. A group of centres characterized by tourism, entertainment and recreation-related industries had the highest population growth. An increasing degree of functional specialization had emerged. In 1961 the regional cities and towns could be classified according to just nine categories. But that had increased to 12 categories by 1991 and to 16 categories by 1996. There had been a fragmentation of functional specialization, reflecting the spatial concentration of activities like tourism, administration and mining. The researchers suggested that the uneven outcomes for regional cities and towns reflected the way the broader focus of economic change had affected specialist functions. That finding suggested that the days of the country town with a wide range of functions were passing, and that economic success now called for specialization in a smaller number of functions.

6.4.2 Typologies of Regional Opportunity and Vulnerability

Baum et al. (1999) developed a multivariate model framework to identify a typology of clusters of community opportunity and vulnerability between 1986 and 1996 across both statistical local areas (SLAs) comprising Australia's mega-metro city regions and also for the large regional cities and towns with populations over 10 000 and the smaller regional towns with populations between 4000 and 10 000. The key factors differentiating between the places of opportunity and the places of vulnerability in terms of how places were coping with socioeconomic transition were found to relate to: (i) levels of human capital and income; (ii) engagement/disengagement in the workforce; and (iii) industry structure, and to population size for the regional towns.

The community opportunity–vulnerability framework and typology of SLAs across Australia's cities and towns was used for further analysis, including a study by Stimson and Baum (2001) to identify the degree to which there are variations between 'opportunity' and 'vulnerable' communities in the incidence of: (i) qualifications and skills in the workforce; (ii) levels of participation in post-secondary education and training; and (iii) the distribution of income including the incidence of household dependence on commonwealth income support and benefits. Significant spatial and functional disparities were identified across the settlement system.

Later research by Baum et al. (2006) investigating typologies of advantage/disadvantage over the decade 1996–2006 produced similar findings to the Baum et al. (1999) study.

6.5 MODELLING DETERMINANTS OF ENDOGENOUS REGIONAL GROWTH

Among regional scientists there has emerged a strong interest in how one might model the relationship between regional economic performance and endogenous factors. That has been discussed, for example, by Stimson and Stough (2007). In Australia, research by Stimson et al. (2004, 2005, 2006) developed an exploratory model investigating determinants of spatial variations in levels of endogenous growth performance across the non-metropolitan local government areas (LGAs) of Australia.

6.5.1 The Model

There is no standard definition of endogenous regional employment growth (or change) in terms of the specification of an agreed measurement variable. The Stimson et al. modelling used the differential or regional shift component derived from a shift-share analysis to measure the dependent variable. A total of 27 independent variables was used in a regression model[7] to identify those factors that were significant in explaining spatial variations in the level of endogenous employment growth performance in non-metropolitan (that is, outside the capital cities) LGAs across the five mainland states (namely, New South Wales, Victoria, Queensland, South Australia and Western Australia).[8] The variables were derived from 1991 and 2001 census data. The model provided some new insights into the degree to which endogenous variables measuring industrial structure, occupational structure, population size and growth, income levels and human capital, plus some geographic location proxies might account for variations in regional endogenous employment growth (and decline) in non-metro regional LGAs across those states over the decade 1991–2001.

Stimson et al. (2004, 2005, 2006) used a two-phase modelling approach: (i) phase 1 used conventional ordinary least squares (OLS) to estimate a general model of regional endogenous growth across regional LGAs in the five mainland states; (ii) phase 2 used a step-wise approach to determine a specific model, with each step involving withdrawing one independent variable from the model. The variable thus deleted has the highest probability that its absolute *t*-value was equal to or greater than 0.05. The model was then regressed and new estimates of the model obtained. That process recurred until the variable with the highest probability that its absolute *t*-value is less than 0.05 was identified. A key feature of a reasonable OLS regression is non-constant variance in the residuals. So the researchers ran tests to evaluate this on the estimated variable and to determine the existence of spatial autocorrelation. The autocorrelation problem was evident in the case of South Australia.

6.5.2 Results[9]

The adjusted *R*-squared values in the specific model were high, ranging from explaining 98 per cent of the variance for South Australia, 96 per cent for Victoria, 92 per cent for Western Australia, 88 per cent for Queensland and 86 per cent for New South Wales. Not surprisingly, Stimson et al. (2005) found differences between the states in the number of significant variables and the mix of independent variables in the specific model. The patterns of residuals for LGAs from the line of best fit were mapped for each state.

The exploratory model results may be summarized as follows:

1. Population was a factor that exerted a strong positive impact in all five mainland states, and population size at the beginning of the decade had an important positive impact in all states except New South Wales.
2. The level of industry sector specialization, and the change in it over time both had an important positive effect in all states except New South Wales, and the structural change index and the dynamics in it over time were important positive factors in Queensland, South Australia and Western Australia.
3. The level of income at the end of the decade 1991–2001 was a significant factor only in Queensland.
4. Only in New South Wales did the unemployment variables have a significant and negative impact.
5. There was a mixed picture regarding the impacts of the degree of concentration of jobs in broad industry sectors, the effects being most apparent in New South Wales and in Western Australia. But there was neither a consistent directional effect for these variables nor for the change over time in their location quotients.

6. There was a particularly marked impact from the incidence of people with university and technical qualifications in New South Wales and Queensland, but to a lesser degree in the other states. The incidence of people with university qualifications at the beginning of the decade had a negative impact, but the change in that incidence over the decade was a positive factor in New South Wales and Western Australia, where the change in incidence of people with technical qualifications also had a positive impact.
7. There was no really discernible pattern in the impact of the incidence of jobs in the Reich (1991) broad occupation categories, except in Victoria where the effects were negative, while in South Australia, Western Australia and Queensland the effects were positive when such a variable was significant.
8. Only in Western Australia and South Australia was it evident that the proxy variables relating to location on or near the coast or proximity to the metropolitan area had a significant effect, and that effect was negative.

6.6 CONCLUSION

This chapter has provided an overview of some of the research conducted in Australia investigating regional performance and in particular the role of regional differences in industrial structure and aspects of human capital as endogenous factors in regional economic performance. The studies reviewed illustrate the importance of understanding the role of spatial scale in regional analysis and the modelling of regional performance.

At the macro, more spatially, aggregated level it is evident that the employment industry continues to shift towards a dominance of the services sectors. Educational levels have been rising and there has been strong growth in the share of jobs in knowledge-intensive activities associated with the 'new economy'. However, educational expansion is not seen to be reflected nationally in changing occupations that have remained relatively stable, although there has been considerable internal change in the occupation structures of industry sectors, with all industries having experienced growth in their shares of highly qualified workers.

The outputs from the research reviewed indicate a close tie between regional industry structure and the size of a regional economy, and also with the degree of remoteness of a region. Not surprisingly, the importance of regional employment in the agriculture, mining and accommodation, cafés and restaurants industry sectors are seen to rise with increasing remoteness. But the relative importance of employment in the technology- and knowledge-intensive industries is seen to decline with remoteness and increase with the size of the regional economy, being most highly concentrated in the largest of the metropolitan cities. While these general relationships seem to be strong, nonetheless there remains a considerable degree of variation across Australia's regions in the relative shares of particular industry groups, and there is considerable variety in the industries in which regions specialize.

There is also considerable variation across regions in the particular industries that have been the main sources of employment growth, with the Bureau of Transport and Regional Economics (2004a) research indicating that the relative shares of employment in particular industries changed depending on what component of the decade 1991–2001 was considered, with the magnitude of change varying from 1991–96 to 1996–2001. The data seem to indicate that, over the decade 1991–2001, a more diverse industrial structure emerged outside the major cities, and the more spatially disaggregated analysis based on LMRs revealed that only 37 out of 425 LMRs experienced a decline in industrial diversity in excess of 1 percentage point, while 228 LMRs had experienced an increase of more than 1 percentage point in their industrial diversity. There was evidence to show that about 20 per cent of the variation in employment rate that occurred across LMRs over that decade could be explained by the industry structure of regional employment in 1991 and subsequent national growth trends in industry. The Bureau of Transport and Regional Economics (2004a, p.45) concluded that those variations might also be due to other endogenous factors such as 'amenity, remoteness, investment, leadership and the region's resource and skills base'.

There was also evidence that it has been those regions with a more highly diverse industry structure that tended to have experienced more stable economic performance than is the case for regions with more specialized industry structures. However, the Bureau of Transport and Regional Economics (2004a) study did point out that its modelling 'does not support the claim that a highly diverse industry structure is associated with greater regional growth products' (p. 46). It would thus seem that: (i) the industry structure of employment in regions in Australia does play an important, but not necessarily dominant, role in explaining regional differences in performance and economic growth; (ii) some convergence is evident; but (iii) regional specialization also remains strong. For example, both the Stimson, Baum et al. (2004) and the Bureau of Transport and Regional Economics (2004a, 2004b) research indicate that a larger regional population size *per se* does not always result in increased industry diversity, just as smaller size does not always create specialization. Increasing diversity of itself may not ensure better performance; rather it might act more to insulate a region's economy from the effects of economic shocks.

It is clear that the rise in education levels nationally was reflected across all the remoteness classes in Australia over the decade 1991–2001, even though the level of educational attainment continues to decline with increasing remoteness and also with a decline in the size of a region or urban centre. It is among the indigenous population where decline is most marked. But it seems that something of an oversupply of skills was emerging in some of the more populated regions, while there was a greater absorption of skills in the regional areas of Australia, and that was reflected through increasing shares of employment in some of the professions across some of regional areas. However, the Stimson, Baum et al. (2004) study pointed to a continuing dichotomy at a general level between the capital cities and regional urban areas in their human capital performance.

The results of the Bureau of Transport and Regional Economics (2004b) research suggested that a degree of equalization was occurring in educational levels across Australia's regions, with some evidence of convergence in skills and qualification outcomes for the more populated regions. But that diminished with increasing remoteness. 'Overall, regions with higher 1991 shares of university educated residents tended to experience higher income growth over the 1991 to 2001 decade' (ibid., p. 42). But the research findings did suggest that 'the relationship between higher education and income growth does not persist indefinitely' (ibid.).

The Stimson, Baum et al. (2004) study showed that across the urban system there seemed to be a positive relationship between the size of an urban place and its level of performance on a set of human capital indices, and there was also a tendency for occupation diversity and skills density to increase with the increasing size of a place. But the relationships for the latter were of a considerably lesser magnitude than for the former, and it was evident that some larger places did not have high levels of human capital performance, and some of them had specialized occupation and skills structures while some smaller places had strong human capital performance and reasonably diverse occupational and skill structures. The overall links, then, between education, skills, occupation levels and regional performance and growth appear to be somewhat more complex than might have been expected.

From the exploratory modelling of determinants of spatial variations in regional endogenous growth performance across the non-metro regions of the five mainland states over the decade 1991–2001 conducted by Stimson et al. (2004, 2005, 2006), the research outcomes demonstrate the importance of explanatory factors relating to industrial structure and industry specialization, population size and population change, levels of human capital, and aspects of industry sector and occupation category concentration of jobs. Such factors have been hypothesized more widely in the regional science literature as being important in explaining differences in regional endogenous growth performance. But the Stimson et al. research found that there were considerable differences between the five mainland states in the degree to which individual independent variables were significant explanatory factors accounting for variations in the regional endogenous growth performance of non-metropolitan LGAs. And there were also some variations between the states in the direction of the impact of some of the variables on regional endogenous growth.

What, then, might be the implications of the findings of the research reviewed in this chapter for regional policy and planning? Four key issues might be proposed:

1. Diversification is important but not a panacea for economic growth, and a 'regional push for greater industrial diversity might better reflect preferences for slow and steady growth over a boom and bust economy' (Bureau of Transport and Regional Economics, 2004a, p. 46).
2. Where people live can certainly affect the diversity of job opportunities with respect to the mix of industry, occupation and skill requirements, and it can affect overall levels of labour market participation and engagement. Thus 'place does matter' (Stimson, Baum et al., 2004, ch. 4).
3. The level of human capital is a factor differentiating the performance of places. Thus 'people skills do matter' (Stimson, Baum et al., 2004, ch. 10:4).
4. Population size does matter, as seen in the degree to which large urban places have more diversified job opportunities across both industry sectors and occupational categories, and larger places have higher levels of human capital performance:

> Large urban places also tend to offer employment opportunities for a greater range of educational attainment skill levels. This is not surprising and most likely it represents a self-selection outcome as the best people seek the better performing places so the direction of causation becomes blurred. (Stimson et al., 2004, ch. 10:5)

An important issue for policy is the degree to which differentiation across regions can be addressed by people-based as against place-based policies and programmes, or by a mixture of both approaches, as has been proposed by O'Connor et al. (2001) and by Baum et al. (1999, 2006). The following points may be made:

1. People-based approaches certainly enhance human capital development, and thus post-secondary education and training become critical. 'And enhancing geographical access to those education and training services also became important' (Stimson, Baum et al., 2004, ch. 10:8).
2. The overwhelming evidence is that investment in human capital development as a people-based policy is associated with advantageous place-based outcomes, as well as advantages for people (Stimson, Baum et al., 2004, ch. 10:8).
3. Place-based interventions are typically oriented towards selective industry assistance, payroll tax exemptions, land deals and the like. But such measures can have detrimental impacts on the economic welfare of populations in particular regions (Industry Commission, 1993, 1996) and industry assistance packages in reality have limited potential for state and local government regional development policy to impact on regional economic activity in the longer term (Giesecke and Maddern, 1997, p. 17).
4. Strategies for regional development 'need to be built upon local comparative advantage, and capitalize on region-specific resources, knowledge and location' (Bureau of Transport and Regional Economics, 2004a, p. 45).

The nature of Australia's space economy is changing rapidly and the processes of change are affecting people and places in differential ways. One of the challenges will be to develop and implement regional policies and strategies that build successful regions and places into even more success. As Stimson (2002, p. 35) has pointed out:

> Inevitably that will require greater selectivity, but would be more likely to result in enhanced national performance and improved competitiveness, giving a better return on limited government resources.

Of course tensions resulting from differential levels of regional performance will continue. The challenge is how best might Australia, with its three-tier system of government, respond with appropriate people-based and place-based policies for all the nation's regions.

ACKNOWLEDGEMENTS

This chapter is based in part on research funded by the Australian National Training Authority and undertaken by a team led by the author. The study also draws on research funded by the Australian Research Council (grant No DP0558277). The author acknowledges the contribution of current and former colleagues – John Mangan, T.-K. (Paul) Shyy, Alistair Robson, Scott Baum, Yolanda Van Gellecum, and Tan Yigitcanlar – to those research projects. As acknowledged in the chapter, the discussion also draws in particular on research conducted by the Commonwealth Government's Bureau of Transport and Regional Economics.

NOTES

1. That would be reversed during the next decade.
2. A coefficient of 100 per cent indicates that employment is fully localized in a single region.
3. As measured by the log of employed persons.
4. That analysis used the Bradley and Gans (1998) Herfindahl index, where an index of 100 per cent represents complete diversification across all industries.
5. Trendle and Shorney (2003) measured regional diversification using an entropy index and a regional instability measure (following the Siegel (1966) method).
6. An SCI of 100 per cent represents a complete reversal of industry structure.
7. The Haynes and Dinc (1997) method is used to derive the regional shift component (REG_SHIF) in a shift-share analysis of employment in 17 industry sectors using the ABS two-digit classification, arriving at the total employment change by an additive procedure, standardizing the additive regional shift in employment by the size of the LGA workforce at the 2001 census. That is necessary because of the wide variation in the population size of LGAs.
8. The numbers of LGAs included in the modelling for each of the five mainland states were: New South Wales $n = 135$; Victoria $n = 46$; Queensland $n = 116$; South Australia $n = 49$; Western Australia $n = 111$.
9. A detailed account of outcomes of this modelling has been published in Stimson et al. (2009), along with full details of the methodology used.

REFERENCES

Adams, P.D. (2002), 'Prospects for Australia's regions', *Sustaining Regions*, **1** (2), 4–16.

Arthur, W.B. (1994), *Increasing Returns and Path Dependency in the Economy*, Ann Arbor, MI: University of Michigan Press.

Barro, R.J. (1990), 'Endogenous technological change', *Journal of Political Economy*, **98**, S71–S102.

Baum, S., K. O'Connor and R. Stimson (2006), *Fault Lines Exposed: Advantage and Disadvantage across Australia's Settlement System*, Melbourne: Monash University ePress.

Baum, S., R. Stimson, K. O'Connor, P. Mullins and R. Davis (1999), *Community Opportunity and Vulnerability in Australia's Cities and Towns: Characteristics, Patterns and Implications*, Brisbane: University of Queensland Press for the Australian Housing and Urban Research Institute.

Beer, A. (1999), 'Regional cities within Australia's evolving urban system, 1991–96', *Australasian Journal of Regional Studies*, **5** (3), 329–48.
Beer, A. (2002), 'Editorial', *Sustaining Regions*, **1** (2), 3.
Beer, A. and A. Maude (1995), 'Regional cities within the Australian urban system, 1961 to 1991', *Urban Policy and Research*, **13** (3), 135–48.
Bradley, R. and J. Gans (1998), 'Growth in Australian cities', *The Economic Record*, **74** (226), 266–78.
Bureau of Transport and Regional Economics (BTRE) (2004a), 'Focus on regions No. 1: industry structure', information paper 49, BTRE, Department of Transport and Regional Services, Canberra.
Bureau of Transport and Regional Economics (BTRE) (2004b), 'Focus on regions No. 2: education, skills and qualifications', information paper 51, BTRE, Department of Transport and Regional Services, Canberra.
Department of Home Affairs and the Environment (1982), 'Australian urban environmental indicators', Australian Government Publishing Service, Canberra.
Draca, M., J. Foster and C. Green (2003), 'Human capital investment and economic growth in the Australian economy. Productivity and regional economic performance in Australia', Queensland Office of Economic and Statistical Research (OESR), Brisbane.
Duranton, G. and D. Puga (2000), 'Diversity and specialisation in cities: why, where and when does it matter?', *Urban Studies*, **37** (3), 533–55.
Garnaut, J., P. Connell, R. Lindsay and V. Rodriguez (2001), 'County Australia: influences on employment and population growth', ABARE Research Report, The Australian Bureau of Agricultural and Resource Economics, Canberra.
Garnett, A.M. and E.T. Lewis (2000), 'Population and labour mobility in rural Australia', *Australasian Journal of Regional Studies*, **6** (2), 157–72.
Giesecke, A.D. and J.R. Maddern (1997), 'Regional government economic policy: assessing the policy instruments', *Australasian Journal of Regional Studies*, **3** (1), 3–18.
Goetz, S.J. and A. Rupasingha (2001), 'The returns to higher education: estimates for the contiguous states', paper presented at the Regional Science Association International, North American Annual Meeting, Charleston, November.
Gordon, I.R. and P. McCann (2000), 'Industrial clusters, complexes, agglomeration and/or social networks', *Urban Studies*, **37** (3), 513–32.
Hanushek, E.A. and D.D. Kimko (2000), 'Schooling, labour-force quality and the growth of nations', *American Economic Review*, **90** (5), 1184–208.
Harrison, H. (1997), 'Trends in the delivery of rural health, education and banking services. National focus', National Farmers Federation Research Paper, vol. II, Canberra, February.
Haynes, K.E. and M. Dinc (1997), 'Productivity change in manufacturing regions: a multi-factor shift-Share approach', *Growth and Change*, **28**, 201–21.
Henderson, J.V., A. Kuncoro and M. Turner (1995), 'Industrial development in cities', *Journal of Political Economy*, **103**, 1067–90.
Hogan, L., P. Berry and S. Thorpe (1999), 'Regional Australia – incomes, industry location and infrastructure', *Australian Commodities*, **6** (4), 674–87.
Industry Commission (1993), 'Impediments to regional industry adjustment', Canberra: Australian Government Publishing Service.
Industry Commission (1996), 'State, territory and local government assistance to industry', draft report, Industry Commission, Melbourne.

Johansson, B., C. Karlsson and R.R. Stough (2001), *Theories and Endogenous Growth: Lessons for Regional Policy*, Heidelberg: Springer Verlag.
Kaufman, R. (1993), 'An empirical exploration of the relation among diversity, stability and performance in economic systems', *Structural Change and Economic Dynamics*, **4** (2), 299–313.
Lande, P. (1994), 'Regional industrial structure and economic growth and stability', *Journal of Regional Science*, **34** (3), 343–60.
Lawson, J. and J. Dwyer (2002), *Labour Market Adjustment in Regional Australia*, Reserve Bank of Australia, Sydney.
Lloyd, R., A. Harding and O. Hellwig (2000), 'Regional divide? A study of incomes in Regional Australia', *Australasian Journal of Regional Studies*, **6** (3), 271–92.
Norris, K. and M. Wooden (1996), 'The changing Australian labour market', Canberra: Australian Government Publishing Service.
O'Connor, K., R. Stimson and M. Daly (2001), *Australia's Changing Economic Geography and Society Dividing*, Melbourne: Oxford University Press.
OECD (1998), *Human Capital Investment: An International Comparison*, Paris: OECD.
OECD (2001a), *The Well-Being of Nations: The Role of Human and Social Capital*, Paris: OECD
OECD (2001b), *Cities and Regions in the Learning Economy*, Paris: OECD.
OECD (2001c), *Does Human Capital Matter for Growth in OECD Countries? Evidence from Pooled Mean-Group Estimates*, Paris: OECD.
Productivity Commission (1998), 'Aspects of structural change in Australia', research report, Ausinfo, Canberra.
Productivity Commission, (2003), 'Trends in Australian manufacturing', research paper, Ausinfo, Canberra.
Quiggin, J. (1999), 'Human capital theory and education policy in Australia', *The Australian Economic Review*, **32** (2), 130–44.
Reich, R.B. (1991), *The Work of Nations*, New York: Vintage Books.
Romer, P.M. (1986), 'Increasing returns and long-run growth', *Journal of Political Economy*, **94**, 1002–37.
Romer, P.M. (1990), 'Endogenous technological change', *Journal of Political Economy*, **98**, S71–S102.
Salt, B. (2001), *The Big Shift: Welcome to the Third Australian Culture*, South Yarra, Vic.: Hardie Grant Books.
Siegel, R. (1966), 'Do regional business cycles exist?', *Western Economic Journal*, **5**, 44–57.
Solow, R.M. (1956), 'A contribution to the theory of economic growth', *Quarterly Journal of Economics*, **70**, 65–94.
Stimson, R.J. (2002), 'Success and stress: regional performance across Australia', keynote address, Inspiring Regional Australia National Conference, Bunbury, October.
Stimson, R. and Baum, S. (2001), 'Patterns of advantage and disadvantage across Australia's communities: a focus on education and human capital', New Horizons in Education, *Journal of World Education Fellowship Australia*, **105**, 9–34.
Stimson, R.J. and R. Stough (2007), 'Issues for modelling regional endogenous growth', in I. Johansson (ed.), *Uddevalla Symposium 2006: Entrepreneurship and Development: Local Processes and Global Patterns*, research reports 2007:01,

revised papers presented at the 9th Uddevalla Symposium, 15–17 June 2006, Fairfax, VA, USA. Trollhättan, Sweden: University West, pp. 589–614.

Stimson, R.J., A. Robson and T.-K. Shyy (2004), 'Shift-share analysis and modelling endogenous growth across Queensland's regions', paper presented at the North American Regional Science Association International, Annual Conference, Seattle, November.

Stimson, R.J., A. Robson and T.-K. Shyy (2005), 'Modelling determinants of spatial variations in regional endogenous growth: non-metropolitan regions in the mainland states of Australia', paper presented at the 45th Congress of the European Regional Science Association, Amsterdam, August.

Stimson, R.J., A. Robson and T.-K. Shyy (2006), 'Modelling regional endogenous growth: an application to the non-metropolitan regions of Australia', paper presented at the international workshop 'Creativity and Smart Policy as Signposts for Innovative Development', Tinbergen Institute, Amsterdam, May.

Stimson, R.J., A. Robson and T-K. Shyy (2009), 'Modelling regional endogenous growth: an application to the non-metropolitan regions of Australia', *Annals of Regional Science*, **43** (2), 379–98.

Stimson, R., R. Stough and B. Roberts (2006), *Regional Economic Development: Analysis and Planning Strategy*, Berlin: Springer Verlag.

Stimson, R., S. Baum, J. Mangan, Y. Van Gellecum, T.-K. Shyy and T. Yigitcanlar (2004), 'Analysing spatial patterns in the characteristics of work, employment and skills in Australia's capital cities and across its regional cities and towns: modelling community opportunity and vulnerability', main report, prepared for the Australian National Training Authority (ANTA), CR-SURF/ANTA 2003 National Project, Centre for Research into Sustainable Urban and Regional Futures, University of Queensland, Brisbane.

Taylor, P.J., G. Catalano and N. Gane (2002), 'A geography of global change: services and cities 2000–01', *GaWC Research Bulletin*, **77**, 1–9.

Trendle, B. (1999), 'Measuring the implications of regional diversification: an application of the portfolio solution framework to Queensland data', *Australian Journal of Regional Studies*, **5** (3), 263–78.

Trendle, B. (2002), 'Regional variation in Queensland's unemployment rate', *Australasian Journal of Regional Studies*, **8** (3), 327–45.

Trendle, B. and G. Shorney (2003), 'The effect of industrial diversification on regional economic performance', paper presented at the Australian and New Zealand Regional Science Association annual conference, Perth.

White, D. (1987), 'Education and the state and federal involvement in educational policy development', La Trobe University, Melbourne.

7. Free versus monitored job search in Sweden

Michael Olsson

Both jobseekers and vacancies are spatially distributed. A jobseeker has accessibility to vacancies and a vacancy has accessibility to applicants, and these accessibility measures vary across locations. Left alone, an individual most often prefers to search for a job close to the present home address. The unemployment benefit rules state rather strict mobility requirements. Using these rules changes the accessibility measures at all places. In other words, monitoring job search affects both the search intensity and the level of competition. This directly affects where a jobseeker finds a job. It is shown that an increased mobility follows from a strict usage of the rules. The increased mobility of individuals implies additional transfer of knowledge and ideas.

7.1 INTRODUCTION

The accessibility concept has been used in many different studies: Johansson et al. (2002) study labour market integration, Johansson et al. (2003) study commuting, Andersson and Ejermo (2005) study knowledge sources and innovativeness of corporations, Karlsson and Olsson (2006) study how to define functional regions, Johansson and Karlsson (2007) study R&D and export diversity, and Andersson and Gråsjö (2009) study representations of space in empirical models.

Geographical mobility is often mentioned as a key method to improve the outcome on the labour market. Labour mobility is fundamental in the Swedish unemployment benefit rules (IAF, 2004; Regeringen, 2006). Both jobseekers and vacancies are spatially distributed. Given a job-search strategy, the accessibility to vacancies varies with residence location and the accessibility to applicants varies with firm location. In this chapter the consequences for the accessibility measures from a strict application of the rules will be identified by comparing three job-search strategies. With enlarged search areas a jobseeker applies for more jobs, but he/she also meets increased competition. Therefore the job-search strategy affects where a jobseeker is likely to find a job. This is shown by expressing the solution to a matching model of the labour market (Olsson, 2009) in terms of these accessibility measures. In this chapter, it is shown that mobility is increased if the rules are followed in the daily work at the Public Employment Service. Moreover, Power and Lundvall (2004) identify labour mobility as the main source for transfer of knowledge and ideas. However, these effects may not be realized, since the present rules are more or less ignored by the Public Employment Service (Riksrevisionen, 2004; IAF, 2005; Olsson, 2008).

7.2 MATCHING JOBSEEKERS AND VACANCIES

There are many forms of unemployment benefits (Vodopivec, 2004), and there are several ways of affecting the geographical mobility of the unemployed. The Swedish unemployment benefit rules focus on the job-search area. An option would be to increase geographical mobility via incentives. It would be possible to pay a jobseeker a substantial allowance for accepting a job relatively far from the present home address. In Sweden (2004), there is a small monetary allowance, and a jobseeker may get help with relocation costs. In addition, vacancies may be moved. In this chapter, neither incentives nor regional policies are studied. Elhorst (2003) surveys many studies targeting the spatial variation in unemployment among labour market regions. In the following, municipalities are the chosen geographical unit. All municipalities together are a set **S**. The municipalities are identified by three indices, $i = j = r \in \{1, 2, \ldots, 289\}$. A jobseeker living in a municipality, i, searches for a job in a set of municipalities, $\mathbf{J}(i) \subset \mathbf{S}$. A vacancy located in a municipality, j, receives applicants from a set of municipalities, $\mathbf{I}(j) \subset \mathbf{S}$.

There are a certain number of jobseekers and vacancies at the start of a period. The total number of jobseekers finding a job during the period, M, is related to the total number of unemployed, U, and the total number of vacancies, V, by the matching function, $M = m(U, V)$. At the end of the period, new jobseeker and new vacancy numbers are added to the existing ones. Pissarides (2000) describes the (long-run) equilibrium unemployment, and Pissarides and Petrongolo (2001) survey the literature on the matching function with special attention paid to the labour market. Moreover, there is a regional dimension to the matching taking place in the labour market (van Ommeren and Rietveld, 2002). Pissarides and Petrongolo (2001, p. 400) write 'location influences matching because of imperfect mobility'. In this chapter, the matching is affected by the spatial distribution of the jobseekers and the vacancies, and the geographical extension of the job-search areas.

Some municipalities may be considered relatively more attractive because of their amenities. A person may choose to live wherever he/she wants as long as he/she does not claim unemployment benefit. As soon as a person receives benefit, this changes, and then a person may have to commute a long distance, commute weekly or move closer to the job. These alternatives take time and money in varying degrees and have social consequences. However, it is possible to continue the search for a job and/or residence with the intention of finding a better combination.

There are exceptions to the rules; e.g. jobseekers with significant travel difficulty are allowed a relatively restricted job-search area. According to the rules, an individual receiving benefit does not have the right to see his or her family every day. That means that he/she may have to accept weekly commuting. In addition, it is stated that a person must be active in removing obstacles to mobility. A jobseeker may not wait until after 100 days to start these activities. In essence, this means that the rules should apply to the majority. In this chapter, hindrances are ignored, since they should be exceptions.

Jobseekers and vacancies may be classified in many ways. The spatial distribution of vacancies certainly differs across occupations. In the same way, the spatial distribution of jobseekers certainly varies across educational classes. It is not the purpose of this chapter to give an exact description of a specific occupation or of a certain educational class. The purpose is to establish the general consequences existing in all occupations and educational classes. In this chapter, it is assumed that all jobseekers have the skills to perform well at all vacant jobs. It is also assumed that long-term unemployment does not affect these skills. The spatial distributions used for analysis are based on these assumptions. In some way, these distributions may be considered as a description of the average situation. The results are robust, such that the outcome would qualitatively be the same for most reasonable spatial distributions. There is also very practical reasoning behind this choice, since occupational data are far from perfect. It is in no way clear which skills a person needs to work in a certain occupation.

In addition to the unemployed, some in employment are searching for a new job. That means that the unemployed face competition from these persons as well. Therefore some of the vacancies would be distributed to persons already employed. Hence this may be regarded as a reduction of the vacancies remaining for the unemployed. Competition from people already working is not introduced into the model since it would not help us in answering the research questions. We are investigating the general consequences created by the unemployment benefit rules, in principle for all conceivable spatial distributions. This competition would simply alter the spatial distribution of the vacancies available for the unemployed. Moreover, another reason is that data of this type are not available. It is not known how many of the people working in a specific location are actively searching for a new job during a period. In addition, the area they are looking in is not known, that is if they are actively searching. Jobseekers and people in employment are compared in Blau and Robins (1990).

Jobseekers without benefit can search for a job without interference from authorities. In the following, this form of job search is labelled free search. As a base case, it is assumed that jobseekers with benefit also search in this way. But a jobseeker with benefit should search according to the rules, and by comparing the outcomes from free search and search according to the rules, the effects of sticking to the rules are clarified. The rules are constructed so that geographical mobility is gradually increased for jobseekers with benefit. As a jobseeker passes 100 days with benefit, Sweden becomes the search area. A jobseeker with fewer days with benefit may restrict the job-search area. However, for most jobseekers the rules in practice imply an expansion of the search area. In order to make individuals use such expanded search areas the search activities have to be supervised. For that reason, search according to the rules is labelled monitored search.

The number of job openings a jobseeker finds depends on the size of the search area. When a jobseeker applies for more jobs, the search is more intensive. In the following I use the term search intensity. The size of the search area also affects the number of applicants per vacancy. In the following I use the term competition. Some jobseekers have a relatively difficult situation on the labour market. They may live in a municipality relatively far from vacancies and with many jobseekers. For other individuals the situation may be better. A jobseeker may live in a municipality with many vacancies in the proximity and few competing jobseekers. Given the spatial distribution of vacancies and jobseekers, an expansion of the job-search area will have different effects depending on location. I focus on the following five hypotheses:

Hypothesis 1 (H1) *By comparing free job search to monitored search using the rules for the short-term unemployed, the effects on the accessibility to job openings per unemployed from using these rules are clarified. The first hypothesis is that the magnitude of this effect is positive and varies among the residence municipalities.*

Hypothesis 2 (H2) *By comparing monitored job search using the rules for the short-term unemployed to monitored job search using the rules for the long-term unemployed, the effects on the accessibility to job openings per unemployed from using these rules are clarified. The second hypothesis is that the magnitude of this effect is positive and varies among the residence municipalities.*

Hypothesis 3 (H3) *By comparing free search to monitored search using the rules for the short-term unemployed, the effects on the accessibility to applicants per job opening from using these rules are clarified. The third hypothesis is that the magnitude of this effect is positive and varies with firm location.*

Hypothesis 4 (H4) *By comparing monitored job search using the rules for the short-term unemployed to monitored job search using the rules for the long-term unemployed, the effects on the accessibility to applicants per job opening from using these rules are clarified. The fourth hypothesis is that the magnitude of this effect is positive and varies with firm location.*

Hypothesis 5 (H5) *The size of the job-search area affects the search intensity and the level of competition. In turn, this changes where a jobseeker is likely to find a job. The final hypothesis is that monitoring job search changes the spatial distribution of the probability to find a job in a specific way: the spatial distribution of the probability to find a job becomes more dispersed around the home.*

7.2.1 Accessibility, Intensity and Competition

A jobseeker lives in a municipality, *i*, and he/she applies to some or all of the vacant jobs located in his/hers search area. An individual compares the job offers, and some are relatively more preferred. In the empirical part, the individual's perception of the accessibility to vacancies per unemployed (in *i*) is estimated by equation (7.1). This measure, A_i^{FS}, is referred to as free search (*FS*) accessibility to vacancies per unemployed. This measure is calculated using the number of vacant jobs in each location, V_j, the commuting distance, t_{ij}, and the appropriate distance friction, λ_{ij}.

$$A_i^{FS} = \sum_j \exp\{-\lambda_{ij} t_{ij}\} V_j / U_i \tag{7.1}$$

The number of job offers is discounted, meaning that a jobseeker on average only applies to a fraction of the available job offers. The underlying assumption is that the jobseekers are likely to wish to commute, as those who work do (Olsson, 2009). It is assumed that the individual does not care if he/she has been unemployed for a short or long period. Hence the individuals' evaluation is considered the same, in both situations. This accessibility measure is calculated using both short-term and long-term unemployed. Three types of commuting are used in this study. A commute may be (a) within the residence municipality, (b) between municipalities within the home region, or (c) between municipalities located in different regions. Johansson et al. (2003) present estimates of different distance frictions for these forms of commuting. For commuting within the home municipality, the distance friction is 0.025. For commuting between municipalities within the home region, the distance friction is set to 0.096. For commuting to a municipality in another region, the distance friction is 0.052. These measures of distance friction are average values for all commuters. In this study, I use aggregate data, so these estimates of distance friction are appropriate. Moreover, I argue that in most occupations, free job search is really local.

In Swedish unemployment benefit rules, it is stated that the short-term (*ST*) unemployed have to apply to each vacancy reached with a 90-minute one-way commute from the home, i.e. $t_{ij} \leq 90 \, \forall j \in \mathbf{J}(i)$. If a municipality, j, is in the search area, $j \in \mathbf{J}(i)$, a jobseeker will apply to all vacant jobs, V_j, in that municipality. The share of the unemployed (living in i) that are short-term unemployed is ς_i. The number of short-term unemployed living in municipality i is $\varsigma_i U_i$. Hence the monitored search (*MS*) accessibility to job offers per short-term unemployed, $A_i^{MS:ST}$, is given by equation (7.2). This accessibility measure is calculated using only short-term unemployed. It is interesting to compare the two measures, A_i^{FS} and $A_i^{MS:ST}$, by calculating the difference: $A_i^{MS:ST} - A_i^{FS}$. A difference identifies the effects on search intensity by enforcing the benefit rules during the first period in unemployment. The first hypothesis (H1) is that the effect of the rules is positive, $A_i^{MS:ST} - A_i^{FS} > 0$. This means that the unemployed are forced to search more intensively for a job. In addition, this effect is likely to vary among the residence municipalities.

$$A_i^{MS:ST} = \sum\nolimits_{j \in \mathbf{J}(i)} V_j / (\varsigma_i U_i) \tag{7.2}$$

At the passage of the hundredth day with benefit, a person has to widen his search area. Then the whole country is considered as the search area, $j \in \mathbf{S}$. If a municipality, j, is in the search area, $j \in \mathbf{S}$, a jobseeker will apply for all vacant jobs, V_j, in that municipality. The share of the unemployed (living in i) that are long-term (*LT*) unemployed is $1 - \varsigma_i$. The number of long-term unemployed living in municipality i is $(1 - \varsigma_i) U_i$. The monitored search accessibility to job offers for the long-term unemployed, $A_i^{MS:LT}$, is given by equation (7.3). It is interesting to compare the two measures, $A_i^{MS:ST}$

and $A_i^{MS:LT}$. The difference $A_i^{MS:LT} - A_i^{MS:ST}$ indicates what the effect is on the search intensity of enforcing the specific benefit rules for the long-term unemployed. The second hypothesis (H2) is that this effect is also positive, $A_i^{MS:LT} - A_i^{MS:ST} > 0$, and varying among the residence municipalities. This means that the intensity is increased at a varying rate across municipalities.

$$A_i^{MS:LT} = \sum\nolimits_{j \in \mathbf{S}} V_j / [(1 - \varsigma_i) U_i] \quad (7.3)$$

A vacancy is located in a municipality, and the applicants come from several municipalities. Above, the accessibility to vacant jobs per unemployed was discussed. In the same manner, a firm with a vacancy has more or less accessibility to applicants per vacancy. Assume that all unemployed may search according to their wish. Then the number of jobseekers actually applying is discounted, meaning that only a fraction of the jobseekers (in *i*) search the vacant jobs in *j*. The free search accessibility to unemployed per vacancy is given by equation (7.4). This is a measure of the level of competition for a job in this municipality.

$$B_j^{FS} = \sum\nolimits_i \exp\{-\lambda_{ij} t_{ij}\} U_i / V_j \quad (7.4)$$

The number of short-term unemployed in a municipality is $\varsigma_i U_i$. A short-term unemployed searches in an area around the residence municipality, $t_{ij} \leq 90 \; \forall i \in \mathbf{I}(j)$. The monitored search accessibility to short-term unemployed per vacancy is given by equation (7.5). The third hypothesis (H3) is that the monitored search accessibility to short-term unemployed exceeds the free search accessibility to unemployed, $B_j^{MS:ST} > B_j^{FS}$. This means that the rules lead to tougher competition for a job. Moreover, this effect is likely to vary among municipalities.

$$B_j^{MS:ST} = \sum\nolimits_{i \in \mathbf{I}(j)} \varsigma_i U_i / V_j \quad (7.5)$$

Short-term unemployed and long-term unemployed compete. The labour market in Sweden has on average 18 unemployed per vacancy (see Section 7.3). It is difficult to find a job and consequently relatively many become long-term unemployed. The number of long-term unemployed in a municipality is $(1 - \varsigma_i) U_i$. A long-term unemployed uses Sweden as the search area, $i \in \mathbf{S}$. The monitored search accessibility to long-term unemployed per vacancy is given by equation (7.6). The fourth hypothesis (H4) is that the difference $B_j^{MS:LT} - B_j^{MS:ST}$ is positive and varying among municipalities. This means that the rules for the long-term unemployed add a large number of applicants to every job. In some places relatively more of the competing jobseekers have had a long period in unemployment.

$$B_j^{MS:LT} = \sum_{i \in \mathbf{S}} (1 - \varsigma_i) \, U_i / V_j \tag{7.6}$$

7.2.2 Competition and the Probability of Finding a Job

Let us start with the case of free search. Then the distance between the home and the location of the vacancy has clear effects regarding how attractive the unemployed finds the job. The weight attached to a job is $\exp\{-\lambda_{ij}t_{ij}\}$. Hence relatively few would search a vacant job located far from home. When a person applies for a job in a municipality j, he/she faces competition, measured by B_j^{FS}. A jobseeker living in a municipality i may apply and the probability that he/she gets a job in j is $\pi_{ij}^{FS} = \exp\{-\lambda_{ij}t_{ij}\}/B_j^{FS}$. This would be true as long as $\Sigma_j \pi_{ij}^{FS} < 1$. These free search probabilities to find a job, π_{ij}^{FS}, will be compared to the probabilities when the search is monitored.

Assume that the unemployment benefit rules are followed to the letter. Then the short-term unemployed and the long-term unemployed living in municipality i have an accessibility to vacancies per unemployed equal to $A_i^{MS:ST}$ and $A_i^{MS:LT}$. However, in each location he/she faces competition from others who are unemployed. In a municipality, j, the firms with a vacancy have an accessibility to unemployed per vacancy equal to $B_j^{MS:ST} + B_j^{MS:LT}$. The model described here has been used to study different forms of job search in Olsson (2009). There the model is discussed in detail. There are two groups of unemployed. The short-term unemployed have to search within the area reached from their home with a commute equal to 90 minutes. The number of short-term (ST) unemployed living in municipality i who find a job in a specific municipality in the search area, $j \in \mathbf{J}(i)$, during the period is $M_{ij}^{ST} = \rho_i^{ST}(\varsigma_i U_i/Z_j)\, V_j$, where the share of the job offers an unemployed can accept equals $\rho_i^{ST} = \min\{1/\Sigma_{r \in \mathbf{J}(i)}(V_r/Z_r), 1\}$, where Z is the number of applicants. The regulations state that people who have had long-term unemployment (LT) shall search all jobs in Sweden. The corresponding expression for the long-term unemployed is $M_{ij}^{LT} = \rho_i^{LT}[(1 - \varsigma_i)\, U_i/Z_j]\, V_j$, where the share of the job offers that are accepted is $\rho_i^{LT} = \min\{1/\Sigma_{r \in \mathbf{S}}(V_r/Z_r), 1\}$.

From the data, it is possible to estimate that 20 periods corresponds to 100 days with benefit. It is possible to calculate the share of the unemployed living in municipality i that has fewer than 20 periods in unemployment as $\varsigma_i = n_i^{ST}/(n_i^{ST} + n_i^{LT})$, where $n_i^{ST} = \Sigma_{d=1}^{20}(1 - \pi_i^{ST})^{d-1}$ and $n_i^{LT} = (1 - \pi_i^{ST})^{20}/\pi_i^{LT}$. The share of the unemployed that are classified as long-term unemployed is $1 - \varsigma_i$. Moreover, the number of searchers applying for a job in municipality j is $Z_j = \Sigma_{i \in \mathbf{I}(j)}\varsigma_i U_i + \Sigma_{i \in \mathbf{S}}(1 - \varsigma_i)\, U_i$.

The solution is found using an iterative process, which can be described by ${}^0\pi_i^{ST}, {}^0\pi_i^{LT} \rightarrow \varsigma_i \rightarrow Z_j \rightarrow {}^1\pi_i^{ST}, {}^1\pi_i^{LT}$ and so on until $\Delta\pi_i^{ST} \approx 0$ and $\Delta\pi_i^{LT} \approx 0$.

Assertion: From the description above, it is seen that the probability that a short-term unemployed finds a job in a specific municipality within the search area, $j \in \mathbf{J}(i)$, is $\pi_{ij}^{ST} = \rho_i^{ST} V_j/Z_j$. In the general case, using equations (7.5) and (7.6), this may be rewritten in the following way:

$$1/\pi_{ij}^{ST} = (B_j^{MS:ST} + B_j^{MS:LT})/\max\{1, \Sigma_{r \in \mathbf{J}(i)}(B_r^{MS:ST} + B_r^{MS:LT})\}.$$

According to the benefit rules, a long-term unemployed must extend the search for a job to all locations in Sweden, $j \in \mathbf{S}$. The corresponding expression is applicable for the long-term unemployed,

$$1/\pi_{ij}^{(LT)} = (B_j^{MS:ST} + B_j^{MS:LT})/\max\{1, \Sigma_{r \in \mathbf{S}}(B_r^{MS:ST} + B_r^{MS:LT})\}$$

In the next section, the situation for the Swedish labour market is presented. There it is shown that there is a significant imbalance, such that the number of unemployed is a multiple of the number of vacancies, at each point in time. In such a labour market, it is extremely rare that an unemployed has to turn down a job offer, due to receiving another job offer. Then, $\pi_{ij}^{ST} = V_j/Z_j$, when $j \in \mathbf{J}(i)$. Moreover, the following relation is directly inferred: $\pi_{ij}^{ST} = 1/(B_j^{MS:ST} + B_j^{MS:LT})$, via equations (7.5) and (7.6). In addition, the same applies to the long-term unemployed: $\pi_{ij}^{LT} = 1/(B_j^{MS:ST} + B_j^{MS:LT})$, $j \in \mathbf{S}$. The assumption is that a long period in unemployment does not in itself reduce the probability of finding a job. When there is a significant lack of vacancies per unemployed, there is a severe fight over the few jobs that exist. The competition consists of some that are short-term unemployed and all that are long-term unemployed. The probability that an unemployed finds a job in a specific municipality is negatively related to the accessibility to applicants per vacancy.

The fifth hypothesis is that monitoring job search affects where unemployed find jobs in a specific way: with free search the probability of finding a job far from the present residence is low. By monitoring job search the probability of finding a job at greater distances from the present home increases.

7.3 DATA

In the application, the time it would take to travel between local authority districts by car is the chosen measure of spatial separation. In Sweden, many people of working age are not working but participating in labour market programmes, studying, on parental leave, ill or retired early. In this chapter, only people registered as unemployed at the Public Employment

Table 7.1 The average number of unemployed, vacancies and unemployed per vacancy in Sweden, at a point in time: total and per municipality, 2004

	Unemployed	Vacancies
Total	242 806	13 507
Min.	33	1
Max.	21 364	2217
Mean	840	47
Median	343	15
Standard deviation	1873	154

Service are considered. It is worth noting that the market share of the Public Employment Service is estimated at approximately 30 per cent (Okeke, 2001), and this market share may vary across space. However, these vacancies are of particular importance, since they represent those that jobseekers can be forced to search, via monitoring and the threat of reduced benefit. The data were delivered by the Swedish National Labour Market Board (AMS) and consist of the number of jobseekers and vacancies in each district at four points in time (at the end of July, August, September and October 2004). To even out small variations, calculations are based on the averages of these four points in time. There may still be seasonal variations and therefore the interpretation based on these data is not necessarily valid through the whole year. However, this has no effect on the main results of this study. In Table 7.1, aggregate information about jobseekers and vacancies is presented. Overall, the situation for a jobseeker can be described as daunting, since there are only 0.06 vacancies per unemployed.

7.4 RESULTS

In Figure 7.1 the free search accessibility to vacancies per unemployed is related to the monitored search accessibility to vacancies per short-term unemployed. In most municipalities the monitored search accessibility exceeds the free search accessibility. In most cases the search intensity increases by following the rules. However, this is not the case for peripheral northern regions. The average value of free search accessibility to vacancies per unemployed is 0.34. The average value for monitored search accessibility to vacancies per short-term unemployed is 5.5. Moreover, the effects of adhering to the rules differ among the municipalities. The magnitude of the increase in search intensity varies across municipalities. This

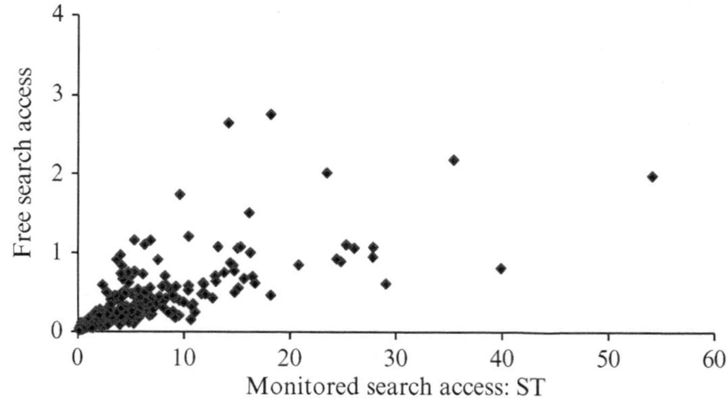

Figure 7.1 *The relation between the free search accessibility to vacancies per unemployed and the monitored search accessibility to vacancies per short-term unemployed*

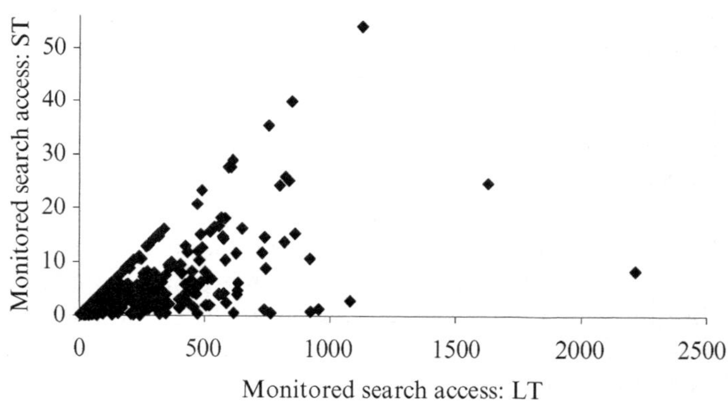

Figure 7.2 *The relation between the monitored search accessibility to vacancies per short-term unemployed and the monitored search accessibility to vacancies per long-term unemployed*

is seen in Figure 7.1, where the slope from the origin varies. This supports hypothesis H1.

On average, the monitored search accessibility to vacancies per long-term unemployed is as high as 293. This means that the rules have a significant effect on search intensity at day 100. The effect is positive for all municipalities. The regulations have stress effects, since they force unemployed to deviate from their most wanted behaviour. The magnitude of this differs across the municipalities. This is clearly seen in Figure 7.2. This supports hypothesis H2.

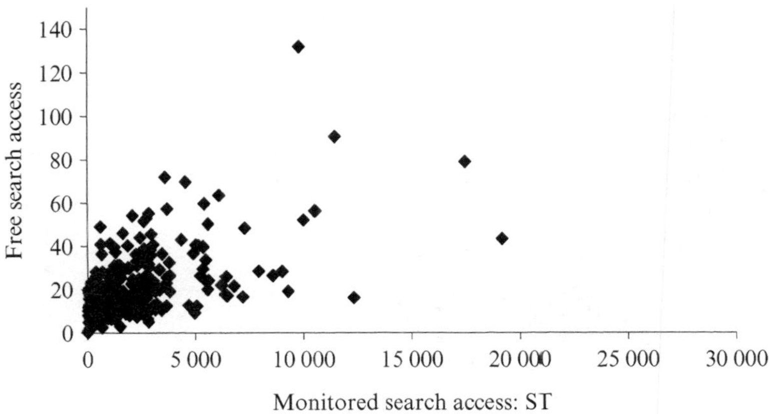

Figure 7.3 *The relation between the free search accessibility to unemployed per vacancy and the monitored search accessibility to short-term unemployed per vacancy*

In Figure 7.3, the free search accessibility to applicants per vacancy is compared to the monitored search accessibility to short-term unemployed per vacancy. The average value of the free search accessibility to applicants per vacancy is 21.7. The average value for the monitored search accessibility to short-term unemployed per vacancy is 2277. It is clearly seen that the effect varies between locations. Hence hypothesis H3 is verified. In other words, monitoring job search increases competition. As was seen in the data section, there is a huge imbalance in the Swedish labour market. Therefore the measures of accessibility to unemployed per vacancy significantly exceed the measures of accessibility to vacancies per unemployed.

Relatively many become long-term unemployed in a labour market with many more unemployed than vacancies. In Figure 7.4 the monitored search accessibility to short-term unemployed per vacancy is compared to the monitored search accessibility to long-term unemployed per vacancy. The average monitored search accessibility to long-term unemployed per vacancy is 4369. This also increases the level of competition. In some locations those that are long-term unemployed are a relatively more important source of applicants. This is readily seen in Figure 7.4. This supports hypothesis H4.

According to the rules, the short-term unemployed have to search in the area reached with a 90-minute commute from the home. For the short-term unemployed living in Skövde, the outcome is seen in Figure 7.5(a). The smallest circle represents a probability equal to 0.00001. The largest circle corresponds to a probability equal to 0.00318. According

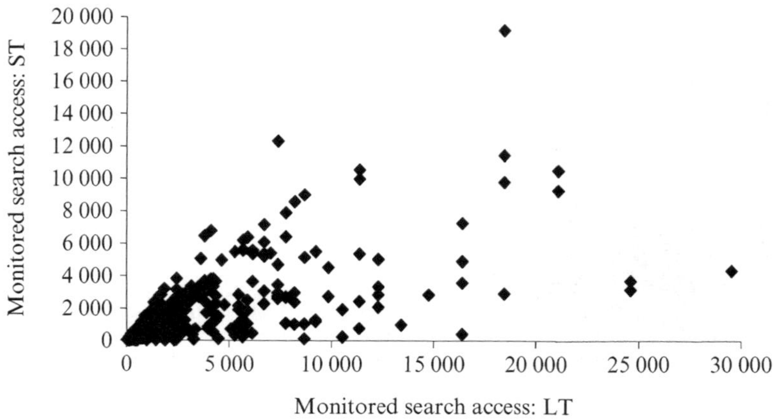

Figure 7.4 The relation between the monitored search accessibility to short-term unemployed per vacancy and the monitored search accessibility to long-term unemployed per vacancy

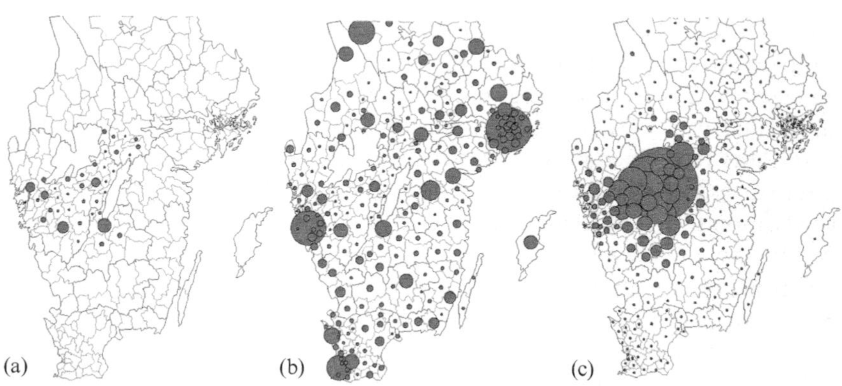

Figure 7.5 Probability of finding a job for a person living in Skövde: (a) for short-term unemployed following the rules; (b) for long-term unemployed following the rules; (c) for short- and long-term unemployed without monitoring

to the rules, long-term unemployed have to search the whole country. The outcome is presented in Figure 7.5(b). The smallest circle represents a probability equal to 0.00001. The largest circle corresponds to a probability equal to 0.02373. In most municipalities the competition over the few vacancies is so fierce that the likelihood of getting one of them is low. Stockholm turns out to be the place with the lowest level of competition. It is relatively easier to get a job in Stockholm, even though it is in absolute terms difficult even there. This would be the result, given that the rules are used in practice. The rules alter the search intensity and the level of competition. If the rules are not used, the result is very different. Then the outcome is determined by the individuals' wishes. For an unemployed that lives in Skövde the outcome of free search is visualized in Figure 7.5(c). The largest circle represents a probability equal to 0.05256. We see that by following the rules the spatial mobility would be increased. This verifies hypothesis H5.

Following the unemployment benefit rules increases (a) search intensity, (b) level of competition, and (c) spatial mobility.

7.5 DISCUSSION

The rules are often not used in the daily work at the Public Employment Service (Riksrevisionen, 2004; IAF, 2005; Olsson, 2008). The reason for this is simply that for most vacancies there are available applicants living close by. In a labour market with many times more unemployed than vacancies, the number of matches will not increase (more than marginally) when the search areas are extended for the jobseekers. The rules are not always used in practice by all handling officers. This is problematic, since only some unemployed have to follow the rules. Not all Swedish citizens like the rules, but it is even the case that the rules lack support within the Public Employment Service. In the daily work, it is often considered to be more important to provide service to the unemployed than to monitor their adherence to the rules.

Labour market policies in Sweden are strongly linked to political parties. The Swedish labour market was unbalanced in 2004, such that there were many more unemployed than vacancies. The Social Democrats lost the election in 2006, which has had strong effects on labour market policies. For example, the unemployment benefit has been reduced. At the same time, there are supporting policies with the aim to increase the demand for labour. These labour market reforms will make the labour market better balanced, but for the moment the negative effects of the financial crisis dominate.

When there is an approximate balance between the number of unemployed and the number of vacancies, an increased search area will increase the number of matches. In such a labour market, not all vacant jobs can be filled by local applicants. In a better-balanced labour market the support for the rules will increase, and the rules will most likely be used more frequently. This is important, since it will lead to a more vibrant economy:

individuals will commute and move to a larger degree, and in so doing transfer knowledge and ideas. It is important to have a better balance on the labour market. With this goal the flexibility of wages may be an additional factor to consider.

Spatial aspects are important and accessibility measures are clearly useful in studies of labour markets and evaluations of labour market policies. In this study, I used aggregate data. It would be interesting to continue this investigation using less aggregated data. One idea would be to divide the data by length of education.

REFERENCES

Andersson, M. and O. Ejermo (2005), 'How does accessibility to knowledge sources affect the innovativeness of corporations? Evidence from Sweden', *Annals of Regional Science*, **39** (4), 741–65.

Andersson, M. and U. Gråsjö (2009), 'Spatial dependence and the representation of space in empirical models', *Annals of Regional Science*, **31** (1), 159–80.

Blau, D.M. and P.K. Robins (1990), 'Job search outcomes for the employed and unemployed', *Journal of Political Economy*, **98** (3), 637–55.

Elhorst, J.P. (2003), 'The mystery of regional unemployment differentials: theoretical and empirical explanations', *Journal of Economic Surveys*, **17** (5), 709–48.

IAF (2004), 'Inspektionen för Arbetslöshetsförsäkringens Föreskrifter om Tillämpningen av §11-lagen (1997:238) om Arbetslöshetsförsäkring Gällande Lämpligt Arbete', Report 2004:3, IAF, The Swedish Unemployment Insurance Board, Katrineholm.

IAF (2005), 'Lämpligt Arbete, IAF:s Redovisning av Tillämpningen av Regelverket för Lämpligt Arbete med Utgångspunkt från IAF:s Föreskrift 2004:3', Report 2005:16, IAF, The Swedish Unemployment Insurance Board, Katrineholm.

Johansson, B. and C. Karlsson (2007), 'R&D accessibility and regional export diversity', *Annals of Regional Science*, **41** (3), 501–23.

Johansson, B., J. Klaesson and M. Olsson (2002), 'Time distances and labour market integration', *Papers in Regional Science*, **81** (3), 305–27.

Johansson, B., J. Klaesson and M. Olsson (2003), 'Commuters' non-linear response to time distances', *Journal of Geographical Systems*, **5** (3), 315–29.

Karlsson, C. and M. Olsson (2006), 'The identification of functional regions: theory, methods and applications', *Annals of Regional Science*, **40** (1), 1–18.

Okeke, S. (2001), 'Arbetsförmedlingens Marknadsandelar 1999 och 2000', Ura 2001:8, Swedish National Labour Market Board (AMS), Stockholm.

Olsson, M. (2008), 'The gap between legislation and daily practice in the Swedish unemployment insurance', *European Journal of Management*, **8** (1), 156–68.

Olsson, M. (2009), 'Matching in the labour market: modelling spatial aspects of the Swedish unemployment benefit rules', *Annals of Regional Science*, **43** (2), 345–63.

Pissarides, C.A. (2000), *Equilibrium Unemployment Theory*, Cambridge, MA: The MIT Press.

Pissarides, C.A. and B. Petrongolo (2001), 'Looking into the black box: a survey of the matching function', *Journal of Economic Literature*, **XXXIX** (2), 390–431.

Power, D. and M. Lundvall (2004), 'Working through knowledge pools: labour market dynamics, the transference of knowledge and ideas, and industrial clusters. Urban studies', **41** (5/6), 1025–44.

Regeringen (2006), http://www.sweden.gov.se/content/1/c6/04/38/62/dbe7bac1.pdf. Accessed 25 August 2006.

Riksrevisionen (2004), 'Arbetslöshetsförsäkringens Hantering på Arbetsförmedlingen', Report RiR 2004:3, Riksrevisionen, Stockholm.

van Ommeren, J. and P. Rietveld (2002), 'A multiregional equilibrium search model for the labour market', Research memorandum 2002–18, Vrije Universiteit, Amsterdam.

Vodopivec, M. (2004), *Income Support for the Unemployed, Issues and Options*, Washington, DC: The World Bank.

PART II

Institutions

8. Regional institutional environment and new firm formation

Kristina Nyström

This chapter uses an institutional approach to investigate the relationship between the regional institutional environment and regional new firm formation. The importance of perceived attitudes regarding private enterprises, local taxes, political majority, the size of the government sector and perceived rules and bureaucracy on new firm formation in 286 Swedish municipalities is investigated. The empirical findings show that perceived positive attitudes toward private enterprises and political governance by a right-bloc majority tend to have positive effects on regional new firm formation. A large local government sector, on the other hand, tends to have negative effects on regional new firm formation. The chapter also explores if the effect of different aspects of regional institutional environment on new firm formation are similar across industries. The pattern in the private service sector industries is most similar to the overall pattern in the economy, while the only variable reflecting the regional institutional environment that influences new firm formation in manufacturing industries is perceived rules and bureaucracy.

8.1 INTRODUCTION

Political and economic institutions underlie and determine the incentive structure in a society. Hence they importantly affect economic performance in a society (North, 1991, 1994). It is undoubtedly the case that the quality of institutions plays an important role for creating economic growth (see e.g. Acemoglu et al., 2001; Rodrik et al., 2004). Stimulating entrepreneurship is by many policy makers regarded as an important way to achieve economic growth. However, as recognized by Wennekers and Thurik (1999), the link between individual micro-level foundations in terms of entrepreneurship and the aggregate growth level needs to be unravelled further.

Unravelling the link between the institutional setting, entrepreneurship and aggregate economic growth can of course be done in several different ways. The institutional differences can of course be expected to vary across countries (see for example Bjørnskov and Foss, 2008; Freytag and Thurik, 2007). In addition, the institutional differences can vary substantially across regions within a country. The role of the region has been put forward as becoming increasingly important. It is argued that economies experience increased globalization, the role of national markets decreases and limits the possibility of using macroeconomic policy tools in order to adjust the economy. In such an environment, regional specialization tends to increase and regions and not countries are the ones competing with each other (e.g. Hallin and Malmberg, 1996).

The Swedish institutional context provides a particularly interesting case for studying the link between institutions and entrepreneurship. The Swedish 'welfare state' is characterized by a large public service sector and extensive social security systems. Henrekson (2005) discuss how welfare state institutions, such as, for example, the large size of the public service sector and the tax structure, reduces the incentives for entrepreneurship. Henrekson and Rosenberg (2001) specifically focus on science-based entrepreneurship and conclude that institutions do not favour the incentives to become an entrepreneur or for existing firms to grow in these industries. However, these studies focus on the aggregate country level and do not consider regional institutional differences. An additional motivation to study the Swedish case is that during the 1990s the Swedish economy has experienced some major deregulations as regards, for example, opening up for more private alternatives in education and health and medical care industries. During the period 1996–2001 employment in the private sector of these sectors in Sweden increased by 40 000 employees. A large part of this increase is due to the establishment of new firms in these sectors (Nyström, 2006a).

Studies focusing on regional new firm formation in Sweden, though not applying an explicit institutional focus include, for example, Davidsson et al. (1994);[1] Karlsson and Nyström (2006); Nyström (2007). This chapter contributes to the empirical knowledge about the link between the regional institutional environment and regional entrepreneurship in terms on new firm formation. The chapter investigates the relationship for the overall economy, as well as investigates if the results differ if we study the manufacturing and private service sector separately. This crude but important distinction is motivated by the fact that regional factors determining regional new firm formation may differ across industries (see e.g. Audretsch and Fritsch, 1999; Armington and Acs, 2002; Davidsson et al., 1994; Nyström, 2007). In addition, the chapter uses the econometric tools that modern spatial econometrics provide, which enable us to handle the presence of spatial interdependency between regions.

The chapter is organized as follows: Section 8.2 outlines the theoretical foundation for the study, i.e. the different types of institutions and how they influence incentives for new firm formation. Moreover, in Section 8.2 the particular regional institutional environment aspects that will be empirically investigated are discussed. Section 8.3 presents the data and the econometric method that will be used in the empirical analysis. Section 8.4 presents the empirical results, and finally the conclusions are presented.

8.2 INSTITUTIONS AND REGIONAL NEW FIRM FORMATION

Before we proceed to elaborate on the institutional setting that influences firm behaviour, we need to say a few words about the concept of the entrepreneur and entrepreneurship in relation to new firm formation. Historically, a number of definitions have been suggested. One of the most commonly used definitions of the entrepreneur is as a risk taker, resource allocator and innovator. These three perspectives all focus on the economic function of the entrepreneur. A frequently used definition of entrepreneurship that incorporates all these functions and also emphasizes the role of institutions is that by Wennekers and Thurik (1999, pp. 46–7), who define entrepreneurship as the

> manifest ability and willingness of individuals, on their own, in teams within and outside organisations, to: perceive and create new economic opportunities and to introduce their ideas in the market, in the face of uncertainty and other obstacles, by making decisions on location, form and use of resources and institutions.

This definition indeed highlights the multidimensional aspects of entrepreneurship and one has to recognize that it is extremely difficult to empirically measure such a multidimensional concept. Measures that are frequently used (but do not cover all the above described dimensions of entrepreneurship) are self-employment rates, new firm formation or innovation in small firms. As previously mentioned, this chapter will use new firm formation as a measure of entrepreneurship.

8.2.1 Institutions and the Behaviour of the Firm

Institutions are commonly depicted as the 'the rules of the game' for individuals or organizations and they can be either characterized as informal or formal. Williamson (2000) in particular discusses the institutions that influence economic activities in firms. He categorizes institutions according to four aspects that will help us elaborate on the relationship between institutions and entrepreneurship. 'Social embeddedness' includes informal institutions, customs, norms and social networks; 'institutional environment' represents the formal rules of the game such as polity, judiciary and bureaucracy; 'institutions of governance' refers to transactions and contracts between firms, and, finally, 'resource allocation and employment' emphasizes the role of institutions in reshaping incentive structures that affect decisions on resource allocation in production. These concepts will be further elaborated on below and related to some previous empirical findings.

Social embeddedness

The concept of social embeddedness refers to, for example, the culture, norms, values, traditions and religion in a society. These institutions determine how different behaviours are rewarded (or punished). Hence they influence people's behaviour and decisions. Social relations include relations to family, friends, colleagues or business relations. These institutions change very slowly. More explicitly discussing how people do business, Granovetter (1985) suggests that the density of social network relations indeed influences what kind of activities and transactions are made. There is now an increasing literature emphasizing the role of social conditions for innovation and entrepreneurship and economic growth.[2] Empirical findings focusing on the effect on the regional level include Baptista (2004), who finds that cultural values in a society, in terms of attitudes toward risk and uncertainty, influence the level of entry regulations in a country. Beugelsdijk and Noorderhaven (2004) investigate 54 European regions and show that regions differ with regard to entrepreneurial attitude and culture, and that these regional characteristics are correlated with regional economic growth. Kangasharju (2000) argues that there might be a stochastic distribution of entrepreneurial talents across regions, which in addition may be enhanced by regional specific factors and hence contribute to explaining the regional variation in entrepreneurship. Finally, Audretsch (2001) identifies entrepreneurial culture as important for nurturing start-ups and growth of US biotech firms. It should be noted that entrepreneurial culture in a region is of course very difficult to measure. Most studies that consider regional culture as a variable in the empirical analysis either measure it indirectly by including regional specific effects or use proxies for regional culture (Beugelsdijk and Noorderhaven, 2004).

Institutional environment

The institutional environment includes the formal rules such as constitutions, regular law and regulations (North, 1991). The institutional environment concerns the definition and enforcement of property rights and contract laws, which are of course fundamental for economic activities and transactions. Secure property rights ensure that people are able to keep the returns of their entrepreneurial activities. In addition, well-defined property rights and contract enforcement reduce the transaction costs associated with doing business (Coase, 1937). The institutional environment includes both the functions of the government as well as the powers of distribution between different levels of government (Williamson, 2000). Consequently, the ability for each region to influence the environment for entrepreneurship is limited by the given level of autonomy.

Institutions of governance

Regardless of the existence of contract laws, many of the contract agreements and dispute settlements are managed directly by the parties involved. In analysing the effect of institutions of governance, transaction cost economics is often used in the analysis (Williamson, 2000). Important decisions include the choice of producing something within the firm or using another firm as supplier. Moreover, the institutions governing product markets influence the competitive environment and decisions on mergers and acquisitions, which of course in the end are important aspects that potential entrants need to consider. In empirical studies it is found that a rigorous regulatory environment of product markets has a negative effect on productivity and new firm formation (Scarpetta et al., 2002). Djankov et al. (2002) investigate the time and money that a firm needs to spend on starting up a business in 85 countries. They find that countries with higher entry costs also have higher levels of corruption and larger unofficial sectors. One of the motivations for entry regulations is the belief that these regulations should improve the quality of the private and public goods produced. This does not seem to be the case, according to Djankov et al. (2002).

Resource allocation and employment

Institutions influence the availability, flexibility and cost of using different resources, such as capital and labour, in the firm. Hence they will also influence the incentives to start a new firm. This fourth level of institutional analysis is the level at which neoclassical economics analysis has operated (Williamson, 2000). Examples of this type of analysis may include studies of the incentives, prices and quantities on the labour and capital markets. Labour market legislation has, for example, the purpose of creating a stable environment for both employers and employees, but may also reduce the incentive to hire people and start a new firm since it affects the cost of labour. In addition, the quality of the financial institutions determines the cost of acquiring capital for investments and seed capital for starting a new firm.

8.2.2 Institutional Impact on New Firm Formation in the Swedish Regional Context

In some respects, the institutional prerequisites are similar across regions in a country, at least considering the second level of institutions previously referred to as the institutional environment, since it refers to the general rules of the game, which are centrally determined and apply to all regions. In Sweden this is, for example, the case with the taxation of capital and labour market legislation. However, there are some important regional differences. In Sweden, there are primarily three different levels of government that need to be considered: national, county and municipality. The decisions taken at the national level of course concern all firms and individuals equally. At the county level the responsibility is mainly to provide health and medical care and public transportation. The range of issues that the municipality is responsible for is much wider, including, for example, education, waste disposal and building permits. Up to now, we have deliberately been vague when using the concept of a region since it can be defined and measured in several different ways. In the empirical part of this chapter the regional dimension corresponds to the municipality. The wider range of issues handled at the municipality level makes it more interesting than the county level as the unit of analysis from an institutional perspective. However, it should be emphasized that the municipality is still an administrative definition, which may not be completely adequate, especially regarding regional market conditions. The following sections will discuss some institutional aspects that differ across Swedish municipalities and that reflect the variables used in the empirical part of the chapter.

Attitudes

The attitudes towards entrepreneurship and being a business owner in general reflect how the social environment responds to entrepreneurship. The institutional embededdness of firms not only includes the business networks that the firm operates in but also its social interaction with other economic and social institutions (Johannisson et al., 2002). From a social point of view, it can be hypothesized that attitudes in different social contexts have more or less impact on regional entrepreneurship. One of the Swedish 'success stories' as regards regional entrepreneurship is the

Gnosjö region located in the south/middle part of Sweden. The region is often compared to regions such as the 'third Italy'. It is claimed that one of the reasons for the success of the entrepreneurial Gnosjö region is the social network, which has formed a local environment with positive attitudes towards entrepreneurship (see, e.g., Wigren, 2003). It should also be noted that the causality could also be the reverse, i.e. successful entrepreneurship positively influence attitudes and local environment.

Local taxes

As previously mentioned, capital incomes are taxed equally regardless of which region the firm is located in. However, a large part of the entrepreneurial income is taxed as wage income (Henrekson, 2005). Since tax on income is determined at the municipality level, it can be regarded as an economic institution that determines the economic payoff of being an entrepreneur in particular regions. However, it should be noted that the variations in tax rate across municipalities are rather small in Sweden and the difference between the municipalities with the highest and smallest tax rates in, for example, the year 2001 is just above six percentage points (see the descriptive statistics presented in Table 8.2). The previously mentioned study by Davidsson et al. (1994) included the local tax rate as an explanatory variable for gross births of establishments per 1000 inhabitants, but this variable did not turn out to be statistically significant in the empirical analysis.

Size of the government sector

One of the aspects of product market institutions is the level of competition. Competition refers not only to competition between firms in the private sector, but also occurs between private firms and the public sector. In certain service sectors such as education and health care the main competitor for a potential entrepreneur is the services provided by the government sector. In a cross-country setting it has been shown that the size of the government sector is negatively correlated with entrepreneurship (Bjørnskov and Foss, 2008; Nyström, 2008). The size of the Swedish government sector and the regulations regarding certain service sectors implies a limited possibility to establish new firms in these sectors. In fact, the Swedish private service sector is much smaller compared to that in many other OECD countries (SOU, 1997, p. 17). Actually, there has been no net growth of employment in the private sector in Sweden since the 1950s (Davidsson and Henrekson, 2002). However, at the regional level there is still some variation in terms of the number of private alternatives in, for example, the health care[3] and education sectors. Different municipalities have, for example, chosen to imply different levels of private alternatives regarding providers of health care (Socialstyrelsen, 2003).

Political power

The institutional environment and institutions of governance can also differ depending on the interests and political agenda of the policymakers. Pierre (1999) argues that the degree of inclusion of organized interests in urban governance differs within nations. This in turn influences the policy outcomes in different regions. This is reflected in the previously mentioned differences in involvement in providing public services or decisions on local tax rates, but there might be additional differences regarding how/if one will encourage private entrepreneurship. If we stylize the political message, delivered from different political parties on the right to left scale, we could argue that parties belonging to the right bloc advertise their policy as friendly towards private enterprises. The previously mentioned study by Davidsson et al. (1994) included explanatory variables on the percentage of socialist voters and the share of Christian Democratic voters in the regions as measures of entrepreneurial culture, but these variables were not found to affect regional new firm formation.

Rules and bureaucracy

For 2006, the World Bank ranks Sweden as number 13 out of 175 countries regarding the ease of starting a business (World Bank, 2006). In order to start a firm, 20 procedures need to be accomplished and the time spent on these start-up procedures is three days. The cost of starting a new business is reported to be 0.7 per cent of income per capita.[4] Among the rules that may be of importance at the local level are building permits, permits to serve alcohol, or rules regarding environmental concerns. There is both a possibility that the rules determined are more or less restrictive in different regions and that they are applied differently. Hence the time and effort that a firm may have to spend on bureaucracy may differ significantly across municipalities. A number of studies have found, on a cross-country basis, that the unfavourable bureaucracy regulations associated with starting a new firm reduce new firm formation (see, e.g., Alfaro and Charlton, 2006; Klapper et al., 2006; Desai et al., 2003). Van Stel et al. (2007), on the other hand, show that administrative considerations (time cost and number of procedures needed in order to start a firm) do not affect the amount of nascent and young entrepreneurs in the economy.

Regional market conditions

In addition to the institutional environment that we expect to influence the number of firms entering a region, regional market conditions are expected to have an important impact on the decision to start a new firm in a particular region. In the empirical part of this chapter a number of measures of the regional market condition will be used.[5] The size of the population in a region can be expected to influence the number of entering firms since it reflects the number of potential customers, but it can also be expected to influence the 'supply' of entrepreneurs. The income level reflects both the demand aspect in terms of buying power of the potential customers but also the possibilities to acquire new venture capital in the region (Reynolds et al., 1994). On the other hand, the income level also reflects the cost of labour for a potential entrepreneur. The unemployment rate may affect entrepreneurship either positively by forcing people into entrepreneurship as an alternative to unemployment, or negatively if unemployment is regarded as an indicator of the economic situation and hence an indicator of decreased demand.

The level of education in a region can be expected to have ambiguous effects on the probability of starting a new firm in a region. From a demand perspective, it is more attractive for a firm to locate in a region with well-educated inhabitants, assuming that they also have higher incomes. It might also be attractive to locate in a region with a highly skilled population if this is the particular type of human capital that the firm needs in order to run the business. This might, for example, be the case for highly innovative firms in early stages of the product life cycle. In general, it is also assumed that the probability of starting a new firm is high among the well educated since they are believed to have better opportunities to perceive and exploit entrepreneurial opportunities. On the other hand, it should be recognized that the opportunity cost of being an entrepreneur (e.g. wage from employment) can be expected to be higher for well-educated people. Actually, the choice to engage in entrepreneurship is a second choice for many Swedish well-educated people in the science and technology industry (Delmar et al., 2003). Finally, the structure of local business in the municipality may affect the number of new firm formations. If the industry structure is characterized by many small firms, it could be expected that the frequency of entry and exit is high in such regions compared to regions with many large firms.

8.3 DATA, DESCRIPTION OF VARIABLES AND ECONOMETRIC METHOD

8.3.1 Data and Description of Variables

In the empirical analysis, several sources are used. The data used to compile firm entry in each municipality are collected by Statistics Sweden. This data set consists of firm-level data. Each firm in the data set is classified according to the Standard Industrial Classification (SIC) system.[6]

All Swedish non-financial enterprises in the corporate sector[7] are included in the data set. This means that all non-financial joint-stock companies, cooperatives, partnerships, limited partnerships, associations and some foundations are included. Each firm in the data set is assigned a unique identification code. If a new identification code appears, this is identified as a firm entry. Further details about this data set can be found in Statistics Sweden (1998) and Nyström (2006b). The numbers of entering firms in each Swedish municipality for 2001 is used in the empirical part of this chapter. The variable measuring the average firm size in each municipality is also compiled from this data set.

The population, income, education and local taxes variables for each municipality have also been collected by Statistics Sweden. These variables are available at www.scb.se. The variables measuring the size of the government sector, unemployment and political majority were recovered from a database called the municipality database, which is a comprehensive data set covering many different aspects of municipality characteristics.[8]

The variables associated with the institutional setting in terms of attitudes and rules and bureaucracy are based on an annual survey[9] conducted by the Swedish Confederation of Enterprises, henceforward SCE. The survey is sent to over 60 000 firms in all Swedish municipalities and the response rate is about 60 per cent. In the survey, among other things, firms are asked about their perception of attitudes regarding private enterprises in their social environment. This includes the attitudes of the general public, local government politicians, municipal employees, the media and the educational system. In addition, the respondents are asked about their perceptions of rules and bureaucracy. The data and further information about how the survey was conducted are available at: www.svensktnaringsliv.se. It should be noted that the responses from this questionnaire reflect the subjective views of the representatives from incumbent firms. However, Djankov et al. (2002) conclude that regarding the importance of administrative regulations, the subjective assessments made by business people reported by World Economic Forum (2001) have a high correlation with the more objective measures provided by Djankov et al. (2002).

In Table 8.1 the variables included in the analysis are defined and the source for each variable is also presented. Several variables suffered from skewness and kurtosis, indicating non-normal distributions. Therefore these variables were used in their logarithmic form in order to avoid severe problems with normality. The data set includes observations from 286 municipalities.[10]

In order to investigate whether the different aspects of the institutional environment are more or less important for manufacturing or private

Table 8.1 Description of variables

Variable	Definition	Source
New firm formation	Number of entering firms in the municipality 2001 (logarithm)	Statistics Sweden
Attitudes	Perceptions of attitudes regarding private enterprises by the general public, the local government politicians, municipal employees, media and educational system respectively in each municipality. The value ranges from 0.2 to 1.2. A higher value implies more positive attitudes. An average of five categories of attitude measures is constructed.	SCE
Tax	Local tax in % in the municipality for 2001	Statistics Sweden
Political majority	Dummy variable taking the value 1 if the municipality is governed by parties defined as right bloc, 0 otherwise	Municipality database
Government sector	Size of the local government sector measured as the number of employed in the local government per capita in the municipality (logarithm)	Municipality database
Rules and bureaucracy	Perceptions of the extent of rules and bureaucracy in municipality. The measure ranges between 1 and 6, where a higher score corresponds to better (fewer) rules and less bureaucracy	SCE
Population	Population in the municipality 2001 (logarithm)	Statistics Sweden
Income	Average income (thousand SEK) in municipality 2001. The measure includes incomes from both employment and business (logarithm)	Statistics Sweden
Education	Share of employees with a university degree in the municipality 2001 (logarithm)	Statistics Sweden
Unemployment	Unemployment rate in the municipality 2001	Municipality database
Firm size	Average firm size in the region 2001 (logarithm)	Statistics Sweden

Table 8.2 Descriptive statistics

	Mean	Std dev.	Min.	Max.	Skewness	Kurtosis
Entry (all industries)	3.499	1.078	1.099	8.618	0.785	4.551
Entry (manufacturing industries)	1.222	0.955	0.000	5.710	0.749	4.318
Entry (private service sector)	3.031	1.175	0.000	8.353	0.629	4.197
Attitudes	0.700	0.206	0.240	1.200	2.614	2.614
Tax	31.096	1.227	27.150	33.170	−0.778	3.081
Political majority	0.321	0.468	0.000	1.000	0.763	1.583
Government sector	4.262	0.167	3.638	4.615	−0.775	4.150
Rules and bureaucracy	3.500	1.196	1.000	6.000	−0.024	2.594
Population	9.823	0.899	7.878	13.534	0.720	3.850
Income	5.152	0.116	4.979	5.818	1.893	8.533
Education	−1.675	0.320	−2.192	−0.575	0.843	3.404
Unemployment	3.399	1.325	1.000	8.500	0.715	3.793
Firm size	2.107	0.419	1.270	3.429	0.629	3.349

service industries, the number of entering firms in a region was also divided into two subsamples. The manufacturing industries include firms with SIC codes 15–37 and the private service sector refers to industries with SIC codes 50–64 and 70–74. Hence it should be emphasized that this implies that, for example, health care and education sectors are not included in the empirical analysis. Table 8.2 presents the descriptive statistics for the variables included in the study. Unless otherwise noted, the descriptive statistics refer to the case when all industrial sectors are included.

8.3.2 Econometric Method

The econometric model was initially specified as a standard linear regression with the entry variable as dependent variable and all the above-described variables as explanatory variables. For some variables, we can expect a quite strong correlation between the explanatory variables. Appendix Table 8A.1 reports the correlation matrix for the variables. The table shows that there is a quite strong correlation between attitudes regarding private enterprises and rules and bureaucracy. In addition, the correlation between income and education is quite high. The question is if these quite strong correlations are severe enough to cause problems with multicollinearity. The possibility of multicollinearity was therefore also investigated by calculating the variance inflation factors (VIF). The average VIF value was 2.55 and none of the VIF values exceeded 5. Hence the VIF values did not exceed 10, which are usually used as a rule of thumb for indicating multicollinearity problems.

However, since some municipalities are located in close proximity to each other, there is a possibility that there may be spatial dependence in such an econometric model. A Moran's test confirms the suspicion of spatial autocorrelation. In the presence of spatial autocorrelation there are two alternative opportunities regarding how to respecify the model, i.e. as a spatial lag model or as a spatial error model. In a spatial lag model, it is assumed that the dependent variable is a function of the dependent variable in the neighbouring municipalities. In a spatial error model there are spatially correlated measurement errors due to omitted explanatory variables that are believed to be spatially correlated (Haining, 2003). Unfortunately, the Moran test does not give any indication about which of the two models should be applied and this choice must instead be made on a theoretical basis and/or by comparing the estimation results of the two models. In our case such a comparison favours the choice of a spatial lag model. In the estimation of the spatial lag model robust standard errors were used in order to control for heteroscedasticity.

8.4 EMPIRICAL FINDINGS

Tables 8.3 to 8.5 present the regression results. In Table 8.3 the number of new firms in all industrial sectors is the dependent variable. Since the institutional perspective is our focus, we start by analysing the variables measuring the institutional environment.[11] Informal institutions represented by the variable measuring the attitudes towards private enterprises have a positive effect on new firm formation. Municipalities governed by the right bloc also have statistically significantly more new firms. However, one must be careful to interpret this result as solely because of a more 'entrepreneurship-friendly policy', since such a dummy variable also may capture additional differences across regions, which also reflect the preferences of the voters. A large local government sector is found to have a negative effect on new firm formation. The local tax rate and the perceived rules and bureaucracy do not, on the other hand, influence new firm formation. All variables, except unemployment, reflecting the regional market conditions are statistically significant. A large population and higher education level in the municipality tend to increase new firm formation. Hence the attraction effect of locating in a municipality with a highly educated labour force seems to outweigh the possible negative effects. A

Table 8.3 Regression results. Dependent variable: new firms in all industries

Variable	Coeff.	Robust std err.	*t*-value
Attitudes	0.440*	0.160	2.75
Tax	−0.006	0.021	−0.26
Political majority	0.105*	0.040	2.61
Local government sector	−0.361*	0.181	−1.99
Rules and bureaucracy	−0.027	0.025	−1.09
Population	1.085*	0.041	26.42
Income	−0.542*	0.266	−2.04
Education	0.343*	0.113	3.04
Unemployment	0.021	0.021	0.97
Firm size	−0.155*	0.058	−2.67
Constant	−1.660	1.975	−0.84
R^2	0.919		
n	286		

Note: * indicates significance at the 5% level. ** indicates significance at the 10% level.

Table 8.4 Regression results. Dependent variable: new firms in manufacturing industry

Variable	Coeff.	Robust std err.	*t*-value
Attitudes	0.194	0.306	0.63
Tax	−0.025	0.041	−0.61
Political majority	0.077	0.080	0.97
Local government sector	0.216	0.410	0.53
Rules and bureaucracy	0.084**	0.045	1.87
Population	0.932*	0.068	13.61
Income	−0.079	0.486	−0.16
Education	−0.290	0.212	−1.37
Unemployment	0.012	0.034	0.36
Firm size	−0.027	0.091	−0.30
Constant	−8.271*	3.799	−2.18
R^2	0.639		
n	286		

Note: As for Table 8.3.

Table 8.5 *Regression results. Dependent variable: new firms in private service sector*

Variable	Coeff.	Robust std err.	*t*-value
Attitudes	0.475*	0.188	2.53
Tax	−0.039**	0.024	−1.65
Political majority	0.108*	0.051	2.11
Local government sector	−0.220	0.203	−1.08
Rules and bureaucracy	−0.022	0.029	−0.75
Population	1.123*	0.044	25.47
Income	−0.551**	0.315	−1.75
Education	0.518*	0.141	3.68
Unemployment	0.033	0.024	1.37
Firm size	−0.171*	0.061	−2.81
Constant	−1.723	2.298	−0.75
R^2	0.903		
n	286		

Note: As for Table 8.3.

high income level in the municipality, on the other hand, seems to reduce new firm formation. Fewer new firms are also established in municipalities with larger average firm size.

The results of these regressions, focusing on new firm formation in the manufacturing industry, are provided in Table 8.4. The table shows that the explanatory variables do not perform as well in explaining the differences in new firm formation in manufacturing industries across regions as they did when including all industrial sectors. The only variables that are statistically significant are population and perceived rules and bureaucracy and the R^2 value for this specification is much lower. The size of the region in terms of the size of the population does positively affect new firm formation. Rules and regulations perceived as well functioning also tend to increase new firm formation. Again, the industrial structure is influential on the pattern of new firm formation. Why is it that rules and bureaucracy seem to be more deleterious to new firm formation in the manufacturing industry? A possible explanation is that the amount of rules and the bureaucracy associated with doing business are not evenly distributed across industries. The administrative costs associated with compliance with rules and regulations has been estimated to be highest for tax law regulation, labour laws and environmental laws (NUTEK, 2004). While the bureaucracy associated with tax laws and labour laws can be expected to be more equally distributed across industries, compliance with environmental laws in terms of bureaucracy might be more important to manufacturing industries.

Table 8.5 presents the results of the regression focusing on the private service sector. The results of this regression are quite similar to the results received in the estimation for all industrial sectors. Hence positive attitudes towards private enterprises seem to encourage new firm formation. Moreover, municipalities governed by a right-bloc majority tend to have more new firms established. On the other hand, the variable measuring the size of the government sector is not statistically significant. For private sector industries, the tax rate seems to be of some importance. The negative sign of the coefficient indicates that a higher local tax rate tends to reduce private sector new firm formation in the municipality. Regarding the variables reflecting the regional market condition, the regressions yield similar results as the estimations including all industrial sectors, i.e. a larger population and a higher level of education in the municipality tend to increase new firm formation, whereas a higher income level and large firm size reduce new firm formation.

8.5 CONCLUSIONS

This chapter has used an institutional framework to explain the regional differences in new firm formation. Believing that entrepreneurship, measured as new firm formation, is a vital factor in economic growth, the institutional prerequisites for entrepreneurship indeed must be regarded as very important. The institutional environment empirically measured in this chapter includes attitudes towards private entrepreneurship, local tax rates, political majority, the size of the government sector and the perceived rules and bureaucracy. In the study, the region is defined as 286 Swedish municipalities. The effect of the institutional variables was analysed controlling for regional market conditions and spatial autocorrelation.

The effects were analysed using firm-level data for 2001, both for all industrial sectors and for two sub samples: the manufacturing industry and the private service sector. At the aggregate level, perceived positive attitudes towards private enterprises and municipalities governed by the right-bloc political majority have a positive effect on new firm formation. However, as previously noted, the impact of the political majority on new firm formation should be carefully interpreted, since there is a possibility that this variable may reflect inherent attributes of the voters residing in the municipality. A large size of the local government sector tends to have a negative effect on new firm formation. This can be interpreted as competition from the government crowding out private entrepreneurship. In the private sector industry, the patterns are rather similar to what was observed for all industrial sectors, except that the size of the local government sector does not show up as statistically significant. Higher levels of local tax rate instead reduce new firm formation in this sector. However, in the manufacturing sector perceived rules and bureaucracy play a more pronounced role. The other institutional variables are in this case of less importance, as are several of the variables reflecting regional market conditions except for the size of the region, which is still of major importance. These findings highlight the fact that different aspects of the institutional environment are not equally important across sectors.

ACKNOWLEDGEMENTS

The author thanks colleagues at the Ratio Institute, participants at the 2007 ISNIE Conference in Reykjavik and participants at the 2007 Uddevalla Symposium for valuable comments on a previous version of this chapter.

NOTES

1. However, it should be noted that the study included some explanatory variables related to the institutional environment, such as variables reflecting entrepreneurial culture and access to role models.
2. See, for example, the literature on enterprise culture (e.g. Amin and Tomaney, 1991) and regional innovation systems (e.g. Cooke et al., 1997; Thomas, 2000).
3. The municipality is responsible for health care for the elderly.
4. Gross national income.
5. For an overview of which factors are expected to influence regional new firm formation, see e.g. Keeble and Walker (1994) and Johnson and Parker (1996).
6. The SIC code at the four-digit level corresponds to NACE Rev. 1.
7. Financial intermediation (SIC codes 65–67), Real estate activities (SIC code 70) and Activities of membership organizations (SIC code 91) are not included in the data set since these sectors are not covered in the data collection made by Statistics Sweden.
8. The Centre Party, The Christian Democrats, the Liberal Party and the Moderate Party are defined as parities belonging to the right on the political scale.
9. The survey was published in 2002. However, it was conducted in the autumn of 2001.
10. In 2001 Sweden consisted of 289 municipalities. However, in the distance matrix necessary for controlling for spatial autocorrelation, information from only 286 municipalities was available. This implies that the municipalities Nykvarn, Bollebygd and Lekeberg are not included in the analysis.
11. Since the dependent and many of the explanatory variables are in their logarithmic form, interpretation of the size of the variables is not always straightforward. In the interpretation of the results, the focus is therefore on the sign and significance of the coefficients.

REFERENCES

Acemoglu, D., S. Johnson and J. Robinson (2001), 'The colonial origins of comparative development: an empirical investigation', *American Economic Review*, **91**, 1369–401.

Alfaro, L. and A. Charlton (2006), 'International financial integration and entrepreneurship', CEPR Discussion Paper no. 755, Centre for Economic Performance, London School of Economics and Political Science.

Amin, A. and J. Tomaney (1991), 'Creating an enterprise culture in the North East? The impact of urban and regional policies of the 1980s', *Regional Studies*, **25**, 479–87.

Armington, C. and Z.J. Acs (2002), 'The determinants of regional variation in new firm formation', *Regional Studies*, **36**, 33–45.

Audretsch, D. (2001), 'The role of small firms in US biotechnology clusters', *Small Business Economics*, **17**, 3–15.

Audretsch, D.B. and M. Fritsch (1999), 'The industry component of regional new firm formation processes', *Review of Industrial Organization*, **15**, 239–52.

Baptista, R. (2004), 'Culture, institutions and government attitudes towards new firm entry', Discussion Papers on Entrepreneurship, Growth and Public Policy, Discussion Paper 2004–39, Max Planck Institute for Research into Economic Systems, Jena.

Beugelsdijk, S. and N. Noorderhaven (2004), 'Entrepreneurial attitude and economic growth. A cross-section of 54 regions', *Annals of Regional Science*, **38**, 199–218.

Bjørnskov, C. and N.J. Foss (2008), 'Economic freedom and entrepreneurial activity: some cross country evidence', *Public Choice*, **134**, 307–28.

Coase, R.H. (1937), 'The nature of the firm', *Economica*, **4**, 386–405.

Cooke, P., G. Uranga and G. Etxebarria (1997), 'Regional innovation systems: institutional and organisational dimensions', *Research Policy*, **26**, 475–91.

Davidsson, P. and M. Henrekson (2002), 'Determinants of the prevalence of start-ups and high growth firms', *Small Business Economics*, **19**, 81–104.

Davidsson, P., L. Lindmark and C. Olofsson (1994), 'New firm formation and regional development in Sweden', *Regional Studies*, **28**, 395–410.

Delmar, F., J. Wiklund and K. Sjöberg (2003), 'The involvement in self-employment among the Swedish science and technology labour force between 1990 and 2000', Research Report A2003:017, Swedish Institute for Growth Policy Studies (ITPS), Stockholm.

Desai, M., P. Gompers and J. Lerner (2003), 'Institutions, capital constraints and entrepreneurial firm dynamics: evidence from Europe', NBER Working Paper no. 10165, Cambridge, MA: National Bureau of Economic Research.

Djankov S., R. La Porta, F. Lopes-de-Silanes and A. Shleifer (2002), 'The regulation of entry', *The Quarterly Journal of Economics*, **67**, 1–37.

Freytag, A. and R. Thurik (2007), 'Entrepreneurship and its determinants in a cross country setting', *Journal of Evolutionary Economics*, **17**, 117–31.

Granovetter, M. (1985), 'Economic action and social structure: the problem of embeddedness', *American Journal of Sociology*, **91**, 481–510.

Haining, R. (2003), *Spatial Data Analysis – Theory and Practice*, Cambridge and New York: Cambridge University Press.

Hallin, G. and A. Malmberg (1996), *Attraktion, Konkurrens och Regional Dynamik i Europa* (Attraction, Competition and Regional Dynamics in Europe), Stockholm: Fritzes.
Henrekson, M. (2005), 'Entrepreneurship: "a weak link in the welfare state"', *Industrial and Corporate Change*, **14** (3), 437–67.
Henrekson, M. and N. Rosenberg (2001), 'Designing efficient institutions for science-based entrepreneurship: lessons from the US and Sweden', *Journal of Technology Transfer*, **26** (3), 207–31.
Johannisson, B., M. Ramírez-Pasillas and G. Karlsson (2002), 'The institutional embeddedness of local inter-firm networks: a leverage for business creation', *Entrepreneurship and Regional Development*, **14**, 297–315.
Johnson, P. and S. Parker (1996), 'Spatial variations in the determinants and effects of firm births and deaths', *Regional Studies*, **30**, 679–88.
Kangasharju, A. (2000), 'Regional variation in firm formation: panel and cross-section data evidence from Finland', *Papers in Regional Science*, **79**, 355–73.
Karlsson, C. and K. Nyström (2006), 'Knowledge accessibility and new firm formation', CESIS Working Paper no. 70, Royal Institute of Technology, Stockholm.
Keeble, D. and S. Walker (1994), 'New firms, small firms and dead firms: spatial patterns and determinants in the United Kingdom', *Regional Studies*, **28**, 411–27.
Klapper, L., L. Laeven and R. Rajan (2006), 'Entry regulation as a barrier to entrepreneurship', *Journal of Financial Economics*, **82**, 591–629.
North, D. (1991), 'Institutions', *Journal of Economic Perspectives*, **5** (1), 97–112.
North, D. (1994), 'Economic performance through time', *American Economic Review*, **84**, 359–68.
NUTEK (2004), *En Kartläggning av Företagens Administrativa Börda* (A Survey of Administrative Burdens for Firms), NUTEK, Stockholm.
Nyström, K. (2006a), 'Den Offentliga Sektorn och Nyföretagandet – Nya Villkor för Nyföretagande och Sysselsättning i Vård, Skola och Omsorg', in D. Johansson and N. Karlsson (eds), *Svensk Utvecklingskraft* (Swedish Development Dynamics), Ratio, Stockholm, pp. 180–205.
Nyström, K. (2006b), 'Entry and exit in Swedish industrial sectors', JIBS Dissertation Series, no. 32, Jönköping International Business School, Jönköping.
Nyström, K. (2007), 'An industry disaggregated analysis of the determinants of entry and exit', *Annals of Regional Science*, **41** (4), 877–96.
Nyström, K. (2008), 'The institutions of economic freedom and entrepreneurship: evidence from panel data', *Public Choice*, **136** (3–4), 269–82.
Pierre, J. (1999), 'Models of urban governance', *Urban Affairs Review*, **34**, 372–96.
Reynolds, P., D. Storey and P. Westhead (1994), 'Cross-national comparisons of the variation in new firm formation rates: an editorial overview', *Regional Studies*, **28**, 343–6.
Rodrik, D., A. Subramanian and F. Trebbi (2004), 'Institutions rule: the primacy of institutions over geography and integration in economic development', *Journal of Economic Growth*, **9**, 131–65.
Scarpetta S., P. Hemmings, T. Tressel and J. Woo (2002), 'The role of policy and institutions for productivity and firm dynamics: evidence from micro and industry data', OECD Economics Department Working Paper No. 329, Paris.

Socialstyrelsen (National Board of Health and Welfare) (2003), 'Nationell Handlingsplan för Hälso- och Sjukvården' (National Action Plan for Health and Medical Services), *Socialstyrelsens Årsrapport 2003*, Stockholm.
SOU (1997), 'Skatter, Tjänster och Sysselsättning' (Taxes, Services and Employment), SOU 1997:17, Ministry of Finance, Stockholm.
Statistics Sweden (1998), 'Financial accounts for enterprises 1996', *Statistiska Meddelanden SM9801 NV11*, Statistics Sweden, Örebro.
Thomas, K. (2000), 'Creating regional cultures of innovation? The regional innovation strategies in England and Scotland', *Regional Studies*, **34**, 190–98.
Van Stel, A., D.J. Storey and A.R. Thurik (2007), 'The effect of business regulation on nascent and young business entrepreneurship', *Small Business Economics*, **28** (2–3), 171–86.
Wennekers, S. and R. Thurik (1999) 'Linking entrepreneurship and economic growth', *Small Business Economics*, **13** (1), 27–55.
Wigren, C. (2003), 'The spirit of Gnosjö – the grand narrative and beyond', JIBS Dissertation Series No. 17, Jönköping International Business School, Jönköping.
Williamsson, O. (2000), 'The new institutional economics: taking stock, looking ahead', *Journal of Economic Literature*, **38**, 595–613.
World Bank (2006), *Doing Business 2006*, available at http://www.doingbusiness.org.
World Economic Forum (2001), *The Global Competitiveness Report 2001–2002*, New York: Oxford University Press.

APPENDIX 8.1

Table 8A.1 Correlation matrix

	Entry (all)	Entry (manufacturing)	Entry (private services)	Attitudes	Tax	Political majority	Government sector	Rules and bureaucracy	Population	Income	Education	Unemployment	Firm size
Entry (all)	1.000												
Entry (manufacturing)	0.801	1.000											
Entry (private services)	0.985	0.756	1.000										
Attitudes	0.266	0.254	0.276	1.000									
Tax	−0.357	−0.273	−0.378	−0.488	1.000								
Political majority	−0.026	−0.044	−0.016	0.368	−0.328	1.000							
Government sector	−0.398	−0.266	−0.401	−0.443	0.718	−0.279	1.000						
Rules and bureaucracy	0.034	0.131	0.045	0.727	−0.325	0.289	−0.248	1.000					
Population	0.942	0.780	0.929	0.217	−0.328	−0.111	−0.382	0.014	1.000				
Income	0.491	0.337	0.450	0.346	−0.541	0.130	−0.677	0.124	0.471	1.000			
Education	0.748	0.522	0.759	0.321	−0.474	0.118	−0.543	0.042	0.712	0.744	1.000		
Unemployment	−0.068	−0.023	−0.069	−0.421	0.428	−0.360	0.538	−0.243	−0.059	−0.479	−0.272	1.000	
Firm size	0.191	0.243	0.179	0.197	−0.097	−0.133	−0.111	0.166	0.295	0.022	−0.007	−0.015	1.000

9. Knowledge, political innovation and referendum

Tsuyoshi Hatori and Kiyoshi Kobayashi

Referenda in which imperfectly informed individuals are called to vote for or against an innovative project can result in inefficient outcomes, as compared to the outcomes that would arise with completely informed individuals. In this chapter, an incomplete information game is presented to investigate the influence of interest groups' voices on individuals' judgements. It is shown that on account of the lack of knowledge of individuals about an innovative project, a limited number of interest groups that disagree with the innovation utilize their voices in strategic fashion and try to prevent a referendum outcome containing the majority will. Alternative institutional designs are introduced to overcome this inefficiency, and some problems regarding a referendum process are discussed.

9.1 INTRODUCTION

Innovations and their adoption are the keys to regional growth and development. Faced with intense interregional and international competition, regional policy makers must find innovative solutions for enhancing the competitive advantage of their regions. Innovations, however, are not the result of a decision by a single policy maker, but follow from the invention of policy options and the search for solutions made interactively by regional agents, including but not limited to a policy maker. This forces us to realize that innovations and their adoption are not immune to the political arena. Indeed, the implementation of innovations depends on regional political systems, in which regional agencies wield power and authority, interact with each other, exchange their knowledge and information, and influence and enact regional policies and decisions. Given this situation, it is important to develop political systems and processes for selecting an innovation according to the general welfare of a region.

Over the past two decades, an era referred to variously as collective decision making, public choice, or social choice, much research has been accumulated in an attempt to build a theory of political systems on social decision-making processes (Arrow, 1963; Downs, 1957; Gibbard, 1969; Mueller, 1997; Riker and Ordeshook, 1968, 1973; Romer and Rosenthal, 1978; Satterthwaite, 1975). Among these, it is shown in a theoretical framework that the most efficient public-good allocation mechanisms can be approximated by a referendum where individuals simply vote for or against a public project (Ledyard and Palfrey, 2002). However, this finding depends on the special condition that a referendum is contested under some ideal situation. It is pointed out that in the real world direct democracy through referenda is fraught with various problems and it is difficult to assume the ideal situation. First, the participants in a referendum are not necessarily rational and deliberative, as assumed in previous research based on the paradigm of rational choice. Indeed, many researchers have suggested that people often fail in making a reasoned choice (Boulding, 1956; Holsti, 1962; Leites, 1951; Lippmann, 1922; Manza et al., 2002). Second, individuals could abstain from voting. If the majority of electorates in a region choose abstention from voting, the vote outcome does not reflect the majority will (Downs, 1957; Ferejohn and Fiorina, 1974; Palfrey and Rosenthal, 1985; Soberg and Tangeras, 2003).

Third, as focused on in this chapter, is the existence of information asymmetries among participants (Lupia, 1992; McKelvey and Ordeshook, 1985). In general, many models and theories developed so far assume that individuals have a level of knowledge about electoral alternatives. Empirical observation, however, suggests that citizens often do not know the outcomes of policies they espouse (Delli et al., 1991; Lupia, 1994; Popkin, 1991). When voters possess incomplete information about proposed alternatives, they may cast a different vote than they would have cast if they had possessed complete information. Consequently, a referendum in the real world may not result in the same outcome as a referendum contested under complete information. That may be particularly true for the case in which innovative projects are contested, because individuals are ill informed about the characteristics of innovations that are designed by making use of expert knowledge. This chapter is focused on the third factor, and examines the likelihood of an inefficient outcome to arise as a consequence of incomplete information. For this purpose, we develop a rational choice model of people's voting behaviour. The model is based on an assumption that people vote rationally in the sense that they each maximize their own utility. It is also assumed that they do not abstain from voting. The reason that we make these assumptions is due to our research motivation to show that if people lack relevant knowledge, even if they cast their votes rationally, a referendum might cause an inefficient outcome. In what follows, we shall define a social decision that coincides with the majority preferences as an efficient outcome, in accordance with Ledyard and Palfrey (2002).

The lack of relevant information at the disposal of individuals will give a more prominent place to the role of available information sources. While voters possess imperfect information on proposed projects, they might have a chance to take cues from other information sources that are easily observable, e.g. other voters, interest groups and poll results, to mention a few. Among them, interest groups are in a distinct position in modern political systems (Cameron and Jung, 1992; Winden, 1999). In fact, diverse influences of interest groups are easily observed in every activity for policy makings (cf. Potters et al., 1997). The presence of interest groups who undertake various actions from rent seeking to information transmission lobbying in attempting to affect political decision making provides uninformed individuals with low-cost information cues. These cues may have a huge influence upon individuals' beliefs, and then their voting behaviours. In this study, we consider interest group endorsement as available information sources for uninformed voters and investigate the impact of voices by interest groups on referendum outcomes.

This chapter presents an incomplete information game incorporating the one-dimensional spatial voting model proposed by Grofman and Norrander (1990) as a sub-model. The analysis of the basic model shows that on account of the lack of knowledge of individuals about an innovative project, a referendum where the individuals are called to vote for or against the project might end up in an inefficient outcome that is different from an outcome produced by completely informed individuals. In particular, it is shown that a limited number of interest groups that disagree with the innovation use their voices and prevent a referendum outcome from coinciding with the majority will. Next, we develop the basic model and derive the equilibrium of the model, which proves an inefficient outcome of the referendum model due to incomplete information. Then alternative institutional designs are introduced to overcome the inefficient referendum outcome, and some problems regarding the referendum process are discussed. A concluding section summarizes the findings.

9.2 THE BASIC MODEL

9.2.1 Assumptions

This section develops a spatial voting model that demonstrates the impact of interest groups' voices on referendum outcomes. Let us consider a referendum process in which $2M - 1$ incompletely informed individuals are called upon to vote either for or against an innovative project that is proposed by a public manager. Majority rule determines a referendum outcome. The basic model assumes that all individuals necessarily vote for or against the project without abstention. Let $N = \{1, \ldots, 2M - 1\}$ denote the set of individuals. The referendum question is phrased so that a vote for 'X' gives an approval to the project, whereas a vote for 'Y' supports the status quo. Respective properties of the two alternatives are represented as one point of the one-dimensional alternative space $\Theta = [0, 1]$. Let $x \in [0, 1]$ denote the project property (alternative X), while $y = 0$ denotes the status quo (alternative Y).

Each individual's preferences over the alternative space are distinguished by the location of his or her most preferred alternative, or ideal point. It is assumed that individual i's ideal point $t_i \in [0, 1]$ $(i \in N)$ is distributed as $t_1 \leq \ldots \leq t_i \leq \ldots \leq t_{2M-1}$. Each individual has symmetric single-peaked preferences with his or her ideal point and prefers an alternative that is closer to the ideal point. Individuals know the location of the status quo $y = 0$, while they do not know the exact location of the project property x. This assumption is based on the fact that a public manager proposes an innovation, and individuals have uncertainty about its desirability. Individuals possess prior beliefs $F(x)$ that represent a subjective probability distribution from which the project property x is drawn. For simplicity, it is assumed that the subjective probability is common knowledge among all the players. Each individual votes for or against the project on the basis of inaccurate beliefs about the project property.

Individuals who are uncertain about a project property can acquire information on preferences or opinions of others, and then use this information to infer how the project will affect their own well-being. In the basic model, it is assumed that m interest groups send their voices to individuals. Such groups may be lobbying groups, companies, mass communication media, political parties and so on, which express their own opinions regarding the public project. Let $R = \{1, \ldots, m\}$ denote the set of interest groups. Interest groups are also endowed with their preferences over the alternative space. Additionally, they are assumed to possess perfect information about the project property. They express their voice about whether the project should be approved or not from the standpoint of their own interests. The voice of an interest group is a statement about which alternative that group prefers the most rather than information regarding the exact location of the project property x. However, they are allowed to send their voice strategically to affect individuals' voting behaviour in accordance with their interests. The distribution of interest groups' ideal point $z_j \in [0, 1]$ $(j \in R)$ is $z_1 \leq \ldots \leq z_i \leq \ldots \leq z_m$. Interest groups are approximately classified into two types according to which alternative they most prefer. In what follows, an interest group that is motivated to approve the project is denoted as a 'progressive group'. On the other hand, an interest group that is motivated to reject the project and maintain the status quo is denoted as a 'conservative group'. Individuals are uncertain as to the ideal point of each interest group. The subjective probability distribution $H(z)$ represents the prior beliefs that individuals have about interest groups' ideal points. This probability distribution is assumed to be of common knowledge among all the players. However, it is assumed that interest groups know the ideal points of other groups. The voices of interest groups are transmitted to all the individuals by incurring statement costs. These costs represent both pecuniary costs such as expenditures on campaigning and soap-box speeches, and non-pecuniary costs such as efforts and time. Individuals can observe the voices of interest groups and their costs.

9.2.2 Foundation of the Model

The utility to an individual i for a project is given by

$$U(x, t_i) = -|x - t_i| \tag{9.1}$$

In the same way, the utility of the individual i for the status quo is denoted by $U(0, t_i)$. This utility function represents that individuals have symmetric single-peaked preferences. This study assumes that a completely informed public manager proposes an innovative project to increase the welfare of individuals, that is,

Assumption 1:

$$U(x, t_M) > U(0, t_M) \tag{9.2}$$

where t_M represents the ideal point of the median voter (majority of individuals). The above condition implies that the public manager possesses an innovative idea and expertise, and is motivated to propose, as a welfare policy, a project coinciding with the majority will. However, this condition is not known by individuals who have inaccurate prior beliefs $F(x)$ about the project property. They choose to vote for or against the project on the basis of the belief $F(x)$. The expected utility of individual i for the project is represented by

$$EU(t_i) = \int_0^1 U(x, t_i)dF(x) \tag{9.3}$$

Regarding the expected utility of the median voter, the following assumption is satisfied:

Assumption 2:

$$EU(t_M) > U(0, t_M) \tag{9.4}$$

This assumption implies that in the initial state, the majority of individuals agree with the project proposed by the welfare manager. We can imagine the situation where the public manager successfully persuades individuals to agree to his proposal.

Before individuals cast votes, interest groups are allowed to give them a piece of information, using their voices in the project. Voices of interest groups, however, require the expenditure of statement costs. If an interest group does not pay the cost, it cannot send its voice to individuals. Thus a strategy of an interest group is composed of two components and is denoted by $s_j = (s_j^1, s_j^2)$. In the first place, an interest group has to decide whether to send its voice or not. The first decision of an interest group is represented by s_j^1, where $s_j^1 = 1$ represents the strategy of sending a voice, and $s_j^1 = 0$ represents the strategy of not sending a voice. In order for an interest group j to send its voice, it has to pay a statement cost c_j. In the model, the statement cost c_j is set exogenously. If an interest group decides to send its voice, it chooses the second component of the strategy, that is, whether to approve the project or not. Let s_j^2 denote the second component of the strategy, where $s_j^2 = 1$ represents approval for the project, and $s_j^2 = 0$ represents opposition to the project. In the case that an interest group chooses not to send its voice ($s_j^1 = 0$), the second strategy of the group is not defined. Let C_p and C_q denote the set of interest groups who decide to approve or disapprove the project respectively,

$$C_p = \{p | (s_p^1, s_p^2) = (1, 1), p \in M\} \tag{9.5}$$

$$C_q = \{q | (s_q^1, s_q^2) = (1, 0), q \in M\} \tag{9.6}$$

Interest groups that are well informed about the project property have the following utility function for the project:

$$W(x, z_i) = -|x - z_i| - s_j^1 c_j \tag{9.7}$$

The utility of an interest group for the status quo is denoted by $W(0, z_j)$. Since an interest group's choice is conditioned on the project property x and its own ideal point z_j, we denote the strategy of an interest group as

$$s_j(x, z_j) = [s_j^1(x, z_j), s_j^2(x, z_j)]$$

Before casting a vote, individuals are allowed to observe the strategies of interest groups and update their own beliefs about the project property x by using Bayes Rule. The updated beliefs are represented as the following expression:

$$F(x|s) = \frac{\int_0^x \text{Prob}(s|u)\,dF(u)}{\int_0^1 \text{Prob}(s|u)\,dF(u)} \tag{9.8}$$

where

$$\text{Prob}(s|u) = \prod_{p\in C_p}\int_{\underline{z}}^{\bar{z}} s_p^1(u, z_p)s_p^2(u, z_p)dH(z_p)\prod_{q\in C_q}\int_{\underline{z}}^{\bar{z}} s_q^1(u, z_q)[1-s_q^2(u, z_q)]dH(z_q) \tag{9.9}$$

After updating their own beliefs, each individual casts a vote. Individuals' strategy is represented by a binary decision v_i, which equals 1 if the individual vote for the project and 0 otherwise. Individuals' choices depend on their own ideal point t_i and the set of strategies of interest groups $s = (s_1, \ldots, s_j)$. Therefore the strategy of an individual is represented by $v_i\,(t_i, s)$.

After a referendum is held, an alternative is determined as a social decision by the majority rule. The outcome function through a referendum is represented by

$$\Phi(v) = \begin{cases} X{:}if \sum_{i=1}^{2M-1} v_i \geq M \\ Y{:}if \sum_{i=1}^{2M-1} v_i < M \end{cases} \tag{9.10}$$

As explained in the next subsection, the referendum outcome is determined by the choice of the median voter. Let us denote the alternative as:

$$\psi(t_M, s) = \begin{cases} X{:}if\ v_M(t_M, s) = 1 \\ Y{:}if\ v_M(t_M, s) = 0 \end{cases} \tag{9.11}$$

The decision-making process of the basic model consists of five stages:

1. A project property x is determined (a public manager proposes an innovative project).
2. Interest groups observing x decide their strategies $s = (s_1, \ldots, s_m)$.
3. Individuals observing the strategies s of interest groups choose their voting strategies $v = (v_1, \ldots, v_{2M-1})$.
4. A referendum outcome a is determined by the majority rule from individuals' voting.
5. The utilities of individuals and interest groups $U = (U_1, \ldots, U_{2M-1})$ and $W = (W_1, \ldots, W_m)$ are determined according to the referendum outcome a.

9.2.3 Equilibrium

As a solution of the basic model, we employ a perfect Bayesian equilibrium. To analyse the equilibrium, however, we incorporate two additional assumptions in the model. First, the basic model assumes that all individuals necessarily cast a vote without abstention. This means that all the individuals always vote as if they are the pivotal voter. This strategy is known to be weakly dominant with respect to the possible strategies of the other individuals. In short, individuals choose their strategies to maximize their expected utility given the strategies of the other individuals and interest groups. Therefore the strategy of an individual who has updated beliefs $F(x|s)$ is represented by

$$v_i(t_i, s) = \begin{cases} 1{:}\mathit{if}\ EU(t_i|s) \geq U(0, t_i) \\ 0{:}\mathit{if}\ EU(t_i|s) < U(0, t_i) \end{cases} \tag{9.12}$$

where $EU(t_i|s)$ is the conditional expected utility of an individual i:

$$EU(t_i, s) = \int_0^1 U(x, t_i)dF(x|s). \tag{9.13}$$

If the assumption of the pivotal voter is satisfied, and all individuals cast a vote according to the strategy (9.12), then the referendum outcome is determined by the choice of the median voter $v_M(t_M, s)$. As a result, the utility of an interest group is represented by

$$EW_j(v_M, s) = W[\psi(t_M, s), z_j] \tag{9.14}$$

The second assumption we impose to define the solution of the model requires the consistency of individuals' beliefs. It is difficult to define an individual's updated beliefs about an information set that he believes should happen with zero probability in equilibrium. This out-of-equilibrium belief cannot be defined by Bayes Rule. With regard to this consistency problem, we adopt the definition offered by Fudenberg and Tirole (1991). Their definition requires that a deviation from equilibria that leads to a zero-probability information set does not imply that the deviating player gets information that he cannot know essentially in this game. This means that 'if the individual is in a zero-probability information set, then he ignores the interest groups' message'.

A perfect Bayesian equilibrium of the basic model is defined as a set of interest groups' strategies $s^* = (s_1^*, \ldots, s_m^*)$, individuals' strategies $v^* = (v_1^*, \ldots, v_{2M-1}^*)$ and individuals' beliefs $F(x|s^*)$ that satisfy the following conditions:

1. For any interest group j, the strategy s_j^* maximizes the expected utility of the interest group j, given the strategy of the median voter v_M^*, and the other interest groups s_{-j}^*.
2. For any individual i, the strategy v_i^* is defined by equation (9.12), given the strategy of interest group s^* and his own beliefs $F(x|s^*)$.
3. The beliefs of individuals are defined by Bayes Rule (9.8) from the strategy of interest group s^*.

In the basic model, there are two cases of perfect Bayesian equilibrium: (1) no interest groups send their voices (this equilibrium is hereafter called 'indifferent equilibrium') and (2) a limited number of conservative groups who oppose the project send their voices (this equilibrium is hereafter called 'disagreement equilibrium').

Indifferent equilibrium

Indifferent equilibrium always exists in the basic model. In this equilibrium, the strategy of any interest group is $s_j^{1*}(x, z_j) = 0$. Since no interest group sends its voice, individuals cannot get any information about the project. As a result, they do not update their beliefs about the project property. The equilibrium strategy of an individual is represented by the strategy (9.12) on the basis of initial beliefs. Under the assumption of symmetric single-peaked preferences of individuals, there exists a critical point that satisfies the condition $EU(t^*) = U(0, t^*)$. The referendum outcome depends on the critical point t^* and the ideal point of the median voter t_M:

$$a = \begin{cases} X{:}\,if\ t_M \geq t^* \\ Y{:}\,if\ t_M < t^* \end{cases} \tag{9.15}$$

If Assumption 2 about the public manager is satisfied, the referendum outcome ratifies the project. Furthermore, Assumption 1 ensures that the outcome is better for the majority of individuals. Thus, while individuals cast their votes based on inaccurate initial beliefs, the referendum outcome coincides with the majority will, as long as Assumptions 1 and 2 with respect to the public managers are satisfied.

Disagreement equilibrium

Let C_q^* denote the set of conservative groups that oppose the project in the disagreement equilibrium. The condition for the existence of this type of equilibrium is

$$\begin{gathered}\int_{\bar{c}^*}^{1} U(x, t_M) dF(x|s_{-q}^*) \geq U(0, t_M) \\ \int_{\bar{c}^*}^{1} U(x, t_M) dF(x|s^*) < U(0, t_M) \\ |-z_q| + c_q \leq |x - z_q|\end{gathered} \tag{9.16}$$

where s_{-q} represents the strategy profile of conservative groups that belong to the set $C_q^* - q$, and $\bar{c}^*$ is the highest cost that conservative groups sending their voices in this equilibrium have to pay. Conservative group $q \in C_q^*$ has an incentive to induce individuals to vote against the project. However, it is beneficial for the group to send its voice only if its voice can affect the voting behaviour of the median voter and change the referendum outcome. The first two conditions represent the necessary conditions that the voice of a conservative group q changes the referendum outcome from ratifying the project to opposing it. Furthermore, the last condition expresses that it is profitable for the conservative group to change the referendum outcome, even if it has to pay the statement costs. If these conditions are satisfied, the conservative group $q \in C_q^*$ opposes the project $s_q^{1*}(x, z_q) = 1, s_q^{2*}(x, z_q) = 0$.

On the other hand, progressive groups that are motivated to carry out the project do not send their voices, that is $s_p^{1*} = 0$. In this equilibrium, individuals observe that interest groups $q \in C_q^*$ pay the statement cost and oppose the project. They can infer that $x \notin [0, \bar{c}^*]$ with respect to the project property. Therefore the updated beliefs of individuals are represented by

$$F(x|s^*) = \frac{\int_{\bar{c}^*}^{x} \prod_{r \in C_q^*} \mu(u, c_r) dF(u)}{\int_{\bar{c}^*}^{1} \prod_{r \in C_q^*} \mu(u, c_r) dF(u)} \tag{9.17}$$

where

$$\mu(u, c_q) = \int_{\underline{z}}^{u - c_q/2} dH(z) \tag{9.18}$$

The choice of an individual i in this equilibrium is represented by the strategy (9.12) on the basis of the updated beliefs (9.17). In this equilibrium, the referendum outcome that results from individuals' votes is $a = Y$. Therefore, according to the voices of the conservative groups $q \in C_q^*$, the project is rejected in the referendum. However, the referendum outcome does not necessarily coincide with the majority will. In particular, if Assumption 1 is satisfied, the referendum ends up in an inefficient outcome that is not better for the majority.

What we have explored can be summed up as follows:

Proposition 1: In the basic model, progressive groups do not send their voices. (For proof see Appendix 9A.1.)

In the disagreement equilibrium, only a limited number of interest groups disagree with a project and prevent a referendum outcome coinciding with the majority will. The result, in which progressive groups do not send their voices in equilibrium, is due to following reason. Since Assumption 1 is satisfied in the basic model, progressive groups that agree to the project can expect a referendum outcome in accordance with their preferences, even if they do not voice their opinion. For conservative groups that disagree with the project, however, a referendum outcome in discordance with their preferences can be expected unless they send their opposing voices. Therefore conservative groups have a strong incentive to oppose the project, even if they have to pay the statement costs. If the referendum outcome is likely to result in project rejection, progressive groups try to influence the outcome to approval by sending their voices. In this context, however, more conservative groups try to prevent the outcome that approves the project. Consequently, in the equilibrium, no progressive groups make their statement. Furthermore, individuals who do not know the ideal point of the interest groups cannot judge whether they should follow interest groups' endorsement or not. As a result, the referendum rejects the project that should be chosen under complete information. Thus the drivers behind an inefficient outcome are (1) the initial state in which the public manager proposes a project, (2) the statement costs that interest groups have to pay in order to send their voices, and (3) uncertainty of individuals about the ideal points of interest groups.

9.2.4 Evaluation of the Effects of Information

Before proceeding, we examine the complete information situations for the sake of evaluating the effects of the lack of information on referendum outcomes. When voters have perfect information, their strategies are represented by

$$v_i(t_i) = \begin{cases} 1{:}if\ U(x, t_i) \geq U(0, t_i) \\ 0{:}if\ U(x, t_i) < U(0, t_i) \end{cases} \tag{9.19}$$

As a result, a referendum outcome depends on the project property x and the ideal point of the median voter t_M:

$$a = \begin{cases} X{:}if\ t_M \geq x/2 \\ Y{:}if\ t_M < x/2 \end{cases} \tag{9.20}$$

Here, if Assumption 1 is satisfied, the vote of the referendum ratifies the project such that $a = X$. Thus it is shown that in a complete information environment, the result of the referendum confirms the innovative project that provides a higher level of social welfare. The analysis of the basic model demonstrates that the lack of knowledge of individuals diminishes the efficiency of referendum systems.

9.3 POLICY TO OVERCOME AN INEFFICIENT REFERENDUM OUTCOME

In the basic model, only a limited number of conservative groups send their voices. In order to realize an efficient outcome through the referendum, it is required to give all the interest groups an incentive to send their voices. This section deals with an alternative policy that makes individuals better informed about a project property and examines the likelihood of attaining votes as if they reflected accurate information. In what follows, two policies are considered in order to tackle the factors that lead to the inefficient outcome in the basic model: (1) a policy to bear the statement cost (Section 9.3.1); and (2) a policy to provide information about the ideal points of interest groups (Section 9.3.2). The former policy gives all the interest groups opportunities to express their voices. For example, it can be expected that the government carries out public hearings or bears advertisement costs. By the latter policy, individuals can know the ideal point of each interest group. For example, we can consider that the government or a third party examines all the statements of interest groups and distinguishes clearly their viewpoints.

9.3.1 Equitable Statement Opportunities

In this section, the policy game A is formulated in order to investigate the effect that the policy providing all the interest groups' equitable statement opportunities has on referendum consequences. In the policy game A, all the interest groups are able to send their voices without any costs. Therefore the decision of an interest group is whether or not it agrees with the project. The strategy of an interest group is represented by a one-component strategy, $s_j(x, z_j)$, which equals 1 if it agrees with the project, 0 otherwise. The set of interest groups who decide to approve or disapprove of the project is denoted as R_p and R_q, respectively:

$$R_p = \{p | s_p = 1, p \in R\} \tag{9.21}$$

$$R_q = \{q | s_q = 0, q \in R\}. \tag{9.22}$$

The utility of an interest group is denoted by

$$\overline{W}(x, z_i) = -|x - z_i| \tag{9.23}$$

Observing the strategies of interest groups, individuals update their own beliefs about the project property x by using Bayes Rule. The updated beliefs

$$F(x|s) = \frac{\int_0^x \text{Prob}(s|u)\,dF(u)}{\int_0^1 \text{Prob}(s|u)\,dF(u)} \tag{9.24}$$

where

$$\text{Prob}(s|u) = \prod_{p \in R_p} \int_{\underline{z}}^{\overline{z}} s_p(u, z_p)\,dH(z_p) \prod_{q \in R_q} \int_{\underline{z}}^{\overline{z}} [1 - s_q(u, z_q)]\,dH(z_q) \tag{9.25}$$

The individuals' voting strategy is represented by a binary decision $v_i(t_i, s)$, which equals 1 if the individual vote for the project and 0 otherwise. According to the assumption of the pivotal voter introduced in the basic model, the strategy of an individual is represented by equation (9.12). Similarly, the referendum outcome is determined by the choice of the median voter as in equation (9.11).

In the policy game A, there exist two cases of perfect Bayesian equilibrium: (1) interest groups do not send their voices on the basis of their private information, i.e. the project property x and their ideal points z_j (this equilibrium is hereafter called 'pooling equilibrium'); and (2) interest groups recommend the alternative that is better for the group on the basis of their private information (this equilibrium is hereafter called 'separating equilibrium').

Pooling equilibrium
Pooling equilibrium always exists in the policy game A. In the pooling equilibrium, the strategy of any interest group is represented by

$$s_j^*(x, z_j) = 1 \text{ or } 0 \text{ (indefinite)} \tag{9.26}$$

The above strategy means that interest groups are indifferent as to what statement about the project they should make. As the voices of interest groups describe no substance of the project, individuals cannot update their beliefs about the project property. Individuals cast a vote on the basis of initial beliefs, represented by equation (9.12) in the indifferent equilibrium. In the pooling equilibrium, since each individual realizes that the voices of interest groups do not transmit any information on the project, the individual ignores what voices interest groups send. Furthermore, this fact drives interest groups to become indifferent as to which voices to send. Under Assumptions 1 and 2, however, the referendum outcome ratifies the project that is better for the majority of individuals, like the indifferent equilibrium of the basic model.

Separating equilibrium
The following condition is required for the existence of the separating equilibrium:

$$EU(t_M|s_j = 1, s_{-j}^*) \geq EU(t_M|s_j = 0, s_{-j}^*) \tag{9.27}$$

where $EU(t_M|s_j = 1, s_{-j}^*)$ and $EU(t_M|s_j = 0, s^*_{-j})$ denote the conditional expected utility on the basis of updated beliefs $F(x|s_j = 1, s_{-j}^*)$ and $F(x|s_j = 0, s_{-j}^*)$, respectively. The above condition reflects the fact that the voice of an interest group can give marginal effects on the voting behaviour of the median voter. In this equilibrium, the strategies of interest groups are represented by

$$s_j^*(x, z_j) = \begin{cases} 1{:}if\,|x - z_j| \leq |z_j| \\ 0{:}if\,|x - z_j| > |z_j| \end{cases} \tag{9.28}$$

The above strategy means that progressive and conservative groups agree and disagree with the project, respectively. Then individuals' beliefs are updated in the following ways:

$$F(x|s^*) = \frac{\int_0^x \mu(u)^{m_X(s^*)}[1 - \mu(u)]^{m_Y(s^*)} dF(\mu)}{\int_0^1 \mu(u)^{m_X(s^*)}[1 - \mu(u)]^{m_Y(s^*)} dF(\mu)} \tag{9.29}$$

where

$$\mu(u) = \int_{u/2}^{\bar{z}} dH(z_j) \tag{9.30}$$

and

$$m_X(s^*) = \|\{p|s_p^* = 1, p \in R\}\| \tag{9.31}$$

$$m_Y(s^*) = \|\{q|s_q^* = 0, q \in R\}\| \tag{9.32}$$

The terms $m_X(s^*)$ and $m_Y(s^*)$ represent the number of progressive and conservative groups, respectively. In policy game A, individuals who cannot distinguish the ideal points of interest groups know just the number of interest groups that endorse each alternative. The strategy of individuals in the separating equilibrium is denoted by expression (9.12) on the basis of updated beliefs (9.29).

The information that individuals can obtain in the separating equilibrium is just the number of interest groups that approve and reject the project, namely, $m_X(s^*)$ and $m_Y(s^*)$. Even if each interest group sends its voice with respect to the desirability of the project, individuals who are uncertain as to the ideal points of interest groups cannot know the correct position of the project property x. Consequently, it can happen that individuals forming incorrect beliefs about the project property vote for the alternative that is not better for them. If the condition for the separating equilibrium is not satisfied, the pooling equilibrium realizes a unique equilibrium. In sum, in any equilibrium in the policy game A, individuals cannot gain the correct information about the project property x and an inefficient outcome can result.

Even in the case when a separating equilibrium exists, the pooling equilibrium might still be realized. As the condition (9.27) is satisfied, however, the former case implies that interest groups can have a substantial influence on the choice of the median voter by sending their voices. Farrell (1993) regards the equilibrium where players adopt an indifferent and ignoring strategy under the condition (9.27) as an irrelevant equilibrium, namely, a 'babbling equilibrium'. In the following analysis, we focus only on the separating equilibrium as long as condition (9.27) is satisfied. If condition (9.27) is not satisfied, however, the pooling equilibrium is always realized as the unique equilibrium.

9.3.2 Disclosing Ideal Points of Interest Groups

In policy game A, individuals are uncertain of the ideal points of interest groups. In this section, we relax this restraint and present the policy game B in order to examine the effect of the policy that informs individuals of the ideal points of interest groups. Also in the policy game B, the assumption of free statement costs remains the same as in policy game A. Then the strategy of an interest group $s_j(x, z_j)$ is whether or not it agrees with the project. On the other hand, the strategy of an individual depends on the ideal points of interest groups. We denote the strategy of an individual as $v_i(t_i, s, z)$, where $z = (z_1, \ldots, z_m)$ represents the set of ideal points of interest groups. The beliefs that an individual updates by observing the strategy of interest groups s and their ideal points z are represented by

$$F(x|s, z) = \frac{\int_0^x \text{Prob}(s|u, z)\,dF(u)}{\int_0^1 \text{Prob}(s|u, z)\,dF(u)} \tag{9.33}$$

where

$$\text{Prob}(s|u, z) = \prod_{p \in R_p} s_p(u, z_p) \prod_{q \in R_q} [1 - s_q(u, z_q)] \tag{9.34}$$

The strategy of an individual is represented by

$$v_i(t_i, s, z) = \begin{cases} 1{:}\textit{if } EU(t_i|s, z) \geq U(0, t_i) \\ 0{:}\textit{if } EU(t_i|s, z) < U(0, t_i) \end{cases} \tag{9.35}$$

where $EU(t_i|s, z)$ is the conditional expected utility of an individual i:

$$EU(t_i, s, z) = \int_0^1 U(x, t_i)\,dF(x|s, z) \tag{9.36}$$

The policy game B has a unique perfect Bayesian equilibrium, in which all the interest groups endorse the alternative that they most prefer, and individuals cast votes on the basis of their own beliefs $F(x|s^*, z)$. In this equilibrium, conservative groups $\{1, \ldots, j^*\}$ oppose the project, and progressive groups $\{j^*, \ldots, m\}$ agree with the project. The critical number j^* is determined by the condition $z_j^* < x/2 < z_j^* + 1$. Furthermore, individuals who know the ideal point of interest groups can infer that $x \in [2z_{j^*}, 2z_{j^*+1}]$ Therefore individuals' beliefs are represented by

$$F(x|s^*, z) = F(x|s^*, z) = \begin{cases} 0 \ (\textit{if}\ x \in [0, 2z_{j^*}]) \\ \dfrac{\int_{2z_{j^*}}^{x} dF(u)}{\int_{2z_{j^*}}^{2z_{j^*+1}} dF(u)} \ (\textit{if}\ x \in [2z_{j^*}, 2z_{j^*+1}]) \\ 1 \ (\textit{if}\ x \in [2z_{j^*+1}, 1]) \end{cases} \quad (9.37)$$

The above expression means that the more closely the ideal points of interest groups are distributed (the smaller distance between the two ideal points of the interest group j^* and $j^* + 1$), the more correct beliefs individuals can possess. Even in this equilibrium, however, individuals cannot acquire the complete information about the project property. In particular, when the ideal points of interest groups are polarized, individuals' beliefs about the project property are not improved only by knowing the distribution of the ideal points of interest groups.

9.3.3 Political Implication

The result of the theoretical analysis in this chapter suggests that the referendum might cause an inefficient outcome even where individuals cast votes rationally and without abstention. As shown in the basic model, if individuals lack the appropriate knowledge regarding an innovative project, the referendum outcome is that (1) individuals and interest groups become indifferent, or (2) a limited number of conservative groups oppose the project, and the project is rejected. Indeed, an innovative project is often in a vulnerable position to the attack of interest groups in conservative philosophies. Then, as shown in our analysis, if no progressive groups that agree with the project make statements, the opinion of conservative groups can be accepted by the majority and consequently the innovative project is always rejected in a region. The policies introduced in this study have the effect of making individuals acquire more accurate information about a project. These policies, however, cannot completely remove the likelihood that an inefficient outcome is realized by the referendum. In particular, if the ideal points of interest groups are polarized and are far from the ideal point of the median voter in a region, the referendum might end up in an inefficient outcome.

Proposition 2: A policy to bear statement costs and disclose ideal points of interest groups cannot attain perfect information, and the referendum might fail in an inefficient outcome.

As explained in Section 9.1, the referendum is a useful device for efficient social decision as long as it is contested under an ideal condition. If individuals do not possess precise knowledge about a proposed project, however, the referendum may produce an unsuitable social decision. Eventually, the inefficiency problem in the referendum will be overcome by reducing the incompleteness of people's knowledge about the project. One of the important roles that public managers should play here is to make individuals informed of a project by providing them with relevant information (Kobayashi et al., 2003).

9.4 CONCLUSIONS

Recently, the use of a referendum in the determination of a public project has become increasingly widespread (cf. Soberg and Tangeras, 2003; Commission on the Conduct of Referendum, 1996). In a democratic system that adopts the majority decision scheme, a referendum is likely to serve as an effective device for social decision making. Empirical observation, however, has often pointed out that innovations hardly obtain majority acceptance in a region, and the optimal solution will not always be implemented by a referendum outcome. The model developed here allows us to evaluate the efficiency and the effectiveness of a referendum mechanism. It shows that informational assumptions are key to the referendum outcomes, and an inefficient outcome, different from the outcome attained when individuals are completely informed, may arise in incomplete information environments. In particular, it shows that where individuals' judgements on the credibility of the groups' voice are based on the groups' efforts (statement cost), a limited number of interest groups utilize their voice in strategic fashion and try to prevent a referendum outcome expressing the majority will. Alternative institutional designs are introduced to overcome the inefficient outcome produced by the referendum, while the limits of these policies are demonstrated. As suggested in the previous paragraph, in order to improve the efficiency of the referendum system, overcoming the lack of information about innovative projects is the demanding task. These results imply that the innovation capabilities of political systems can be improved by sharing decentralized knowledge and information among regional agencies.

The analytical results obtained in this study rely upon the several assumptions of the model. The framework presented in this study can be extended to various directions, towards the development of a theory of political systems. The following subjects remain for future studies. First, we assumed rational voting behaviour of individuals. However, psychological and emotional factors might prevent them from making a reasoned choice. Second, we should investigate the issue of abstention. If many individuals choose to abstain from casting a vote, majority preferences might not be reflected in the referendum outcome. Third, communications among individuals are not modelled. Interactions among individuals could have an enormous effect on the formation of public opinion in a region.

REFERENCES

Arrow, K.J. (1963), *Social Choice and Individual Values*, 2nd edn, New Haven, CT: Yale University Press.

Boulding, K.E. (1956), *The Image*, Ann Arbor, MI: University of Michigan Press.

Cameron, C.M. and J.P. Jung (1992), 'Strategic endorsements', mimeo, New York: Columbia University.

Commission on the Conduct of Referendum (Chair: P. Nairn) (1996), 'Report of the Commission on the Conduct of Referendum', London: Electoral Reform Society and Constitution Unit.

Delli, C., X. Michael and S. Keeter (1991), 'Stability and change in the United States public's knowledge of politics', *Public Opinion Quarterly*, **55**, 583–612.

Downs, A. (1957), *An Economic Theory of Democracy*, New York: Harper and Row.

Farrell, J. (1993), 'Meaning and credibility in cheap talk games', *Games and Economic Behavior*, **5**, 514–31.

Ferejohn, J.A. and M.P. Fiorina (1974), 'The paradox of not voting: a decision theoretic analysis', *American Political Science Review*, **68**, 525–36.

Fudenberg, D. and J. Tirole (1991), 'Perfect Bayesian equilibrium and sequential equilibrium', *Journal of Economic Theory*, **53**, 236–60.

Gibbard, A. (1969), 'Manipulation of voting schemes: a general result', *Econometrica*, **41**, 587–601.

Grofman, B. and B. Norrander (1990), 'Efficient use of reference group cues in a single dimension', *Public Choice*, **64**, 213–27.

Holsti, O. (1962), 'The belief system and national images: a case study', *Journal of Conflict Resolution*, 6, 244–52.

Kobayashi, K., K. Matsushima and T. Hatori (2003), 'Providing policy information and citizen learning', *Proceedings of the 2003 IEEE Systems, Man and Cybernetics Conference* (CD-ROM).

Ledyard, J.O. and T.R. Palfrey (2002), 'The approximation of efficient public good mechanisms by simple voting schemes', *Journal of Public Economics*, **83**, 153–71.

Leites, N. (1951), *The Operational Code of the Politburo*, New York: McGraw-Hill.

Lippmann, W. (1922), *Public Opinion*, New York: Macmillan.

Lupia, A. (1992), 'Busy voters, agenda control and the power of information', *American Political Science Review*, **86**, 390–403.

Lupia, A. (1994), 'Shortcuts versus encyclopedias: information and voting behavior in California insurance reform elections', *American Political Science Review*, **88**, 63–76.
Manza, J., F.L. Cook and B.I. Page (eds) (2002), *Navigating Public Opinion: Polls, Policy, and the Future of American Democracy*, Oxford: Oxford University Press.
McKelvey, R.D. and P.C. Ordeshook (1985), 'Elections with limited information: a fulfilled expectations model using contemporaneous poll and endorsement data as information sources', *Journal of Economic Theory*, **36**, 55–85.
Mueller, D. (ed.) (1997), *Perspectives on Public Choice: A Handbook*, Cambridge: Cambridge University Press.
Palfrey, T.R. and H. Rosenthal (1985), 'Voter participation and strategic uncertainty', *American Political Science Review*, **79**, 62–78.
Popkin, S.L. (1991), *The Reasoning Voter: Communication and Persuasion in Presidential Campaigns*, Chicago, IL: University of Chicago Press.
Potters, J., R. Sloof and F. Winden (1997), 'Campaign expenditures, contributions and direct endorsements: the strategic use of information and money to influence voter behavior', *European Journal of Political Economy*, **13** (1), 1–31.
Riker, W.H. and P.C. Ordeshook (1968), 'A theory of the calculus of voting', *American Political Science Review*, **62**, 25–43.
Riker, W.H. and P.C. Ordeshook (1973), *An Introduction to Positive Theory*, Englewood Cliffs, NJ: Prentice-Hall.
Romer, T. and H. Rosenthal (1978), 'Political resource allocation, controlled agendas and the status quo', *Public Choice*, **33** (4), 27–43.
Satterthwaite, M.A. (1975), 'Strategy-proofness and Arrow's conditions: existence and correspondence theorems for voting procedures and social welfare functions', *Journal of Economic Theory*, **10**, 187–217.
Soberg, M. and T. Tangeras (2003), 'Voter turnout in direct democracy: theory and evidence', Working Paper 596, The Research Institute of Industrial Economics, Stockholm.
Winden, F. (1999), 'On the economic theory of interest groups: towards a group frame of reference in political economics', *Public Choice*, **100**, 1–29.

APPENDIX 9A.1

9A.1 Proof of Proposition 1

First, we identify the conditions that progressive and conservative groups choose to send their voices, respectively.

(a) A progressive group (p) sends its voice if:

$$EU(t_M|s_j^1 = 0, s_{-j}) < U(0, t_M) \tag{9A.1}$$

$$EU[t_M|(s_j^1 = 1, s_j^2 = 1), s_{-j}] \geq U(0, t_M) \tag{9A.2}$$

$$-|x - z_j| - c_j \geq -|z_j| \tag{9A.3}$$

(b) A conservative group (q) sends its voice if:

$$EU(t_M|s_j^1 = 0, s_{-j}) \geq U(0, t_M) \tag{9A.4}$$

$$EU[t_M|(s_j^1 = 1, s_j^2 = 0), s_{-j}] < U(0, t_M) \tag{9A.5}$$

$$-|z_j| - c_j \geq -|x - z_j| \tag{9A.6}$$

The first two conditions (a) and (b) represent the necessary condition that the voice of progressive (conservative) group changes the referendum outcome from opposing (ratifying) the project to ratifying (opposing) it. The last condition represents that it is profitable for a progressive (conservative) group to change the referendum outcome, even if it has to pay the statement cost.

Second, we prove that different types of interest groups do not send their voices simultaneously in the equilibrium. Suppose, contrary to this, that the equilibrium strategies s^* in which the group j agrees with the project ($s_j^{1*} = 1, s_j^{2*} = 1$), and the group j' opposes the project ($s_{j'}^{1*} = 1, s_{j'}^{2*} = 0$). From (9A.2) and (9A.5), the equilibrium requires the following conditions:

$$EU[t_M|(s_j^{1*} = 1|s_j^{2*} = 1), s_{-j}] \geq U(0, t_M) \tag{9A.7}$$

$$EU[t_M|(s_{j'}^{1*} = 1|s_{j'}^{2*} = 0), s_{-j'}] < U(0, t_M) \tag{9A.8}$$

Here, as the right-hand sides of the above expressions are the same, both conditions cannot be satisfied. As a result, either type of progressive and conservative groups sends their voices in equilibrium.

Finally, we show that sending its voice is not a dominant strategy for a progressive group. From the above argument, we know that there are two cases, one in which progressive groups $p \in C_p^*$ ratify the project (case 1), or the other in which conservative groups $q \in C_q^*$ oppose the project (case 2). Consider case 1. Then, (9A.3) requires $x \notin [0, \bar{c}^*]$,where $\bar{c}^*$ is the maximum of endorsement costs of groups $p \in C_p$. Accordingly, (9A.1) and (9A.2) are:

$$\int_{\bar{c}^*}^{1} U(x, t_M) dF(x|s_p^1 = 0, s_{-p}^*) < U(0, t_M) \qquad (9A.9)$$

$$\int_{\bar{c}^*}^{1} U(x, t_M) dF[x|(s_p^{1*} = 1, s_p^{2*} = 1), s_{-p}^*] \geq U(0, t_M) \qquad (9A.10)$$

From the assumptions of the model, (9A.9) means that the expected value of the project property x increases following the voices by groups $C_p^* - p$. The expected value, however, satisfies:

$$E[x|s_p^1 = 0, s_{-p}^*] \leq \int_{c_p^*}^{1} x dF(x) \leq \int_{0}^{1} x dF(x) \qquad (A9.11)$$

This means that the expected value decreases by the groups $C_p^* - p$, and as a result this contradicts the condition (9A.9). Thus, case 1 does not occur in the equilibrium of the basic model.

9A.2 Equilibrium of the Policy Game A

The best response of an interest group j ($j = p$ for a progressive group and q for a conservative group) to the strategy of the median voter is: (1) when $v_M(t_M, 1, s_j) = 1$, $v_M(t_M, 0, s_j) = 0$ then $s_p^*(x, z_p) = 1$ for a progressive group, and $s_q^*(x, z_q) = 0$ for a conservative group; (2) when $v_M(t_M, 1, s_j) = v_M(t_M, 0, s_j)$, then $s_j^*(x, z_j) = 0$ or 1 ($j = p, q$); (3) when $v_M(t_M, 1, s_j) = 0$, $v_M(t_M, 0, s_j) = 1$, then $s_p^*(x, z_p) = 0$ for a progressive group, and $s_q^*(x, z_q) = 1$ for a conservative group. Case (3) requires the median voter to understand that the voice approving the project means to oppose it, and that the voice opposing the project means to approve it. This behaviour is called 'neologistic', and describes the situation of no agreement on the meaning of the voices by interest groups. While the meaning of messages is an important matter for human communications, it is not the main concern of this chapter. Thus we focus on the non-neologistic equilibrium and exclude case (3) from equilibrium. In case (2), the group is indifferent about which voice to send, and the median voter does not base his choice on such a voice. This is the case of pooling equilibrium. This equilibrium, called 'babbling equilibrium', always exists as the voter has no motivation to rely on the voices of interest groups if these groups do not provide useful information, and interest groups have no motivation to send their voices based upon their information if they are ignored. Finally, case (1) requires the following conditions:

$$EU[t_M|(s_j = 1, s^*_{-j})] \geq U(0, t_M) > EU[t_M|(s_j = 0, s^*_{-j})]. \quad (9A.12)$$

As no statement cost is assumed in the policy game A, however, even in the case of $EU[t_M|(s_j = 1, s^*_{-j})] = EU[t_M|(s_j = 0, s^*_{-j})]$, interest groups' strategy (1) can be their best response. Therefore the necessary condition for separating equilibrium is:

$$EU[t_M|(s_j = 1, s^*_{-j})] \geq EU[t_M|(s_j = 0, s^*_{-j})] \quad (9A.13)$$

10. Economic evaluation of pre- and post-discounting fee systems

Kakuya Matsushima and Kiyoshi Kobayashi

10.1 INTRODUCTION

Thanks to the innovation of information technology (IT), various financial settlement systems are developing rapidly. With the advance of IT, it is possible to set various fare systems for both public transportation and toll roads, e.g. the IC (integrated circuit) settlement service for railway companies and the ETC (electronic toll collection) system for highways. Thanks to such high-level settlement technology, a new system can be introduced where both consuming and travelling behaviours can be bundled. Consumers' behaviour of buying something with their credit cards has the effect of releasing their personal information to credit card companies. On the other hand, firms also reveal their information to credit card companies by offering settlement services with credit cards. Each stakeholder who attends this transaction can acquire information about other stakeholders by using this settlement system. In that sense, settlement services by credit card can be considered as an 'information club'.

Once we see bundling service between consuming and travelling as an information club, indirect effects that are produced by settlement services in transportation markets can be analysed. People who enjoy settlement services by credit card automatically send fruitful information that they are frequent consumers of the service. Firms who join the information club can send information to consumers who are involved in the club more effectively, which reduces transaction costs. In addition, when both transportation firms and retailers join the information club, both travelling and consuming behaviours, which were treated independently, can be bundled. This means that both travelling and consuming behaviours, which are distributed in both a spatial and temporal manner, are linked.

In this chapter, the main focus is on pre- and post-discounting fee systems in transportation services. Consumers who participate in the programme may change not only their travelling behaviours, but also their consuming behaviours, which may affect regional economies. In general, those services can be achieved with settlement systems by credit card. When consumers pay transportation fares by credit card, various means for discount fares can be considered because the fare is settled in a fixed period, e.g. once a month. That gives consumers flexible usage of transportation services; they may change their travel behaviour, including where to visit to consume services.

As a first step, we focus on the point that transportation fares are post-paid with settlement system by credit card. The risk-sharing structure between the firms providing transportation services and the customers of the pre- and post-paid systems are theoretically investigated. The pre-paid systems refer to the complete contracts that have to be established before service transactions, while the post-paid systems refer to the incomplete contracts where the application of the prespecified fare structure is described in the contract, and the actual payments are conditional upon actual consumption by the consumers. A three-period contract model is formulated to investigate the impacts of the pre- and post-paid systems upon the firm's profit and the consumers' surplus. The chapter concludes that social surplus can always be improved by introducing the post-paid system in addition to the conventional price systems.

In this chapter, the risk-sharing structure with transportation firms and households in pre- and post-discounting fee systems is analysed to show the economic benefit of these systems. First, let us call systems where households pay fees before they consume services 'pre-discounting' fee systems. Train passes and pre-paid cards are samples of pre-discounting fee systems. Households purchase options to consume the transportation service (hereafter, pre-discounting ticket) in advance. Those who purchase tickets can consume the service free of charge within the effective period of the ticket. Pre-discounting tickets can be classified into (1) tickets with fixed effective period (e.g. train passes) and (2) those without any effective period (e.g. a book of coupons and pre-paid cards). Consumers forgo the right to compensation in the case of unused tickets. The first type of pre-discounting ticket is analysed in this chapter. Households bear the risk of use of transportation services (hereafter, demand risk) when they purchase train passes. Firms obtain a fixed amount of profit in a certain period, while households enjoy the benefit from discounted fees, but bear the demand risk. Discounted fees can be considered as the compensation for the loss of monetary liquidity of part of their income.

On the other hand, the system where households pay discounted fees based on how much they have consumed the service is called the post-discounted fee system. ETC systems in highways and settlement services with IC cards for private railways in Kansai area, Japan (Surutto Kansai PiTaPa) are examples of this type of system. Rules about fee payment after

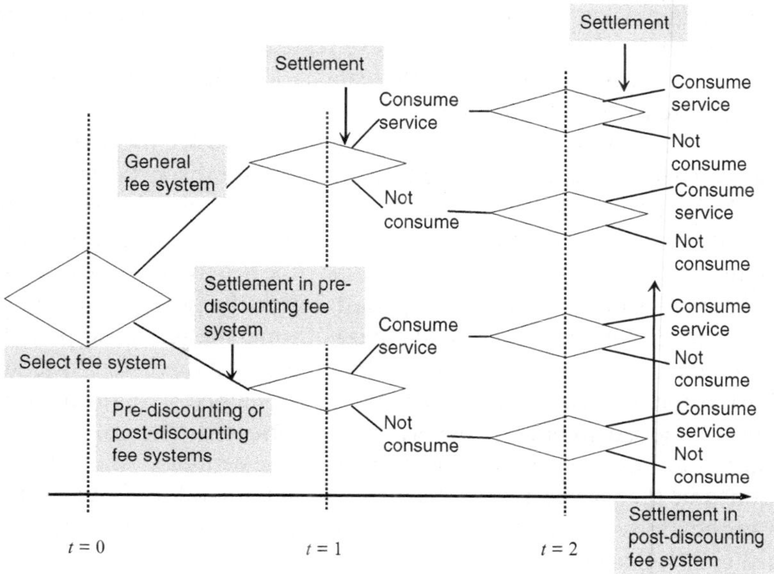

Figure 10.1 Structure of the model

the consumption of services (hereafter, discounted fee menu) are proposed in advance for the post-discounted fee system. Households make a contract about the menu with the service provider before they consume the service. The contract about the discounted fee menu is made at this point, while that about the amount of money they will pay is made later. As only the discounted fee menu is written in the contract, the amount of the transaction cannot be included in the contract. The amount of the fee is notified when it is settled based upon private information about their service use, which makes its possible to introduce various methods of discounting. As it is necessary to process a large amount of information about individuals' behaviour, we cannot introduce the post-discounted fee system without high-level financial settlement technologies.

The basic structure of the two types of systems is explained with the three-period contract model shown in Figure 10.1. In period 0, a contract about the consumption of transportation service is made between households and the firm. Transportation services are consumed in both periods 1 and 2. In period 0, households cannot accurately predict their behaviour in the future as they bear demand risk for service consumption. The contract about the transaction for the pre-discounted ticket is made in period 0. Contents of this contract cannot be changed after period 0 as it is fixed when the contract is made. Households that do not purchase pre-discounted ticket have the option to decide whether they will consume the transportation service after they have realized the value of trip utility (hereafter, selection option). Households may lose the selection option if they purchase the pre-discounted ticket.

On the other hand, contracts about the discounted fee menu are made in period 0 with the post-discounted fee system. As transportation fees are notified after period 2 based upon how frequently households consume the service, they have the selection option in both periods 1 and 2. Households that consume the service in period 1 can enjoy the benefit from fee discount if they also consume the service in period 2 with the post-discounted fee system. This means that households that consume the service in period 1 are given the option about discounted fees in period 2 (hereafter, discount option). If these households consume the service in period 2, the discount option is exercised and the fee in period 2 is discounted. The firm bears the amount of fee discount; that is, the firm bears the demand risk. If they do not consume the service in period 2, this option is abandoned. As we have seen in the above discussion, both systems have different structures with regard to risk sharing.

There is empirical research on how loyalty programmes affect households' consumption (Nako, 1997; Sharp and Sharp, 1997; Bolton et al., 2000; Yi and Jeon, 2003; Lewis, 2004; Taylor and Neslin, 2005; Kivetz et al., 2006; Meyer-Waarden, 2007). The results of these studies suggest that these programmes have significant effects upon consumers' consuming behaviours. However, they cannot explain the structure of their effects. There is also related theoretical research to tackle the effect of frequent-flyer programmes upon economies (Cairns and Galbraith, 1990; Banerjee and Summers, 1987; Caminal and Matutes, 1990; Fudenberg and Tirole, 2000). For example, Caminal and Claici (2007) show that frequent-flyer programmes are business-stealing devices that tend to enhance competition, in the sense of generating lower average transaction prices and higher consumer surplus. But these studies do not explain the role of these programmes as contracts between households and firms, and do not analyse households' behaviours from the perspective of option theory.

There is also research on optimal rationing systems of transportation services in the field of operations research. In particular, there are many studies that analyse overbooking problems and pre-paid discount airline ticket (Beckmann, 1958; Subramanian et al., 1999; Chatwin, 1999; McGill and Ryzin, 1999). They study reservation systems that maximize the firm's profit or social surplus. However, households' demand distribution is exogenously given in these, so they do not have an equilibrium concept that can analyse the interaction between households' behaviours and the firm's behaviour. Other studies also analyse optimal price systems under demand uncertainty (Sherman and Visscher, 1999; Harris and Raviv, 1981; Miravete, 2005) and optimal rationing mechanisms of services under fixed prices (Carlton, 1979, 1991). Matsushima and Kobayashi (2003) propose a model to measure the economic benefit of a reservation system with an endogenous mechanism of the interaction between households' and the firm's behaviour. All this research only considers the pre-paid discounting system, and does not consider post-paid systems, as does our study.

The remainder of the chapter is organized as follows. Section 10.2 presents the benchmark model, and Section 10.3 explains the pre-paid and post-paid discounting fare systems to analyse individuals' behaviour regarding transportation services. In Section 10.4, monopolistic firms' behaviour is explained. Section 10.5 concludes.

10.2 THE BENCHMARK MODEL

10.2.1 Assumptions

Let us explain the basic structure of the pre-paid and post-paid discounting fare systems by the three-period model (see Figure 10.1). In period 0, a contract regarding transportation service is made between a monopolistic transportation firm and households. In periods 1 and 2, households have chances to consume transportation services. As households have demand risk for consuming the service, they cannot estimate accurately their future behaviours. With a pre-paid system, a contract is made to sell and buy pre-discounting ticket in period 0. As the contents of the contract are fixed in period 0, those households that buy discount ticket bear the demand risk. If they do not buy discount tickets, they have the option to decide whether to consume transportation services after they observe demand risk in both periods 1 and 2. Households receive discount fares by purchasing discount tickets and give up the selection option.

On the other hand, households make contracts about the use of a menu for discount fares in period 0 with the post-paid system. As the exact amount of the fare is fixed only after period 2, depending upon how they consume services, they have selection options in both periods 1 and 2. For those households that consume the service in period 1 and also consume the service in period 2, the fare is discounted with a post-paid system. That is, households that consume the service in period 1 have the right to discount in period 2 (hereafter, the discount option). The firm bears the cost of the discount. The firm has demand risk with the post-paid system.

If households with discount option do not consume the service in period 2, the firm need not to bear the discount cost as the discount option is given up.

In the benchmark model, households pay the fare for transportation services whenever they consume the service. Assume that the fare is set as $p \geq 0$. This fare system without any discount in the benchmark model can be written as $\Gamma(p)$. Households have two alternatives: to consume the service or do something else. Utility acquired when other behaviours are selected is called reserved utility, which is distributed along a probabilistic distribution function.

10.2.2 Households' Behaviour

Let us express sub-utility when households make trips in period $i(i = 1, 2)$ as $r_i = r - p$, and reserved utility in period $i(i = 1, 2)$ as $s_1 = s - u$ and $s_2 = s - v$. r and s are definite utility and regarded as 0 for simplicity. u is stochastic reserved utility when they do another activity in period 1, which is distributed according to a distribution function $f(u)$. The reserved utility becomes $\hat{u}$ at the beginning of period 1. v is reserved utility when they do another activity in period 2, which is distributed according to the same distribution function $f(v)$. The reserved utility becomes $\hat{v}$ at the beginning of period 2. Assume also that u and v are independent. Households' utility can be written as

$$U = Y - \min\{p, u\} - \min\{p, v\} \tag{10.1}$$

where Y indicates generalized income. The second and third term on the right-side hand of the linear utility function (10.1) show that households choose activities that require a smaller cost in period 1 and 2, respectively. At the beginning of period 2, reserved utility $\hat{v}$ is fixed. Households' behaviour can be written as follows:

$$\left.\begin{array}{ll}\text{consume the service} & \text{when } p \leq \hat{v} \\ \text{not consume the service} & \text{when } p > \hat{v}\end{array}\right\} \tag{10.2}$$

Let us focus upon period 1. At the beginning of the first period, $\hat{u}$ is fixed, but $\hat{v}$ is still uncertain. The probability that they consume the transportation service in period 2 when v is distributed along the probabilistic density function $f(v)$ is

$$\pi = \text{Prob}(p \leq v) = \int_p^{\infty} f(v)dv = 1 - F(p) \tag{10.3}$$

$F(v)$ is the distribution function of $f(v)$. Let us define households' expected disutility $E[V(p)]$ with service fare in the second period as p. When they consume the service, they pay service fare p, and bear disutility v when they do not consume the service. Partial disutility in period 2 $V(p)$ is then:

$$V(p) = \max\{-p, -v\} \tag{10.4}$$

Expected disutility in period 2 measured in period 1 is

$$E[V(p)] = E[\max\{-p, -v\}] = -p + \int_0^p F(v)\,dv \tag{10.5}$$

Households' decision making in period 2 can be regarded as a real option, where they consume the service only when reserved disutility v is smaller than the fare of transportation service p. Therefore expected disutility in the second period $E[V(p)]$ consists of the fare for the service $-p$ and the value of the selection option to consume the service in the second period $\int_0^p F(v)\,dv$, from the definition of $E[V(p)]$, $E[V(p)] \leq 0$.

In the benchmark model, fares for the service in both periods are fixed as p. At the beginning of period 1, reserved disutility $\hat{u}$ is fixed. Households that consume the service in the first period have expected utilities $EU^e(p)$ when they consume the service and $EV^e(p)$ when they do not consume the service:

$$\begin{aligned} EU^e(p) &= -p + E[V(p)] \\ EV^g(p) &= -\hat{u} + E[V(p)] \end{aligned} \tag{10.6}$$

Households may decide whether or not to consume the service by comparing p and $\hat{u}$ when u and v are independent.

10.2.3 Expected Disutility and the Demand Function

Let us denote the border of reserved disutility u where households decide whether to consume the service or not 'critical disutility'. Critical disutility in the first period is

$$\alpha = p \tag{10.7}$$

and their behaviour in the first period can be shown as follows:

$$\left.\begin{array}{ll} \text{consume the service} & \text{when } u \leq \alpha \\ \text{not consume the service} & \text{when } u > \alpha \end{array}\right\} \tag{10.8}$$

Critical disutility in the second period is also expressed as follows:

$$\beta = p \tag{10.9}$$

and their behaviour in the second period is

$$\left.\begin{array}{ll} \text{consume the service} & \text{when } u \le \beta \\ \text{not consume the service} & \text{when } u > \beta \end{array}\right\} \tag{10.10}$$

In period 0, reserved disutilities u and v are still uncertain. Households' expected utility $E[W(p)]$ measured in period 0 can be derived in the same way as equation (10.5):

$$E[W(p)] =$$

$$Y + E[\max\{-p + E[V], -u + E[V]\}] = Y - 2p + 2\int_0^p F(v)\,dv \tag{10.11}$$

By setting total number of household at 1, the number of households that consume the service in the first period $x(p)$ and those that do not consume the service $y(p)$ are:

$$x(p) = y(p) = 1 - F(p) \tag{10.12}$$

10.3 PRE-PAID AND POST-PAID DISCOUNT FARE SYSTEM AND HOUSEHOLDS' BEHAVIOUR

10.3.1 Pre-paid and Post-paid Discount Fare Systems

The model to show households' decision making under pre-paid and post-paid systems is formulated. They enter into a contract with the transportation firm about the use of the discount fare system in period 0. With the pre-paid system, the lump-sum fare P through the first and second periods is paid in period 0 when they enter into the contract. Assume that they cannot cancel the contract in periods 1 and 2. With the post-paid system, on the other hand, they pay total fares at the end of the second period depending upon the result of service use. The transportation firm can design various fare systems as it will charge households only after it has information about their use thorough all periods. This chapter discusses a post-paid discount system where the service fare in the second period is discounted based upon behaviour in the first period.

10.3.2 Pre-paid System

Households can purchase discount tickets in period 0 with the pre-paid system. Assume that the price of the discounted fare ticket is $P(\leq 2q)$. Let us indicate the pre-paid system, which is operated together with the benchmark system, $\Gamma^{pre}(P)$. When households purchase pre-paid discounts ticket in period 0, they pay nothing in the second period as the fare was already charged and settled in period 0. Those who did not purchase pre-paid tickets have to pay p in order to consume the service in the second period. Disutility in the second period can be expressed as follows:

When they purchase the pre-paid ticket,

$$\left.\begin{array}{ll} 0 & \text{when they consume the service} \\ -\hat{v} & \text{when they do not consume the service} \end{array}\right\} \qquad (10.13a)$$

When they do not purchase the pre-paid ticket,

$$\left.\begin{array}{ll} -p & \text{when they consume the service} \\ -\hat{v} & \text{when they do not consume the service} \end{array}\right\} \qquad (10.13b)$$

As the domain of disutility is $[0, \infty]$, households that purchase the pre-paid ticket always consume the service in the second period. Households that purchase the pre-paid ticket bear the expected disutility

$$E[V_2^y] = 0 \qquad (10.14)$$

The superscript y indicates households that purchase the pre-paid ticket. On the other hand, expected disutility in the second period measured in period 0 when they do not purchase the ticket is

$$E[V_2^n(p)] = -p + \int_0^p F(v)dv \qquad (10.15)$$

where subscript n shows the case when they do not purchase the pre-paid ticket.

Next, let us consider the behaviour in the first period. Households that purchase the ticket have the following expected disutility in the first period:

$$E[V_1^y] = 0 \qquad (10.16)$$

and for those who do not purchase the pre-paid ticket:

$$E[V_1^n(p)] = -p + \int_0^p F(u)\,du \tag{10.17}$$

The next step is to consider households' behaviour in period 0. They have two strategies: (1) to purchase the pre-paid discount ticket with fare P; and (2) not to purchase the pre-paid ticket and to pay fare p whenever they consume the service. Expected disabilities in both cases are as follows:

$$\begin{aligned} \overline{EU^y}(P) &= -P \\ \overline{EV^n}(p) &= -2p + 2\int_0^p F(v)\,dv \end{aligned} \tag{10.18}$$

They decide whether to purchase the pre-paid ticket or not by comparing both disutilities. The condition that they purchase the pre-paid ticket in period 0 is

$$P \leq 2p - 2\int_0^p F(v)\,dv \tag{10.19}$$

The second term on the right-hand side of equation (10.19) shows the quasi-option value by holding their decisions about the first and the second periods in period 0. In other words, purchasing the pre-paid ticket in period 0 brings about commitment to future behaviours. In order to have the incentive to purchase the pre-paid ticket, the discount of fare $2p - P$ should be larger than the option value.

Expected utility of households measured in period 0 is

$$E[W^{pre}(P)] = Y + E[\max\{\overline{EU^y}(P), \overline{EU^n}(P)\}] \tag{10.20}$$

$$= \begin{cases} Y - P & \text{when eq. (10.19) is satisfied} \\ Y - 2p + 2\int_0^p F(v)\,dv & \text{when eq. (10.19) is not satisfied} \end{cases}$$

When equation (10.19) is satisfied, all households purchase pre-paid tickets. The number of households that consume the service is expressed as follows:

$$x^{pre}(P) = y^{pre}(P) = 1 \tag{10.21}$$

On the other hand, when equation (10.19) is not satisfied, no households purchase the pre-paid tickets. Then the number of households that consume the service is the same as the benchmark model:

$$x^{pre}(P) = y^{pre}(P) = x(p) = y(p) \tag{10.22}$$

10.3.3 Post-paid System

Next, let us consider a case where the post-paid discount system is introduced. To be specific, consider a case where the fare for the first period is set at $\overline{p}$ and the fare for the second period is discounted at $\overline{q}$ ($\overline{q} < \overline{p}$) for the households that consumed the service in the first period. Those who did not consume the service in the first period are charged $\overline{p}$, on the other hand. This means that the results of households' behaviours in the first period affect their behaviours in the second period. We call this type of post-paid discount system $\Gamma^{post}(\overline{p}, \overline{q})$.

Households' behaviour in the second period can be expressed as follows:

When they consume the service in the first period:

$$\begin{cases} \text{consume the service} & \text{when } \overline{q} \leq \hat{v} \\ \text{do not consume the service} & \text{when } \overline{q} > \hat{v} \end{cases} \tag{10.23a}$$

When they do not consume the service in the first period:

$$\begin{cases} \text{consume the service} & \text{when } \overline{p} \leq \hat{v} \\ \text{do not consume the service} & \text{when } \overline{p} > \hat{v} \end{cases} \tag{10.23b}$$

Next, go back to the first period and evaluate expected disutility in the second period. Expected disutilities in the second period are:

$$\begin{aligned} E[V^e(\overline{p}, \overline{q})] &= -\overline{q} + \int_0^{\overline{q}} F(v)\,dv \\ E[V^g(\overline{p}, \overline{q})] &= -\overline{p} + \int_0^{\overline{p}} F(v)\,dv \end{aligned} \tag{10.24}$$

Expected utilities when households consume the service and do not consume the service in the first period are:

$$\begin{aligned} \overline{EU^e}(\overline{p}, \overline{q}) &= -\overline{q} + \int_0^{\overline{q}} F(v)\,dv - \overline{p} \\ \overline{EU^g}(\overline{p}, \overline{q}) &= -\overline{p} + \int_0^{\overline{p}} F(v)\,dv - \hat{u} \end{aligned} \tag{10.25}$$

Critical disutility $\overline{\alpha}$ where households consume the service in the first period is

$$\overline{\alpha} = \overline{q} + \int_{\overline{q}}^{\overline{p}} F(v)\,dv \tag{10.26}$$

where $\overline{q} \leq \overline{\alpha} \leq \alpha = \overline{p}$. Expected utility measured in period 0 is expressed as

$$\begin{aligned} E[W^{pos}(\overline{p}, \overline{q})] &= Y + E[\max\{\overline{EU^{e}}(\overline{p}, \overline{q}), \overline{EU^{g}}(\overline{p}, \overline{q})\}] \\ &= Y - (\overline{p} + \overline{q}) + \int_{0}^{\overline{q}} F(v)\,dv + \int_{0}^{\overline{\alpha}} F(u)\,du \end{aligned} \tag{10.27}$$

Evaluating the difference between expected utility in the benchmark system and in the post-paid system, the following equation can be derived:

$$E[W^{pos}(\overline{p}, \overline{q})] - E[W(\overline{p})] = (\overline{p} - \overline{q}) - \int_{\overline{q}}^{\overline{p}} F(v)\,dv - \int_{\overline{\alpha}}^{\overline{p}} F(u)\,du \tag{10.28}$$

The first and second terms of the right-hand side of equation (10.28) are a decrease in expected utility in the second period from fare discount $\overline{p}$ to $\overline{q}$. The third term shows the expected cost to acquire the discount option through consuming the service in the first term. Next, let us calculate the expected number of households that consume the service with the post-paid system. The number of households that consume the service in the first period is

$$x^{pos}(\overline{p}, \overline{q}) = \int_{\overline{\alpha}}^{\infty} f(u)\,du = 1 - F(\overline{\alpha}) \tag{10.29}$$

There are two types of consumers of the service in the second period; one that consumes the service both in the first and second period (type 1), and one that consumes the service only in the second period (type 2). Expected numbers of households of both types are

$$\begin{aligned} y^{ee}(\overline{p}, \overline{q}) &= \int_{\overline{\alpha}}^{\infty} f(u)\,du \int_{\overline{q}}^{\infty} f(v)\,dv = [1 - F(\overline{\alpha})][1 - F(q)] \\ y^{ge}(\overline{p}, \overline{q}) &= \int_{0}^{\overline{\alpha}} f(u)\,du \int_{\overline{q}}^{\infty} f(v)\,dv = F(\overline{\alpha})[1 - F(\overline{p})] \end{aligned} \tag{10.30}$$

Therefore the number of households that consume the service in the second period is

$$y^{pos}(\overline{p}, \overline{q}) = y^{ee}(\overline{p}, \overline{q}) + y^{ge}(\overline{p}, \overline{q}) =$$

$$[1 - F(\overline{\alpha})][1 - F(q)] + F(\overline{\alpha})[1 - F(\overline{p})] \tag{10.31}$$

10.4 THE EFFECT OF A RISK-SHARING STRUCTURE UPON HOUSEHOLDS' SURPLUS

Compare all systems $\Gamma(p)$, $\Gamma^{pre}(P)$, $\Gamma^{post}(\bar{p}, \bar{q})$ to focus upon the effect of risk sharing on households' surplus. A firm's optimization of discount fares is considered in the next section. Assume the following relation in order to compare households' surplus.

$$P = \bar{p} + \bar{q} \text{ and } p = \bar{p} \tag{10.32}$$

The result of the analysis that shows the effect of differences in every type of fare upon households' surplus and the number of households that consume the transportation service can be seen in Table 10.1.

First, compare the number of households that consume the service. The following proposition can be derived.

Proposition 1: Assume that equation (10.32) is satisfied. The following relations hold among the expected number of households that consume the transportation service in both periods under every system:

1. When $P \leq 2p - 2\int_0^p F(v)\,dv$:

Table 10.1 Comparison of fare systems

Fare system		Households' surplus	Number of households that consume the service in the first period	Number of households that consume the service in the second period
$\Gamma(p)$		$Y - 2p + 2\int_0^p F(v)\,dv$	$1 - F(p)$	$1 - F(p)$
$\Gamma^{pre}(P)$	When eq. (10.19) is satisfied	$Y - P$	1	1
	When eq. (10.19) is not satisfied	$Y - 2p + 2\int_0^p F(v)\,dv$	$1 - F(p)$	$1 - F(p)$
$\Gamma^{post}(\bar{p}, \bar{q})$		$Y - (\bar{p} + \bar{q}) + \int_0^q F(v)\,dv + \int_0^{\bar{\alpha}} F(u)\,du$	$1 - F(\bar{\alpha})$	$[1 - F(\bar{\alpha})][1 - F(q)] + F(\bar{\alpha})[1 - F(\bar{p})]$

$$x(p) \leq x^{pos}(\overline{p}, \overline{q}) < x^{pre}(P) = 1$$
$$y(p) \leq y^{pos}(\overline{p}, \overline{q}) < y^{pre}(P) = 1$$

2. When $2p - 2\int_0^p F(v)\,dv < P \leq 2\int_0^\infty vF(v)\,dv$:

$$x^{pre}(P) = x(p) \leq x^{pos}(\overline{p}, \overline{q}) < 1$$
$$y^{pre}(P) = y(p) \leq y^{pos}(\overline{p}, \overline{q}) < 1$$

3. When $2\int_0^\infty vF(v)\,dv < P$:

$$x^{pos}(\overline{p}, \overline{q}) \geq x(p) = x^{pre}(P) \geq 0$$
$$y^{pos}(\overline{p}, \overline{q}) \geq y(p) = y^{pre}(P) \geq 0$$

When the transportation firm sets the pre-paid ticket price low enough to satisfy equation (10.19), all households consume the service. Introducing the post-paid discount system increases the number of households that consume the transportation service in comparison with the benchmark system. As all households purchase the ticket even if they bear demand risk when the price of the pre-paid ticket is low enough, the number of households becomes larger in the pre-paid system. On the other hand, the number of households that consume the service under a post-paid system, where the firm bears the demand risk, increases as the pre-paid ticket price increases.

Next, let us compare expected utilities under every system.

Proposition 2: Assume that equation (10.32) is satisfied. The following relations hold among the expected utility of households that consume the transportation service under every system.

1. When $P \leq 2p - 2\int_0^p F(v)\,dv$:

$$E[W(p)] \leq E[W^{pre}(P)] \leq E[W^{pos}(\overline{p}, \overline{q})]$$

2. When $2p - 2\int_0^p F(v)\,dv < P$:

$$E[W^{pre}(P)] = E[W(p)] \leq E[W^{pos}(\overline{p}, \overline{q})]$$

This proposition states that households' surplus under the post-paid system is always larger than that under the benchmark or pre-paid system as long as equation (10.32) is satisfied. Households can use both the selection option and the discount option under the post-paid system. Therefore expected utility is largest under the post-paid system. On the other hand, households can use the discount option while they lose the selection option under the pre-paid system. Under the benchmark system, they have the selection option but do not use the discount option.

The order of expected utilities under every system depends upon the difference between the two options. When equation (10.19) is satisfied, all households consume the service by applying the pre-paid system. When equation (10.19) is not satisfied, on the other hand, no households purchase the pre-paid discount ticket, which means $E[W^{pre}(P)] = E[W(p)]$.

10.5 THE MONOPOLISTIC FIRM'S BEHAVIOUR

10.5.1 The Benchmark System

Propositions 1 and 2 hold when equation (10.32) is satisfied. However, when the transportation firm decides the fare under profit-maximization behaviour, equation (10.32) is not necessarily satisfied under every system. In the following, assume that the monopolistic transportation firm sets its fare through profit maximization.

Under the benchmark system, the profit of the firm is expressed as follows:

$$\Pi(p) = 2(p - c)x(p) - d = 2(p - c)[1 - F(p)] - d \quad (10.33)$$

where c is marginal cost and d is fixed cost. Assume that p^* exists which satisfies the following first-order condition for profit maximization, and that it also satisfies the second-order condition for profit maximization:

$$-(p^* - c)f(p^*) + 1 - F(p^*) = 0 \quad (10.34)$$

From equation (10.34), the following equation holds:

$$p^* - c = \frac{1 - F(p^*)}{f(p^*)} \geq 0 \quad (10.35)$$

Optimal benchmark fare p^* is expressed as follows:

$$p^* = \left(\frac{\rho}{\rho - 1}\right)c \quad (10.36)$$

where ρ is the price elasticity of demand that satisfies

$$\rho = -\frac{\dfrac{dx(p)}{dp}}{\dfrac{x}{p}} = \frac{pf(p)}{1 - F(p)} \tag{10.37}$$

From equation (10.37), $\rho > 1$. The optimal benchmark fare can be derived by multiplying mark-up ratio $\rho/(\rho - 1)$ by marginal cost c. The firm's profit is

$$\Pi(p^*) = 2(p^* - c)[1 - F(p^*)] - d \tag{10.38}$$

and households' surplus is

$$E[W(p^*)] = Y - 2p^* + 2\int_0^{p^*} F(v)\,dv \tag{10.39}$$

In order to allow the firm to retain its behaviour, its profit should be positive. Hereafter, assume that the firm's profit is positive.

10.5.2 Pre-paid System

Consider a pre-paid discount system where the pre-paid discount fare is P and the benchmark fare is p^*. As no households purchase pre-paid tickets if equation (10.19) is not satisfied, consider a case where equation (10.19) is satisfied in the following. Profit maximization of the firm is expressed as

$$\begin{aligned} &\max_P \Pi^{pre}(P, p^*) = (P - 2c) - d \\ &\text{subject to } P \leq 2p^* - 2\int_0^{p^*} F(v)\,dv \end{aligned} \tag{10.40}$$

Therefore the optimal pre-paid discount fare $P^*(p^*)$ given benchmark fare p^* is determined as the maximum value that satisfies condition (10.19). That is,

$$P = 2p^* - 2\int_0^{p^*} F(v)\,dv \tag{10.41}$$

Taking the difference between profit under the pre-paid system and that under the benchmark system, we shall have the following equation:

$$\Pi^{pre}[P^*(p^*) - p^*] - \Pi(p^*) = 2(p^* - c)F(p^*) - 2\int_0^{p^*} F(v)\,dv \tag{10.42}$$

In order that the firm has an incentive to adopt pre-paid system, its profit should become larger than that under the benchmark system if it introduces the pre-paid system. The necessary condition for the pre-paid system to be adopted is

$$\int_0^{p^*} F(v)\,dv \leq (p^* - c)F(p^*) \tag{10.43}$$

When condition (10.43) is not satisfied, only the benchmark system is adopted. Therefore the optimal behaviour of the firm is written as follows:

$$\begin{cases} \text{adopt } \Gamma^{pre}[P^*(p^*), p^*] & \text{when eq. (10.43) holds} \\ \text{adopt } \Gamma(p^*) & \text{when eq. (10.43) does not hold} \end{cases} \tag{10.44}$$

Households' surplus when $\Gamma^{pre}[P^*(p^*), p^*]$ is adopted is:

$$E\{W^{pre}[P^*(p^*), p^*]\} = Y - 2p^* + 2\int_0^{p^*} F(v)\,dv = E[W(p^*)] \tag{10.45}$$

10.5.3 Post-paid System

Profit maximization of the firm under a post-paid system is expressed as follows:

$$\max_P \Pi^{pre}(\bar{p}, \bar{q}) = (\bar{p} - c)[x^{pos}(\bar{p}, \bar{q}) + y^{ge}(\bar{p}, \bar{q})] + (\bar{q} - c)y^{ee}(\bar{p}, \bar{q}) \tag{10.46}$$
$$\text{subject to } \bar{p} \geq \bar{q}$$

First-order conditions for profit maximization are $\partial\Pi^{pos}/\partial\bar{p} = 0$ and $\partial\Pi^{pos}/\partial\bar{q} = 0$. Let us indicate optimal fares which satisfy the conditions above as (p°, q°). Then the following equation holds:

$$q^\circ < p^* < p^\circ \tag{10.47}$$

The firm's profit, households' surplus, and the number of households that consume the service can be derived in the same manner.

From the discussion above, the following proposition holds:

Proposition 3: The following equations are satisfied for fare systems:

$$\Gamma(p^*), \Gamma^{pre}[P^*(p^*), p^*], \Gamma^{post}(p^\circ, q^\circ),$$

$$\Pi(p^*) \leq \Pi^{post}(p^\circ, q^\circ) \text{ and } E\{W^{pre}[P^*(p^*), p^*]\} \leq E[W(p^*)]$$

As shown in this proposition, the firm can increase its profit with a post-paid system. On the other hand, it cannot always increase its profit with a pre-paid system. Additionally, households' surplus does not improve with a pre-paid system. With a post-paid system, the fare in the second period q° is smaller than the fare in the benchmark system p^*. On the other hand, p° is larger than p^*, which reduces welfare of households that consume the service only in the first period. Therefore, whether households' surplus increases or not with the introduction of a post-paid system cannot be determined. From the discussion above, it can be said that a post-paid system has a comparative advantage. However, a policy to incentivize the firm to reduce the fare is necessary in introducing a post-paid system.

10.5.4 Fee Regulation and Social Surplus

As Proposition 3 suggested, the expected profit of the firm always increases while households' surplus does not necessarily improve when the monopolistic firm sets the fee level freely. We consider fee regulation in order to prevent the decrease in households' surplus. Although we can consider various ways to regulate the fee, let us consider a post-discounted fee system $\Gamma^{post}(\bar{p}^*, \bar{q})$ where the fee at period 0, $\bar{p}$, is regulated as the same as the optimal fee with systems without any discount p^*. Table 10.1 also indicates both the expected profit of the firm and the social surplus of households under $\Gamma^{post}(\bar{p}^*, \bar{q})$. Social surplus under $\Gamma^{post}(\bar{p}^*, \bar{q})$ is always larger than that under $\Gamma(p^*)$. Therefore all households adopt the post-discounted fee system $\Gamma^{post}(\bar{p}^*, \bar{q})$ if both systems $\Gamma(p^*)$ and $\Gamma^{post}(\bar{p}^*, \bar{q})$ are available. Let us indicate the marginal disutility as $\alpha^*(\bar{p}^*, \bar{q})$ with which utility level households are indifferent whether they consume the service or not at period 1 when the post-discounted fee system is introduced. The profit of the firm under $\Gamma^{post}(\bar{p}^*, \bar{q})$ is written as

$$\begin{aligned}
&\Pi^{post}(\bar{p}^*, \bar{q}) \\
&= (\bar{p}^* - c)x^{post}(\bar{p}^*, \bar{q}) + (\bar{p}^* - c)y^{ge}(\bar{p}^*, \bar{q}) + (\bar{q} - c)y^{ee}(\bar{p}^*, \bar{q}) - d \\
&= (\bar{p}^* - c)\{1 - F[\alpha^*(\bar{p}^*, \bar{q})]\} + (\bar{q} - c)\{1 - F[\alpha^*(\bar{p}^*, \bar{q})]\}[1 - F(\bar{q})] \\
&\quad + (\bar{p}^* - c)F[\alpha^*(\bar{p}^*, \bar{q})][1 - F(\bar{p}^*)] - d \qquad (10.48)
\end{aligned}$$

The profit maximization problem of the monopolistic firm is expressed as

$$\max \{\Pi^{post}(\bar{p}^*, \bar{q})\} \quad \text{subject to } \bar{p}^* \geq \bar{q} \tag{10.49}$$

The optimal solution to the problem above is expressed as $\bar{q}^*(\bar{p}^*)$ and the profit of the firm as $\Gamma^{post}[\bar{p}^*, \bar{q}^*(\bar{p}^*)]$. If we focus on the fact that $\bar{\alpha}^*[\bar{p}^*, \bar{p}^*(\bar{p}^*)] = \bar{p}^*$ is satisfied, $\Pi^{post}(\bar{p}^*, \bar{p}^*) = \Pi(\bar{p}^*)$ is derived from the definition of the profit (10.48). Therefore the general fee system $\Gamma(p^*)$ is a special case of the post-discounted fee systems and the following equation is satisfied:

$$\Pi^{post}[\bar{p}^*, \bar{q}^*(\bar{p}^*)] \geq \Pi(\bar{p}^*) \tag{10.50}$$

That is, the firm is more profitable if it introduces the post-discounted fee system.

In considering equation (10.34), the following equation is satisfied around $(\bar{p}^*, \bar{q}) = (p^*, p^*)$:

$$\frac{d\Pi^{post}(p^*, p^*)}{dq} \tag{10.51}$$

$$\begin{aligned} &= -(p^* - c)f(p^*)\{1 - F(p^*)\}F(p^*) + \{1 - F(p^*)\}^2 \\ &\quad -(p^* - c)f(p^*)\{1 - F(p^*)\}^2 - f(p^*)\{1 - F(p^*)\}(p^* - c) \\ &= -\{1 - F(p^*)\}^2 < 0 \end{aligned}$$

If the firm makes $\bar{q}$ smaller, its profit increases as $\bar{q} = p^*$, which results in $\bar{q}^*(\bar{p}^*) < p^*$. Households' surplus with fees $[\bar{p}^*, \bar{q}^*(\bar{p}^*)]$ is

$$E[W^{post}(\bar{p}^*, \bar{q}^*(\bar{p}^*))] = \tag{10.52}$$

$$Y - (\bar{p}^* + \bar{q}^*(\bar{p}^*)) + \int_0^{\bar{q}^*(\bar{p}^*)} F(v)\,dv + \int_0^{\bar{\varepsilon}^*(\bar{p}^*, \bar{q}^*(\bar{p}^*))} F(u)\,du$$

With Proposition 2 and $\bar{q}^*(\bar{p}^*) < p^*$, the following equation is satisfied:

$$E[W^{post}(\bar{p}^*, \bar{q}^*(\bar{p}^*))] \geq E[W(p^*)] \tag{10.53}$$

Therefore all households are motivated to adopt the post-discounted fee system.

Social surplus under each fee system $\Gamma(p)$, $\Gamma^{pre}(P, p)$ and $\Gamma^{post}(\bar{p}, \bar{q})$ can be written as follows:

$$SW(p^*) = \Pi(p^*) + E[W(p^*)] \tag{10.54a}$$

$$SW^{pre}[P(p^*), p^*] = \tag{10.54b}$$

$$\Pi^{pre}[P(p^*), p^*] + E\{W^{pre}[P(p^*), p^*]\}$$

$$SW^{post}[p^*, \bar{q}^*(p^*)] = \tag{10.54c}$$

$$\Pi^{post}[p^*, \bar{q}^*(p^*)] + E\{W^{post}[p^*, \bar{q}^*(p^*)]\}$$

These discussions are summarized as the following Proposition 4.

Proposition 4: The following equations are satisfied for three fee systems $\Gamma(p)$, $\Gamma^{pre}(P, p)$ *and* $\Gamma^{post}(\bar{p}, \bar{q})$:

$$\Pi(p^*) \leq \Pi^{post}[\bar{p}^*, \bar{q}^*(\bar{p}^*)],$$

$$E\{W^{pre}[P^*(p^*), p^*]\} = E[W(p^*)] \leq E\{W^{post}[\bar{p}^*, \bar{q}^*(\bar{p}^*)]\}$$

$$SW(\bar{p}^*) \leq SW^{post}[\bar{p}^*, \bar{q}^*(\bar{p}^*)]$$

The profit of the firm always increases if it adopts the post-discounted fee system $\Gamma^{post}[\bar{p}^*, \bar{q}^*(\bar{p}^*)]$. *As households' surplus increases, social surplus is also better off. On the other hand, the profit does not necessarily increase with introduction of the pre-discounted fee system.*

10.6 CONCLUSION

This chapter compares and evaluates the economic effect of introducing pre-paid and post-paid discount systems. The results suggest that both the firm's profit and households' surplus increase with the post-paid system. On the other hand, the pre-paid system always increases the firm's profit, but households' surplus does not increase with the pre-paid system. The transportation firm may set the benchmark fare higher to enclose households, which reduces their welfare. Moreover, the post-paid system has a comparative advantage against the pre-paid system both in households' surplus and social surplus.

The theoretical results shown above can be achieved only on the assumptions in this chapter. There is some future research to be tackled. First of all, this chapter assumes homogeneity in households' preference. As a result, edge solutions where all or no households consume the service are derived with the pre-paid system. It is necessary to analyse the firm's behaviour with interaction between the discount fare and the normal fare when households are heterogeneous. Second, this research can be extended to a multiple-period model with interaction between households' decision process in different periods. This type of extension is necessary when we analyse fare systems in which past behaviours affect future behaviours. Third, more extensions are necessary to analyse the effect of settlement technologies and the post-paid fare system upon economies. For example, a system where the discount option can be used for other goods should be considered. Last, empirical research to reinforce our theoretical results is necessary. More research on how to accumulate households' behavioural data efficiently and sufficiently should be performed.

REFERENCES

Banerjee, A. and L. Summers (1987), 'On frequent flyer programs and other loyalty-inducing arrangements', Technical Report 1337, Cambridge, MA: Harvard Institute of Economic Research.
Beckmann, M.J. (1958), 'Decision and team problem in airline reservation', *Econometrica*, **26**, 134–45.
Bolton, R., P. Kannan and M. Bramlett (2000), 'Implications of loyalty program membership and service experiences for customer retention and value', *Journal of the Academy of Marketing Science*, **28** (1), 95–108.
Cairns, R. and J. Galbraith (1990), 'Artificial compatibility, barriers to entry, and frequent-flyer programs', *Canadian Journal of Economics*, **23** (4), 807–16.
Caminal, R. and A. Claici (2007), 'Are loyalty-rewarding pricing schemes anti-competitive?', *International Journal of Industrial Organization*, **25** (4), 657–74.
Caminal, R. and C. Matutes (1990), 'Endogenous switching costs in a duopoly model', *International Journal of Industrial Organization*, **8**, 353–73.
Carlton, D.W. (1979), 'Contracts, price rigidity, and market equilibrium', *Journal of Political Economy*, **87**, 1034–61.
Carlton, D.W. (1991), 'The theory of allocation and its implication for marketing and industrial structure: why rationing is efficient?', *Journal of Law and Economics*, **XXXIV**, 231–61.
Chatwin, R. (1999), 'Continuous-time airline overbooking with time-dependent fares and refunds', *Transportation Science*, **33**, 182–91.
Fudenberg, D. and J. Tirole (2000), 'Customer poaching and brand switching', *RAND Journal of Economics*, **31** (4), 634–57.
Harris, M. and A. Raviv (1981), 'A theory of monopoly pricing schemes with demand uncertainty', *American Economic Review*, **71**, 347–65.
Kivetz, R., O. Urminsky and Y. Zheng (2006), 'The goal-gradient hypothesis resurrected: purchase acceleration, illusionary goal progress, and customer retention', *Journal of Marketing Research*, **43**, 39–58.
Lewis, M. (2004), 'The influence of loyalty programs and short-term promotions on customer retention', *Journal of Marketing Research*, **43** (3), 281–92.
Matsushima, K. and K. Kobayashi (2003), 'Reservation of transportation services under uncertainty', *Selected Proceedings of the 9th World Conference on Transport Research*, Elsevier Science, CD-ROM.

McGill, J.I. and G.J.V. Ryzin (1999), 'Revenue management: research overview and prospects', *Transportation Science*, **33**, 233–56.

Meyer-Waarden, L. (2007), 'The effects of loyalty programs on customer lifetime duration and share-of-wallet', *Journal of Retailing*, **83** (2), 223.

Miravete, E.J. (2005), 'The welfare performance of sequential pricing mechanisms', *International Economic Review*, **46**, 1321–60.

Nako, S. (1997), 'Frequent flyer programs and business travellers: an empirical investigation', *Logistics and Transportation Review*, **28**, 395–410.

Sharp, B. and A. Sharp (1997), 'Loyalty programs and their impact on repeat-purchase loyalty patterns', *International Journal of Research in Marketing*, **14**, 473–86.

Sherman, R. and M. Visscher (1999), 'Nonprice rationing and monopoly price structures when demand is stochastic', *The Bell Journal of Economics*, **13**, 254–62.

Subramanian, J., S. Stidham Jr and C.J. Lautenbacher (1999), 'Airline yield management with overbooking, cancellations and no-shows', *Transportation Science*, **33**, 147–67.

Taylor, G.A. and S. Neslin (2005), 'The current and future sales impact of a retail frequency reward program', *Journal of Retailing*, **81**, 293–305.

Yi, Y. and H. Jeon (2003), 'The effects of loyalty programs on value perception, program loyalty and brand loyalty', *Journal of the Academy of Marketing Science*, **31**, 229–40.

PART III

The global context

11. Clustering and the location of multinational enterprises: an exploration of financial services in London

Gary A.S. Cook and Naresh R. Pandit

This chapter examines the small but growing literature that offers explanations for multinational enterprise (MNE) location in clusters. It tests the propositions of this literature against the findings of a study that compares MNEs and non-MNEs regarding the advantages and disadvantages of a location in the City of London financial services cluster, which has an extraordinarily large MNE component. As such it makes a contribution towards current efforts to bridge the gap between the established theories of MNE and those of industrial clustering. The evidence presented is based on 39 semi-structured interviews with very senior managers across seven major subsectors of the financial services industry in London and 310 postal questionnaires. The primary conclusion is that MNEs and non-MNEs have different and multiple motives for locating in the cluster. MNEs perceive significantly higher benefits of close proximity in terms of competing with rivals and benchmarking against them compared to non-MNEs. Moreover, they perceive significantly higher benefits of close proximity in terms of ease of communication and ability to have face-to-face contact than non-MNEs, undermining popular 'death-of-geography' arguments. There are two auxiliary conclusions. For MNEs, because strong clusters have disadvantages (e.g. congestion) and because advantages can change over time, MNEs need to continually assess which activities they need to locate in a cluster. The second auxiliary conclusion is that for MNEs, clusters may provide advantages over and above those available to non-MNE competitors.

11.1 INTRODUCTION

Research on the foreign direct investment (FDI) activities of MNEs has a long and rich tradition (Dunning, 2003). Research on the advantages, disadvantages and processes that arise in business clusters has a similar tradition (Marshall, 1890; Porter, 1998). Whilst it is clear that there is a considerable amount of MNE FDI in clusters (Kozul-Wright and Rowthorn, 1998), and that this activity is increasing (Nachum, 2003), the body of research on this interface is small (Birkinshaw and Solvell, 2000). However, it is growing fast in the face of increased globalization, deregulation and advances in information and communication technology (ICT), all of which have begun to prompt a re-evaluation of the spatial organization of MNE activity. This study asks three related questions:

1. What theoretical reasons have been advanced that might explain the high level of MNE activity in the London financial services cluster?
2. How and why are the advantages, disadvantages and processes that arise in the London cluster similar and different for MNEs and non-MNEs?
3. To what extent do the answers to question (2) support, contradict or extend the explanations given in the extant literature identified in (1)?

The chapter is structured as follows. Section 11.2 reviews the literature on the MNE FDI/clusters interface. Section 11.3 provides a concise history of the City, emphasizing the rise of MNE FDI in the postwar period. Section 11.4 details the methodology of the study. Section 11.5 presents the findings and discusses these in relation to the literature on the MNE FDI/clusters interface. A final section concludes.

11.2 LITERATURE ON THE MNE FDI/CLUSTERS INTERFACE

From the perspective of the MNE, a better understanding of agglomeration is desirable because performance may improve if certain activities are located in clusters where higher levels of productivity (Henderson, 1986; Porter, 1998) and innovation (Baptista and Swann, 1998; Porter, 1998) may be achievable. A better understanding of agglomeration will also help the MNE decide which activities not to locate in clusters. Since clusters are usually expensive and congested locations (Swann et al., 1998), unless an activity needs to be located in a cluster, it will pay the MNE to move it elsewhere. These reasons, coupled with the trends of increased globalization, deregulation and advances in ICT, mean that MNEs are increasingly employing cluster-based thinking to inform their investment and location decisions (Enright, 1998). At one extreme, there are MNEs that locate entire activities, including headquarters, in a cluster (Birkinshaw, 1996) and at the other, there are MNEs that place only certain activities in clusters while moving other activities to non-clustered locations (Enright, 2000).

There is a growing body of more specific evidence that shows that MNEs are attracted to clusters (Gong, 1995; Head et al., 1995, 1999; Wheeler and Mody, 1992) and that MNE FDI in clusters is increasing (Nachum, 2003). This evidence suggests that 'liability of foreignness' (Zaheer, 1995) – disadvantages faced by firms in foreign locations due to unfamiliarity and inferior access to local assets – is being compensated by the advantages of cluster location. These advantages may be categorized as those that are available to all firms at a location ('general cluster advantages') and those that are of particular benefit to MNEs ('MNE cluster advantages'). Under the first category, beyond so-called 'fixed effects' (Swann et al., 1998) – advantages that exist at a location that are not a function of the co-presence of related firms and institutions (e.g. climate, time-zone and cultural capital) – there are advantages that are directly related to the co-presence that exists within a cluster, referred to as economies of agglomeration.

These can emanate on the demand or supply side and are extensively detailed in Porter (1998), Swann et al. (1998) and Pandit and Cook (2005).

What are the 'MNE cluster advantages'? There is a large literature that attempts to generally explain MNE FDI in terms of the benefits that certain locations provide for investing MNEs. Dunning (1993) presents an FDI typology differentiating between investments that are 'natural-resource-seeking', 'market-seeking', 'efficiency-seeking' and 'strategic-asset-seeking'. More recently, he has drawn from economic geography (Dunning, 1998) to elaborate the location element of his 'OLI' (ownership–location–internalization) framework by incorporating clusters thinking.

On the subject of MNE location in clusters, Birkinshaw and Hood (2000) find such activity to be rational as subsidiaries located in clusters make greater strategic contributions to parent companies than subsidiaries that are not located in clusters. Enright (1998) elaborates a typology of such contributions. 'Listening posts' aim to absorb knowledge from the cluster and then disseminate it within the wider enterprise (Dupuy and Gilly, 1999). Nachum and Keeble (2003) state that the ability to tap into cluster-specific knowledge is particularly important when that knowledge is tacit. 'Stand-alone corporate portfolio investments' serve as centres for particular business activities perhaps benefiting from the reputation spill-over of a particular location. Nachum (2000a, p. 370) supports this line of thinking by commenting on the increased importance and autonomy of foreign subsidiaries:

> The hierarchical structure, which was common amongst most TNCs in the past, has become inadequate in the more recent decades when knowledge creation by all parts of the TNC has become essential for competitive success . . . Greater autonomy for the affiliates is increasing the potential for local linkage formation and the transfer of technology and skills between the affiliates and other firms in the near locality, sometimes independent from the headquarters and the TNCs as a whole.

Another type is the subsidiary that 'supplies products and activities' for the MNE's other activities, and finally there is the subsidiary that absorbs 'skills and capabilities' from the cluster and then transfers these to the wider enterprise. Beaverstock's (1994) study of multinational banks elaborates this type of MNE FDI by finding that such firms benefit from the ability to transfer skills and capabilities between subsidiaries in their worldwide operations through international personnel movements. This may be particularly the case when an industry has more than one prominent location and so the MNE may benefit from locating in all prominent locations in order to pick up skills and capabilities in one to pass on to the others. Nachum and Keeble (2003) point further to the advantage of a subsidiary absorbing a cluster's culture and then disseminating it to its other parts.

A further motivation for MNEs locating in clusters is provided by Harrison (1994). He argues that a cluster location may enable MNEs to concentrate on their core competences and outsource non-core activities to specialist suppliers that are geographically proximate. Nachum (2000a, p. 370) provides support for this argument, finding that

> In the process of internal reorganization of the production and externalisation of certain activities, TNCs have come to rely heavily on the supply of goods and services from other firms and have become considerably more dependent on linkages with them.

In the process of internal reorganization of the production and externalization of certain activities, transnational corporations (TNCs) have come to rely heavily on the supply of goods and services from other firms and have become considerably more dependent on linkages with them. Similarly, Nachum and Keeble (2003) argue that MNEs will locate in clusters to benefit from the highly specialized, non-standard inputs that are available there.

Although this typology encourages us to think of MNEs 'taking' from clusters, we should guard against such a conclusion. Studies by Dunning (2000), Head et al. (1995), Nachum (2000a) and Wheeler and Mody (1992) show that MNEs can play a major role in cluster development and evolution. Indeed, Birkinshaw and Hood's (2000) analysis of the characteristics of 229 foreign-owned subsidiaries located in clusters finds that such subsidiaries are more embedded and more internationally oriented than subsidiaries that are not located in clusters. Another caveat is that, as with most typologies, the types should not be thought of as mutually exclusive (Markusen, 1996). An MNE may invest in a cluster for more than one reason, although it is likely that one reason will dominate the others.

Before reporting the empirical results, let us define the City and describe what activity takes place there, emphasizing its MNE dimension.

11.3 THE CITY OF LONDON

The City of London is best understood as a wholesale financial services centre (Coggan, 2002) with core activities in banking, insurance and fund management supported by a panoply of activities including legal services, accounting, management consultancy, advertising, market research, recruitment, property management, financial printing and publishing, and the provision of electronic information (IFSL, 2004). Technically, the 'City of London' refers to the 'square mile' around the Bank of England. Although this remains the geographic core of the cluster, developments to the east, west and north have extended the centre to the extent that the term 'the City' is now often used to refer to the cluster as a whole and not just the square mile (Golding, 2001). There are five distinctive sub-concentrations (see Figure 11.1). First, Canary Wharf to the east, which is the home of some of the largest investment banks. Second, the very dense 'square mile' that is the original City of London featuring banks, insurance and law firms. Third, a less dense West end concentration featuring banks near Mayfair and advertising in Soho. Fourth, an incipient concentration north of the City featuring services such as architecture and business support. Finally, a concentration that lies in between the City and the West End, consisting of law firms located in close proximity to the law courts. Together these interdependent sub-concentrations employ some 369 000 people (Corporation of London, 2004) and make up the City of London financial services cluster.

The cluster fits the generic definition arrived at by the Department of Trade and Industry after an extensive review of the clusters literature:

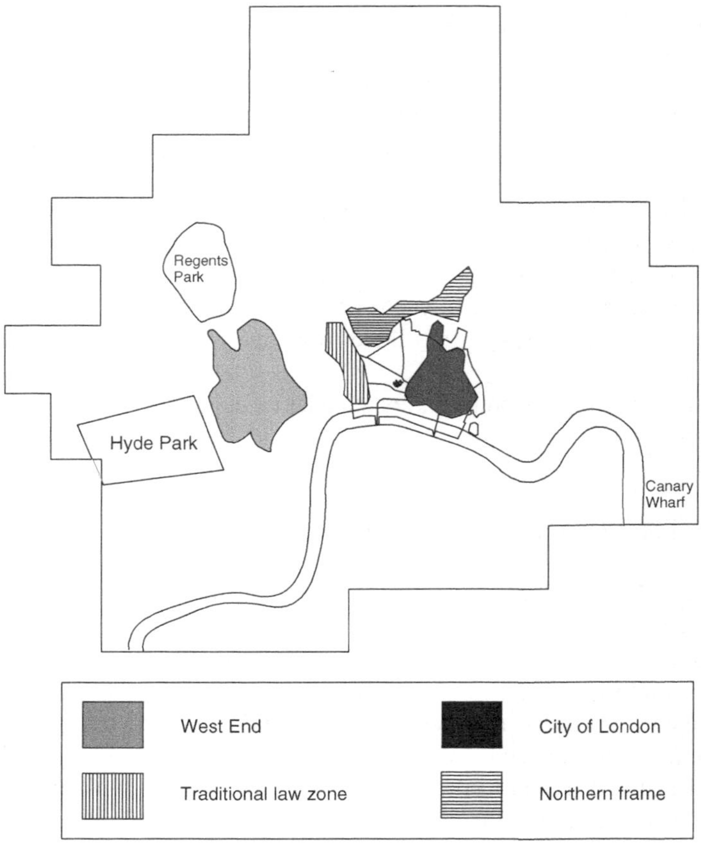

Source: Taylor et al. (2003).

Figure 11.1 The London financial services cluster

> A geographic concentration of competing, collaborating and *interdependent* companies and *institutions* which are connected by a system of market and non-market links. (DTI, 1998, p. 22, emphasis added)

This definition has at least four strengths. First, it does not relate to a single industry; rather it merely requires that companies in a cluster are interdependent in some way. Second, a cluster is defined not just in terms of companies but also supporting institutions. Third, non-market linkages are emphasized. These, born out of a common culture and trust, are known to be important with respect to productivity and innovation. Finally, the definition encourages us to think of clusters as complex systems of industrial organization that confer sustainable competitive advantage on incumbents. A weakness of the definition is that it is imprecise in at least two important ways: it provides little guidance on the required quantity or quality of incumbents and linkages in a cluster; and it provides no guidance on the geographic scope of a cluster. A rebuttal is that as clusters are complex and polymorphous phenomena (Gordon and McCann, 2000; Markusen, 1996), any generic definition will necessarily be vague.

Three financial centres are ranked together as the most important in the world: London, New York and Tokyo (Roberts, 1994; Sassen, 1991, 1999). There are three major differences between London and the other two (Nachum, 2003). First is the share of financial services activity controlled by foreign ownership, which is much lower in New York and Tokyo (for example, the number of foreign banks in London, New York and Tokyo was 573, 275 and 93 respectively in 2000). Second, London is more international in its outlook, with a much higher percentage of foreign business. In contrast, New York's and Tokyo's strength relates to the strength of their domestic economies and currencies. London's unique position is that its strength is independent of its domestic economy and currency. Third, the UK and so London has a more liberal policy attitude to foreign ownership (Morgan, 1997).

The City's current attractiveness as a centre for MNE FDI and its position as the world's most important international financial services is the result of developments in the postwar period, in particular the growth of the 'euromarkets'; 1963, when the first Eurodollar bond was issued by Warburgs, was, according to Kynaston (2001, p. 275), 'the most important year since 1914 in the history of London as an international financial centre'. In 1957, 'Regulation Q' had been introduced in the USA and this artificially capped the interest rate that could be paid on dollar deposits in the USA. In response, dollar deposits searched for better returns and found them at European banks trading in the more loosely regulated City of London. By the end of 1964, Kynaston (2001) estimates that the majority of 44 foreign dollar issues worth $681 million had been made in London. Very importantly, currency and location had been decoupled (HM Treasury, 2003); the City's strength would now be independent of the strength of the UK economy and currency. The size of London's euromarkets increased in the 1970s as US banks used them to recycle OPEC (Organization of Petroleum Exporting Countries) countries' large surpluses of 'petrodollars'. The parallel developments of investment banking and investment institutions in the late 1960s and 1970s further enhanced the City's strength. The ground for London's role as an international financial services centre, and so its attractiveness to MNE FDI, had been prepared. A subsequent development in the late

1970s and 1980s – deregulation – then triggered a substantial rise in MNE FDI in the City (Augar, 2000; Coggan, 2002; Golding, 2001; Hamilton, 1996; Kynaston, 2001).

In 1979, exchange controls were abolished and full competition was introduced in to the banking sector by 1980. These changes paved the way for foreign, mainly US, banks to take over UK firms to establish their European time-zone wholesale operations in the City. As a result, 'foreign firms' investment came to dominate London's wholesale markets – "the City as FDI"' (HM Treasury, 2003, p. 31). The term 'Big Bang', although initially used to refer to the deregulation in 1986 of the London Stock Exchange when trading was automated, has become associated with the general modernization and deregulation of London's financial markets brought on by the 1986 Financial Services Act. It was the first major deregulation of this type in Europe: 'This focus on competitiveness meant that foreign investment was encouraged, resulting in *most* of the leading wholesale institutions being foreign owned' (HM Treasury, 2003, p. 31, emphasis added). Clark (2002, p. 438) concludes:

> London is an 'industrial district' that has attracted and retained firms whose home location could place them elsewhere in the world (in the US and Europe for example). Indeed, for many such firms, locating and developing a significant presence in London has been a conscious locational choice made both in relation to competitors and related firms, and in relation to the preferences and needs of UK and European customers.

Clark's advocacy of London as a rational choice for MNE FDI is supported by Nachum's (2000b) analysis of the profitability and failure of City firms between 1975 and 2000. She finds that the profit margin of UK financial services firms was 0.132 compared with 0.147 for foreign financial services firms and that of 313 failures over the period, 214 were UK and 99 foreign. Accordingly, in line with Enright (2000), and against Porter (1990), it seems that the conditions within a cluster that attract foreign companies will not necessarily foster local companies to the same extent. Whilst the City of London attracts many world-class foreign financial services firms, it has not spawned nearly as many domestic equivalents.

11.4 METHODOLOGY

Data were collected via a postal questionnaire survey and via in-depth face-to-face interviews. For the questionnaire survey, 1500 questionnaires were posted to companies engaged in banking, investment banking, insurance and fund management, and to companies providing related support: legal services, accounting, management consultancy, advertising, market research, recruitment, property management, financial printing and publishing, and the provision of electronic information. The firms included in the sampling frame were those known to be operating within a 500-metre buffer extending beyond the boundaries of the City of London and Canary Wharf. The sample was selected using a stratified method. A total of 100 per cent of the largest 350 financial services firms were selected. These were identified primarily from a database supplied by the specialist information provider Market Locations. The remaining 1150 firms were drawn at random from the rest of the Market Locations database (using a random number generator). A total of 310 usable questionnaires was returned, a response rate of just over 20 per cent. Each postal questionnaire case was coded as MNE or non-MNE and then chi-squared tests (cross-tabulations) were run to look for differences and similarities between the two subsamples. A concern was that the differences and similarities revealed would be due to firm size and not multinationality, with MNEs generally being larger than non-MNEs. Size analysis[1] revealed this not to be the case; that is, the differences and similarities reported in the next section are not due to size. However, there were some interesting differences between small and large MNEs that will be reported.

The interview survey was designed to provide qualitative evidence complementing the quantitative data gathered by the postal questionnaire. Senior executives in leading organizations within key subsectors were identified using 2001/02 sources, for example *The Banker*, London Investment Banking Association (LIBA), International Financial Services London (IFSL) and invited to participate. While most firms were large by international and London standards, prominent small, specialized organizations were included. In total, 39 interviews were conducted across seven sectors. The interview data were coded numerically and sorted by both sector and location variables.

11.5 RESULTS

11.5.1 Postal Questionnaire

In Table 11.1 we see three interesting patterns indicated by the boxes. The first pattern indicates cluster advantages that accrue to non-MNEs more than to MNEs. With respect to reputational benefits of a cluster location, well-known MNEs will have a reputation that is independent of location. Non-MNEs, however, are subject to higher information asymmetries and therefore will

Table 11.1 MNE and non-MNE cluster advantages

	Cluster advantages			
	More important to		More important to	
	MNEs	Non-MNEs	Large MNEs	Small MNEs
Your address is important to being perceived as credible		*		
It is the best place to be to take market share from rivals				
You benefit from being close to market-leading customers				
Your customers external to London find it easier to locate you		**		
Customers external to London find it easier to interact with you		*		
You benefit from being near leading competitors	***		**	
You benefit from a strong, skilled labour supply	*		**	
You benefit from being near professional bodies		*		
Ability to find firms who will supply bespoke services				
Ability to access real-time information on market trends				
Local rivalry among competitors is a powerful spur	**		**	
Ability to benchmark against competitors	***		**	
Support from local government				
Access to venture capital				
Knowledge transfer from the City's 'financial atmosphere'				
Proximity to a relevant exchange or physical marketplace		**	**	

Notes:
* Significant/very close to significance at 10%.
** Significant at 5%.
*** Significant at 1%.

rely to a greater extent on their address as a signal of their credibility. The second and third significant results within the first pattern link with the reputational spillovers that non-MNEs seek. Further down the non-MNE results column we see that non-MNEs benefit more from being close to professional bodies. This may be due to the greater embeddedness within the cluster. The finding on proximity to a relevant exchange or physical marketplace is difficult to interpret and may be caused by sector-specific effects.

The second box contains cluster advantages that benefit MNEs more than non-MNEs. Very significantly, MNEs benefit more from being near leading competitors. This finding fits Enright's (1998) listening post and skills and capabilities-absorbing motives for MNE FDI in clusters. The finding also fits Knickerbocker's (1973) argument that in an uncertain environment, oligopolists will find that the safest thing to do is to copy rivals, and this benchmarking is easier within a cluster. Finally, the finding fits with Amin and Thrift's (1992) point that location in global nodes is important, not least because it affords the opportunity to make sense of a complex and fast-changing environment through dialogue with other leading players in the industry. This is underscored by the fact that this advantage is more important to large MNEs. The fact that local rivalry and ability to benchmark against competitors are significantly more important to MNEs than to non-MNEs is consistent with all the preceding points and indicates the importance of strategic intent in the location decision among MNEs.

The finding that MNEs benefit more from the strong, skilled labour supply that is available in a cluster fits Enright's (1998) skills and capabilities-absorbing motive. As one would expect, this advantage is also more important to larger MNEs.

With respect to cluster disadvantages (Table 11.2), the first result (by row) suggests that MNEs resent a high price for a credible address that they need less than non-MNEs. This finding complements the reputation results in Table 11.1. The second and third results on infrastructure and environmental quality are difficult to interpret. Regarding the fourth result, one would expect non-MNEs to be more concerned about national transport links. Also, larger MNEs may have more than one office in the UK and so will protest similarly. The fifth result is in line with Castells's (1996) space-of-flows reasoning, which places emphasis on the ease of movement of personnel and ideas.

In general, the results reported in Table 11.3 support Porter's (1998) clusters paradox and Audretsch's globalization irony (Audretsch, 1998). The advantages of close proximity to other firms is clearly more important to MNEs. The first result (by row) suggests the greater importance of international alliances for MNEs, while the second result underlines the importance of common cultures and sensemaking at global nodes

Table 11.2 MNE and non-MNE cluster disadvantages

	Cluster disadvantages			
	More important to		More important to	
	MNEs	Non-MNEs	Large MNEs	Small MNEs
Cost of business premises	*			
The UK's current position outside the eurozone				
Local infrastructure (including buildings)		**	**	
Access to venture capital				
Availability of staff with language skills				
Competition on cost/price				
Environmental quality and pollution		*		
National transport links		**	**	
International transport links	*		***	
State of the Underground				
Government regulation				

Notes:
* Significant/very close to significance at 10%.
** Significant at 5%.
*** Significant at 1%.

Table 11.3 Close proximity to other firms

	Close proximity to other firms			
	More important to		More important to	
	MNEs	Non-MNEs	Large MNEs	Small MNEs
It is easier to build relationships of trust and cooperation				
We generally have complementary expertise with such firms	*			
Easier to communicate because of common understanding of business	**		**	
It is easier to build and maintain personal contacts				
Multidisciplinary teams can be assembled more quickly				
The ability to have face-to-face contact	*			

Notes:
* Significant/very close to significance at 10%.
** Significant at 5%.
*** Significant at 1%.

(Amin and Thrift, 1992). The fourth result suggests that it is important for high-level employees to be close to one another. A commonplace in the literature is that face-to-face contact is most valued for exchange of tacit, non-standardized and complex information, which is apt to be particularly important in the strategy and operations of leading MNEs.

11.5.2 Interview Survey

Results from the interview survey also shed light on our research questions. We have begun to categorize quotations as MNE and non-MNE. The following quote from an MNE bank provides evidence of Enright's (1998) stand-alone corporate portfolio investment and skills and capabilities motives for MNE location in clusters.

> We're here for two reasons – one is that we have an ambition to be an international bank and you can't be an international bank unless you have something in London. The other is that the exposure to London markets and London personnel and the ways of doing things in London is something we want to gain experience of and communicate through the rest of the . . . Group. (MNE bank)

The following is another quotation from an MNE bank that provides evidence of the skills and capabilities motive.

> there is a skills base, people both front and back office, that exists in London that you'd probably have difficulty finding elsewhere in the volumes you need to support the industry. So because the industry's grown up and evolved in the City, then around it you have a large pool of skilled resource in the areas you need it and some of those areas are quite specific. So that's the major point. (MNE bank)

The final quotation from an MNE law firm provides evidence of market-seeking and marketplace-seeking investments.

> There is an awful lot of business that is done which is joint business between institutions. There is more and more now of large transactions which are done jointly and the risk is spread then between different organizations. So there's a need not only for you to get yourself together with a client but to get those proposing the solution together. (MNE law firm)

11.6 CONCLUSION

This chapter has focused on the extraordinary concentration of MNE FDI in the City of London financial services cluster. It has examined the small but growing literature that suggests motives for MNE location in clusters and has attempted to relate these motives to the findings of a study that compares MNEs and non-MNEs regarding the advantages and disadvantages of location in the City of London financial services cluster. The primary conclusion is that MNEs and non-MNEs have different and multiple motives for locating in the cluster. There are two auxiliary conclusions. For MNEs that are cluster incumbents, because strong clusters have disadvantages (high expense and congestion) and because advantages can change over time, the MNE needs to continually assess which activities they need to locate in a cluster and which can be elsewhere (Buckley and Ghauri, 2004). Clark (2002, p. 437) corroborates, finding that in wholesale financial services industry

> Firms assess and re-assess time-after-time the costs and benefits of particular locations. This is especially true of Anglo-American 'bulge-bracket' financial houses that maintain and manage their global operations on a daily basis.

An example of this process is the movement of activity out of the City's core during the 1970s. During that decade London companies such as Clerical Medical, Sun Life and NatWest Life moved the less knowledge-intensive aspects of their business out of London to Bristol to save costs (Pandit and Cook, 2003). Similarly, we are now observing certain investment banking activity moving out of London to India. Research by IFSL (2005) finds that such 'offshoring' is most appropriate when the activity in question is characterized by no face-to-face servicing requirement, low social networking requirements, high information content, a work process that is telecommutable and Internet enabled, high wage levels relative to the destination country, and low set-up barriers.

The second auxiliary conclusion is that for MNEs that are not located in relevant clusters, clusters may provide advantages over and above those available to non-MNE competitors.

Just over a decade ago, O'Brien (1991, pp. 1–2) declared the 'end of geography' in financial services, stating:

> Geographic location no longer matters in finance, or much less than hitherto . . . For financial firms, this means that the choice of geographical location can be greatly widened, provided that an appropriate investment in information and computer systems can be made . . . There will be forces seeking to maintain geographical control . . . Yet, as markets and rules become integrated, the relevance of geography and the need to base decisions on geography will alter and often diminish.

Whilst this prediction may have great applicability to retail financial services, this study finds that wholesale financial services remain sticky in increasingly slippery space. Thus, as Enright (2000, pp. 115–16) states:

> as transportation and communications improve, as technology becomes more widely dispersed, and as barriers to trade and investment fall, some industries become more dispersed over geographic space. In other industries and activities, however, the same forces foster geographic concentration by allowing firms and locations to exploit specific sources of competitive advantage over even wider geographic areas . . . This logic concludes that as competition globalizes, the geographic or location-specific sources of competitive advantage will tend to become more, not less, important.

Whilst London's initial advantage may have been one of historical legacy, as 'the centre of Empire' (Clark, 2002), a London location continues to be important in order to have face-to-face contact and build trusting relationships that enable important interfirm linkages among local firms, particularly those with complementary expertise, which above all translate into the ability to provide high-level services to clients.

NOTE

1. For the purposes of this analysis, size was measured as being greater than 100 employees (large) or less than or equal to 100 (small): 100 was the 75th percentile for the sample. There were 14 firms with 100 employees, then just a few firms between 100 and 120; therefore it was also a natural break point. Only eight non-MNEs had over 100 employees; therefore this group could not be included in the analysis.

REFERENCES

Amin, A. and N. Thrift (1992), 'Neo-Marshallian nodes in global networks', *International Journal of Urban and Regional Research*, **16**, 571–87.

Audretsch, D.B. (1998), 'Agglomeration and the location of innovative activity', *Oxford Review of Economic Policy*, **14** (2), 18–29.

Augar, P. (2000), *The Death of Gentlemanly Capitalism*, London: Penguin.

Baptista, R.M.L.N. and G.M.P. Swann (1998), 'Do firms in clusters innovate more?', *Research Policy*, **27**, 527–42.

Beaverstock, J.V. (1994), 'Re-thinking skilled international labour migration: world cities and banking organizations', *Geoforum*, **25**, 323–38.

Birkinshaw, J.M. (1996), 'How multinational subsidiary mandates are gained and lost', *Journal of International Business Studies*, **27**, 467–96.

Birkinshaw, J.M. and N. Hood (2000), 'Characteristics of foreign subsidiaries in industry clusters', *Journal of International Business Studies*, **31**, 141–54.

Birkinshaw, J.M. and O. Solvell (2000), 'Preface', *International Studies of Management and Organization*, **30**, 3–9.

Buckley, P.J. and P.N. Ghauri (2004), 'Globalisation, economic geography and the strategy of multinational enterprises', *Journal of International Business Studies*, **35**, 81–98.
Castells, M. (1996), *The Rise of the Network Society*, Oxford: Blackwell.
Clark, G.L. (2002), 'London in the European financial services industry: locational advantages and product complementarities', *Journal of Economic Geography*, **2** (4), 433–54.
Coggan, P. (2002), *The Money Machine: How the City Works*, London: Penguin.
Corporation of London (2004), *City Economy Digest*, issue 1, February, London: Corporation of London.
DTI (1998), 'Our competitive future: building the knowledge driven economy', Cmnd. 4176, London: HMSO.
Dunning, J.H. (1993), *Multinational Enterprises and the Global Economy*, Wokingham, UK: Addison-Wesley.
Dunning, J.H. (1998), 'Location and the multinational enterprise: a neglected factor?', *Journal of International Business Studies*, **29**, 45–66.
Dunning, J.H. (2000), 'The eclectic paradigm as an envelope for economic and business theories of MNE activity', *International Business Review*, **9**, 163–90.
Dunning, J.H. (2003), 'The key literature on IB activities: 1960–2000', in A.M. Rugman and T.L. Brewer (eds), *The Oxford Handbook of International Business*, Oxford: Oxford University Press, pp. 36–69.
Dupuy, C. and J.-P. Gilly (1999), 'Industrial groups and territories: the case of Matra Marconi Space in Toulouse', *Cambridge Journal of Economics*, **23**, 207–25.
Enright, M.J. (1998), 'Regional clusters and firm strategy', in A.D. Chandler, O. Solvell and P. Hagstrom (eds), *The Dynamic Firm: The Role of Technology, Strategy and Regions*, Oxford: Oxford University Press, pp. 315–42.
Enright, M.J. (2000), 'Regional clusters and multinational enterprises', *International Studies of Management and Organization*, **30**, 114–38.
Golding, T. (2001), *The City: Inside the Great Expectation Machine*, London: Prentice-Hall.
Gong, H. (1995), 'Spatial patterns of foreign investment in China's cities, 1980–1989', *Urban Geography*, **16**, 198–209.
Gordon, I.R. and P. McCann (2000), 'Industrial clusters: complexes, agglomeration and/or social networks?', *Urban Studies*, **37**, 513–32.
Hamilton, A. (1996), *The Financial Revolution*, London: Penguin.
Harrison, B. (1994), *Lean and Mean: The Changing Landscape of Corporate Power in the Age of Flexibility*, London: The Guilford Press.
Head, K., J.C. Ries and D.L. Swenson (1995), 'Agglomeration benefits and location choices: evidence from Japanese manufacturing investments in the United States', *Journal of International Economics*, **38**, 223–47.
Head, K., J.C. Ries and D.L. Swenson (1999), 'Attracting foreign manufacturing: investment promotion and agglomeration', *Regional Science and Urban Economics*, **29**, 197–218.
Henderson, J.V. (1986), 'Efficiency of resource usage and city size', *Journal of Urban Economics*, **19**, 47–70.
HM Treasury (2003), 'The location of financial activity and the euro', London: HM Treasury.
International Financial Services London (2004), 'International financial markets in the UK', May (available at www.ifsl.org.uk).

International Financial Services London (2005), 'Offshoring of services: impact and implications', March (available at www.ifsl.org.uk).

Knickerbocker, F.T. (1973), *Oligopolistic Reaction and the Multinational Enterprise*, Cambridge, MA: Harvard University Press.

Kozul-Wright, R. and R. Rowthorn (1998), 'Spoilt for choice? Multinational corporations and the geography of international production', *Oxford Review of Economic Policy*, **14**, 74–92.

Kynaston, D. (2001), *The City of London: Volume IV: A Club No More 1945–2000*, London: Pimlico.

Markusen, A. (1996), 'Sticky places in slippery space: a typology of industrial districts', *Economic Geography*, **72**, 293–313.

Marshall, A. (1890), *Principles of Economics*, London: Macmillan.

Morgan, G. (1997), 'The global context of financial services: national systems and the international political economy', in G. Morgan and D. Knights (eds), *Regulation and Deregulation in European Financial Services*, Basingstoke: Macmillan Business, pp. 14–41.

Nachum, L. (2000a), 'Economic geography and the location of TNCs: financial and professional service FDI to the USA', *Journal of International Business Studies*, **31**, 367–85.

Nachum, L. (2000b), 'Global financial centres in an era of globalisation', Working Paper series of the Geneva Association for the Study of Insurance Economics, no. 233.

Nachum, L. (2003), 'Liability of foreignness in global competition? Financial service affiliates in the City of London', *Strategic Management Journal*, **24**, 1187–208.

Nachum, L. and D. Keeble (2003), 'Neo-Marshallian clusters and global networks: the linkages of media firms in Central London', *Long Range Planning*, **36**, 459–80.

O'Brien, R. (1991), *Global Financial Integration: The End of Geography*, London: Pinter/Royal Institute of International Affairs.

Pandit, N.R. and G.A.S. Cook (2003), 'The benefits of industrial clustering: insights from the British financial services industry at three locations', *Journal of Financial Services Marketing*, **7**, 230–45.

Pandit, N.R. and G.A.S. Cook (2005), 'The clustering of the British financial services industry', in B. Johansson, C. Karlsson and R.R. Stough (eds), *Industrial Clusters and Inter-Firm Networks*, Cheltenham, UK and Northampton, MA, USA: Edward Elgar, pp. 173–99.

Porter, M.E. (1990), *The Competitive Advantage of Nations*, London: Macmillan.

Porter, M.E. (1998), 'Clusters and competition: new agendas for companies, governments, and institutions', in M.E. Porter, *On Competition*, Boston, MA: Harvard Business School Publishing, pp. 197–288.

Roberts, R. (ed.) (1994), *Global Financial Centres*, vol. II, Camberley, UK and Brookfield, US: Edward Elgar.

Sassen, S. (1991), *The Global City: New York, London, Tokyo*, Princeton, NJ: Princeton University Press.

Sassen, S. (1999), 'Global financial centres', *Foreign Affairs*, **78**, 75–87.

Swann, G.M.P., M. Prevezer and D. Stout (eds) (1998), *The Dynamics of Industrial Clustering: International Comparisons in Computing and Biotechnology*, Oxford: Oxford University Press.

Taylor, P.J., J.V. Beaverstock, G. Cook, N. Pandit, K. Pain and H. Greenwood

(2003), *Financial Services Clustering and its Significance for London*, London: Corporation of London.
Wheeler, D. and A. Mody (1992), 'International investment location decisions', *Journal of International Economics*, **33**, 57–76.
Zaheer, S. (1995), 'Overcoming the liability of foreignness', *Academy of Management Journal*, **38** (2), 341–64.

12. Globalization and distribution of exports

Börje Johansson and Désirée Nilsson

During the 1980s, many economists started to use the term globalization as a catchword for an increased interaction between countries in world trade. The literature does not provide a clear definition of globalization. We set up a number of criteria and formulate hypotheses about globalization that we explore for Swedish export flows during the years 1965–2000. Globalization, in this study, is referred to as increases in country diversity, extended transport radii, less effect of distance on trade flows, and the ratio of exports to the importing countries' incomes. The results from the empirical analysis do not support the hypotheses of increasing trade globalization. It is rather the case that export flows are becoming more internationally regionalized.

12.1 INTRODUCTION

What is economic globalization? The literature does not offer a clear definition of the concept. However, in this connection one often refers to integration, openness and the mobility of production factors. The extent of openness (export and import as a ratio to GDP) is continuously increasing since many countries in the world are opening up to international trade. Free trade agreements, customs unions and other types of cooperation between countries are also constantly being established. The integration of financial markets has been just as extensive as that of the commodities market. This study will consider only the global integration of the commodities market by focusing on the aggregate export flows of one small open economy, Sweden. It provides a perspective of nearly 40 years, from 1965 to 2000.

In this study we classify globalization as increases in country diversity, extended transport radii, less effect of distance on flows, and the allocation of exports being related to the importing countries' incomes. The aim of this chapter is to investigate whether Swedish exports are more globalized today than they were 40 years ago. We formulate three criteria and seven hypotheses about globalization that we investigate in the empirical analysis.

Economic globalization is not a new phenomenon. Many would argue that it started as early as the second half of the nineteenth century and then declined with the start of World War I (Taylor, 2002; Kenwood and Lougheed, 1999). Two major causes are attributed to the fast integration of global markets during the initial period of globalization: rapidly declining transportation costs and improved communication conditions.[1] Further technological development in these areas has stimulated the ongoing wave of globalization that started in the 1950s. Scholars have argued that gradual reductions in transportation and other transaction costs as a share of commodity values continue to reduce the importance of distance (Andersson et al., 1993; Welfens, 1999). However, many studies – like this one – indicate that distance still plays a significant role in the interaction between countries (cf. Rietveld and Vickerman, 2004; Bröcker and Rohweder, 1990). Sceptical authors state that the turn of the twenty-first century represents merely a return to a world trade situation that was observed about a century ago (Baldwin and Martin, 1999; Krugman, 1995).

Why focus on exports? Welfens (1999) presents a view implying that both export coverage and import penetration should be considered as examples of globalization, although he limits his statements to the OECD countries. Following Heckscher (1957), export flows are based on scale economies and comparative advantages. As such they can be expected to be much less diversified than import flows. Import flows, on the other hand, represent the diversity of the entire world economy. In this view, import patterns represent both diversification and novelty, whereas export flows from any particular country will be more limited in scope and more invariant over time.

Accepting Heckscher's conclusion that imports are more diversified than exports, we still consider a study of a country's export flows as an appropriate starting point in our endeavour to examine to what extent the period 1965–2000 represents a change towards more globalized trade. Sweden is a small open economy, dependent on the exchange of products on the international market. Export statistics were collected from the UN Comtrade database and GDP data from the World Bank.

Since 1965 Sweden has increased its export share of GDP from 21 per cent to about 47 per cent in 2000 (World Bank, 2004). During the same time period, the structure of exports has shifted towards a larger share of machinery and transport equipment. The share of crude materials in Swedish exports has decreased considerably. The most drastic changes in the Swedish economy have been the deregulation of the financial market in the 1980s. Foreign direct investments (FDI), both inflows and outflows, have been increasing ever since, and in the late 1990s flows increased dramatically. Previous studies of Swedish globalization have therefore mainly focused on the development of FDI. Karpaty and Kneller (2005) study the development of FDI and export flows. They find that inflows of FDI generally have a negative effect on the domestic firm's likelihood to export.

The results indicate that Swedish exports reflect international regionalization rather than globalization. Export flows have become increasingly concentrated to the European countries. Swedish exports as a ratio of world demand have also decreased during the 1990s, while the dampening effect of distance remains at the same level as in the mid-1970s.

The subsequent section presents the theoretical background and delineates the criteria and related hypotheses about globalization. Section 12.3 analyses how well the criteria are met, using statistics on Swedish export flows during the years 1965–2000. The results are summarized in the concluding section (Section 12.4), where suggestions for further research are also provided.

12.2 THEORY OF TRADE DIVERSITY AND MEASURES OF GLOBALIZATION

This section introduces, defines and examines variables and relations that will be empirically analysed in Section 12.3. The perspective is the same throughout the chapter: we study one exporting country and its relations with customer countries.

12.2.1 A Model of Import Demand and Exporters' Behaviour

This section delineates a connection between the export supply performance of firms and the import demand behaviour of firms and agents in countries. The flow of products from an exporting country is limited by the demand in each importing country. Let X_r denote the flow, in value terms, from one specific exporting country to country r. Import demand in country r may be modelled by considering the GDP of that country, Y_r, representing the purchasing power or the import capacity in this country. In a demand function we also need to consider prices. The variable p_r may denote the aggregate average export price for the flow X_r, or the deviation of the price from the average export price. In addition to the demand capacity and prices, we also need to account for the transaction distance, denoted by d_r. We can then formulate the following model of how the export flow to every country r may be determined:

$$X_r = \hat{\alpha} Y_r^{\beta} \exp(-\varphi d_r - \phi p_r) \tag{12.1}$$

Equation (12.1) can be interpreted as the exporting country's market potential of country r (Johansson and Karlsson, 2001; Lakshmanan and Hansen, 1965). $Y_r^{\beta} \exp(-\varphi d_r - \phi p_r)$ represents country r's 'demand budget' for imports and $\hat{\alpha}$ the fraction of demand budget allocated to deliveries from the exporting country. $\hat{\alpha}$ indicates the average ratio of a country's export to receiving countries demand potential. β is a scale parameter reflecting a possible nonlinearity of demand. Observe that if β deviates from unity, export flows will not be proportional to the size of GDP. In the exponential term of equation (12.1), $-\varphi d_r$ represents the influence of transaction distance on demand. The larger φ, the larger the transaction costs, and hence the smaller the market potential or the accessible market. The ϕ parameter transforms the price variable to the same scale as the transaction distance variable. Moreover, the transaction distance is often reflected in the average export price. Thus d_r and p_r are likely to display a strong covariation. The expression in equation (12.1) may be thought of as a market accessibility measure, incorporating variables that influence the ease of access of exporting firms to demand potentials around the world.[2]

In a complementary setting, equation (12.1) describes export supply behaviour. In this setting we assume that the behaviour of exporters can be described by a random choice preference function of the following type:

$$U_r = \psi_r - \varphi d_r - \phi p_r + \varepsilon_r \tag{12.2}$$

where U_r denotes the preference value associated with export supply to country r. Preferences for the exporter is generally denoted by profits, and the goal of the exporter is to attain the highest possible profit. ψ_r is an attractiveness factor that may reflect the size of demand or number of customers in country r. The error term ε_r is a random term that we assume to be extreme-value distributed. Given this specification, the probability of selling to country r, q_r, can be described by the following share formula (Ben-Akiva and Lerman, 1985):

$$q_r = x_r = X_r/X = \exp(V_r)/\sum_r \exp(V_r) \tag{12.3}$$

where $V_r + \varepsilon_r = U_r$. Taking the logarithm of equation (12.3) then yields $\ln X_r = \psi_r - \varphi d_r - \varphi p_r + \ln X - \ln \Sigma_r \exp(V_r)$, and let us assume that

$\psi_r = \ln \sigma + \beta \ln Y_r$. Both $\ln X$ and $\ln \Sigma_r \exp(V_r)$ can be treated as constants that can be added to σ, yielding $\alpha = \ln \sigma + \ln X - \ln \Sigma_r \exp(V_r)$. Setting $\alpha = \ln \hat{\alpha}$, we obtain formula (12.1).

It is often difficult to attain proper representation of the price variable, but because of its correlation with the distance the price effect is still incorporated to some extent. Thus the model that will be used in the empirical application is

$$X_r = \hat{\alpha} Y_r^{\beta} \exp(-\varphi d_r) \tag{12.1a}$$

where the price variable has been excluded. In the empirical section equation (12.1 a) is logarithmically transformed for the estimation

$$\ln X_r = \alpha + \beta \ln Y_r - \varphi d_r + \varepsilon_r \tag{12.4}$$

12.2.2 Indicators of Globalization and Country Diversity

The fundamental question posed in this chapter is whether we can find indications of globalization in export flows from Sweden. Trade globalization will, for a start, be related to the number of different destinations and whether the average export distance has increased. Has the number of links increased over time and have exporters increased the radius of distribution? Hence, by simply counting the number of destinations and calculating the average export distance over time, a first indication of globalization can be provided. The first criterion for globalization that we set up is:

Criterion 1 (Number of and distance to export destinations): in a more globalized setting one can expect that the number of links increases as economies become more integrated in the world economy. Thus, with the progress of globalization the number of export destinations for a country increases. As economies become more integrated, distance is likely to exert a smaller effect on trade flows. This would be manifested in an increase of the average export distance to destinations. The following hypotheses consistent with globalization can be formulated:

(a) The number of export destinations increases.
(b) The average export distance increases.

Our prime concern is to investigate the distribution of aggregate export flows to destinations. Diversity can be given a further dimension if we also consider the distribution of products across destinations. The issue of distribution that we are interested in is whether it follows the allocation of world income. Complete diversity would emerge if export flows were directed to each import market in proportion to the relative size of that market, and distance should not have any influence. In such a case the world market would be completely global.[3] To create a measure that may capture complete diversity, first recall that $x_r = X_r/X$ denotes a share value that can be interpreted as a probability, since $\Sigma_r x_r = 1$. The distribution of the share values can be described by the function $-\Sigma_r x_r \ln x_r$, which is a concave function. Letting M denote the number of possible export destinations, this function attains its maximum, at $\ln M$, when $x_r = 1/M$ for all r (see, e.g., Theil, 1963). In relation to the introduced distribution function, one may go one step further and formulate the information measure $C = \Sigma_r x_r \ln (x_r/y_r)$ where $y_r = Y_r/Y$. This measure reaches its optimal distribution at $C = 0$, when $x_r = y_r$ for all r (Theil, 1963; Snickars and Weibull, 1977). The measure assesses the deviation from perfect distribution of export flows, which would be in accordance with y_r. The function is convex to the origin, whether it approaches from above (if the export share, x_r, is larger than the relative size of the demand, y_r) or below (if the export share, x_r, is smaller than the relative size of the demand, y_r). On the basis of this, a second criterion is obtained:

Criterion 2 (Complete diversity): in this case, country diversity is measured by $C = \Sigma_r x_r \ln (x_r/y_r)$. First, we examine which groups of countries contribute most to the observed C-value. The hypothesis is that globalization has increased between 1965 and 2000, and we expect this to be evident in gradually reduced C-values during the time period. Thus the criterion provides the following hypothesis consistent with globalization:

(c) Exports are distributed in correspondence with the distribution of world income.

The previous criterion explored complete diversity without any influence of distance. We may also examine proportional distribution after accounting for the effect of transaction distance on trade flows. The transaction distance is likely to display an influence on the expected size of export to a particular destination. Research has found varying results on the effect of distance on international exchanges (Andersson et al., 1993; Welfens, 1999; Rietveld and Vickerman, 2004. Bröcker and Rohweder, 1990). Criterion 3 below applies a model where proportional diversity can be estimated, and where also the effect of transaction distance is included:

Criterion 3 (Distance-dependent diversity): This criterion refers to equation (12.4), $\ln X_r = \alpha + \beta Y_r \ \varphi d_r + \varepsilon_r$. This criterion requires that α is

Table 12.1 Criteria and hypotheses about globalization

Criterion	Name	Hypotheses consistent with globalization
1	Number of and distance to export destinations	(a) The number of export destinations increases with time (b) The average export distance increases with time
2	Complete diversity	(c) Exports are distributed in correspondence with the distribution of world income
3	Distance-dependent diversity	(d) Exports as a fraction of world income are significantly different from zero and less than 1 (e) Exports as a fraction of world income increase over time (f) The scale parameter, β, is insignificantly different from 1 (g) The distance parameter, φ, decreases over time

significant and $\alpha < 0$, which is the same as $0 < \hat{\alpha} < 1$ since $e^{\alpha} = \hat{\alpha}$. If the parameter is negative and significantly different from zero, this indicates that exports from a country constitute a fraction of world income. The estimated β parameter needs to be significant and close to or equal to 1, $\beta \approx 1$, to indicate proportional country diversity. Moreover, increasing globalization may also be reflected by decreasing values of α ($\hat{\alpha}$ increases) as well as by falling values of φ over time. The following hypotheses consistent with globalization and proportional distribution of exports can be formulated:

(d) Exports as a fraction of world income are significantly different from zero and less than 1.
(e) Exports as a fraction of world income increase over time.
(f) The scale parameter, β, is insignificantly different from 1.
(g) The distance parameter, φ, decreases over time.

The criteria presented above and the associated hypotheses are summarized in Table 12.1. Keep in mind that globalization is intended to be indicated by diversity in export destinations, extended export radius and proportional distribution of exports on the associated links. The empirical section that follows will provide answers to the hypotheses concerning trade globalization.

12.2.3 Data and Statistical Sources

The export statistics used in the empirical analysis were collected from the UN Comtrade database (classification SITC rev.1) for the period 1965–2000. GDPs (constant US dollars, 1995 prices) were collected from the World Development Indicators, World Bank, and the distance measure comes from the Centre d'Études Prospectives et d'Informations Internationales (CEPII).[4]

12.3 EXAMINING EXPORT DESTINATION DIVERSITY

This section examines the criteria formulated for examining globalization of a country's exports. Some of the criteria are analysed by dividing the world into geographical areas: Europe (subdivided into the Nordic area, Northern Europe, Southern Europe and Eastern Europe); North America; Central/South America; Africa; Asia and the Pacific Ocean (see Appendix 12A.1).

12.3.1 Criterion 1: Number of and Distance to Export Destinations

The first criterion of globalization investigates the diversity of exports by simply counting the number of destinations that Swedish products are exported to. Since the 1960s the world has changed considerably. One geographical area that has seen radical changes is Europe. There are multiple examples of countries that have disintegrated into smaller units. The most drastic change was (and is) the dissolution of the Soviet Union, but we can also recall the turmoil in the Balkans and the peaceful split of Czechoslovakia. These changes on the European map call for caution in the interpretation of this criterion. Table 12.2 presents the number of export destinations in the different geographical areas between 1965 and 2000.

The number of destinations of Swedish exports has increased from 122 in 1965 to 194 in 2000. The largest percentage increase has occurred in Eastern Europe, where the number has increased from 5 to 18. The number of export destinations has also increased significantly in Central/South America, Africa and Asia. Several of the countries on these continents have opened up to international trade during the past four decades. During this period Sweden has also started to export to new destinations in the Pacific Ocean.

The increase in the number of export destinations, shown in Table 12.2,

Table 12.2 Number of export destinations in each geographical area

	1965	1970	1975	1980	1985	1990	1995	2000
Europe	23	23	23	25	25	26	40	42
Nordic area	4	4	4	4	4	4	4	4
Northern	6	6	6	8	8	9	9	11
Southern	8	8	8	8	8	8	9	9
Eastern	5	5	5	5	5	5	18	18
North America	3	3	3	3	3	3	3	3
Central/South America	23	26	28	32	32	35	37	37
Africa	40	42	45	46	46	46	48	53
Asia	23	26	32	32	32	33	42	42
Pacific Ocean	10	11	11	13	13	13	16	17
Total	122	131	142	151	151	156	186	194

Table 12.3 Average Swedish export distance in kilometres, weighted by export shares, 1965–2000

	1965	1970	1975	1980	1985	1990	1995	2000
Average export distance	2706	2628	2700	2853	3035	2657	2926	2903

can partly be explained by the rewriting of the map of Eastern Europe and the liberalization of trade in the same area. Geographic proximity also contributes to the development of exports to that region. Trade liberalization of countries in Central/South America, Africa and Asia has also provided Sweden with new export destinations. Hence Swedish exports have become more globalized in the sense that Sweden exports to more destinations in 2000 than it did in 1965.

The next question is whether the average export distance has also increased during the time period. Table 12.3 shows the average export distance in kilometres. The export distance increases continuously until 1985 and plunges in 1990, to return to larger values in 1995 and 2000. The long-term trend indicates an increase in weighted average export distance, which can be interpreted as an increase in globalization of Swedish export flows. The shift in the structure of exports (se Figure 12A.1 in Appendix 12A.1), away from crude materials to include more of machinery and transport equipment, may have contributed to extending the reach of export flows from Sweden. The average export distance stretches just beyond the borders of Europe.

12.3.2 Criterion 2: Complete Diversity

Criterion 2 investigates the distribution of exports and to what extent it diverts from complete diversity. The distribution of exports is related to the distribution of world income. In a hypothetical world where integration is complete it may be argued that exports from a country may be distributed consistently with relative import demand in destination countries. Distance and other friction variables, such as common language, free trade agreements and cultural affinity would then not have an effect on the distribution. Criterion 2 specifies an information-theoretical measure $C = \Sigma_r x_r \ln(x_r/y_r)$, where the export share, x_r, is related to the income share, y_r. The findings relating to how this measure has developed over time are presented for various geographic areas in Table 12.4. Globalization, in the form of trade diversification, would be manifested in a C-value that approaches zero. The overall observation is that exports from Sweden are not distributed in proportion to the relative size of GDP for the importing countries. It is rather the case that the measure indicates a distance effect, where the Nordic countries and the North European countries receive disproportionally more exports from Sweden than what is motivated by their relative demand capacity. In addition, there does not seem to be any development towards more globalization with GDP-proportional export flows as the twenty-first century begins. The total value of C fluctuates over the years but it displays a larger deviation from complete diversity in 2000 than in 1965.

Table 12.4 Complete diversity as indicated by $C = \Sigma_r x_r \ln(x_r/y_r)$

	1965	1970	1975	1980	1985	1990	1995	2000
Europe	0.644	0.768	0.827	0.793	0.777	0.863	0.758	0.856
Nordic area	0.581	0.659	0.709	0.649	0.649	0.570	0.498	0.527
Northern	0.079	0.129	0.126	0.152	0.143	0.276	0.224	0.233
Southern	−0.016	−0.021	−0.010	−0.013	−0.016	0.014	0.002	0.022
Eastern	0.000	0.001	0.002	0.005	0.001	0.003	0.034	0.074
North America	−0.117	−0.107	−0.092	−0.100	−0.107	−0.101	−0.103	−0.107
Central/South America	−0.014	−0.015	−0.012	−0.009	−0.008	−0.012	−0.016	−0.015
Africa	0.012	0.051	0.053	0.034	0.019	0.008	0.001	0.001
Asia	−0.025	−0.032	−0.031	−0.019	−0.033	−0.050	−0.067	−0.067
Pacific Ocean	−0.005	−0.005	−0.003	0.012	0.004	0.005	0.010	0.003
Total	0.599	0.756	0.825	0.710	0.652	0.713	0.583	0.671

The lack of globalization, according to this measure, comes mainly from the concentration of Swedish exports to the Nordic countries. The focus of exports to these countries has been fairly consistent since the 1960s. The results also indicate an increase in the focus of exports to countries in Northern Europe that does not correspond to their share of world income. This is caused by Sweden's close trade affinity (small transaction distance) with destinations in the Nordic and Northern European areas. A similar tendency of disproportional distribution of Swedish exports appears for the Eastern and Southern European countries. Several of the Eastern European countries are situated close to Sweden (such as Estonia, Latvia, Lithuania and Poland). Studies of the exchange of goods between the Baltic Sea countries (henceforth abbreviated BSC)[5] have displayed high intensity, and the cultural and historical links that exist in the region promote further exchange in the area (Peschel, 1993, 1998; Hacker and Einarsson, 2003). The trade liberalization of these countries and the geographic proximity to them explains the drastic rise in the *C*-value for them after 1990.

Swedish exports to North America have consistently displayed a negative value of *C*, which means that the export shares to the countries in this region are less than their share of world income. This indicates that there is demand potential in the USA, Canada and Mexico that firms in Sweden may try to take advantage of. There seem to be similar export potentials for Swedish exports to Asia.

Recall that the number of export destinations in Central/South America has increased continuously since 1965. However, the degree of complete diversity of export flows has remained fairly constant. The value of *C* is close to zero for exports to Africa and the Pacific Ocean.

Thus the results in Table 12.4 present a strengthening of the concentration of Swedish exports to the European countries, which include the Nordic area, Northern, Southern and Eastern Europe. The results of Criterion 2 rather indicate regionalization than globalization.

12.3.3 Criterion 3: Distance-dependent Diversity

In Criterion 3, globalization refers to the fraction of world income. How large is the portion of world income that is used on exports from Sweden?

Globalization will grow if this fraction increases over time, indicating that Swedish products are becoming more important on the world market. The method applied for this criterion is regression analysis, where ordinary least squares (OLS) is used. The equation estimated is $\ln X_r = \alpha + \beta \ln Y_r + \varphi d_r + \gamma BSC_r + \varepsilon_r$, where a dummy variable representing the BSC is added to equation (12.1) and e^{α} represents the share parameter. The reason for this is the displayed increase in concentration of export flows to the Nordic countries as well as to the Northern and Eastern European countries, revealed in the complete diversity measure of the previous section. The results from this estimation are presented in Table 12.5.

A proportional distribution of export flows is indicated if β is close to or equal to 1. Some degree of globalization is present if the share parameter is significantly different from zero, and proportional distribution is indicated if β is insignificantly different from 1. In addition, globalization can also be shown by a decrease in the distance parameter φ.

The results show that the share parameter, α, is significantly different from zero. The β parameter has high *t*-values and increases over time. In other words, export elasticity with respect to world income is increasing. Proportional distribution of exports, with respect to income, is accepted for the years 1965–1990, since the β parameter is insignificantly different from 1. However, we need to reject proportional distribution for the years 1995 and 2000, as the observed export intensity has the form of a size-biased globalization. Export flows increasingly tend to concentrate on large markets. The change in the structure of exports, towards a larger share of machinery and transport equipment and away from crude materials (see Figure 12A.1 in Appendix) may be a contributing factor to the orientation of export flows towards larger markets. The distance parameter φ does show a tendency of increased globalization, in the form of reduced friction, between 1975 and 1995, but thereafter trade friction increases markedly in 2000.

The dummy for the *BSC* displays a significant and positive effect on trade flows from Sweden. The effect seems to be decreasing during the time period, even if some fluctuations are present after 1980. Swedish exports as a fraction of world income are smaller in 2000 compared with the level in 1965. The ratio to world income was considerably higher between 1975 and 1990, peaking in 1980. The development of the share parameter in the 1970s and 1980s is also connected with changes in the distance effect on trade flows. When the share parameter drastically increases between 1970 and 1975, the effect of distance also increases. However, the pattern changes during the 1990s when the negative effect of distance is still strong and even increasing, while the share of world income decreases. The smaller share parameter indicates that, as world income increases, Sweden is not able to fully compete for the extra demand potential.

12.3.4 Summary and Assessment of Results

Table 12.6 again presents the criteria and hypotheses about globalization and answers them by either rejection or acceptance. Out of the

Table 12.5 *Distance-dependent diversity as presented by* $lnX_r = \alpha + \beta lnY_r + \varphi d_r + \gamma BSC_r + \varepsilon_r$

	1965	1970	1975	1980	1985	1990	1995	2000
$\ln Y_r$	0.973	0.991	0.964	0.984	1.001	1.001	1.058[a]	1.087[b]
	(14.57)***	(16.24)***	(16.34)***	(19.79)***	(22.29)***	(25.06)***	(27.81)***	(29.61)***
BSC_r	2.555	2.492	2.147	1.964	2.211	1.669	1.868	1.667
	(8.52)***	(7.98)***	(8.13)***	(9.31)***	(10.71)***	(4.01)***	(4.77)***	(4.00)***
d_r	−0.026	−0.052	−0.116	−0.120	−0.101	−0.102	−0.081	−0.117
	(1.01)	(2.06)**	(4.13)***	(4.54)***	(4.06)***	(4.02)***	(3.53)***	(5.76)***
α	−7.304	−7.395	−5.468	−5.427	−6.145	−5.941	−7.421	−7.884
	(4.37)***	(4.78)***	(3.61)***	(4.31)***	(5.18)***	(5.61)***	(8.03)***	(8.59)***
Obs.	88	97	106	125	133	141	169	176
R^2	0.80	0.78	0.77	0.85	0.85	0.87	0.88	0.89

Notes:
Robust *t*-statistics in parentheses.
*** significant at 1%.
** significant at 5%.
[a] and [b] indicate significant difference from 1 at 10% and 1% respectively.
Dependent variable: ln*Exp*.

Table 12.6 Summary of results

Criterion	Name	Hypotheses about globalization	Provisional result of analysis
1	Number of and distance to export destinations	(a) The number of export destinations increases with time	Accept
		(b) The average export distance increases with time	Accept
2	Complete diversity	(c) Exports are distributed in correspondence with the distribution of world income	Reject
3	Distance-dependent diversity	(d) Exports as a fraction of world income are significantly different from zero and less than 1	Accept
		(e) Exports as a fraction of world income increase over time.	Reject
		(f) The scale parameter, β, is insignificantly different from 1	Accepted for 1965–90, rejected for 1995 and 2000
		(g) The distance parameter, φ, decreases over time	Reject

seven hypotheses, only three can be accepted for the development of Swedish exports during the past 40 years. Sweden exports to more destinations in the world in 2000 than it did in 1965. The average export distance, weighted by export shares, extends just beyond the borders of the European countries. We also found that Swedish exports as a ratio of world income are significantly different from zero. A fourth hypothesis, Hypothesis (f) (Criterion 3), can be accepted during the years 1965–1990 but not for 1995 and 2000. This means that Sweden, during the 1990s, increasingly concentrates export flows to larger markets. Thus there is a size-biased distribution of export flows.

The remaining hypotheses are rejected. The distribution of export flows from Sweden is becoming increasingly concentrated to the European countries. The dissolution of the Soviet Union and the trade liberalization of the Eastern European countries have opened up new markets in the proximity of Sweden. The BSC display strong affinity to Sweden, though it seems to be diminishing. Results also show that Sweden is losing ground in the competition for increasing demand potential in the world. During the 1990s world demand grew especially in countries at a long distance from Sweden. The effect of distance on export flows seems to remain at approximately the same level since 1975. This means that the dampening effect of trade frictions has been fairly stable over the years.

12.4 CONCLUSIONS

There is little support for the argument that Swedish exports are becoming more globalized. Results in this study rather indicate the opposite, that exports are becoming more concentrated to specific geographical areas, primarily Europe. Only three of the seven hypotheses consistent with globalization that we formulated could be accepted; a fourth hypothesis was accepted for the earlier years.

This study has explored only the development of export flows from Sweden. A natural step would be to perform the same type of analysis on other countries. Further suggestions for studies of globalization of export flows should apply a more disaggregated level, so that, for example, product diversity can be considered. Product diversity in export flows means that different product groups are exported on each link. Patterns of globalization may vary depending on the product groups considered.

NOTES

1. In addition to technical advances, changes in the political arena played a significant role in the globalization process (Taylor, 2002).
2. Besides distance and commodity prices influencing demand potentials, there are a number of other variables, such as common language, cultural affinity and free trade agreements, that may improve the availability of markets.
3. Rodrik (2000) discusses the concept of complete international economic integration where markets for goods, services and factors of production are perfectly integrated in the world economy. In this hypothetical world, distance, country borders and other friction variables have no influence on international exchanges.
4. The distance measure is calculated using the great circle formula, which applies longitudes and latitudes of the most important city or of the country's official capital.
5. Countries included in the definition of BSC are Norway, Finland, Estonia, Latvia, Lithuania, Russia, Poland, Germany and Denmark.

REFERENCES

Andersson, Å.E., D.F. Batten, K. Kobayashi and K. Yoshikawa (1993), 'Logistical dynamics, creativity and infrastructure', in Å.E. Andersson, D.F. Batten, K. Kobayashi and K. Yoshikawa (eds), *The Cosmo-Creative Society: Logistical Networks in a Dynamic Economy*, Berlin: Springer Verlag.

Baldwin, R.E. and P. Martin (1999), 'Two waves of globalisation: superficial similarities, fundamental differences', NBER Working Paper No. W6904.

Ben-Akiva, M. and S. Lerman (1985), *Discrete Choice Analysis: Theory and Application to Travel Demand*, Cambridge, MA: MIT Press.

Bröcker, J and H.C. Rohweder (1990), 'Barriers to international trade: methods of measurement and empirical evidence', *The Annals of Regional Science*, **24** (4), 289–305.

CEPII (2002), Centre d'Études Prospectives et d'Informations Internationales Bilateral Distance Data, http://www.cepii.fr/anglaisgraph/bdd/distances.htm, retrieved 1 March 2002.

Comtrade (2006), United Nations Commodity Trade Statistics Database, retrieved 1 October 2006.

Hacker, R.S. and H. Einarsson (2003), 'The pattern, pull, and potential of the Baltic Sea trade', *The Annals of Regional Science*, **37** (1), 15–29.

Heckscher, E. (1957), *Svenskt Arbete och Liv – Från Medeltiden till Nutiden*, Stockholm: Bonnier.

Johansson, B. and C. Karlsson (2001), 'Geographic transaction costs and specialisation opportunities of small and medium-sized regions: scale economies and market extension', in B. Johansson, C. Karlsson and R.R. Stough (eds), *Theories of Endogenous Regional Growth: Lessons for Regional Policies*, Heidelberg: Springer Verlag.

Karpaty, P. and R. Kneller (2005), 'Demonstration or congestion? Export spillovers in Sweden', GEP Research Paper 05/ 44, Nottingham.

Kenwood, A.G. and A.L. Lougheed (1999), *The Growth of the International Economy 1820–2000: An Introductory Text*, London: Routledge.

Krugman, P. (1995), 'Growing world trade: causes and consequences', *Brookings Papers on Economic Activity*, **1**, 327–62.

Lakshmanan, T.R. and W.G. Hansen (1965), 'A retail market potential model', *Journal of the American Institute of Planners*, **31** (2), 134–43.

Peschel, K. (1993), 'Perspectives of regional economic development around the Baltic', in L. Lundqvist and L.O. Persson (eds), *Visions and Strategies in European Integration. A North European Perspective*, Berlin: Springer Verlag, pp. 19–31.

Peschel, K. (1998), 'Perspectives of regional development around the Baltic', *The Annals of Regional Science*, **32**, 299–320.

Rietveld, P. and R. Vickerman (2004), 'Transport in regional science: the "death of distance" is premature', *Papers in Regional Science*, **83**, 229–48.

Rodrik, D. (2000), 'How far will international economic integration go?', *Journal of Economic Perspectives*, **14** (1), 177–86.

Snickars, F. and J.W. Weibull (1977), 'A minimum information principle: theory and practice', *Regional Science and Urban Economics*, **7** (1–2), 137–68.

Taylor, A.M. (2002), 'Globalization, trade, and development: some lessons from history', NBER Working Paper No. W9326.

Theil, H. (1963), *Economics of Information Theory*, Amsterdam: North-Holland.
Welfens, P.J.J. (1999), *Globalization of the Economy, Unemployment and Innovation: Structural Change, Schumpeterian Adjustment, and New Policy Challenges*, Heidelberg: Springer Verlag.
World Bank (2004), *World Development Indicators*, Washington, DC: World Bank.

APPENDIX 12A.1 CATEGORIZATION OF COUNTRIES INTO GEOGRAPHICAL AREAS

Nordic area (4)
Denmark
Finland
Iceland
Norway

Northern Europe (11)
Austria
Belgium
Faroe Isles
France
Germany
Greenland
Ireland
Luxembourg
Netherlands
Switzerland
United Kingdom

Southern Europe (9)
Andorra
Cyprus
Greece
Israel
Italy
Malta
Portugal
Spain
Turkey

Eastern Europe (18)
Albania
Belarus
Bosnia and Herzegovina
Bulgaria
Croatia
Czech Rep.
Estonia
Hungary
Latvia
Lithuania
Poland
Romania
Russian Federation
Serbia and Montenegro
Slovakia
Slovenia
FYR of Macedonia
Ukraine

North America (3)
Canada
Mexico
USA

Central/South America (37)
Antigua and Barbuda
Argentina
Aruba
Bahamas
Barbados
Belize
Bermuda
Bolivia
Brazil
Cayman Islands
Chile
Colombia
Costa Rica
Cuba
Dominica
Dominican Rep.
Ecuador
El Salvador
Grenada
Guatemala
Guyana
Haiti
Honduras
Jamaica
Neth. Antilles
New Caledonia
Nicaragua
Panama
Paraguay
Peru
Saint Kitts and Nevis
Saint Lucia
Saint Vincent and the Grenadines
Suriname
Trinidad and Tobago
Uruguay
Venezuela

Africa (53)
Algeria
Angola
Benin
Botswana
Burkina Faso
Burundi
Cameroon
Cape Verde
Central African Rep.
Chad
Comoros
Congo
The Ivory Coast
Dem. Rep. of the Congo
Djibouti
Egypt
Equatorial Guinea
Eritrea
Ethiopia
Gabon
Gambia
Ghana
Guinea
Guinea-Bissau
Kenya
Lesotho
Liberia
Madagascar
Malawi
Mali
Mauritania
Mauritius
Morocco
Mozambique
Namibia
Niger
Nigeria
Rwanda
São Tomé and Principe
Senegal
Seychelles
Sierra Leone
Somalia
South Africa
Sudan
Swaziland
Togo
Tonga
Tunisia
Uganda
United Rep. of Tanzania
Zambia
Zimbabwe

Asia (42)
Afghanistan
Armenia
Azerbaijan
Bahrain
Bangladesh
Bhutan
Cambodia
China
China, Hong Kong
China, Macao SAR Dem. People's Rep.
Georgia
India
Iran
Iraq
Japan

Jordan
Kazakhstan
Kuwait
Kyrgyzstan
Lao People's Dem. Rep.
Lebanon
Libya
Maldives
Mongolia
Myanmar
Nepal
Oman
Pakistan
Qatar
Rep. of Korea
Rep. of Moldova
Saudi Arabia
Sri Lanka
Syria
Tajikistan
Thailand
Turkmenistan
United Arab Emirates
Uzbekistan
Viet Nam
Yemen

Pacific Ocean (17)

Australia
Brunei Darussalam
Fiji
French Polynesia
Indonesia
Kiribati
Malaysia
Marshall Islands
N. Mariana Islands
New Zealand
Palau
Papua New Guinea
Philippines
Samoa
Singapore
Solomon Islands
Vanuatu

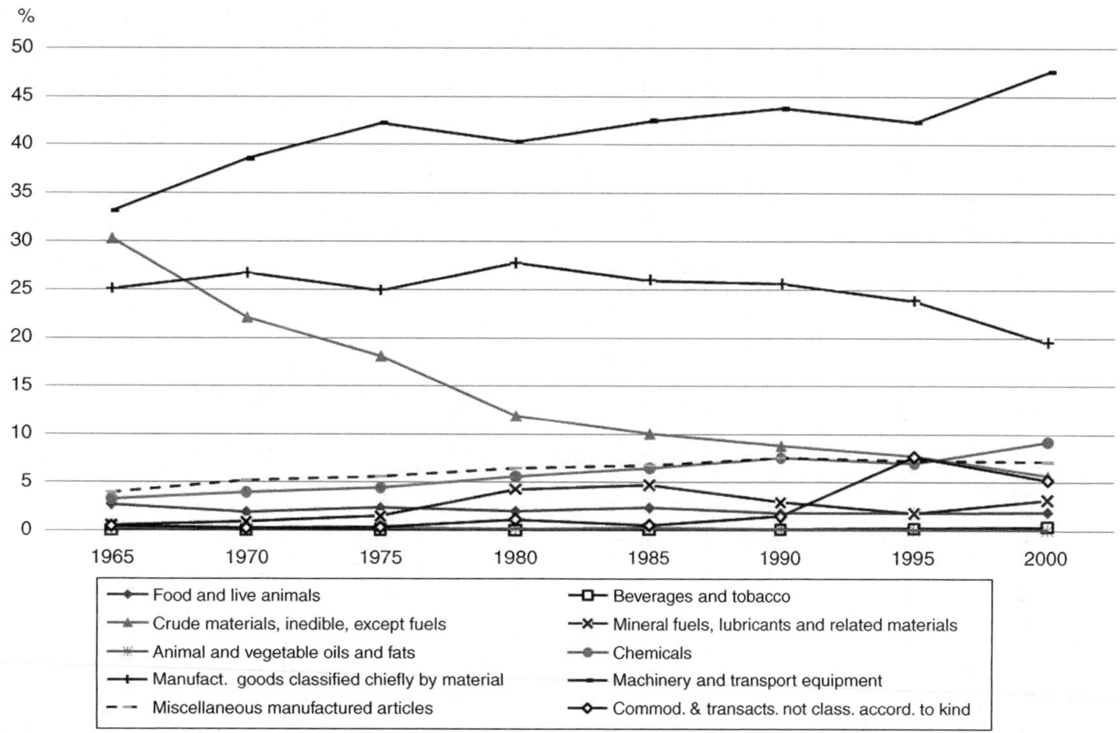

Source: Comtrade, SITC rev 1, United Nations.

Figure 12A.1 Export structure, share (%)

13. Firm performance and international trade – evidence from a small open economy

Martin Andersson, Sara Johansson and Hans Lööf

Despite a growing interest in firm-level analyses of international trade from both theorists and empiricists, papers providing thorough analyses of firms' trading activities and their relation to firm performance are rare. The literature is dominated by stylized facts from the USA, a large country with a significant share of the world market. This chapter resolves this imbalance and presents a comprehensive analysis of Swedish firms' trade. Sweden is a small open economy with a limited domestic market. Its neighbour countries have similar traits (language, culture, formal and informal institutions) and Swedish firms presumably face low entry costs not only to the rest of Scandinavia but also the Baltic countries. Sweden thus constitutes an interesting case. The chapter makes a twofold contribution: (1) based on detailed data on Swedish firms over a sequence of periods, we present stylized facts about their engagement in international trade and contrast them to findings from other countries, the USA in particular. Our data cover information on both export and import activities across products and markets for each and every firm, such that we can provide a complete picture of the firms' international trading activities and their variation across products and markets; (2) we extend previous analyses by examining the elasticity of productivity with respect to both export and import activities, respectively. Moreover, we perform static panel estimations (ordinary fixed effects) and dynamic estimations using the Arellano–Bond estimation procedure. We find evidence of both 'learning by exporting' and 'learning by importing', the former being stronger than the latter. Our findings on 'learning by importing' are consistent with previous research pointing to trade in intermediate capital goods being a significant vehicle for international technology diffusion.

13.1 INTRODUCTION[1]

Detailed micro-level data on international trading activities by manufacturing plants showed that (i) there are large within-industry variations among plants in terms of their export involvement and (ii) there are marked differences in characteristics between exporting and non-exporting plants (Bernard and Jensen, 1995). There is a series of papers on how different characteristics of individual firms affect their export activities (see Wagner, 2007; Greenaway and Kneller, 2007; Tybout, 2003 for surveys). Particular emphasis is put on the relationships between productivity, entry and survival in export markets. Several studies from different countries show that exporters are larger, more productive and have higher skill and capital intensity.[2] In short, firms engaged in international trade show better performance than firms operating solely on domestic markets.

There are two alternative but not mutually exclusive explanations for the observed differences between exporters and non-exporters (Wagner, 2007). The first is that the most productive firms self-select into foreign markets because they are in a better position to recover sunk costs associated with foreign sales. Such a self-selection hypothesis has been suggested by, e.g., Clerides et al. (1998), Aw et al. (1998) and Bernard and Jensen (1999). The second is that firms engaged on international markets acquire knowledge and technology via 'learning by exporting' such that exports have positive feedback effects on firms' knowledge and technology accumulation. Although there are studies pointing to 'learning by exporting' – e.g. Castellani (2002), Castellani and Zanfei (2003), Criscuolo et al. (2004) – the predominant finding in the literature is self-selection, i.e. *ex ante* productivity advantages of exporters (Bernard et al., 2007).

The self-selection hypothesis holds that firms located in dense regions with richness in human talent and R&D investments are in a better position to be able to penetrate foreign markets. There is ample evidence that firms located in large and dense regions benefit from agglomeration economies; i.e. characteristics of the local environment of firms may spur their productivity. This would imply that functional regions may be a breeding ground for firms' entry into international markets.

The current chapter has an indirect link to characteristics of regions. It analyses attributes of firms engaged in international trade, which may provide an indication of the kind of milieus that favour firms' internationalization. Based on detailed data on Swedish firms' over a sequence of periods (1997–2004), we present stylized facts about Swedish firms' engagement in international trade and contrast them with findings from other countries, the USA in particular. A merit of our data is that they cover information on both export and import activities across products and markets for each and every firm. This allows us to provide a complete picture of the firms' international trading activities and their variation across products and markets. Despite the large literature, studies providing a comprehensive picture of firms' trading activities in terms of exports, imports, geographical scope and distribution across different product groups etc., are rare. Most existing studies are limited to information on aggregate export activities with a breakdown on neither markets nor products. One reason for this is simply that there are few internationally comparable data sets providing the pertinent information. The bulk of papers on productivity differences between exporters and non-exporters rely for instance on export indicators in the form of exporter dummy variables (or similar). Analyses of firms' total trading activities are at present limited to a few countries, most typically the USA. To our knowledge, Bernard et al.'s (2007) analysis of US 'Firms in international trade' is the only study of firms' trading activities that covers exports, imports and their respective geographical scope and distribution across products. Bernard et al. (2007, p. 2) state:

> In discussing the origins and implications of international trade, economists emphasize competitive advantage, increasing returns to scale and consumer love of variety, but pay relatively little attention to the firms that actually drive trade flows. Yet engaging in international trade is an exceedingly rare activity: of the 5.5 million firms operating in the United States in 2000, just 4 percent were exporters. Among these exporting firms, the top 10 percent accounted for 96 percent of total US exports.

In view of the characteristics of the Swedish economy – small domestic market, neighbouring Scandinavian countries (with similar language and culture) to which Swedish firms presumably face low entry costs – Sweden provides an interesting contrast to the US experience. Second, we analyse the relationships between firm performance and trading activities. We extend previous analyses by examining the elasticity of productivity with respect to both export and import activities respectively; we perform static panel estimations (ordinary fixed effects) and dynamic estimations using the Arellano–Bond estimation procedure. The vast majority of the analyses to date are confined to exports. Yet imports constitute a significant part of firms' trading activities, and results from empirical analyses advancing trade as a vehicle for international technology diffusion point to a direct link between imports and productivity at the firm level (see, *inter alia*, Keller's survey in 2004).

In all our estimations we make use of the geographical dimension in the data as well as the breakdown by products to test whether these dimensions of both export and import activities have significant effects on productivity. We condition on a number of firm characteristics influencing productivity, such as human and physical capital and ownership structure. The empirical analyses are based on a balanced panel of 22 264 firm-level observations for the period 1997–2004.

The basis for our empirical analysis of the relationship between exports and productivity draws on both the self-selection hypothesis and the hypothesis on 'learning by exporting'. The conceptual framework for our analysis of the role of imports builds on the literature on international technology diffusion (see, e.g., Kortum, 1997; Eaton and Kortum, 1999, 2002; Keller, 2004; Coe and Helpman, 1995; Lööf, 2007). The econometric analysis allows us to draw conclusions regarding magnitude of both 'learning-by-exporting' and 'learning-by-importing' effects.

As stated above, our analysis is based on Swedish data. This makes it an interesting case since Sweden is a small open economy. The limited domestic market – about 9 million inhabitants – can be expected to imply an average higher export intensity (at least on the assumption of scale economies in production). Moreover, Sweden is interesting because there are some countries for which costs of initiating exports are presumably relatively small for Swedish firms (such as other neighbouring Scandinavian countries, Baltic countries).

The remainder of the chapter is organized as follows: Section 13.2 presents our theoretical framework. The first part focuses on the implications of firms' export activities of the combination of sunk costs of entry and firm heterogeneity as regards productivity. The second part is devoted to the relationship between imports and productivity. In Section 13.3 we present our data. Section 13.4 describes and motivates our estimation strategies and Section 13.5 presents our results. Section 13.6 concludes.

13.2 THEORETICAL BACKGROUND

13.2.1 Exports and Productivity – Self-selection and Learning by Exporting

Trade theory has historically been marked by the absence of individual firms. In standard Ricardian and Heckscher–Ohlin models, firms are seldom mentioned even if they do operate (in perfect competition) in the background. The new trade theory initiated by Krugman (1979, 1980), based on the Dixit and Stiglitz (1977) model of monopolistic competition have firms explicitly, but builds on representative firms.

To explain the observed heterogeneity across firms within the same industry in terms of export participation, one needs to focus on firms and their export decisions and move from models based on representative firms to models based on heterogeneous firms. Variations in export participation across firms can be explained by a combination of (i) sunk costs associated with entry on export markets and (ii) heterogeneity in the underlying characteristics of firms (Greenaway and Kneller, 2007). Likewise, heterogeneity across exporters in terms of the extent of penetration of geographic markets can be explained by market-specific sunk costs of entry and heterogeneity among exporters. Several newly developed models have exactly these features. For instance, Bernard et al. (2003) present a model that builds on Eaton and Kortum (2002) with Ricardian differences in technological efficiency between producers. Melitz (2003) develops a dynamic monopolistic competition model with heterogeneous firms and fixed costs of exporting, and derives intra-industry reallocation effects of trade. In a model with the same market structure, Chaney (2008) introduces fixed entry costs and transport cost per geographic market. Moreover, Eaton et al. (2004) develop a model with heterogeneous firms, entry costs for each market and transport costs.

All of these models incorporate self-selection, such that exports require an *ex ante* productivity advantage. We illustrate a basic model set-up below, following Helpman et al. (2007) and Chaney (2008). We simplify by assuming only two countries: home (h) and foreign (f).

A firm located in h faces no transport costs on sales in h. However, sales in f are subject to (i) transport costs and (ii) a fixed (sunk) entry cost F. All consumers in h and f have CES preferences. Demand for a product i in h, $z_{i,h}$, is given by:

$$z_{i,h} = \frac{\tilde{p}_{i,h}^{-\sigma}}{P_h^{1-\sigma}} Y_h \qquad P_h \equiv \left(\sum\nolimits_{j \in N_h} \tilde{p}_{j,h}^{1-\sigma} \right)^{\frac{1}{1-\sigma}} \tag{13.1}$$

where $\tilde{p}_{i,h}$ denotes the (cif) price of product i faced by consumers in market h and Y_h is the income in the same market. P_h represents the (ideal) price index in h. Of the products in the set $N_h = \{1, \ldots, n\}$, some are produced domestically and some are imported from other f. All firms in h and f produce distinct products. Exports from market h to market f are associated with iceberg transport cost, $t > 1$, and a fixed entry cost, $F > 0$. The cost of a firm i in h producing for f is

$$c_{i,f} = \frac{\beta}{\gamma_i} t z_{i,f} + F \tag{13.2}$$

where β/γ_i denotes firm i's marginal cost. The magnitude of its marginal cost depends on the firm's productivity, γ_i, such that firms with higher productivity have lower marginal cost. The cost of supplying goods to the domestic market is, however, $c_{i,h} = (\beta/\gamma_i)z_{i,h}$. The markets for final products are characterized by monopolistic competition. Each firm maximizes profits and faces a downward-sloping demand curve in each geographic market. A firm located in h will obey the following pricing rule for products exported to f:

$$\widetilde{p}_{i,f} = \frac{\sigma}{1-\sigma}\frac{\beta}{\gamma_i}t \tag{13.3}$$

Profit-maximizing firms will export as long as they can at least break even on their export flows. For a firm i located in h, the profits generated by exporting to f are

$$\pi_{i,f} = \widetilde{p}_{i,f}z_{i,f} - \frac{\beta}{\gamma_i}z_{i,f}t - F \tag{13.4}$$

All firms will supply their respective domestic market. By setting (13.4) equal to zero, solving for γ_i and making use of (13.1) and (13.3), we derive a productivity threshold as regards exports:

$$\hat{\gamma}_{df} = \alpha\left(\frac{F}{Y_f}\right)^{\frac{1}{\sigma-1}}\left(\frac{t}{P_f}\right) \tag{13.5}$$

where α is a selection of constant parameters. Equation (13.5) represents the productivity level necessary for the gross profits to recover the fixed entry cost. The fixed (sunk) cost associated with export implies that the number of firms exporting to f depends on the magnitude of the productivity threshold in combination with the productivity distribution of the firms in the origin country.

The partial equilibrium expression in (13.5) implies that productivity differences between exporters and non-exporters depend on a number of factors: (i) the magnitude of fixed entry costs; (ii) transport costs; (iii) degree of competition in the destination (expressed by the price index); and (iv) the market size in the destination. Since (i)–(iv) are expected to differ from destination to destination, it is important to recognize the geographical dimension of firms' export activities. In fact, if a country faces low productivity thresholds to certain destinations because of, e.g., a common border, institutions (formal and informal), language etc., one would not expect *a priori* to observe large productivity differences between exporters and non-exporters. If productivity thresholds among markets differ substantially, differences among firms that export to different destinations can be much larger than differences between non-exporters and exporters overall. Self-selection also operates from market to market, provided that productivity thresholds differ.

Self-selection due to *ex ante* productivity differences in combination with sunk costs of entry is one explanation for the observed productivity differences between exporters and non-exporters. Another explanation (not excluding self-selection) is 'learning by exporting'. This hypothesis states that firms with sales on international markets are more exposed to knowledge and technology, such that exports have positive feedback effects on firms' knowledge and technology accumulation. Although empirical evidence of such effects is weak, there are several plausible mechanisms through which exporting can have a positive impact on a firm's productivity. A specific example is marketing costs. It is well known in the marketing literature that success in certain markets implies lower costs of penetrating other markets, which stems from consumers evaluating products after their success in other markets (see Takada and Jain, 1991). A firm that has successfully penetrated a 'lead' market with high media coverage typically faces lower costs of penetrating 'follower' markets: e.g. all else equal, a new consumer durable good can be easier to sell in Asia if it has successfully been adopted by US consumers. Export success to one country can thus translate into lower costs of penetrating other 'follower' markets, which boosts productivity through lower costs.

13.2.2 Imports and Productivity – Knowledge Flows and International Technology Diffusion

As with exports, it can be expected that imports are subject to fixed costs. Establishing a trading relation with foreign suppliers is costly. Basic transaction cost theory (Williamson, 1979) suggests that the establishment of exchange agreements with foreign suppliers is associated with costs. An exchange agreement is typically preceded by a search process for potential suppliers, inspection of goods, negotiation and contract formulation, etc. These activities are associated with costs that are irrevocably committed, i.e. sunk costs (Johansson and Westin, 1994). Therefore productive firms may self-select into importers. Hence a self-selection hypothesis regarding imports is also likely to be observed.

However, there is ample empirical evidence pointing to a 'learning-by-importing' effect in the form of technology diffusion. The literature suggests that international trade and foreign direct investment (FDI) are important means by which technologies diffuse. The majority of existing studies on 'international technology diffusion' are conducted at the country level, whose set-up is more often than not akin to the seminal work by Coe and Helpman (1995). In these kinds of studies, total factor productivity (TFP) of an industry in a country is expressed as a function of domestic R&D and foreign R&D, where foreign R&D is accessed through imports of capital goods. The imports of capital goods are in turn weighted by the R&D intensity of the industry producing those capital goods in the origin countries, respectively. The conceptual framework for measuring cross-country technology diffusion in this manner is based on Aghion and Howitt (1992), Grossman and Helpman (1991), Kortum (1997), Eaton and Kortum (1999, 2002) and Keller (2004).

Trade in intermediate goods is a natural mechanism through which technology diffuses. If import of intermediate capital goods is an important means by which technologies are transmitted, it follows that the productivity of the firms in the economy can be related to their import of intermediates from foreign countries.

Keller (2004) outlines a simplified model based on Grossman and Helpman (1991) and Rivera-Batiz and Romer (1991) of how imports of intermediate goods affect domestic productivity. The basic idea is akin to Romer (1990) in that new intermediate goods are outcomes from investments in R&D. A domestic firm can then access foreign R&D by importing the intermediate goods produced in the foreign country. Let the production function of a representative firm be a standard Cobb–Douglas:

$$y = AL^{\alpha}I^{1-\alpha} \quad 0 < \alpha < 1 \tag{13.6}$$

where A is a constant and L is labour. I is a sub-production function and represents a composite index of intermediate goods, z:

$$I = \left(\sum_{i \in n^e} z_i^{1-\alpha} \right)^{\frac{1}{1-\alpha}} \tag{13.7}$$

where n^e is the number of intermediate capital goods employed by the firm and may be a subset of all intermediate goods in the world economy. If the intermediate goods are symmetric, the stock of capital can be written as $k = n^e z$ and the right-hand side of (13.7) can be expressed as $(n^e)^{\alpha/(1-\alpha)}k$. This means that (13.6) can be rewritten to read:

$$y = AL^{\alpha}k^{1-\alpha}(n^e)^{\alpha} \tag{13.8}$$

Total factor productivity (TFP) is then given by:

$$\ln TFP \equiv \ln y - \ln(l^{\alpha}k^{1-\alpha}) = \ln A + \alpha \ln n^e \tag{13.9}$$

Equation (13.9) states that the total factor productivity of a firm is increasing in the number of capital goods employed in production. The relationship to technology stems from the basic assumption in Romer (1990): each capital good is based on a unique design, developed in an R&D process. By importing capital goods, then, a firm can indirectly access technologies developed in foreign countries. Hence equation (13.9) provides a theoretical foundation for a positive relationship between imports and productivity. It can be hypothesized that imports is a natural case where self-selection and learning operate simultaneously.

13.3 DATA AND DESCRIPTIVE STATISTICS

The data in this chapter consist of a balanced panel of 22 264 firm-level observations in Sweden for the period 1997–2004. The panel is restricted to manufacturing firms. The original data set covers all manufacturing firms in Sweden. In order to calculate labour productivity we have eliminated all firms with zero employees. In addition, we only consider firms that are observed during the whole period 1997–2004.

Table 13.1 presents summary statistics of the data for the period 1997–2004. Four different categories of corporate structure ownership are considered: foreign-owned multinational enterprises, MNEs, domestically owned enterprises, domestically owned uninational enterprises (firms belonging to a group with affiliates only in Sweden) and non-affiliate firms. The range of employment in the investigated firms is 1–20 090.

Analysing US data, Bernard et al. (2007) suggest that exporting is a relatively rare activity. Only 15 per cent of firms active in industries more predisposed to export (manufacturing, mining and agricultural sectors) were exporters in the year 2000. In stark contrast, the exporters' share in the small open Swedish economy was 83 per cent in year 2004. The corresponding share among importers was 82 per cent.

The US data reveal that a large fraction of the firms (42 per cent) exports only one product and an even larger share (64 per cent) exports only to one country. However, these exporters represent only a small share of aggregate exports (0.4 per cent and 3.3 per cent, respectively). A very small share of the firms (11.9 per cent) accounts for the vast majority of the aggregate export value (92.2 per cent). Interestingly, The top 10 per cent of firms by size in Swedish manufacturing 2004 accounted for 67.7 per cent of the aggregate manufacturing employment, 77.1 per cent of value added, 82.6 of export value and 78.8 per cent of import value. Moreover, despite

Table 13.1 Summary statistics, number of observations 22264

	Mean	Std dev.	Min.	Max.
Foreign MNE	18.4	38.7	0	100
Domestic MNE	27.5	44.6	0	100
Domestic UNI	25.4	43.5	0	100
Domestic NAF	28.6	45.1	0	100
Employment	139	593	1	20090
Value added	94866	624536	−1293000	2.75e+07
Investment ME*	10950	80963	−69560	4951183
Investment total	53577	363049	0	1.55e+07
Invest ME/sales	4.2	79.8	−10.1	89.6
Human capital	5.8	8.7	0	100
Exporters, share	82.9	37.7	0	100
Export value	1.64e+08	1.57e+09	0	7.67e+10
Export volume	8930132	6.37e+07	0	1.82e+09
Number of export destinations	14.8	18.1	0	168
Number of export products	17.6	36.0	0	692
Importers, share	81.6	38.7	0	100
Import value	6.08e+07	4.91e+08	0	2.15e+10
Import volume	6379	6.02e+07	0	1.79e+09
Number of import destinations	7.8	8.2	0	118
Number of import products	23.9	41.6	0	593

Note: ME = Machinery equipment.

that, the largest firms reduced their share of employment between 1997 and 2004, their share of both import value and export value increased. The average number of both traded products and international trade destinations is considerably higher among Swedish firms than their US counterparts. During the period we study, the average number of export and import destinations was 14.8 and 7.8, respectively. The typical Swedish manufacturing firm exported 17.6 products and imported 23.9 products (see Table 13.1).

Tables 13.2(a) and (b) 13.3(a) and (b) display exporting Swedish manufacturing firms by industry and corporate ownership structure in 1997 and 2004.

Looking first at the industry classes, a large heterogeneity in the relative export intensity (export value per employee) number of export and number of export destinations is shown (see Tables 13.2(a) and 13.2(b). Considering the corporate ownership structure, two interesting findings appear. First, it is shown that foreign-owned MNEs are more oriented towards the international market compared to Swedish MNEs, Swedish UNIs and Swedish non-affiliated firms. Second, between 1997 and 2004 foreign MNEs took over a considerable fraction of the Swedish firms

Table 13.2(a) Exporting and by Swedish manufacturing firms, 1997

		% of firms	Export, share of firms	Relative export intensity[a]	Number of export prod.	Number of export dest.
15	Food and beverages	8.5	43.9	21.4	8.3	4.7
17–19	Textiles, apparel, leather	4.4	99.2	44.6	25.2	13.1
20	Wood products	5.4	76.8	70.0	7.9	7.78
21	Pulp and paper	3.4	100.0	86.2	16.1	24.9
22	Printing	4.6	67.7	9.7	7.1	5.42
23–24	Petr. and chemical	5.5	100.0	94.8	29.9	21.8
25	Plastics and rubber	6.8	97.4	41.9	13.6	13.2
26	Non-metallic minerals	2.4	94.0	43.7	17.3	15.7
27	Basic metals	3.4	97.9	100.0	25.3	21.3
28	Fabr. metal products	17.2	64.6	24.8	7.7	7.6
29	Mach. and equipment	16.9	88.8	69.5	19.7	20.1
30–33	Comp. and electronic	11.0	94.8	54.8	20.3	18.7
34–35	Transportation	5.7	96.8	58.5	30.2	12.7
36	Furniture and related	5.1	91.6	43.2	12.7	13.0
	Aggregate manuf.	100.0	82.9		16.2	17.7

Note: [a] Export value per employee.

Table 13.2(b) Exporting and by corporate ownership structure firms, 1997

	% of firms	Export, share of firms	Relative export intensity[a]	Number of export prod.	Number of export dest.
Foreign-owned MNE	10.5	98.9	100.0	33.4	27.6
Dom.-owned MNE	26.9	97.7	89.4	25.5	22.8
Dom.-owned UNI	24.8	83.6	47.8	9.1	8.7
Dom.-owned NAF	37.8	67.3	36.5	7.2	6.7
Aggregate manufac.	100.0	82.9		16.2	17.7

Note: As for Table 13.2(a).

observed in the sample in year 1997. The result was that their share of the sample increased from 10.5 per cent to 23.2 per cent. Since the major target of the takeover policy was non-affiliated firms, the fraction of these firms decreased from 37.8 per cent to 22.7 per cent.

Tables 13.4(a) and (b) and 13.5(a) and (b) present descriptive statistics on importing in 1997 and 2004, respectively. As might be expected, the heterogeneity found among the exporters is shown also among

CARDIFF UNIVERSITY
PRIFYSGOL CAERDYDD

University
Library Service

Gwasanaeth Llyfrgell
y Brifysgol

Additional library opening hours

From Monday 13th June until Sunday 18th September

Aberconway Library

Monday to Friday: 5pm – 9pm

Saturday & Sunday: 10am – 5.30pm

Arts and Social Studies Library

Saturday: 10am - 5.30pm

Users who are only able to visit after 5pm or at weekends can request books to be transferred from other libraries to these sites.

Please ask at any library enquiry desk.

Table 13.3(a) *Exporting and by Swedish manufacturing firms, 2004*

		% of firms	Export, share of firms	Relative export intensity[a]	Number of export prod.	Number of export dest.
15	Food and beverages	8.4	43.6	24.9	8.0	5.0
17–19	Textiles, apparel, leather	4.3	99.1	45.9	29.9	14.2
20	Wood products	5.4	77.0	57.1	8.2	8.6
21	Pulp and paper	3.5	100.0	87.6	13.9	25.2
22	Printing	4.5	69.2	11.5	8.4	6.3
23–24	Petr. and chemical	5.4	100.0	100.0	27.5	23.4
25	Plastics and rubber	6.9	97.8	50.2	15.2	15.7
26	Non-metallic minerals	2.4	93.8	36.4	18.1	14.1
27	Basic metals	3.3	97.8	98.8	22.0	21.2
28	Fabr. metal products	17.3	65.1	31.1	8.6	8.9
29	Mach. and equipment	17.2	89.0	64.5	22.3	22.5
30–33	Comp. and electronic	10.8	94.8	55.8	25.0	23.1
34–35	Transportation	5.6	97.3	57.1	36.2	15.1
36	Furniture and related	5.1	91.3	39.8	14.5	13.0
	Aggregate manufacturing	100.0	83.2		17.7	15.4

Note: As for Table 13.2(a).

Table 13.3(b) *Exporting and by corporate ownership structure firms, 2004*

	% of firms	Export, share of firms	Relative export intensity[a]	Number of export prod.	Number of export dest.
Foreign-owned MNE	23.2	98.5	100.0	27.9	23.9
Dom.-owned MNE	27.8	97.6	90.4	27.2	23.4
Dom.-owned UNI	26.3	77.8	36.1	8.7	8.3
Dom.-owned NAF	22.7	55.7	24.7	5.8	5.2
Aggregate manufac.	100.0	83.1		17.7	15.4

Note: As for Table 13.2(a).

importers. It is noteworthy that foreign MNEs are distinct from all three categories of Swedish firms in terms of export intensity. The average foreign MNE's import value per employee is about twice as large or more compared to Swedish firms. In addition, foreign MNEs import a larger number of products compared to both Swedish MNEs and non-MNEs.

Table 13.4(a) Importing and by Swedish manufacturing firms, 1997

		Import, share of firms	Relative import intensity[a]	Number of import prod.	Number of import dest.
15	Food and beverages	47.2	46.4	18.8	4.7
17–19	Textiles, apparel, leather	99.1	80.5	37.7	13.0
20	Wood products	70.1	14.6	7.2	7.8
21	Pulp and paper	100.0	67.7	38.8	24.9
22	Printing	58.2	26.6	11.3	5.4
23–24	Petr. and chemical	100.0	100.0	49.8	21.8
25	Plastics and rubber	97.3	46.7	20.0	13.2
26	Non-metallic minerals	95.5	56.4	27.1	15.7
27	Basic metals	97.8	86.4	35.0	21.3
28	Fabr. metal products	61.4	24.3	8.7	7.6
29	Mach. and equipment	88.3	29.1	21.1	20.1
30–33	Comp. and electronic	95.0	39.2	28.7	18.7
34–35	Transportation	94.3	56.7	41.10	12.7
36	Furniture and related	88.8	30.5	19.0	13.0
	Aggregate manuf.	816.0		22.8	13.8

Note: [a] Import value per employee.

Table 13.4(b) Importing and by corporate ownership structure firms, 1997

	Import, share of firms	Relative import intensity[a]	Number of import prod.	Number of import dest.
Foreign-owned MNE	98.6	100.0	52.1	27.6
Dom.-owned MNE	97.3	53.8	37.1	22.8
Dom.-owned UNI	82.2	34.0	12.7	8.7
Dom.-owned NAF	65.2	36.2	11.1	6.8
Aggregate manuf.	81.6		22.8	13.8

Note: As for Table 13.4(a).

13.4 PRODUCTIVITY, EXPORTS AND IMPORTS

13.4.1 Empirical Model and Estimation Strategy

In the regression analyses we restrict attention to firms with at least ten employees. This gives us 56 957 observations. We first conduct seven

Table 13.5(a) Importing and by Swedish manufacturing firms, 2004

		Import, share of firms	Relative import intensity[a]	Number of import prod.	Number of import dest.
15	Food and beverages	47.2	37.2	19.0	5.1
17–19	Textiles, apparel, leather	99.2	71.9	40.4	14.2
20	Wood products	70.3	14.9	8.1	8.6
21	Pulp and paper	100.0	82.2	35.4	25.2
22	Printing	59.8	21.2	10.7	6.3
23–24	Petr. and chemical	100.0	100.0	40.5	23.4
25	Plastics and rubber	97.8	45.4	19.5	15.7
26	Non-metallic minerals	95.3	44.5	32.0	14.1
27	Basic metals	97.7	80.9	33.0	21.3
28	Fabr. metal products	61.9	30.9	9.9	8.93
29	Mach. and equipment	88.6	28.6	23.5	22.5
30–33	Comp. and electronic	95.2	47.5	36.3	23.1
34–35	Transportation	94.7	93.9	42.1	15.1
36	Furniture and related	88.1	36.3	21.0	13.0
	Aggregate manufacturing	81.8		24.5	15.5

Note: As for Table 13.4(a).

Table 13.5(b) Importing and by corporate ownership structure firms, 2004

	Import, share of firms	Relative import intensity[a]	Number of import prod.	Number of import dest.
Foreign-owned MNE	98.5	100.0	43.6	23.9
Domestically owned MNE	97.2	56.5	33.9	23.4
Domestically owned UNI	77.9	32.5	12.0	8.3
Domestically owned NAF	59.0	35.4	7.5	5.2
Aggregate manufacturing	81.8		24.5	15.5

Note: As for Table 13.2(a).

regressions where the sensitivity of labour productivity with respect to different trade variables is estimated by employing the random effects specification of the generalized least squares (GLS) estimator. In these estimations firm characteristics, such as human and physical capital, corporate ownership structure and firm size, are controlled for along with industry- and time-specific effects.

The very general model used in the analysis is the following:

$$y_{it} = \alpha_{it} + x_{it}'\beta_{it} + u_{it}, \quad i = 1, \ldots, N, t = 1, \ldots, T \qquad (13.10)$$

where y_{it} is a scalar dependent variable, x_{it} is a K* 1 vector of independent variables, u_{it} is a scalar distributed term, i indexes firm in a cross-section and t indexes time. The random effects model that will be applied assumes that the unobservervable individual effects are random variables that are distributed independently of the regressors:

$$y_{it} = \alpha_i + x_{it}'\beta + \varepsilon_{it}, \quad i = 1, \ldots, N, t = 1, \ldots, T \qquad (13.11)$$

where α_i are random variables that capture unobservable heterogeneity ε_{it} is iid (independent and identically distributed) over i and t, assumed to be independent of x, and β is a K* 1 column vector to be estimated.

The dependent variable (y_i) is log value added per employee, or labour productivity. The relationships between export and productivity on the one hand, and import and productivity on the other, are analysed separately. We use the following trade variables:

- a dummy variable indicating whether or not the firm is an exporter or importer, respectively;
- log of trade (export or import) value per employee;
- log of trade (export or import) volume per employee;
- a set of dummy variables for the number of traded products according to four different classes;
- a set of dummy variables for the number of countries with which the firm trade according to four classes.

In addition to observations of trading activities, we control for a large set of firm attributes that theoretical and empirical literature suggests will influence labour productivity, i.e. human capital, physical capital, firm size and corporate ownership structure. Human capital is measured as the fraction of the workers with a university degree and the physical capital variables are measured as the log of the gross investment per employee. The corporate ownership structure is defined according to the four different categories described above and firm size is controlled for by dummy variables reflecting four different size classes. In order to control for industry effects and time trend, we include 14 industry indicators and eight year dummies in the model.

To deal with possible simultaneity we apply the instrumental-variable estimator. To derive consistent estimates of equation (13.2) in the presence of endogeneity, we must find an instrumental variable that is uncorrelated with the disturbances and highly correlated with the endogenous regressor. We follow Baum (2006) and instrument the trade variables with lags and use robust regressions that cause the two-step GMM (generalized method of moments) estimator to compute efficient estimates. Test statistics inform us that the second and third lag of the trade variable in general fulfil this requirement. In some cases we have to extend the lag structure to the fourth lag. The drawback here is that the observations in our unbalanced panel are reduced to 26 640–19 542 observations, depending on the lag structure.

13.4.2 Results

This section presents the regression estimates from the GLS estimator and the two-step GMM procedure. The results from the 28 regressions estimated by GLS and GMM respectively are summarized in Table 13.6 (export) and Table 13.7 (import).

Focusing initially on the relationship between exporting activities and labour productivity, the results of these regressions are summarized in Table 13.6. In column (1) the GLS estimates are presented whereas column (2) shows the GMM estimates. The main message from Table 13.6 is that exporters are more productive, irrespective of export indicator and model specification. All estimates are highly significant and both models (GLS and GMM) produce more or less identical results.

Row 1 in Table 13.6 reports the elasticity of labour productivity with respect to the dummy variable, indicating whether or not the firm is engaged in export activities. On average, exporters have 5 per cent higher labour productivity than non-exporters, which is consistent with a vast body of previous empirical findings based on firm-level data. The results in rows 2 and 3 indicate that the productivity premium of exporters is lower when the export-related explanatory variables are defined in terms of export intensity. A 1 per cent increase in export value per employee predicts a productivity premium of 2 per cent whereas a 1 per cent increase in export quantity per employee suggests a modest productivity premium of 1 per cent.

The coefficients estimates reported in row 4 and downwards show that the export premium is increasing in the number of products that firms are exporting. A firm that exports 1–3 products has on average 4 per cent higher labour productivity than a non-exporting firm, whereas the typical firm that sells 4–8 products on foreign markets has a productivity that is 6.6

Table 13.6 The relationship between log value added per employee and exports. GLS random effects model and two-step GMM model

Equation	GLS, RE Obs. 56 607	GMM Obs. 26 640–19 542
1. Export dummy	0.049 (0.005)***	0.051 (0.008)*** L.3
2. Log export value per employee	0.022 (0.000)***	0.021 (0.001)*** L.3
3. Log export volume per employee	0.011 (0.000)***	0.011 (0.001)*** L.3
4. Number of export products		
0	Reference	–
1–3	0.040 (0.005)***	–
4–8	0.066 (0.006)***	–
9–	0.102 (0.007)***	–
0–7	–	Reference
8–	–	0.073 (0.012) *** L.4
5. Number of export destination		
0	Reference	–
1–4	0.041 (0.005)***	–
5–13	0.082 (0.007)***	–
13–	0.153 (0.008)***	–
0–7	–	Reference
8	–	0.098 (0.008)***
Covariates	Included	Included

Note: (L.3) Instrumented by 2–3 lags and using 26 640 observations; (L.4) Instrumented by the 2–4 lags and using 19 542 observations.

per cent higher than the average firm, which only operates on the domestic market. Firms with foreign sales contain 9 or more products have a productivity premium over non-exporters of 10.2 per cent. The results obtained with the GMM estimator (column 3) give similar results: firms that export 8 products or more have 7.3 per cent higher labour productivity than firms exporting between 0 and 7 products.[3] This result is consistent with the finding that the production of different products is associated with different levels of fixed costs and profitability for firms, such that low-productivity firms produce fewer products associated with low levels of fixed costs.

The estimated parameters associated with the export dummy variables for different destination countries show that the export premium for labour productivity is increasing in the number of countries which firms export to.

Table 13.7 The relationship between log value added per employee and imports. GLS random effects model and two-step GMM model

Equation	GLS, RE Obs. 56 607	GMM Obs 26 640
1. Import dummy	0.044 (0.004)***	0.086 (0.009)*** L.3
2. Log import value/ per employee	0.015 (0.000)***	0.027 (0.001)*** L.3
3. Log import volume per employee	0.010 (0.000)***	0.011 (0.000)*** L.3
4. Number of import products	0.001 (0.000)***	0.001 (0.000)*** L.3
0	Reference	–
1–3	0.033 (0.004)***	–
4–8	0.076 (0.006)***	–
9–	0.133 (0.008)***	–
0–7	–	Reference
8–	–	0.080 (0.008)*** L.3
5. Number of import countries		
0	Reference	–
1–4	0.044 (0.005)***	–
5–13	0.119 (0.007)***	–
13–	0.175 (0.009)***	–
0–7	–	Reference
8–	–	0.098 (0.008)*** L.3
6. Log import (value/product) per employee	0.016 (0.000)***	0.020 (0.001)*** L.3
7. Log import value/destination per employee	0.015 (0.000)***	0.017 (0.000)*** L.3
Covariates	Included	Included

Note: (L.3) Instrumented by 2–3 lags and using 26 640 observations.

According to the GLS estimates, productivity is 4 per cent higher for firms that export to 1–4 countries compared to non-exporters. The same figure for firms exporting to 4–8 countries is 7 per cent, whereas it is 15 per cent for firms exporting to at least 13 countries. With the GMM estimator we find that the average firm that trades with 8 or more countries has 10 per cent higher labour productivity than a reference group consisting of firms with 0–7 export products. These results provide strong support for models of exports with asymmetric countries and asymmetric sunk costs of entry (as in, e.g., Chaney, 2008 and Helpman et al., 2007). In such models self-selection occurs from market to market. Firms will enter all markets whose productivity threshold is lower than their own productivity level. Because of this, firms enter markets according to a hierarchy where firms with low productivity serve a limited number of markets of low order, i.e. low-productivity thresholds, whereas firms with higher productivity can export to a larger number of markets (of higher order). These models predict the pattern observed in Table 13.6. Results thus show that productivity is key for both number of export products and number of destination countries.

Turning to the relationship between productivity and import behaviour, Table 13.7 presents the results from estimations of the regressions of labour productivity on import indicators and firm characteristics. The covariates are the same as in the regressions, including the export variables above. Overall, the results for imports correspond to those obtained for exports. Labour productivity is 4.4 per cent higher for importers compared to non-importers. Taking into account that productivity and import might be simultaneously determined – as suggested by the literature on international technology diffusion (Keller, 2004) – and employing an instrumental variable estimator (GMM), the size of the coefficient estimate for the import indicator is 8.6 per cent. This difference is much larger than that for exports and indicates that simultaneity is important to control for in the case of imports. Also, a 1 per cent higher import value per employee is estimated to imply a 1.5 per cent (GLS) and 2.7 per cent (GMM), respectively, higher labour productivity. The elasticity of labour productivity with respect to import volume per employee is about 1 per cent in both model specifications.

Furthermore, as in the case of exports, the import premium is increasing in the number of import products as well as in the number of import countries. A manufacturing firm that imports 9 or more products is predicted to have about 13 per cent higher labour productivity than a non-importing firm according to the GLS estimates, and the GMM estimate yields a corresponding coefficient of 8 per cent where the reference firms is importing 0–7 products.

Similar to exports, the productivity premium of importers with respect to labour productivity increases more with expansions in geographical scope than with extensions in number of import products. The GLS estimates imply that the productivity premium is almost three times larger for firms importing from 5–13 countries than for firms importing from 1–4 foreign markets. For firms importing from 13 markets or more the estimated productivity mark-up over non-importing firms is 17.5 per cent. The GMM estimates with a three-year lag structure for the instruments shows that a firm that imports from 8 or more countries is expected to have 9.8 per cent higher labour productivity than a firm that imports from 0–7 countries.

Addressing the estimated influence of the control variables on labour productivity, the estimated parameters associated with the control variables are almost identical in the export and import regressions. Not surprisingly, human capital and physical capital have a significant positive impact on labour productivity. Foreign-owned MNEs have on average a higher productivity than domestic MNEs. MNEs have on average higher productivity than firms belonging to a domestic corporation and non-affiliated firms. Moreover, firms in the largest size class (more than 250 employees) have a higher labour productivity than firms in lower size classes.

Taken together, the results presented in Tables 13.6 and 13.7 show that there is a strong and significant positive relationship between trade and productivity levels at firm level. In both export and import activities productivity premiums are growing with the variety in traded goods and trading markets.

13.5 CONCLUDING DISCUSSION

This chapter has presented a comprehensive description of Swedish firms' engagement in international trade, i.e. trading activities by firms located in a small, open economy that shares borders with a set of countries with similar traits. Also, the relationship between firm performance and trading activities was examined.

Our results from the overall description of Swedish firms' exports and imports show that the concentration of Sweden's (a small open economy) trade flows to a small set of large firms (multinationals) resembles the pattern found in other studies. However, our results illustrate that the export (import) intensity measured as the share of firms engaged in export (import) is significantly larger in Sweden compared to the USA. This indicates the importance of acknowledging the geographical scope of firms' export activities. In a country facing low productivity thresholds to certain destinations because of, e.g., common borders, institutions (formal and informal) and language – which is the case for Sweden's relation to other Scandinavian countries and the Baltic countries – one would not expect *a priori* to observe large productivity differences between exporters and non-exporters. Cross-country comparisons need to acknowledge geography.

The econometric analysis showed that there is a marked relationship between international trade and productivity at the firm level.

Interestingly, our results imply that it is not merely a matter of being an exporter or non-exporter. The geographical scope of a firm's export and import activities was shown to be a significant explanatory variable for firms' productivity.

Our results imply both a 'learning-by-exporting' and 'learning-by-importing' effect. The latter effect is consistent with imports of capital goods being a significant vehicle for technology diffusion. It is more difficult to pin down what mechanisms operate behind the former effect, but they suggest that exposure to foreign markets spurs a firm's knowledge and technology accumulation.

The chapter has an indirect link to the role of characteristics of regions for firms. The analyses of attributes of firms engaged in international trade may provide an indication of the kind of milieus that favour firms' internationalization. Overall the results suggest that firms located in dense regions with rich human talent and R&D investments are in a better position to be able to penetrate foreign markets, because such regions may stimulate the productivity of the firms they host.

NOTES

1. This is a version of a paper previously published 2008 in the *Review of World Economics*, **144**(4), 774–801, with the title 'Productivity in international trade – evidence from a small open economy'.
2. These findings have, *inter alia*, inspired novel perspectives on the relationship between trade and aggregate productivity. Melitz (2003) introduces heterogeneous firms (marginal cost heterogeneity) in the general DS framework and shows how exposure to trade leads to reallocations towards firms with high productivity. In this model gains from trade come from selection effects (the least productive firms are outcompeted) rather than scale effects (firms increase their production and materialize scale economies) from trade liberalizations.
3. In order to specify the GMM estimation in an appropriate way, we use another classification than in the GLS estimation.

REFERENCES

Aghion, P. and P. Howitt (1992), 'A model of growth through creative destruction', *Econometrica*, **60** (2), 323–51.

Andersson, M. (2007), 'Entry Costs and Adjustments on the Extensive Margin – An Analysis of how Familiarity Breeds Exports', *CESIS Working Paper Series in Economics and Institutions of Innovation*, no. 81, Royal Institute of Technology, Stockholm.

Aw, B.Y., S. Chung and M.J. Roberts (1998), 'Productivity and the decision to export: micro evidence from Taiwan and South Korea', NBER Working Paper Series, no. 6558, National Bureau of Economic Research, Cambridge, MA.

Baum, C.F. (2006), *An Introduction to Modern Econometrics Using Stata*, College Station, TX: Stata Press.
Bernard, A.B. and J.B. Jensen (1995), 'Exporters, jobs and wages in US manufacturing 1976–1987', *Brookings Papers on Economic Activity, Microeconomics*, 67–112.
Bernard, A.B and J.B. Jensen (1999), 'Exceptional exporter performance: cause, effect or both?', *Journal of International Economics*, **47**, 1–25.
Bernard, A.B., J. Eaton, J.B. Jensen and S. Kortum (2003), 'Plants and productivity in international trade', *American Economic Review*, **93**, 1268–90.
Bernard, A.B., J.B. Jensen, S.J. Redding and P.K. Schott (2007), 'Firms in international trade', NBER Working Paper Series, no. 13054, National Bureau of Economic Research, Cambridge, MA.
Castellani, D. (2002), 'Export behavior and productivity growth: evidence from Italian manufacturing firms', *Review of World Economics*, **138**, 605–28.
Castellani, D. and A. Zanfei (2003), 'Technology gaps, absorptive capacity and the impact of inward investments on productivity of European firms', *Economics of Innovation and New Technology*, **12**, 555–76.
Chaney, T. (2008), 'Distorted gravity – the intensive and extensive margins of international trade', *American Economic Review*, **98** (4), 1707–21.
Clerides, S., S. Lach and J. Tybout (1998), 'Is learning by exporting important? Micro-dynamic evidence from Colombia, Mexico and Morocco', *Quarterly Journal of Economics*, **113**, 903–47.
Coe, D.T. and E. Helpman (1995), 'International R&D spillovers', *European Economic Review*, **39** (5), 859–87.
Criscuolo, C., J. Haskel and M.J. Slaughter (2004), 'Why are some firms more innovative? – Knowledge inputs, knowledge stocks and the role of global engagement', mimeo, Tuck School of Business, Hanover, NH.
Dixit, A.K. and J.E. Stiglitz (1977), 'Monopolistic competition and optimum product diversity', *American Economic Review*, **67**, 297–308.
Eaton, J. and S. Kortum (1999), 'International technology diffusion: theory and measurement', *International Economic Review*, **40**, 537–70.
Eaton, J. and S. Kortum (2002), 'Technology, geography and trade', *Econometrica*, **70**, 1741–79.
Eaton, J., S. Kortum and F. Kramarz (2004), 'Dissecting trade: firms, industries and export destinations', *American Economic Review*, **94**, 150–54.
Greenaway, D. and R. Kneller (2007), 'Firm heterogeneity, exporting and foreign direct investment', *Economic Journal*, **117**, 134–61.
Grossman, G. and E. Helpman (1991), *Innovation and Growth in the Global Economy*, Cambridge, MA: MIT Press.
Helpman, E., M.J. Melitz and Y. Rubinstein (2007), 'Estimating trade flows: trading partners and trading volumes', NBER Working Paper Series, no. 12927, National Bureau of Economic Research, Cambridge, MA.
Johansson, B. and L. Westin (1994), 'Affinities and frictions of trade networks', *The Annals of Regional Science*, **28** (3), 243–61.
Keller, W. (2002), 'Trade and the transmission of technology', *Journal of Economic Growth*, **7**, 5–24.
Keller, W. (2004), 'International technology diffusion', *Journal of Economic Literature*, **42**, 752–82.
Keller, W. and R. Acharya (2007), 'Technology Transfer through Imports', *NBER Working Paper Series*, no. 13086, National Bureau of Economic Research, Cambridge, MA.

Kortum, S. (1997), 'Research, patenting, and technological change', *Econometrica*, **65**, 1389–420.
Krugman, P. (1979), 'Increasing returns, monopolistic competition and international trade', *Journal of International Economics*, **9**, 469–79.
Krugman, P. (1980), 'Scale economies, product differentiation, and patterns of trade', *American Economic Review*, **70**, 950–59.
Lööf, H. (2007), 'Technology spillovers and innovation – the importance of domestic and foreign sources', CESIS Working Paper Series in Economics and Institutions of Innovation, no. 83, Royal Institute of Technology, Stockholm.
Markusen, J. (2002), *Multinational Firms and the Theory of International Trade*, Cambridge, MA: MIT Press.
Melitz, M.J. (2003), 'The impact of trade on intra-industry reallocations and aggregate industry productivity', *Econometrica*, **71**, 1695–725.
Rivera-Batiz, L. and P. Romer (1991), 'International trade with endogenous technological change', *European Economic Review*, **35**, 971–1001.
Romer, P. (1990), 'Endogenous technological change', *Journal of Political Economy*, **98**, 71–102.
Takada, H. and D. Jain (1991), 'Cross-national analysis of diffusion of consumer durable goods in Pacific Rim countries', *The Journal of Marketing*, **55** (2), 48–54.
Tybout, J. (2003), 'Plant and firm level evidence on "new" trade theories', in E.K. Choi and J. Harrigan (eds), *Handbook of International Trade*, Oxford: Basil Blackwell.
Wagner, J. (2007), 'Exports and productivity – a survey of the evidence from firm level data', *World Economy*, **30**, 60–82.
Williamson, O. (1979), 'Transaction-cost economics: the governance of contractual relations', *Journal of Law and Economics*, **22**, 233–61.

14. Imports, R&D and local patent production

Urban Gråsjö

The purpose of this chapter is to analyse the effects of national and international knowledge flows on innovative activity. Therefore a knowledge production function is estimated with patent applications in Swedish municipalities as the measure of innovation. The knowledge resources applied are R&D investments and high-valued imports. In order to account for the importance of proximity, the knowledge resources are expressed as accessibilities. The total accessibility of a municipality is decomposed into local, intraregional and interregional accessibility. The main results indicate that knowledge resources in a given municipality tend to have a positive effect on the innovative activity of another municipality, given that the municipalities belong to the same functional region. Thus the results of the analysis indicate that knowledge flows transcend municipal borders, but that they tend to be bounded within functional regions. This result holds for both R&D investments and high-valued import products.

14.1 INTRODUCTION

Knowledge is a key concept in today's society, and it is easy to understand why. One explanation is that investments in knowledge, e.g. education, and research and development (R&D), are assumed to be very important for the promotion of economic growth. To thoroughly explain what factors are significant in the knowledge production process is therefore fundamental.

A basic feature of economic activities is their tendency to be concentrated geographically, which is particularly true for activities related to knowledge production. In some regions knowledge production is strongly represented, while other regions have no knowledge production at all. Therefore it is surprising that many studies of how knowledge is produced and transferred use countries instead of regions (or municipalities) as the research unit. There is strong evidence that knowledge transfers are to a high extent dependent on face-to-face interaction. The volume of knowledge flows depends on the interaction possibilities at different spatial scales. This chapter assumes that it is important to identify a number of such spatial scales based on the character of the generalized spatial interaction costs. In particular, the chapter claims that there are three spatial scales that are of special pertinence: (i) the local scale, which allows several interactions per day; (ii) the intraregional scale – the commuting scale – which allows for daily interaction; and (iii) the interregional scale, which allows only for a limited number of planned interactions per month or year.

Furthermore, despite the fact that knowledge tends to spill over in space, there have been very few attempts to model the spillovers in continuous space. The reach of the spillovers from the knowledge source is often modelled with geographical concentric rings with distances reported in kilometres or, even more simply, with neighbours. As an alternative, the present study elaborates by an accessibility approach, which discounts the interaction potentials using travel time distances and time sensitivity parameters, which are different for different spatial scales. By this approach it is possible to highlight the knowledge potential of each spatial unit with proper consideration of the fact that the more distant a knowledge source is, the less it contributes to the knowledge potential in a given location. The locations in this study are municipalities separated into functional regions. Then it is possible to define the accessibility on three spatial levels: accessibility (i) within a municipality; (ii) to municipalities within a functional region; and (iii) to municipalities outside the functional region.

Gråsjö (2006) uses the accessibility approach to examine to what extent R&D affects the patenting capacity in Swedish municipalities. One dimension that has not been taken into consideration in Gråsjö (2006) is the potential impact from abroad. A representative study where international knowledge spillovers are in focus is Coe and Helpman (1995), which is based on the theoretical model developed by Grossman and Helpman (1991). They emphasize the role of international trade in goods as the main channel of international knowledge spillovers. They find that foreign R&D capital stock weighted by the trade partners' import shares has a significant impact on total factor productivity, implying the existence of international knowledge spillovers. Numerous studies following the framework of Coe and Helpman (1995) have identified international spillovers of some form.[1] The impact of knowledge spillovers on the regional level is, however, very often left out in these studies.

A natural extension of the work conducted in Gråsjö (2006) is to empirically test a model that, besides R&D investments within the nation, also includes knowledge flows from abroad. As a proxy for international knowledge flows, this study uses the share of high-valued import products per employed. Hence, the empirical question analysed in the study is:

> To what extent can accessibility to R&D and high-valued imported products explain the knowledge output (measured by the number of patent applications per employed) in Swedish municipalities?

The remaining parts of the chapter are organized as follows: in Section 14.2 the theoretical framework is presented. The accessibility concept and the empirical model used are presented in Section 14.3. Section 14.4 presents the data and estimation methods. Section 14.5 contains the estimation results from the regressions. The chapter ends with the main conclusions of the empirical findings.

14.2 THEORETICAL FRAMEWORK

The framework for analysing the importance of knowledge and knowledge spillovers for innovative activity is usually based on the knowledge production function of Griliches (1979). According to Romer (1990), knowledge spillovers arise because knowledge is a partially excludable and non-rival good. It is non-rival in the sense that one agent can use it without limiting its use by others in knowledge production, and partially excludable given the possibility of preventing its use in production by others by means of patenting. The non-excludable part of knowledge seems correctly defined if it is assumed to have two portions: a perfectly accessible part consisting of already established knowledge elements (obtainable via scientific publications, patent applications, etc.); and a novel, tacit element, accessible only by interactions among actors in an innovation system.[2] This tacit element of knowledge and the accompanying importance of face-to-face contacts are supported in the growing literature on geographical knowledge spillovers, where it is evident that knowledge is not freely accessible to everybody engaged in research (as stated in Romer, 1990).

Several studies in the literature have used firm-level data in a knowledge production framework to investigate localized knowledge spillovers. Jaffe et al. (1993) use patent citations in order to examine the extent to which knowledge spillovers are geographically localized and find evidence of localization effects within USA states. With panel data from the US and Japan, Branstetter (2001) estimates the relative impact of intra-national and international knowledge spillovers on innovation and productivity at the firm level. The empirical results suggest that knowledge spillovers are primarily intranational in scope. International knowledge spillovers have also been addressed in trade and growth literature. International trade can be seen as a channel of technology transfer either through imports of intermediate products and capital equipment (Feenstra et al., 1992) or through learning by exporting to industrial countries (Clerides et al., 1998). Several studies have looked for international knowledge spillovers driven by imports. According to Keller (2004), overall evidence supports the notion that importing is associated with technology spillovers. Coe et al. (1997) find positive productivity effects for technology diffusion from highly industrialized to less developed countries. Xu and Wang (1999) emphasize that imports of differentiated capital goods (machinery) have a positive impact on productivity, while Keller (2000) came to the same conclusion for specialized machinery imports. Compared to imports, there is much less evidence of knowledge spillovers through learning-by-exporting. According to Keller (2004), learning by exporting effects have been found in the case study literature, whereas authors of econometric studies take a much more sceptical view.

The overall assessment is that imports promote productivity and innovative capacity through international knowledge spillovers. According to Keller (2000), the import of specialized inputs might facilitate learning about the product, spurring imitation or innovation of a competing product. However, the choice of the import variable carrying the useful knowledge varies widely in the literature and is more or less an empirical question. It is obvious that not all imported products have an impact on the ability to innovate. Consequently, in these types of studies the imports used are often limited to machinery inputs for manufacturing industries (see, e.g., Keller, 2000). This study uses the share of imports with a high price as a possible variable to explain innovation. With this variable, imports in specific manufacturing industries are heavily represented (see Appendix 14A). Furthermore, the vast majority of earlier empirical studies analyse the role of international knowledge spillovers (e.g. imports) on innovation using aggregated models for the whole national economy. However, the fact that knowledge activities are spatially concentrated ought to be acknowledged, since it is well established that knowledge flows are bounded in space.

There are several possible ways to measure and account for geographical proximity and the accompanying knowledge spillovers. Jaffe (1989) introduces a geographical coincidence index between public and private sector research. Anselin et al. (2000) implement an approach on US data to formalize spatial externalities by combining spatial dependence and spatial heterogeneity in spatial regimes. They distinguish between 'connected' and 'isolated' metropolitan statistical areas (MSAs), i.e. MSAs that are within or beyond a given distance threshold. Thus the geographic reach of knowledge spillovers is linked to a distance decay effect. Autant-Bernard (2001), Acs et al. (2002) and Bottazzi and Peri (2003) compare different geographical levels by introducing external research stock occurring on the periphery of a particular area. A geographical area's innovation capacity is therefore related to internal R&D effort but also to spillovers flowing from research activities in neighbouring areas. Bottazzi and Peri (2003) also use distance (in kilometres) between different regions when investigating the importance of geographical proximity for knowledge spillovers. The present study uses an accessibility approach as an instrument to discount the spillover effects spatially. There are several different accessibility approaches and the one chosen can be referred to a class called 'gravity-based measures'.[3] Weibull (1976) narrowed down the measurement of accessibility to those that satisfy certain axioms.

A core concept when it comes to determine the reach of knowledge spillovers is the functional region. The definition of a functional region is based on the spatial interaction patterns of economic agents in a country. It is characterized by its density of economic activities, social opportunities and interaction options (Ciccone and Hall, 1996; Johansson, 1997). Density is a positive factor for the individual firm since it creates accessibility to suppliers, potential buyers and other actors. Accessibility is obtained by a combination of density and infrastructure, which facilitates particularly high factor mobility within the functional region's border. Disregarding fixed resources such as land and natural resources, the major factor that sets the spatial border of a functional region is usually the labour force and its propensity to commute. The geographical interaction costs between different marketplaces for work are for households, in principle, equal to the total costs for moving between marketplaces, that is, between different labour markets. According to this conceptualization, functional regions become equal to local labour markets (Karlsson and Stough, 2002). Earlier studies dealing with spatial knowledge spillovers have normally been based on a division in administrative regions, which do not need to be functional regions.

There has been a discussion in the literature about relevant output measures of innovation. Jaffe et al. (1993) have used a 'paper trail' of patent citations to track the direction and intensity of spillovers. Peri (2002) argues that this approach can only identify intensity and direction of knowledge flows, and not R&D externalities. Moreover, citations do not capture non-codified knowledge flows and embodied knowledge flows, which could be important sources of localized spillovers, as Saxenian (1991) and Audretsch and Feldman (1996) argue. The two most common and frequently used innovation indicators are R&D effort (measured by expenditures on R&D

or persons carrying out R&D) and the number of patented inventions. According to Kleinknecht et al. (2002), these two measures have more weaknesses than is often assumed. One obvious disadvantage is that R&D is an input of the innovation process and says very little about the output. Patents may be good indicators of the technology creation, even if not all new innovations are patented, but they do not measure the economic value of the technologies (Hall et al., 2001). In contrast to proxies of innovation activities such as R&D effort or patents, literature-based innovation output measures provide a direct indicator of innovation (Acs et al., 2002; Kleinknecht et al., 2002). Screening the new product announcements in trade and technical journals generates literature-based innovation output indicators. The advantage of these indicators is that they document the actual commercialization of technical ideas. Nevertheless, Acs et al. (2002) show, in a comparison between patents and the literature-based output measure, that patents provide a fairly good measure of innovative activity in a knowledge production context.

14.3 THE ACCESSIBILITY CONCEPT AND THE EMPIRICAL MODEL

14.3.1 Modelling Spatial Dependence with Accessibilities

In this chapter, the empirical analysis is based on a spatial cross-regressive model (cf. Rey and Montouri, 1999) with accessibility variables on the right-hand side. In such a model, the extent of spatial dependence is revealed by the magnitude and significance of the estimated parameters associated with the accessibility variables (Andersson and Gråsjö, 2006).[4] The method with accessibilities in knowledge production has been used in a series of papers, (see, e.g., Gråsjö, 2005; Andersson and Ejermo, 2004a, 2004b; Andersson and Karlsson, 2005).

The accessibility of location i to itself and to $n - 1$ surrounding locations is defined as the sum of its internal accessibility to a given opportunity X and its accessibility to the same opportunity in other locations (not only neighbours):

$$A_i^X = x_1 f(c_{i1}) + \ldots + x_i f(c_{ii}) + \ldots + x_n f(c_{in}) \qquad (14.1)$$

where A_i^X is the total accessibility of location i and x_i is a measure of an opportunity X. The opportunities used in this study are conducted R&D and import products with high prices. $f(c)$ is the distance-decay function that determines how the accessibility value is related to the cost of realizing the opportunity. A very common way of calculating an accessibility value when the accessibility is interpreted as potential of opportunity is to use an exponential distance-decay function (see, e.g., Martellato et al., 1998), and then $f(c)$ takes the following form:

$$f(c_{ij}) = \exp\{-\omega t_{ij}\} \tag{14.2}$$

where t_{ij} is the time distance between location i and j, and ω is a time sensitivity parameter. The value of ω in (14.2) depends on whether the interaction is local, intraregional (between locations in a region), or interregional (location i and j in different regions). It is apparent that the accessibility value may improve in two ways, either by an increase in the size of the opportunity, x_j, or by a reduction in the time distance between location i and j. If the total accessibility to a specific opportunity is decomposed into local, intraregional and interregional accessibility, then:

$$A_i^X = A_{iL}^X + A_{iR}^X + A_{iOR}^X \tag{14.3}$$

where

$A_{iL}^X = x_i \exp\{-\omega_L t_{ii}\}$; local accessibility to opportunity X for location i,
$A_{iR}^X = \Sigma_{r \in R, r \neq i} x_r \exp\{-\omega_R t_{ir}\}$; intraregional accessibility to opportunity X for location i,
$A_{iOR}^X = \Sigma_{k \notin R} x_k \exp\{-\omega_{OR} t_{ik}\}$; interregional accessibility to opportunity X for location i.

r defines locations within the own region R (where municipality i is located), and k defines locations in other regions.

The accessibility concept has several advantages. First, it incorporates 'global' spillovers and does not only account for the impact from neighbours or locations within a certain distance band. Second, the separation of the total effect into local, intraregional and interregional spillovers captures potential productive knowledge flows between locations and clarifies the inferential aspects. Third, distance is often measured by physical distance, but a better way to measure it is to use the time it takes to travel between different locations (Beckmann, 2000). Time distances are also crucial when it comes to attending business meetings and also to reach spatial borders of labour markets (see Johansson and Klaesson, 2001 for the Swedish case). Thus accessibility provides a connection between the functional and the spatial component of an urban system (Bertuglia and Occelli, 2000). It defines the range and temporal organization of economic opportunities available in space as well as the cost of overcoming space in order to explore the opportunities in different locations. Accessibility accounts for the size of an opportunity in a location and discounts the value of the opportunity with time distance in a way that reflects the willingness to explore that opportunity given its size and distance. Accessibility is also a robust operational measurement tool that makes spatial proximity operational (Karlsson and Manduchi, 2001).

14.3.2 The Empirical Model

The research unit in this study is the municipalities in Sweden. Hence the locations referred to in equations (14.1)–(14.3) are municipalities. The regions are local labour market (LLM) regions. NUTEK's (1998) definition of LLM regions is used as the empirical counterpart to functional regions. According to this classification, there are 81 functional regions in Sweden. An LLM region consists, in most cases, of a number of municipalities that are connected through intensive commuting flows. In the sparsely populated areas in Sweden these regions often consist of single municipalities. Each LLM provides the firms in the region short time distances for travel between different locations, in most cases less than 50 minutes. The average time distance is 20–30 minutes (Johansson et al., 2002). LLM regions are delineated based on the intensity of intraregional commuting flows and are in this sense characterized by a high frequency of intraregional interaction. The borders of an LLM region are distinguished by a sharp decline in the intensity of such flows. Hence LLM regions can be conceived as arenas for face-to-face interaction and milieus for the generation and diffusion of innovation ideas.

In accordance with the discussion in Section 14.2, the following variables are used for municipality i in the empirical model:

Dependent variable: Number of patent applications per 10 000 employed aged 16–74.

Explanatory variables: Local (intramunicipal), intraregional and interregional accessibility to:

- university and company R&D;
- the share of the number of import products with a price greater than 1000 SEK per kg. With 1000 SEK per kg as a cut-off value, approximately 16 per cent of the products imported into the Swedish municipalities have a price that exceeds this limit (see Appendix 14.A).[5]

In order to investigate the importance of R&D and high-valued import products, the first choice would be to estimate one equation with a single regression using the accessibilities on all three geographical levels as exogenous variables. This, however, is not possible because of problems with multicollinearity between the intraregional variables and the interregional variables. Therefore two separate specifications are estimated:

$$Pat_i = a + b_1 A^Z_{iL} + b_2 A^Z_{iR} + b_3 A^Z_{iOR} + b_4 A^{R\&D}_{iL} + b_5 D^{pub}_i + b_6 D^{agr}_i + b_7 D^{LM}_i + b_8 D^{LR}_i + u_i \quad (14.4)$$

and

$$Pat_i = a + b_1 A^Z_{iL} + b_2 A^{R\&D}_{iL} + b_3 A^{R\&D}_{iR} + b_4 A^{R\&D}_{iOR} + b_5 D^{pub}_i + b_6 D^{agr}_i + b_7 D^{LM}_i + b_8 D^{LR}_i + u_i \quad (14.5)$$

where

Pat_i = number of patent applications per 10 000 employed aged 16–74 in municipality *i*
A^Z_{iL} = local (intramunicipal) accessibility to high-valued import products in municipality *i*
A^Z_{iR} = intraregional accessibility to high-valued import products in municipality *i*
A^Z_{iOR} = interregional accessibility to high-valued import products in municipality *i*
$A^{R\&D}_{iL}$ = local (intramunicipal) accessibility to R&D in municipality *i*
$A^{R\&D}_{iR}$ = intraregional accessibility to R&D in municipality *i*
$A^{R\&D}_{iOR}$ = interregional accessibility to R&D in municipality *i*
D^{pub}_i = dummy variable for large public sector employment
D^{agr}_i = dummy variable for large agricultural sector employment
D^{LM}_i = dummy variable for largest municipality in an LLM region
D^{LR}_i = dummy variable for other municipalities in a large LLM region.

Employment structure is controlled for with dummies for a large employment share in agricultural and a large employment share in the public sector. Large share of agricultural employment is defined as 5 per cent or higher and large share of public sector employment as 35 per cent or higher. Moreover, each LLM region consists of a central municipality, normally a larger city, and a corresponding hinterland of smaller municipalities. This structure implies systematic differences between the municipalities in the hinterland and the central municipality in terms of the relative size of different accessibilities. All municipalities are classified into three groups according to their position in their respective LLM region. The first group of municipalities is constituted by the largest municipality in each of the 81 LLM regions. These are the municipalities with the highest rank in their respective regions and there are thus 81 municipalities in this category. The second group consists of other municipalities in large LLM regions. An LLM region with at least 100 000 inhabitants is considered as a large LLM region. This group contains 142 municipalities. The third group consists of 65 municipalities and includes other municipalities in small LLM regions. Dummy variables D_i^{LM} and D_i^{LR} are included in the model to control for the different types of municipalities.

In what municipalities or regions is it more probable to find beneficiary knowledge flows? The properties that, according to Johansson and Andersson (1998), are of importance for a region's knowledge production and innovating capacity are high accessibility to (i) educated workforce, (ii) R&D competence, (iii) information about new product introductions, (iv) customers prepared to try out new products and (v) suppliers of specialized components and services.[6] It is possible to argue that properties (iii)–(v) to a higher degree characterize regions where importing activity is high. Hence the hypothesis is that companies that together produce a large number of patents are located in municipalities (in large functional regions) with high accessibility to high-valued import products and/or R&D. This implies that the parameter estimates of the local and/or intraregional accessibilities are supposed to be positive and statistically significant.

14.4 DATA AND ESTIMATION METHOD

14.4.1 Data and Descriptive Statistics

The data concerning the number of patent applications are taken from the European Patent Office. Statistics Sweden collects data on performed R&D in universities and companies, and the National Road Administration in Sweden is the data source when it comes to commuting time between and within Swedish municipalities.

- The number of patents per 10 000 employed in the municipalities of Sweden is a yearly average of the years 1998 and 1999.
- The share of high-valued import products in the municipalities of Sweden is a yearly average of the years 1997 and 1998.
- The accessibilities to R&D are yearly averages and these are computed using the sum of conducted R&D in universities and

companies measured in man-years during the period 1994–98 for Swedish municipalities.[7]

Data on the commuting time between and within municipalities in 1990 and 1998 are used for calculating the accessibility variables. In these calculations the time sensitivity parameter value ω_L is set to 0.02, ω_R to 0.1 and ω_{OR} to 0.05 (see equation 14.3). Johansson et al. (2003) estimated these values by using data on commuting flows within and between Swedish municipalities in 1990 and 1998. The intraregional commuting trips are those that are most time sensitive (hamper the propensity to travel the most) and have consequently the highest parameter value (ω_R = 0.1). Table 14.1 reports descriptive statistics of the variables in equations (14.3) and (14.4). Note especially the large amount of zeroes for the dependent variable.

14.4.2 Choice of Estimation Method

A problem with the data is the large proportions of zeroes of the dependent variable. Thus the number of patents per 10 000 employed is a censored variable, which make a Tobit specification proper to use. The Tobit model (Tobin, 1958) assumes a latent dependent variable, y_i^*, that is not directly observed. Y_i is, however, observed and is defined as:

$$y_i = y_i^* \text{ iff } y_i^* > c \tag{14.6}$$

$$y_i = c \text{ iff } y_i^* \leq c \tag{14.7}$$

where c denotes the lower bound below which y_i^* is censored. y_i^* is assumed to be generated by the canonical linear regression model such that:

$$y_i^* = \beta' x_i + \varepsilon_i \tag{14.8}$$

where x_i denotes a vector of regressors and β a corresponding vector of parameters. The error terms are assumed to be independent and identically distributed (iid), $\varepsilon_i \sim N(0, \sigma^2)$. In this case, the lower bound is zero, $c = 0$. Neglecting such a lower bound can lead to biased and inconsistent parameter estimates.

As a complement to the Tobit model, estimations are also conducted using the quantile regression technique. The municipalities are most likely heterogeneous in their patenting abilities. Thus the effects of the variables explaining the abilities do not have to be, and probably are not, the same for all municipalities.[8] It could be the case that municipalities with low

Table 14.1 Descriptive statistics, municipalities in Sweden (n = 288)

Variable	No. of zeroes	Min	Max	Median	Mean	Std dev.
Number of patents per 10 000 employed	73	0	48.19	2.803	4.897	6.585
Local accessibility to imports	0	0.0005	0.315	0.103	0.113	0.060
Intraregional accessibility to imports	25	0	1.054	0.041	0.097	0.167
Interregional accessibility to imports	0	2.8e–06	0.727	0.193	0.210	0.139
Local accessibility to R&D	117	0	3656.1	0.180	60.86	355.8
Intraregional accessibility to R&D	49	0	2373.7	3.412	134.4	349.0
Interregional accessibility to R&D	0	0.0006	1081.5	32.23	110.4	179.8
Dummy, largest municipality in region	207	0	1	0	0.281	0.450
Dummy, municipalities in largest regions	146	0	1	0	0.493	0.501
Dummy, agriculture	197	0	1	0	0.316	0.466
Dummy, public sector	162	0	1	0	0.437	0.497

patenting levels do not experience the same effect from an accessibility increase of, for example, R&D as municipalities with high patenting levels. Quantile regression enables the estimation of any conditional quantile of the dependent variable as a function of the explanatory variables. By estimating the marginal effects of the explanatory variables for different quantiles, a more complete description of the relationship between dependent and explanatory variables is achieved. Koenker and Bassett (1978) originally recommended quantile regressions to solve the problem with errors that are not normally distributed. The quantile regression model expresses the conditional quantile as a linear function of explanatory variables.[9] For an arbitrary quantile, θ, the model specification is:[10]

$$y_i = x_i'\beta_\theta + \varepsilon_{\theta i} \tag{14.9}$$

where β_θ is a vector of regression parameters associated with quantile θ, x_i is a vector of independent variables, y_i is the dependent variable and $\varepsilon_{\theta i}$ is the error term. The conditional quantile, θ, of y_i given x_i is $Q_\theta(y_i|x_i) = x_i'\beta_\theta$. The only necessary assumption concerning $\varepsilon_{\theta i}$ is $Q_\theta(\varepsilon_{\theta i}|x_i) = 0$. The quantile regression estimate for β_θ is the value of β_θ that solves the following minimization problem:

$$\min_\beta \frac{1}{n}\left(\sum_{i:y_i \geq x_i'\beta} |y_i - x_i'\beta|\theta + \sum_{i:y < x_i'\beta} |y_i - x_i'\beta|(1 - \theta) \right) \tag{14.10}$$

The weights of the residuals in equation (14.10) are different for different quantiles. For the median regression, 50 per cent of the residuals are negative and 50 per cent are positive and then all residuals get equal weights.[11] However, when estimating the 75th percentile, 75 per cent of the residuals are negative and 25 per cent are positive. The negative residuals are weighted by 0.25 and the positive residuals by 0.75.

Quantile regression is especially useful in the presence of heteroscedasticity, because the marginal effects of the covariates, given by β_θ, may differ for different quntiles, θ. In the special case where the errors are homoscedastic, the marginal effects will be the same across quantiles, although the intercept will differ. Koenker and Bassett (1982) proposed a method to estimate the variance–covariance matrix. But Rogers (1992) and Gould (1992) argued that this method underestimates the standard errors if the residuals are heteroscedastic. Gould (1992) suggested a bootstrap resampling procedure to overcome this problem. The procedure is standardized in Stata statistical package.[12]

When the dependent variable y is censored, its θth quantile is unaffected by the censoring if the regression function $x'\beta_\theta$ is in the uncensored region (Chay and Powell, 2001). For this reason, estimation results in the following section are reported only for quantiles above the 25th percentile (25 per cent of the observations of the dependent variable are zero). Regressions are then conducted for every fifth quantile (Q30, Q35, . . . , Q95). If the parameter estimates of the accessibility variables are not statistically significant for any conditional quantile, then no result is presented. The parameter estimates of the statistically significant dummy variables can be found in Appendix 14B. In order to solve the heteroscedasticity problem for the quantile regressions, bootstraps with 3000 replications are conducted.

14.5 ESTIMATION RESULTS

The parameter estimates of the variables in equations (14.4) and (14.5) are reported in Table 14.2.

The estimates in the table show that local accessibility to high-valued imports and R&D affect the patenting capacity in the municipalities. The parameter estimates are significant and positive in both specifications. Likewise, the parameter estimates of the intraregional accessibilities variables come out as significant and positive. The interregional effects are also positive, but not statistically significant (95 per cent confidence level). Thus, consistent with previous literature and theory, spatial proximity matters for establishing a productive link between R&D efforts and patent applications. The results in Table 14.2 indicate that this pattern also is true of high-valued imports. The parameter estimates of the dummy variables have all the expected signs. The coefficient estimates of the dummies for a large agricultural and public sector are negative, while the estimates are positive for the largest municipality in the region and municipalities in the largest regions. However, it is only the public sector dummy that is statistically significant.

The marginal effects from the quantile regressions are graphically displayed in Figure 14.1. The three diagrams to the left show the statistically significant accessibilities of equation (14.4). To the right, the significant accessibilities of equation (14.5) are presented. The 95 per cent confidence bands from bootstrapped estimation errors in the quantile regressions are shown as dotted lines. Consequently, given a specific quantile, if both the upper and the lower confidence limits are either above or below zero, then the parameter estimate is statistically significant for the quantile in question.

As can be seen in Figure 14.1, the quantile regression results are in general similar to the Tobit estimates. Starting with the local accessibility to

Table 14.2 Tobit estimates of the parameters in equations (14.4) and (14.5). Dependent variable: number of patents per 10000 employed, n = *288*

Variable	Eq. (14.4) Marg. effect (*t*-value)	Eq. (14.5) Marg. effect (*t*-value)
Constant	−0.858	0.400
	(−0.57)	(0.32)
Local accessibility to imports	19.66	20.34
	(2.79)	(2.83)
Intraregional accessibility to imports	12.84	–
	(4.03)	
Interregional accessibility to imports	4.88	–
	(1.61)	
Local accessibility to R&D	0.0035	0.0044
	(4.04)	(5.74)
Intraregional accessibility to R&D	–	0.0050
		(3.29)
Interregional accessibility to R&D	–	0.0044
		(1.67)
Dummy, largest municipality in region	0.745	0.516
	(0.68)	(0.48)
Dummy, municipalities in largest regions	1.77	1.60
	(1.55)	(1.39)
Dummy, agriculture	−1.60	−1.94
	(−1.75)	(−1.84)
Dummy, public sector	−1.90	−2.09
	(−2.24)	(−2.49)
Wald $chi^2(8)$	100.92	113.60
(Prob > chi^2)	(0.00)	(0.00)

R&D ((c) and (e)), the marginal effects are approximately 0.004. However, the effects are not statistically significant for the municipalities corresponding to the higher quantiles. Hence it cannot be proved that local accessibility to R&D has an effect on the patenting capacity in the municipalities where the number of patents per 10000 employed is high. The intraregional accessibilities are also rather stable ((b) and (f)). The marginal effects are approximately 10 for high valued imports and 0.005 for R&D. It could be the case that intraregional accessibility to either R&D or high-valued imports is of greater importance for the municipalities with the highest patenting levels per employed, but these effects are not statistically significant. The quantile regressions are especially informative in Figure 14.1(a) and (d), where the marginal effects of local accessibility

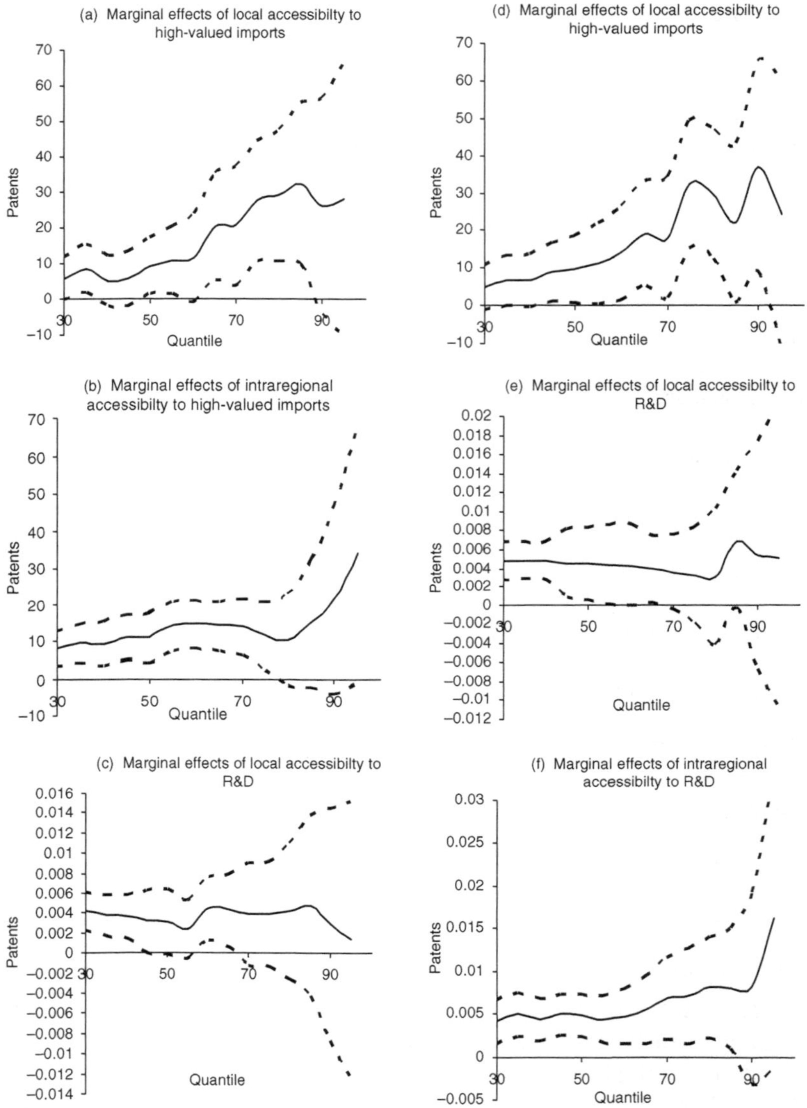

Figure 14.1 *Quantile regression estimates of the parameters in equations (14.4) and (14.5). Dependent variable: number of patents per 10 000 employed,* n = *288*

Equation (14.4)	Equation (14.5)
Pse R^2: 0.147–0.261	Pse R^2: 0.156–0.272

to high-valued imports are displayed. Here it is obvious that the marginal effects are increasing in magnitude, with the largest effects in the upper tail of the distribution of the dependent variable. However, the effects are not statistically significant for all conditional quantiles.

14.6 CONCLUSIONS

Knowledge is maintained as a core variable for innovation and growth in a large set of contemporary theories. However, the accessibility to knowledge resources differs between locations. If knowledge is not easily accessible at every point in space, the location of knowledge production and the characteristics of knowledge flows become critical issues in understanding economic growth.

This chapter has used an accessibility model to analyse the relationship between knowledge and innovation on regional/local level. The number of patent applications per 10 000 employed in a municipality was used as a measure of innovative activity. The knowledge resources applied in the model were (i) R&D conducted at universities and companies and (ii) the share of high-valued import products. The imports were used to account for the possible impact from abroad. A precise definition of accessibility was introduced and calculations were based on actual travel time distances. The total accessibility of a municipality was divided into three types: (i) local (intramunicipal) accessibility; (ii) intraregional accessibility; and (iii) extraregional accessibility. Using data at the municipality level in Sweden, the analysis has shown that this division gives a clear indication of spatial dependence in the sense that the knowledge resources in a given municipality tend to have a positive effect on the innovative activity of another municipality, given that the municipalities belong to the same functional region. Thus the results of the analysis indicate that knowledge flows transcend municipal borders, but that they tend to be bounded within functional regions. This result holds for both R&D investments and high-valued import products.

The estimations in the analysis were conducted with two different regression techniques. The Tobit procedure was chosen because several municipalities have zero registered patents. The quantile regression method was used in order to investigate the heterogeneity among the Swedish municipalities. With quantile regression, a comparison of the importance of the knowledge resources at different quantiles is possible, that is, the resources' importance in municipalities with different patenting levels. The results from the quantile regressions indicate that the local accessibilities are of greater importance for municipalities with lower patenting activity. In contrast, the intraregional accessibilities are important for all municipalities, but especially for the municipalities where patenting activity is high.

As shown in this chapter, knowledge accessibility is formed by the location pattern of knowledge resources combined with infrastructure. The interesting conclusion from this is that since both infrastructure investments and location decisions, and hence knowledge accessibility, can be influenced by policy, so can the phenomena dependent on knowledge accessibility. Thus the results of the analysis suggest that policies can affect innovation through location incentives and infrastructure investments. Which of these strategies is more or less efficient is a question for further research.

NOTES

1. For example, Lichtenberg and van Pottelsberghe de la Potterie (1998) examined the same estimations adding foreign direct investment. Coe et al. (1997) analysed the effect of North–South trade on international spillovers. Engelbrecht (1997) considered the role of human capital.
2. Polanyi (1966) refers to two types of knowledge: codified knowledge and tacit knowledge.
3. See, e.g., Handy and Niemeier (1997) or Baradaran and Ramjerdi (2001).
4. Another strategy to account for substantive spatial dependence is to use a model with a spatially lagged dependent variable, which will tell us how the output yi is affected by the outputs in other (neighbouring) localities. Thus the cross-regressive model is restricted to certain mechanisms of transmission, but will therefore also allow for more precise conclusions.
5. The number of imported products depends of course on how disaggregated the data are. The imports are registered by product according to the Combined Nomenclature (CN) classification system (8-digit level).
6. Andersson (1985) refers to the regions that have characteristics (i)–(v) as C-regions, stressing that their economic milieu has a rich endowment of communication, cognitive capacity and creativity.
7. In Sweden there are two major performers: private companies and universities. Together they account for about 95 per cent of all R&D in Sweden. This implies that the rest of the public sector and R&D institutes play a very limited role indeed in Swedish R&D.
8. In Varga (1998, 2000a, 2000b, 2001) the heterogeneous economic activity in US metropolitan areas is emphasized. Varga stresses that a 'critical mass' of economic agglomeration, which mainly can be found in big municipalities, is needed in order to expect substantial effects of university research on regional innovation.
9. This is analogous to the OLS regression, where the conditional mean of a random variable is expressed as a linear function of explanatory variables.
10. See, e.g., Buchinsky (1998).
11. Koenker and Bassett (1978) state that the conditional median in a regression is more efficient than the least squares estimator for any distribution for which the median is more efficient than the mean.
12. The procedure is called the design matrix bootstrap (see Gould, 1992 for further details).

REFERENCES

Acs, Z., L. Anselin and A. Varga (2002), 'Patents and innovation counts as measures of regional production of new knowledge', *Research Policy*, **31**, 1069–85.

Andersson, Å.E. (1985), *Kreativitet: Storstadens Framtid* (Creativity: The Future of the Metropolis), Stockholm: Prisma.

Andersson, M. and O. Ejermo (2004a), 'How does accessibility to knowledge sources affect the innovativeness of corporations? – Evidence from Sweden', *Annals of Regional Science*, **39** (4), 741–65.

Andersson, M. and O. Ejermo (2004b), 'Sectoral knowledge production in Swedish regions 1993–1999', in C. Karlsson, P. Flensburg and S.-Å. Hörte (eds), *Knowledge Spillovers and Knowledge Management*, Cheltenham, UK and Northampton, MA, USA: Edward Elgar, pp. 143–70

Andersson, M. and U. Gråsjö (2006), 'On the specification of regression models with spatial dependence – an application of the accessibility concept', CESIS Working Paper Series in Economics and Institutions of Innovation, no. 51, Royal Institute of Technology, Stockholm.

Andersson, M. and C. Karlsson (2005), 'Knowledge accessibility and regional economic growth', CESIS Working Paper Series in Economics and Institutions of Innovation, no. 40, Royal Institute of Technology, Stockholm.

Anselin, L., A. Varga and Z. Acs (2000), 'Geographic and sectoral characteristics of academic knowledge spillovers', *Papers of Regional Science*, **79**, 435–45.

Audretsch, D.B. and M.P. Feldman (1996), 'R&D spillovers and the geography of innovation and production', *American Economic Review*, **86** (3), 630–40.

Autant-Bernard, C. (2001), 'The geography of knowledge spillovers and technological proximity', *Economics of Innovation and New Technology*, **10**, 237–54.

Baradaran, S. and F. Ramjerdi (2001), 'Performance of accessibility measures in Europe', *Journal of Transportation and Statistics*, **3**, 31–48.

Beckmann, M. (2000), 'Interurban knowledge networks', in D.F. Batten, C.S. Bertuglia, D. Martellato and S. Occelli (eds), *Learning, Innovation and the Urban Evolution*, London: Kluwer Academic Publishers, pp. 127–35.

Bertuglia, C. and S. Occelli (2000), 'Impact of new information technologies on economic–spatial systems: towards an agenda for future research', in D.F. Batten, C.S. Bertuglia, D. Martellato and S. Occelli (eds), *Learning, Innovation and the Urban Evolution*, London: Kluwer Academic Publishers, pp. 237–54.

Bottazzi, L. and G. Peri (2003), 'Innovation and spillovers in regions: evidence from European patent data', *European Economic Review*, **47**, 687–710.

Branstetter, L. (2001), 'Are knowledge spillovers international or intranational in scope? Microeconometric evidence from Japan and the United States', *Journal of International Economics*, **53**, 53–79.

Buchinsky, M. (1998), 'Recent advances in quantile regression models: a practical guideline for empirical research', *Journal of Human Resources*, **33** (1), 88–126.

Chay, K.Y. and J.L. Powell (2001), 'Semiparametric censored regression models', *Journal of Economic Perspectives*, **15**, 29–42.

Ciccone, A. and R.E. Hall (1996), 'Productivity and the density of economic activity', *The American Economic Review*, **86**, 54–70.

Clerides, S., S. Lach and J. Tybout (1998), 'Is learning-by-exporting important? Micro-dynamic evidence from Colombia, Mexico and Morocco', *Quarterly Journal of Economics*, **113**, 903–47.

Coe, D.T. and E. Helpman (1995), 'International R&D spillovers', *European Economic Review*, **39**, 859–87.
Coe, D.T., E. Helpman and A.W. Hoffmaister (1997), 'North–South R&D spillovers', *Economic Journal*, **107**, 134–49.
Engelbrecht, H.J. (1997), 'International R&D spillovers, human capital and productivity in OECD economies: an empirical investigation', *European Economic Review*, **41**, 1479–88.
Feenstra, R.C., J.R. Markusen and W. Zeile (1992), 'Accounting for growth with new inputs: theory and evidence', *American Economic Review*, **82** (2), 415–21.
Gould, W.W. (1992), 'Quantile regression with bootstrapped standard errors', *Stata Technical Bulletin*, **9**, 19–21.
Gråsjö, U. (2005), 'Accessibility to R&D and patent production', Working Paper Series in Economics and Institutions of Innovation 37, CESIS (Centre of Excellence for Science and Innovation Studies), Royal Institute of Technology, Stockholm.
Gråsjö, U. (2006), 'Spatial spillovers of knowledge production', JIBS Dissertation Series, no. 034, Jönköping International Business School.
Griliches, Z. (1979), 'Issues in assessing the contribution of R&D to productivity growth', *Bell Journal of Economics*, **10**, 92–116.
Grossman, G. and E. Helpman (1991), *Innovation and Growth in the Global Economy*, Cambridge, MA: MIT Press.
Hall, B., A. Jaffe and M. Trajtenberg (2001), 'The NBER patent citations data file: lessons, insights and methodological tools', NBER Working Paper Series, no. 8498, National Bureau of Economic Research, Cambridge, MA.
Handy, S.L. and D.A. Niemeier (1997), 'Measuring accessibility. An exploration of issues and alternatives', *Environment and Planning A*, **29**, 1175–94.
Jaffe, A.B. (1989), 'Real effects of academic research', *American Economic Review*, **79**, 957–70.
Jaffe, A.B., M. Trajtenberg and R. Henderson (1993), 'Geographic localization of knowledge spillovers as evidenced by patent citations', *Quarterly Journal of Economics*, **108**, 577–98.
Johansson, B. (1997), 'Regional differentials in the development of economy and population', in C. Sörensen (ed.), *Empirical Evidence of Economic Growth: The Centre–Periphery Discussion*, The Expert Committee of Danish Ministry of Interior, Copenhagen, pp. 107–62.
Johansson, B. and Å.E. Andersson (1998), 'A Schloss Laxenburg model of product cycle dynamics', in M.J. Beckmann, B. Johansson, F. Snickars and R. Thord (eds), *Knowledge and Networks in a Dynamic Economy*, Heidelberg: Springer Verlag, pp. 181–219.
Johansson, B. and J. Klaesson (2001), 'Förhandsanalys av Förändringar i Transport-och Bebyggelsesystem', (Ex Ante Analyses of Changes in Transport and Housing Systems), Jönköping International Business School, Jönköping (mimeo).
Johansson, B., J. Klaesson and M. Olsson (2002), 'Time distances and labour market integration', *Papers in Regional Science*, **81**, 305–27.
Johansson, B., J. Klaesson and M. Olsson (2003), 'Commuters' non-linear response to time distances', *Journal of Geographical Systems*, **5**, 315–29.
Karlsson, C. and A. Manduchi (2001), 'Knowledge spillovers in a spatial context', in M. Fischer and J. Fröhlich (eds), *Knowledge, Complexity and Innovation Systems*, Heidelberg: Springer Verlag, pp. 101–23.

Karlsson, C. and R.R. Stough (2002), 'Introduction: regional policy evaluation in the new economic geography', in B. Johansson, C. Karlsson and R.R. Stough (eds), *Regional Policies and Comparative Advantage*, Cheltenham, UK and Northampton, MA, USA: Edward Elgar, pp. 1–21.
Keller, W. (2000), 'Do trade patterns and technology flows affect productivity growth?', *World Bank Economic Review*, **14**, 17–47.
Keller, W. (2004), 'International technology diffusion', *Journal of Economic Literature*, **XLII**, 752–82.
Kleinknecht, A., K. van Montfort and E. Brouwer (2002), 'The non-trivial choice between innovation indicators', *Economics of Innovation and New Technology*, **11**, 109–21.
Koenker, R. and G. Bassett (1978), 'Regression quantiles', *Econometrica*, **46** (1), 33–50.
Koenker, R. and G. Bassett (1982), 'Robust tests for heteroscedasticity based on regression quantiles', *Econometrica*, **50**, 43–61.
Lichtenberg, F. and B. van Pottelsberghe de la Potterie (1998), 'International R&D spillovers: a comment', *European Economic Review*, **42**, 1483–91.
Martellato, D., P. Nijkamp and A. Reggiani (1998), 'Measurement and measures of network accessibility: economic perspectives', in K. Button, P. Nijkamp and H. Priemus (eds), *Transport Networks in Europe; Concepts, Analysis and Policies*, Cheltenham, UK and Northampton, MA, USA: Edward Elgar, pp. 161–80.
NUTEK (1998), 'Småföretag och Regioner i Sverige 1998 – Med ett Tillväxtperspektiv för hela Landet' (Small Businesses and Regions in Sweden 1998 – With a Growth Perspective for the Whole Country), report 1998:35, Supplement B 1998:10, NUTEK (Swedish Agency for Economic and Regional Growth), Stockholm.
Peri, G. (2002), 'Knowledge flows and knowledge externalities', CESIfo Working Papers, no. 765, Center for Economic Studies & Ifo Institute for Economic Research, Munich.
Polanyi, M. (1966), *The Tacit Dimension*, London: Routledge and Kegan Paul.
Rey, S. and B. Montouri (1999), 'US regional income convergence – a spatial econometric perspective', *Regional Studies*, **33**, 143–56.
Rogers, W.H. (1992), 'Quantile regression standard errors', *Stata Technical Bulletin*, **9**, 16–19.
Romer, P. (1990), 'Endogenous technological change', *Journal of Political Economy*, **98**, S71–S102.
Saxenian, A. (1991), *Regional Advantage: Culture and Competition in Silicon Valley and Route 128*, Boston, MA: Harvard Publishing.
Tobin, J. (1958), 'Estimations of relationships for limited dependent variables', *Econometrica*, **26**, 24–36.
Varga, A. (1998), *University Research and Regional Innovation: A Spatial Econometric Analysis of Academic Technology Transfers*, Boston, MA: Kluwer Academic Publishers.
Varga, A. (2000a), 'Local academic knowledge spillovers and the concentration of economic activity', *Journal of Regional Science*, **40**, 289–309.
Varga, A. (2000b), 'Universities in local innovation systems', in Z. Acs (ed.), *Regional Innovation, Knowledge and Global Change*, New York: Pinter, pp. 139–52.
Varga, A. (2001), 'Universities and regional economic development: does

agglomeration matter?' in B. Johansson, C. Karlsson and R.R. Stough (2001), *Theories of Endogenous Growth Lessons for Regional Policy*, Berlin: Springer Verlag, pp. 345–67.

Weibull, J. (1976), 'An axiomatic approach to the measurement of accessibility', *Regional Science and Urban Economics*, **6**, 357–79.

Xu, B. and J. Wang (1999), 'Capital goods trade and R&D spillovers in the OECD', *Canadian Journal of Economics*, **32**, 1258–74.

APPENDIX 14A NUMBER OF IMPORTED PRODUCTS TO SWEDISH MUNICIPALITIES FOR DIFFERENT INDUSTRIAL SECTORS (YEARLY AVERAGE 1997–98)

Sector, prod-sni97	No. of import products, price > 1000 SEK/ kg	No. of import products	Share (%)
01 Agricultural establishments and establishments for related services	84	6104	1.4
02 Forestry and related services	5	640	0.8
05 Fishermen, fish farmers and related service companies	32	613	5.2
10 Coal mines; peat industry	2	71	2.8
11 Crude petroleum, natural gas extraction and related service comp.	1	12	8.3
12 Uranium and thorium mines	6	64	9.4
13 Metal ore mines	43	970	4.4
14 Other mines and quarries	99	11 889	0.8
15 Food product and beverages	2	43	4.7
16 Tobacco	770	16 167	4.8
17 Textiles	2268	19 309	11.7
18 Wearing apparel; fur industry	226	5905	3.8
19 Tanneries; luggage, handbags, footwear etc.	37	3671	1.0
20 Wood and products of wood, cork, cane etc., except furniture	155	5314	2.9
21 Pulp, paper and paper products	1268	6192	20.5
22 Publishers and printers; other industry for recorded media	73	919	7.9
23 Coke, refined petroleum products and nuclear fuel	1927	21 362	9.0
24 Chemicals and chemical products	776	13 262	5.9
25 Rubber and plastic products	605	7572	8.0
26 Other non-metallic mineral products	653	9269	7.0
27 Basic metals	2141	18 341	11.7
28 Fabricated metal products, except machinery and equipment	5733	32 932	17.4
29 Machinery and equipment n.e.c.	2305	4226	54.5

Sector, prod-sni97	No. of import products, price > 1000 SEK/ kg	No. of import products	Share (%)
30 Office machinery and computers	4536	16562	27.4
31 Electrical machinery and apparatus n.e.c.	5127	9285	55.2
32 Radio, television and communication equipment and apparatus	7016	13154	53.3
33 Medical, precision and optical instruments, watches and clocks	231	3910	5.9
34 Motor vehicles, trailers and semi-trailers	375	2115	17.7
35 Other transport equipment	1296	12779	10.1
36 Furniture; manufacturing n.e.c.	6	26	23.1
40 electricity, gas, steam and hot water works	141	397	35.5
92 Recreational, cultural and sporting establishments	91	320	28.4
93 Other service establishments	0	1	0.0
Total	38030	243396	15.6

APPENDIX 14B

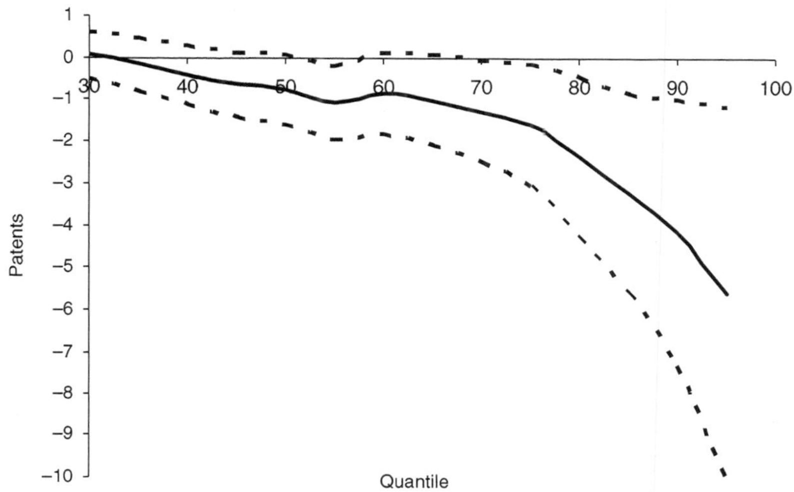

Figure 14B.1 Marginal effects of public sector employment (eq. 3.4)

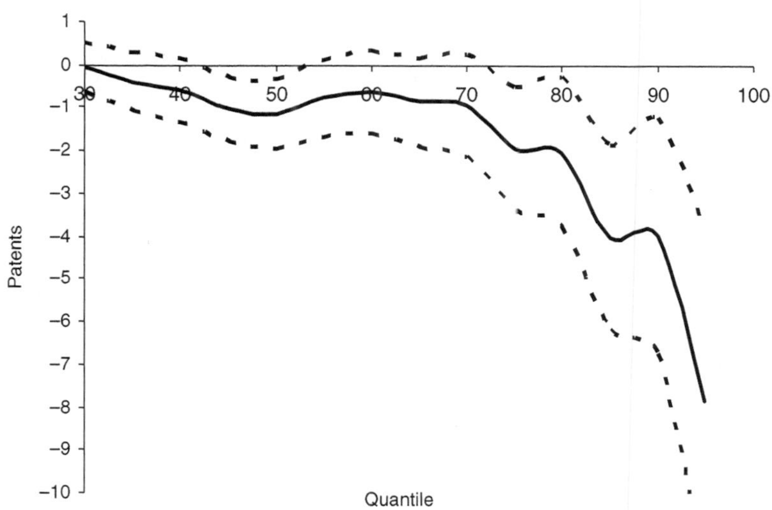

Figure 14B.2 Marginal effects of public sector employment (eq. 3.5)

Index